PRAISE FOR REX WEYLER AND *THE JESUS SAYINGS*

"Weyler extracts a core message, devoid of talk of miracles or the supernatural, by a 'radical, Aramaic-speaking, Jewish Jesus.' This Jesus defines the kingdom of God as within. Righteousness resides in generosity. Purity is not mere external ritual, but internal." — *Globe and Mail*

"A knockout book... Weyler deconstructs one of the most highly constructed figures in the Western world. By the end Jesus appears as a wise and humble teacher, advocating self-awareness and social compassion."
— *Vancouver Observer*

"Weyler has impeccable credentials for spiritual readers: co-author of *Chop Wood, Carry Water* and author of *Blood of the Land* and *Greenpeace: The Inside Story*, he is also co-founder of Greenpeace International. In *The Jesus Sayings*, Weyler is wonderfully effective at coming to terms, for the well-informed common reader, with the historically likely realities of Jesus, taking into account not only orthodox Christian resources but so-called apocryphal sources, historical criticism, and recent archaeology. The result is not a 'Greenpeace Jesus' but a complex and historically more satisfying figure." — *Library Journal*

"The critically acclaimed [Rex Weyler] is also a supreme storyteller who writes with warmth, insight, and integrity. . . . [*The Jesus Sayings*] is a well-organized, compelling overview of the past few decades of more than 120 years of the scholarly search for the flesh-and-blood 'historical' Jesus."
— *Vancouver Sun*

"This book scores high points in readability, relevance, and insight. Weyler shows us that Jesus still has the power to inspire, and that it is up to us to make sure this inspiration draws out the best in humanity, and not the worst." — *Pacific Rim Review of Books*

"Weyler takes his readers on a historical tour of the ancient sources, describing how the earliest accounts of the life and message of Jesus grew over time and in response to changing circumstances. Weyler has done his research and is a good storyteller." — *Montreal Gazette*

"In Weyler's survey of the latest research, Jesus emerges as a revolutionary sage, a man for the ages whose 'words and deeds are sublime' . . . Weyler's Jesus fits comfortably with the historical figure now envisaged by almost all scholars. Living without care for the future, keeping all assets in common, giving all we have to the poor, are other key parts of the authentic teaching as identified by Weyler and others." — *Maclean's*

"Rex Weyler liberates the historical Jesus to tell the Christian origin story anew. He speaks truth to power in this solid and exciting re-telling of the diversity, politics, and mythology behind the origins of Christianity. There is integrity and trustworthiness in this work and in this author, whose history of activism helped launch the global Greenpeace movement. Read this book." — Matthew Fox, author of *One River, Many Wells*; *Original Blessing*; and *The Coming of the Cosmic Christ*

"Rex Weyler is a master journalist and storyteller, who brings us face to face with the Jesus who walked the earth, changed Western civilization, and remains relevant to modern readers." — John Izzo, author of *The Five Secrets You Must Discover Before You Die*

"[A] thoroughly engaging account of the search for the authentic voice of the Galilean . . . well-researched and captivating . . . An important contribution to our understanding of early Christianity." — Barrie Wilson, author of *How Jesus Became a Christian*

THE JESUS SAYINGS

THE QUEST FOR HIS AUTHENTIC MESSAGE

REX WEYLER

ANANSI

To my father, John (Jack) Richardson Weyler

First published in hardcover in 2008 by House of Anansi Press Inc.

This edition published in 2009 by
House of Anansi Press Inc.
110 Spadina Avenue, Suite 801
Toronto, ON, M5V 2K4
Tel. 416-363-4343 • Fax 416-363-1017
www.anansi.ca

Distributed in Canada by
HarperCollins Canada Ltd.
1995 Markham Road
Scarborough, ON, M1B 5M8
Toll free tel. 1-800-387-0117

Distributed in the United States by
Publishers Group West
1700 Fourth Street
Berkeley, CA 94710
Toll free tel. 1-800-788-3123

House of Anansi Press is committed to protecting our natural environment.
As part of our efforts, this book is printed on paper that contains
100% post-consumer recycled fibres, is acid-free, and is processed chlorine-free.

13 12 11 10 09   1 2 3 4 5

Library and Archives Canada Cataloguing in Publication

Weyler, Rex, 1947–
The Jesus sayings : the quest for his authentic message/Rex Weyler.

Includes bibliographical references and index.
ISBN 978-0-88784-819-3

1. Jesus Christ — Teachings. 2. Jesus Christ — Historicity.
I. Title.

BS2415.W42 2009   232   C2008-906430-5

Library of Congress Control Number: 2008938533

Cover design: Paul Hodgson
Text design and typesetting: Ingrid Paulson

 Canada Council
for the Arts
Conseil des Arts
du Canada

 ONTARIO ARTS COUNCIL
CONSEIL DES ARTS DE L'ONTARIO

We acknowledge for their financial support of our publishing program the Canada Council for the Arts, the Ontario Arts Council, and the Government of Canada through the Book Publishing Industry Development Program (BPIDP).

Printed and bound in Canada

CONTENTS

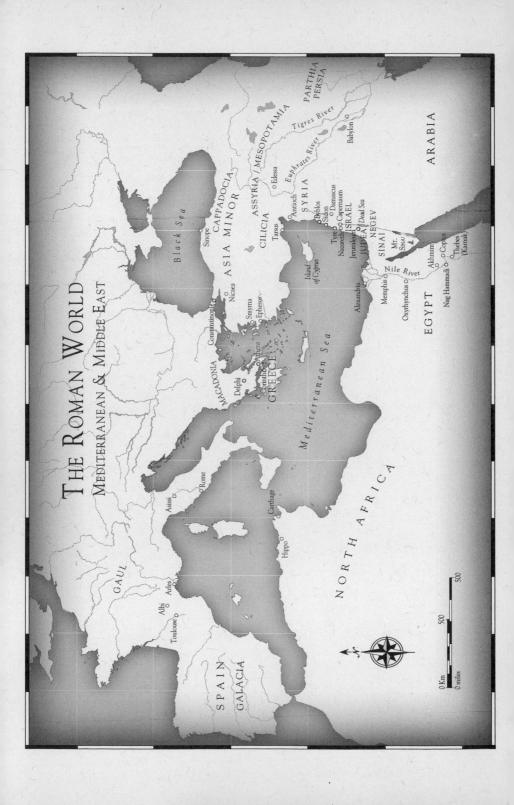

The Roman World
Mediterranean & Middle East

PARTHIA / PERSIA

ARABIA

Black Sea

CAPPADOCIA

ASIA MINOR

ASSYRIA / MESOPOTAMIA

Tigres River

Euphrates River

Babylon

CILICIA

SYRIA

Sinope

Nicaea

Smyrna

Ephesus

Edessa

Tarsus

Antioch

Damascus
Byblos
Sidon
Capernaum
Tyre
Nazareth
Jerusalem
Dead Sea
ISRAEL
JUDEA
NEGEV
SINAI
Mt.
SINAI

*Island
of Cyprus*

Constantinople

MACEDONIA

Delphi

Corinth
Cenchreus
GREECE

Alexandria

Memphis

Nile River

Oxyrhynchus

Akhmim
Nag Hammadi
Coptos
Thebes
(Karnak)

EGYPT

Rome

Assisi

Carthage

Hippo

Mediterranean Sea

NORTH AFRICA

GAUL

Arles
Albi
Toulouse

SPAIN
GALACIA

0 Km
500

500
0 miles

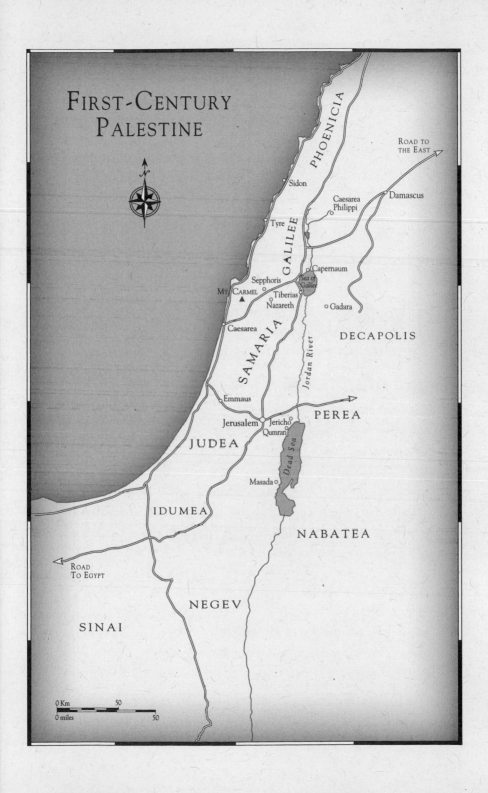

FIRST-CENTURY
PALESTINE

ROAD TO
THE EAST

PHOENICIA

Sidon

Caesarea
Philippi

Damascus

Tyre

GALILEE

Capernaum

Sepphoris

Sea of
Galilee

MT. CARMEL

Tiberias

Nazareth

Gadara

Caesarea

SAMARIA

DECAPOLIS

Jordan River

Emmaus

Jerusalem

Jericho

PEREA

Qumran

JUDEA

Dead Sea

IDUMEA

Masada

NABATEA

ROAD
TO EGYPT

NEGEV

SINAI

0 Km   50
0 miles   50

TIMELINE OF THE JESUS RECORD

The text record of Jesus' sayings includes two sets of dates: (1) the approximate date of the oldest surviving manuscript, and (2) the presumed date that scholars believe an earlier first edition was composed. For example, the oldest extant *Thomas* fragments are from about 200 C.E., but based on language style, scholars believe the originals appeared between 30 and 60 C.E. Most text dates below refer to presumed composition unless otherwise stated. Ancient historical dates are approximate unless tied to established physical events such as the destruction of Jerusalem in 70 C.E. All historical dates for Jesus are approximate; his birth could have occurred anytime between 10 B.C.E. and 10 C.E. Historians generally place his birth in Galilee before the death of Herod in 4 B.C.E.

I. INFLUENCES ON JESUS STORIES

Between 5000 B.C.E. and the birth of Jesus, humanity evolved from hunting and gathering to agricultural communities and to urban life. Advances in writing and travel triggered an information explosion of written laws, legends, philosophies, and histories. Communities attempted to describe cycles of rebirth, fertility, mystery, male and female deities, duality, and primal unity. Wisdom schools examined nature, the movements of celestial bodies, personal knowledge, and social interaction. Society stratified into classes: urban, male kings and priests dominating rural communities and nomadic peasants.

c. 1350 B.C.E.   Semitic tribes in Canaan and Sinai
One king, one God: Akhenaten in Egypt
Vedic Sanskrit hymns and wisdom tradition in India
Mitra, Mithras origins in India and Iran

930–900   Jewish kingdom divided: Israel and Judea
Zarathustra (Zoroaster) in ancient Iran, Mithraism

900–700   Jewish prophets: Elijah, Isaiah, Micah

700–300   Axial Age of wisdom schools
Lao Tzu, Gautama Buddha, Confucius
Marzeah Papyrus, oldest Hebrew manuscripts
Thales, Pythagoras, Socrates, Aristotle: nature and inquiry
Plato, Sophists: dualism, mind/body, spirit/matter separated
Diogenes the Cynic: mocking power and elite society

540–530   Persian King Cyrus conquers Babylon
Exiled Jews return to Jerusalem under Persian authority·

300–100   Dead Sea Scrolls, Old Testament manuscripts

63   Rome conquers Judea

37–4   Herod the Idumean rules Israel and Judea under Rome

II. LIFE AND DEATH OF JESUS: C. 7 B.C.E.–30 C.E.

7–2 B.C.E.   Births of John the Baptist and Jesus
Judas bar Ezekias, Athronges, messiah-rebels in Galilee

4 B.C.E.–39 C.E.   Reign of Herod Antipas in Galilee and Judea
Roman emperors Augustus, Tiberius, Caligula

20–30 C.E. Protests against Pilate over idols and embezzling temple funds
John the Baptist and Jesus teach, and are executed by Antipas
and Pilate, repectively

III. JESUS' LEGACY REMEMBERED, RECORDED, REDACTED

30–60 C.E. The oral tradition decades: memories and legends of Jesus
The earliest Jesus saying anthologies collected
First layer of *Thomas* sayings: light inside, seek and find
Q sayings: blessed poor, turn the cheek, mustard seed
Fayyum fragment: Peter's denial, cock crows
Oxyrhynchus 1224: pray for your enemies
Egerton Gospel: healing a leper, not lip service but action
Hebrews Gospel: Jesus as incarnate Wisdom
Crucifixion stories, source for *Peter* and *John* gospels

49–56 Seven authentic Paul letters: Jesus as messiah, "Christos"

60–70 Miracle anthology, now embedded in *Mark* and *John*
Egyptians Gospel: asceticism, unity of male/female
Thomas anthology expanded
Execution of James, brother of Jesus, in Jerusalem

66–70 Jewish revolt against Rome
Destruction of Jerusalem, dispersed Jewish refugees

70–80 Dialogues: Jesus sayings recorded as conversations with disciples
Earliest *Mark* Gospel, without resurrection
Dialogue of the Saviour source: Jesus, Judas, Matthew, Mary
Oxy. 840 dialogue, Jesus and Pharisees: purify inside, not outside

75–95 Josephus writing Jewish history in Rome

85–95 Gospels that rely on Q sayings, *Mark,* and *Peter* crucifixion
Matthew in Syria, first edition without birth story
Luke Gospel appears in Aegean churches, Ephesus, Corinth

90–120 Popular hope for an imminent return of Jesus falters
John first edition: promotes faith in Jesus as a god, future return
James letter: denounces faith that lacks good deeds
Didache: Community rules, rituals, offices, functions
Letters ascribed to Paul: Colossians, Ephesians, 2 Thessalonians
Revelations: apocalypse, vision of end time, divine judgement
Pliny and Tacitus mention Christian sects, but not Jesus

120–130 Earliest surviving manuscript of a gospel story
P52 fragment depicts Jesus before Pilate
"I came to witness the truth," parallels the *John* Gospel

IV. GOSPEL WARS: EIGHTY FACTIONS OF JESUS FOLLOWERS, ROMAN SUPREMACY

100–150 Roman Church letters attributed to patriarchs and bishops
Clement letter: resurrection, faith, obedience to the church
Barnabas epistle: Anti-Jewish new covenant, "antichrist"
Ignatius letters: attack Jews, promote "catholic" authority
Polycarp letter: promotes resurrection, denounces Satan
Pastoral letters attributed to Paul: Timothy 1 and 2, Titus.

120–140 *John* Gospel second edition: adds opening (1:1–18) and ending (21)
John 15–17 added: authority over all people; so the world may believe
Didache second edition: conforming to *Mark*, *Matthew*, and *Luke*
Acts of Apostles: Pentecost, Paul's mission, and clashes with apostles

120–180 Diversity of poor, peasant, mystic, non-Roman gospel writers
Ebionites, the poor: Jesus was human, he chose us, rejected sacrifices
Nazorean Gospel: give to the poor, prayer requesting daily bread
Mary Gospel: seek within, mind, nature, vision, community conflict
Peter Gospel: pre-60 crucifixion, Joseph of Arimathea, Mary
    Magdalene
Marcion: seeks a historical Jesus, claims Acts is inaccurate
Basilides describes Jesus' message: love all, desire nothing
Carpocrates, Valentinus: Jesus was human, men and women
    are equal

160–200   Irenaeus: promotes only four gospels, denounces Valentinus
     and Marcion
    Athenagoras, Tatian, Theophilus: Christianity without Jesus
    Justin Martyr: virgin birth, son of God, last supper, devils
    Celsus, *True Reason*: critiques Christian plagiarism and
     faulty logic

150–300   Gnostic Jesus followers writing in Syria and Egypt
    Gospel of Truth: Father is within, the wise, children,
     they are truth
    Apocalypse of Peter: corrupted teaching vs. good fruit
    Sophia of Jesus Christ: Jesus' consort Wisdom, seven women
     disciples
    Philip Gospel: Jesus the Nazorean, kissing Mary, unity of
     male/female.
    Apocryphon and Apocalypse of James: attributed to Jesus'
     brother

250–325   Rise of Roman-sponsored archbishops, the metropolitans
    Arius vs. Athanasius: Was Jesus a human or deity or both?
    Roman emperor Constantine and his court scribe Eusebius
    Council of Nicaea, formation of Constantine's state religion

340–380   Earliest surviving complete New Testament Bible manuscripts
    Athanasius's Easter letter: proclaims an orthodox canon
    Panarion: Epiphanius denounces eighty factions or "heresies"

380–400   Roman bishops claim authority over all Christians and Jesus
     literature
    Spanish bishop and ascetic Priscillian executed
    Purge of competing books, Alexandria Library burned,
     heretics executed
    Siricius, Bishop of Rome, first to be called Pope (father)
    Vulgate: Latin Bible

385–430   Augustine in Milan, converts to Roman Catholicism
    Doctrines of original sin, just war for God, papal infallibility
    Egyptian monks secretly bury the *Mary*, *Thomas*, and
     Gnostic texts

V. MEDIEVAL AND MODERN UNDERSTANDING OF JESUS

350–600   German tribes settle Europe: Goths, Vandals, Franks, Angles
Popes share power with Ostrogoth kings in Italy
Jewish and Christian dispersion throughout Europe

600–1000   Islam expands from Arabia to Spain, Palestine, and India
Charlemagne expands Christian empire from Spain to Rome,
   to Saxony
Raiders: Vikings, Hungarian Magyars, Arab Saracens
   dominate Europe
Non-Roman Jesus followers thrive, Bogomils and Cathars,
   "pure ones"

1090–1400   German–papal alliance dominates Europe
Christian crusades against Islamic states
Pope Innocent III: German-Italian aristocrat, eradicates Cathars
Francis of Assisi: patrician follows modesty and mission of Jesus
Pope Gregory IX, establishes the Inquisition, torture, executions
Extermination of pagans, women healers, Jews, and Moors
   in Europe

1350–1700   Reformation of religion and Renaissance of art and science
Chaucer mocks the papal selling of relics and indulgences
Printing press: new information explosion
Martin Luther protests papal corruption, reformed churches
   in Europe
Copernicus, Kepler, Galileo describe movement of planets
   and moons
Christian extermination continues against scientists, healers, Jews
Quakers, Mennonites, Amish seek authentic, peaceful
   Christianity

1700–1900   Scholarship liberated from control of the churches
Jean Leclerc, *Historia Ecclesiastica*: Gospel writers used sources
Hermann Reimarus, D. F. Strauss: historical vs. mythical Jesus
Herbert Marsh, Johannes Weiss: lost sayings collection "Q"
Thomas Jefferson distinguishes Jesus teachings from later doctrine
Bernard Grenfell and Arthur Hunt discover Logia Iēsou sayings

1900– present: The search for a historically accurate Jesus
Albert Schweitzer: *The Quest for the Historical Jesus*
Discovery of *Mary*, *Thomas*, Gnostic texts, buried for
1,500 years
John Kloppenborg, Burton Mack: layers in gospel source Q
Geza Vermes, E. P. Sanders: Jesus in a Jewish context
Elaine Pagels, Karen King, Margaret Starbird:
Mary Magdalene
John Dominic Crossan, Marcus Borg, and others: historical
Jesus examined
Robert W. Funk and the Westar Institute: analyzing Jesus
sayings, deeds
Matthew Fox, David Steindl-Rast: gender-equal, respectful
Jesus devotion

INTRODUCTION

A REAL JESUS

> We are all thieves; we have taken the Scriptures in words,
> and know nothing of them in ourselves.
>
> MARGARET FELL, QUAKER CO-FOUNDER, 1652

A child is born into the world and, before it even recognizes itself as a unique individual, the child hears stories: tales of relatives, ancestors, deities, heroes, and ethical lessons about what happens to those who do the wrong or right things, according, of course, to the storyteller. But the child does not yet know about the proclivities of storytellers. Young innocents take everything literally.

At the age of four, I recall opening the tiny, coloured cardboard doors of an Advent calendar that hung on my bedroom wall, on the frozen Wyoming prairies in the days before television. No chocolates waited behind the little doors in 1951, just pictures of a shepherd boy, an angel, three kings, a lamb, and a star as we approached Christmas day. My father had come from a family of German Lutherans, my mother from French and Irish Catholics. We lived in an oil-field compound in the Big Horn River basin, where each little house was painted in the company colours, white with blue trim.

As far as I could tell, my sister Kaye, two years older, was in charge of Christmas. She would tell me when it was my turn to open the little door, just before bedtime. She explained to me that this was the countdown to the birth of baby Jesus. Of course, we also counted down to the opening of the gifts that accumulated under the little fir sapling we had retrieved with our father from the snowy foothills across the creek. Kaye showed me how to find my own name on the wrapping and how to shake the presents, guessing what treasure might be inside.

The anticipation must have overwhelmed all other stories in my mind, because my only boyhood supernatural vision was rather mundane. I did not yet understand the relationship between Santa and Jesus. I did not know that the gifts symbolized the public generosity encouraged by a peasant in Galilee two millennia earlier. On Christmas Eve, we opened the last miniature coloured door to find the infant looking at us from his straw blanket. Before going to bed, I took one final look out the window into the black, starry night. There, in vivid silhouette, I saw not the Infant Saviour or Holy Mother but Santa Claus in the sky, his sleigh, the reindeer, and the huge bundle of toys for all the good children. According to my mother, who still tells the story, I ran through the house shouting, "I see him, I see him!" I flung open the front door, felt the icy prairie wind in my face, and once again witnessed the vision: Santa arriving in the starlight. I pointed and shrieked so that my family would see also.

"Yes, yes, well then, you better go to bed," my mother said. She ushered me away, and my father closed the door on the frozen darkness. I climbed into my bunk, far too excited to sleep. My sister directly below whispered quietly, reminding me to say my prayers, which I did, although I always shuddered at the same verse: "If I die before I wake."

ELIZABETH AND FRANCESCO

By the time I entered school, we lived in Tulsa, Oklahoma, home of the infamous Pentecostal, faith-healing evangelist Oral Roberts, who had allegedly raised a boy from the dead. In spite of our Protestant father, we were considered Catholics, second-class citizens in 1950s Oklahoma. We still did not own a television, but the family next door did, and after school we watched Mighty Mouse and Popeye cartoons with the neighbour children. Their father, a pastor in the church, despised Catholics and forbade his children to associate with us. Their mother was more tolerant, but one day she ran into the television room whispering, "You kids have to go, quickly, now." As we rushed out the back door, we could hear the father entering through the front. We never returned and had to get our own television.

I became perhaps the worst altar boy in our modest parish, stumbling over Latin phrases, inattentive to the proper time for ringing bells, tripping over my black cassock, and standing when I should kneel. The priests had favourite boys, but I was not among them. I imagined eternal suffering in hell for my transgressions. Sometimes I was too terrified to sleep at night. In spite of these troubles, I admired two Christian heroes. The first, my grandmother, introduced me to the second.

Each summer, when I was in elementary school, my family drove from Tulsa to my grandparents' home on lush Chapala Street in Santa Barbara, California. There, at age thirteen, on a screened wooden porch, I awoke to the sound of doves in the avocado tree and the smell of eucalyptus in the warm, salty predawn air. In the kitchen I would find Elizabeth, my mother's mother, working by the warm oven as the daily bread baked. My grandmother let me spread freshly cooked apricots on a sheet of dough, add nuts and raisins, dust with sugar and cinnamon, and roll the morning's sweet pastries.

I do not recall Elizabeth ever lecturing me or anyone else about proper behaviour. She inspired others by the sheer radiance of her humanity. As a farm girl in Michigan, she had read about the Arizona Territory, where it supposedly never snowed, and dreamed of going there. After high school, she took a teaching job to save money, but the first thing she ever bought was an indoor water pump for her mother. In 1902, at the age of eighteen, she took a train west, stopping to work in Hastings, Nebraska, where she spent two months attending to a dying woman. She would later marry the woman's grandson, Irish farmer Thomas Goodwin, my grandfather.

She taught school in Hadden, Arizona, but when her mother died, she returned to Michigan and brought her younger, disabled sister west to care for her. In our family, we referred to her as Saint Elizabeth. She remained a devout Catholic, prayed daily for others, and at the end of each month, gave whatever remained in her bank account to various Christian missionaries. She let me do the math, so each would receive a fair share. When it did not come out even, she would say, "We'll give the extra to the Poor Clares."

As a widow, at the age of ninety-six, Elizabeth cooked hot lunches and delivered them to the retirement home for the "elderly," most of them twenty years her junior. She fed and encouraged the lonely until the day she died in 1982. Elizabeth never asked for anything in return for her generosity and thereby created a realm of heaven around her. She served as my first religious hero, my measure of righteousness, and the one person who most genuinely embodied the teachings of Jesus as I understood them at age thirteen. During that summer, Elizabeth gave me a short biography of Saint Francis, and in the evenings, on the back porch by a lemon tree, I read the life story of my second childhood religious hero, the humble friar from Assisi.

The now-famous Francesco di Bernardone was born in 1182 to his mother Pica and father Pietro, a cloth merchant in central Italy,

who named him Francesco as a gesture to his wealthy French cus-
tomers. At the age of nineteen, Francis enlisted in the Assisi army,
fought neighbouring Perugia in the Tiber valley, and was captured
at Collestrada. A year in captivity and a serious illness ignited a
spiritual epiphany within the merchant's son. He felt compelled to
follow Jesus' instructions to disciples in the *Gospel of Matthew*: Go
out two by two, heal the sick, take no gold or silver, no bread, no bag,
and no second tunic. Thereafter, he lived his life as a modest messenger of peace and compassion. At the age of twenty-seven, he
walked 1,400 kilometres from Assisi to Rome with eleven followers,
obtained an audience with a reluctant Pope Innocent III, and gained
permission to establish a new religious order, today known as the
Franciscans, who live without personal possessions.

Two features struck me about Francesco's story. First, his life
reminded me of my grandmother as a model of the honest spiritual life. Secondly, I cringed at the gulf between his unassuming
generosity of spirit and the dubious character of Pope Innocent III,
a wealthy aristocrat with a taste for political power. The biography
of Saint Francis that I read as a child only hinted at this clash of
ethical values, and at thirteen I had no real appreciation for the
depth of the contradiction. Still, I wondered how to reconcile these
two embodiments of Jesus' message. Much later, I would discover
the more chilling details about the career of Pope Innocent.

ONE DAY IN CATECHISM

Our family moved from Tulsa to Denver, Colorado, where Catholics
enjoyed more social esteem. However, I lived in a predominantly
Jewish neighbourhood, learned to sing "Hava Nagila" for the school
concert, and won the 1963 grade nine city basketball championship
on a largely Jewish team. Not only were two of my Jewish team-
mates dead eye long-range shooters, they also were keen students,
and we traded typical teenage conjectures on philosophy. In this

multicultural environment, like most of my peers, I began to harbour doubts about the stories I had been told regarding the origin and operation of the universe.

I considered an idea that probably occurs to many young people faced with the problem of supernatural punishment and reward: Perhaps I'm better off to believe what I'm told, even if it seems improbable, since the reward of believing correctly, eternal bliss in heaven, is infinitely better than what might come of correctly not believing. Furthermore, doubt poses the monumental, if unlikely, risk of perpetual torture in hell. This, I learned later, is the famous "Pascal's Wager," posed by seventeenth-century French mathematician Blaise Pascal. Even as a youth, I realized that one persistent fact defeats this gambler's logic: There are many versions of deities all over the world, so even if we imagine it safer to believe in God, which god should we believe in? What if I believed in God, but chose the wrong version?

I still attended catechism classes every Sunday, where the Christian doctrines were explained to us by Sister Catherine. In the Roman Catholic tradition, "catechism" means "learning by means of questions and answers." Why, I asked Catherine, would God consign an innocent baby to hell, simply for being born in the wrong place and taught to believe in the wrong god? This seemed unfair to the poor pagan children in China or India. As I understand it, I told the nun, someone could rob, cheat, and steal through life, repent at the end, and go to heaven. "Yes," Catherine agreed graciously. And an innocent child in China could be kind and generous, die before ever hearing of Jesus or being baptized, and be barred from heaven? The nun knew the correct ecclesiastic response: "We can't fully know God's plan." And so there the question remained, and my youthful reasoning caved in on itself. I'm supposed to believe this *because* I can't understand it? Perhaps I had been presumptuous, but I felt better when I learned in my catechism reading that renowned thirteenth-century scholar Thomas Aquinas had agonized over the same problem. In the end, he hypothesized that a merciful God would not consign innocent babies, even those who died without being purged of Original Sin through baptism, to hell. These innocents, Aquinas imagined, must dwell in limbo, a place between heaven and hell, alongside virtuous but unbaptized pagans such as Plato and Moses, born before Jesus had come to explain things.

Limbo is not to be confused with purgatory, a transitory place, according my first Catholic encyclopedia, "of temporal punishment for those who, departing this life in God's grace, are not entirely free from venial faults." Purgatory is an opportunity to "reach perfection," like a prep school for heaven. In the Middle Ages, the idea of doing time in purgatory until one had "fully paid" for one's transgressions led to the selling of indulgences, reducing a sinner's sentence, while enriching the church, pope, or parson, a practice mocked by Chaucer and protested by Martin Luther. Later, seventeenth-century Protestants spawned multifarious versions of purgatory. Some claimed it is instantaneous and painless, others that it is infinitely painful but instantaneous, or the "God's-One-Second-in-Hell" theory.

Limbo, on the other hand, allegedly provided a permanent resting place for good, but unbaptized, innocents. In 1992, Pope John Paul II would urge Catholic theologians to come up with a "more coherent and illuminating doctrine." Although it doesn't make sense that a deity with the power to create the universe would reward a despicable scoundrel and punish an innocent child, the Vatican could hardly tolerate the idea of virtuous pagans in heaven with Catholics, which would cast doubt on Original Sin and undermine the role of baptism. Still, the theologians have not resolved the question, leaving Plato, Moses, and those innocent pagan babies in at least a metaphorical limbo.

I attended high school in Midland, Texas, pursued science and mathematics, and became a physics undergraduate at Occidental College in Southern California in the fall of 1966. After my first year in college, I spent the summer as an apprentice engineer at Lockheed Aerospace. In this top-secret environment, at the height of the Vietnam War, I grew uncomfortable, not knowing what I might be working on. Perhaps, I thought, I could be drawing circuits for a doomsday machine. I decided to become a journalist, and when I returned to Occidental College I dropped physics and took up literature and history. While studying Christianized Europe in the late Middle Ages, I revisited my old friend Francis of Assisi and his nemesis, the Pope in Rome. I now glimpsed the full horror of religion's dark side.

INNOCENT OF WHAT?

During the twelfth century, Europe witnessed epic shifts in power. The once great Byzantine Empire had been expelled from Italy, Muslim Arabs took Palestine, and Christian Europe launched four crusades against these rivals. Pope Innocent III, from a family of Italian and German aristocrats, expanded papal power beyond Italy until he commanded the selection of a German emperor and could issue decrees to the kings of France and England. He then sent his armies to eradicate all known heretics in the realm. By "heretics" he meant those who believed doctrines not approved by him. Innocent described himself as "lower than God, but higher than man," insisting, "Every cleric must obey the Pope, even if he commands what is evil; for no one may judge the Pope." At the apogee of papal authority in Europe, commanding evil became a high and savage art.

The year Francis visited Rome, Innocent launched a crushing military campaign against non-Catholic Jesus followers in southern France, thus beginning the long, tragic Inquisition. His target, the Cathars, believed in living by the teachings of Jesus, but not by Rome's dictates. Many Cathars, or "pure ones," remained strictly non-violent even to animals, much like Francis in Italy. They believed people should read the words of Jesus in their own language, not necessarily in Latin, and they rejected the church doctrine of a physical resurrection. The Cathars considered the relics sold by Roman clergy to be demonic idols.

In the summer of 1209, 10,000 papal soldiers marched 200 kilometres south from Lyon to Montpellier, then west through the Garonne valley toward rural Cathar communities around Toulouse and Albi. The army surrounded Béziers, a town of 10,000 citizens where a congregation of 500 Cathars reportedly lived. The papal authority, Abbot Arnaud-Amaury, demanded that the Cathars be turned over, and when the citizens refused, he ordered the town destroyed. According to a report by one Caesar von Heisterbach, soldiers asked how to distinguish loyalists from heretics. "*Caedite eos! Novit enim Dominus qui sunt eius,*" the good abbot declared, "Slay them all! God will know his own." The papal soldiers reportedly tortured and mutilated their victims before executing all 10,000. Stories of the terrorism spread before the advancing army. People fled from their villages, and by fall, Innocent's soldiers had taken Limoux, Castelnaudary, Castres, Fanjeaux, Lombers, Montréal, and Albi.

Innocent died seven years later, Francis died in 1226, and both their traditions lived on. In 1229, Innocent's cousin, Pope Gregory IX, officially established the Inquisition in Toulouse, endowing his inquisitors with unlimited authority to suppress alleged heretics, and pressing Francis's order, the Franciscans, into the vile service as inquisitors. Later, Pope Innocent IV formally authorized torture, and his interrogators devised inspired implements of pain to elicit confessions and collect names of new suspects. Clever inquisitors often used their authority to steal property, settle grudges, or satisfy their sexual fetishes. A few surviving Cathars hid out and fought back until the papal army overran their last stronghold, at Quéribus, in 1255, slaughtering every last man, woman, and child.

Meanwhile, Rome also eradicated Jews and Moors. Surviors fled to Spain, but the Inquisition followed them. Propagandists spread rumours that Jews caused plagues by poisoning wells and drove nails through stolen Eucharist wafers to "crucify Jesus again." England expelled Jews, Parisians burned the Talmud, and in Germany, the army of a Christian knight called Rindfleisch boasted of exterminating 30,000 Jews in six months. For the next five hundred years, throughout Europe, both Catholic and Protestant Christians tormented and executed Jews, Muslims, scientists, mathematicians, and common healers accused of witchcraft.

According to the 1867 Vatican journal *La Civiltà Cattolica*, the Pope in Rome serves as Christ's vicar on earth, "the dispenser of spiritual graces, the giver of the benefits of religion, the upholder of justice, and the protector of the oppressed." How is one able to reconcile this claim with the facts of history?

I recoiled at the disparity between the lives of Francis and my grandmother compared to those who claim to possess religious authority. Even today we hear a persistent echo of church leaders gone wrong: sexual abuse in native residential schools, nearly cultish pedophilia by pastors and priests, millions of abuse victims worldwide, Ponzi scams passed off as "investments in the Lord," moralistic hatred from radio and television evangelists, and cheerleading for war, all supposedly in the name of Jesus. Most Christians, of course, remain peace-loving, innocent, and gracious citizens, but for those in authority, religion appears to offer no immunity from the corrupting influence of power.

The examples of Elizabeth and Saint Francis cast my earliest ideal of spirituality in action. Later, in my twenties, I learned of the Buddha, Mahatma Gandhi, Dorothy Day, Martin Luther King,

Susan B. Anthony, and others who transformed spiritual insight into acts of peace and compassion. I began attending Quaker meetings near the college, and was inspired by their pacifist tradition. I refused a draft call to Vietnam, which caused rifts within my family, but my aging grandmother Elizabeth told me, "You do what you know is right." Meanwhile, the question haunted my thoughts: Where does religion go wrong? Specifically, how did the teachings of Jesus go so wrong? And ultimately, what was the original, authentic message of the peasant Jesus in Galilee?

A REAL JESUS?

In 1973, I landed my first journalism job as a reporter in Canada. In 1980, I began researching a book I co-authored, *Chop Wood, Carry Water*, surveying the wisdom of humanity's spiritual traditions and applying that wisdom to modern, everyday life. I travelled to Mount Saviour Monastery in Elmira, New York, to interview Benedictine brother David Steindl-Rast. Born in Vienna in 1926, Steindl-Rast earned a Ph.D. from the University of Vienna and had recently participated in public discussions with Zen teacher Shunryu Suzuki Roshi. We spent a rousing afternoon in the garden talking about spirituality and the human predicament. Eventually, I asked the burning question: How did he reconcile his commitment to Christianity with the atrocities of church history, the Inquisition, the burning of women healers, and the pedophilia scandals? He issued a sad, heartfelt sigh. "I know," he said. "Terrible things have been done in the name of Jesus. However, I remain loyal to Christianity because this is the tradition through which I discovered spirit. The Buddhists discover spirit through their tradition, Hindus through theirs. Jesus discovered spirit through the Jewish tradition in which he grew up."

Jesus' testimony about discovering spirit appears in the elusive record of his words and deeds. This book seeks the authentic sayings of Jesus, his message, and mission. For some Christians this might seem absurdly simple: Just look in any red-letter edition of the Bible for the sayings of Jesus. But if we compare parallel passages, we find that the four canonical Gospels — *Matthew, Mark, Luke, and John* — do not present consistent accounts. The Gospels contradict one another, record aphorisms and parables of Jesus in different words, place them in different narrative scenes, and reinterpret them. The contradictions are not trivial.

The voice of Jesus survived decades of oral transmission before written records appeared, and then centuries of revision thereafter. Jesus wrote nothing and spoke in Aramaic. The gospel authors composed in Greek, and we possess no evidence linking those writers to historical persons. Some forty years elapsed between the execution of Jesus and the first written narrative accounts. The earliest surviving complete manuscripts of the popular gospels appear three centuries later. Scholars presume for good reasons that versions of the gospels appeared earlier than the surviving manuscripts, but we possess no originals and hundreds of variant copies. We might wonder then: How accurately did the message of Jesus survive decades of spoken discourse and centuries of revision?

In the mid-second century, in the port city of Sinope on the Black Sea, a wealthy shipowner, Marcion, son of a Christian church elder, searched the record for a historical Jesus. Marcion's writings were destroyed, so we know him only through his orthodox critics, who denounced him. The *Catholic Encyclopedia* still considers him "the most dangerous foe Christianity has ever known." Conversely, translator Ernest Evans depicts Marcion as a genuinely curious scholar, whose movement survived "persecution, Christian controversy, and imperial disapproval for several centuries." The search for an authentic Jesus, distinct from orthodox interpretation, reappeared with the tenth-century Bulgarian Bogomils, who lived modestly and believed in a human Jesus, and the French Cathars obliterated by the armies of Pope Innocent III.

The Inquisition and its aftermath forestalled research into the historic Jesus until the eighteenth century, when previously unknown manuscripts began emerging from Egypt and the Levant. In 1760, German linguist Hermann Reimarus observed that distinctive language in ancient texts helped him distinguish later doctrine from the most likely words of a first-century Jesus. Thus began what modern researchers call the "quest for the historical Jesus." Reimarus posed two questions for himself and his academic colleagues: Which events reported in the Gospels actually happened? And, what ideas and teachings from the surviving record can be traced to the historical Jesus? They are fair questions. They do not preclude other interesting questions — such as, what do gospel stories mean metaphorically? — but they remain important and relevant today.

During the twentieth century, historians and scholars developed advanced methods of analyzing language to reveal layers of borrowing and revision in ancient manuscripts. The *Matthew* and *Luke* gospels, for example, appear to copy the *Mark* account and other early collections of sayings. Portions of these earlier sources have been discovered in manuscript fragments, but archaeologists continue to look for the remaining "lost gospels." Meanwhile, startling new texts — the gospels of *Mary*, *Thomas*, *Philip*, and others — have risen from their desert graves to provide fresh sources of Jesus' sayings. Some 200 significant historical accounts contribute to the search for the sayings and deeds of Jesus, taking us far beyond the boundaries of New Testament Gospels.

Rare physical artifacts also inform our search. In *Excavating Jesus*, a book published in 2001, John Dominic Crossan and Jonathan Reed discuss these clues and pose another question: Why did the Jesus movement arise in first-century Israel? Their investigations probe social events that triggered popular resistance to Roman domination and inspired the message of Jesus. In the present book, I raise two more questions, presuming that we might approach some understanding of Jesus' authentic message. How did that message get confused or misrepresented? And what relevance does that message offer us in the twenty-first century?

"Some of the words attributed to Jesus were not actually spoken by him," writes Robert J. Miller, editor of *The Complete Gospels*. "While this is not news to scholars, it is news to the...public." In the course of this book, we will examine the research of scholars such as Miller, Crossan and Reed, Elaine Pagels, Burton Mack, Bart D. Ehrman, Karen L. King, Margaret Starbird, Nicholas Wright, Robert W. Funk, and many others. We will scrutinize the work of academic associations such as the Westar Institute's Jesus Seminar and the Committee for the Scientific Examination of Religion's Jesus Project. These scholars attempt to answer the questions raised by Reimarus: What can we reasonably say about the historical Jesus, and what did this person teach?

WAYS OF KNOWING

In 1981, the United States of America launched a new attack submarine, armed with cruise missiles and nuclear warheads, named *Corpus Christi*, the body of Christ. In the days thereafter, as far as I could discover, not a single journalist mentioned the dreadful irony. Neither the Vatican nor American televangelists publically objected to naming the world's most advanced killing machine after Jesus. Years later, following polite objections from dismayed Christians, the U.S. Navy changed the name to the *City of Corpus Christi*, perhaps to clarify that they did not intend the actual Prince of Peace.

I would not want to hurt the feelings of any true believer — whether Hindu, Muslim, Christian, or Shinto — but the time has long since arrived for modern society to reckon with the misuse of religion and the horrors perpetrated in the name of religion. In the West, perhaps it is time to rediscover what Jesus, a poor Jewish peasant from Galilee, actually said.

As we examine the historical record, this book will pose the typical historian's questions: Who says? Who corroborates the story? What credentials does the witness possess? Simultaneously, we must ask the ethnologist's questions: What human truths do the myths and stories reveal, regardless of their historicity? We will recognize, in other words, that myth, legend, popular narrative, bias, and even intentional manipulation of facts reveal underlying truths about human experience. In her book *The Battle for God*, Karen Armstrong points out that ancient cultures possessed "two ways of thinking, speaking, and acquiring knowledge, which scholars have called *mythos* and *logos*...complementary ways of arriving at truth, and each had its special area of competence."

Mythos — parables, legends, and metaphors — addresses timeless meaning, unconscious emotion, and cultural insights that cannot be contained in collections of facts. *Logos* — rationality, science, and logic — describes natural processes, cause and effect, and historical events. First-century culture was far more influenced by *mythos* than we are today. Our modern culture is dominated by *logos*, by science and engineering. Our society is so committed to rational facts that we have almost lost the ability to discuss spiritual feelings unless we also imagine that our metaphors are literally true. Myth is the tool that allows people to examine deep, taboo, unpopular, or radical ideas without exposing themselves to retribution. There is a saying among writers: If you really want to tell the truth, you better write fiction.

Crossan points out that ancient gospel writers had no intention of writing history. "They are writing gospel," he reminds us. "If you read a gospel as giving you straight history you are denying what it claims to be, namely good news." Our word "gospel" is a translation of the Greek word *euaggelion*, meaning "good announcement." A gospel is an uplifting story, not history. Furthermore, ancient writers typically borrowed stories, merged scenes, and conflated characters. This is not unusual. We face the identical challenge, for example, in researching the authentic sayings of Pythagoras, Socrates, or the Buddha.

Difficulties arise, however, when people confuse *mythos* and *logos*, or use cultural myth to impose public policy. I do not consider it a threat, or any of my business, for example, if a devout Hindu believes that the god Indra really came to earth as Rama and made common cause with Hanuman the monkey king. However, I do care if he or she wages war on all people who don't share this belief. I care if he or she uses myth to divide humanity and manipulate others toward violence. If someone believes that Muhammad actually rode a white horse to heaven or that a god in heaven dictated books to humans, there may be no harm; however, there certainly is harm if that person presumes the right to eradicate populations in the name of those beliefs. The problem with confusing myth and history is that one's metaphors are doomed to clash with the heartfelt metaphors of other people.

In pursuing history, we need not sacrifice the wonder of myth. We do not have to take myth, parables, or fables literally to absorb their meaning. *Logos* and *mythos*, history and metaphor, work together simultaneously to reveal truth. The key involves looking behind the metaphors to witness humanity's authentic struggles between power and vulnerability, oppression and justice, men and women, vision and longing. Our stories, from the Sumerian tale of Gilgamesh to J. R. R. Tolkien's *Lord of the Rings*, use mythology in this way to portray very real human experiences and emotions.

A TIMELESS PRESENCE

The first decade of the twenty-first century has witnessed a revival of secular and agnostic reactions to violence among fundamentalist Christians, Jews, Muslims, and Hindus. In our era of religious tolerance, books such as *The God Delusion* by Richard Dawkins, *God Is Not Great* by Christopher Hitchens, or *The Battle for God* by Karen Armstrong have broken the taboo against critiquing religion, especially religious doctrines used to rationalize violence, injustice, depravity, and greed. Such open discussion signals a healthy change, but some faithful adherents to these religions fear that losing long-held doctrines about deities will erode our ethical foundations.

One of the more thoughtful authors in this genre, Sam Harris (*The End of Faith* and *Letter to a Christian Nation*), makes a strong case that religion is not the basis of our compassion or ethics. Common citizens everywhere, even without religion, know how to treat people with respect, while passages from the Quran or Bible are relentlessly employed to justify violence. The Book of Deuteronomy in the Jewish Torah, adopted by Christianity as the Old Testament, insists we stone our children to death if they profess belief in the wrong deities. We would like to believe that human society has moved beyond such doctrines, but religious bloodshed appears daily on our television screens to remind us how far we have to go. "Questions about morality are questions about happiness and suffering," Harris writes, and "People make religion out of the full fabric of their lives, not out of mere beliefs."

Religious tolerance remains a hallmark of civilized society, but pandering to religious hypocrisy does not. We are not forced to choose sides between blind faith in ancient doctrines, on the one hand, and rationalist denial of people's spiritual experiences on the other. A vast and glorious landscape exists between the extremes of religious fundamentalism and absolute rationalism.

That landscape is populated by individuals such as Somali-Dutch author Ayaan Hirsi Ali, speaking out for the liberation of Muslim women; Dominican and Episcopal scholar Matthew Fox, declaring a "new reformation" of Christian spirituality; and the Dalai Lama, urging all humanity to seek "inner disarmament."

As a journalist, I have participated in social and ecological movements, helping to research and tell stories that I felt were important. I have observed that perhaps the greatest impediment to social change is often spiritual immaturity and blunders of the ego — pride, fear, and greed — not mistakes of theory or tactics. The social-justice mentors who have inspired me work from spiritual maturity, not from political dogma: Gandhi, Dorothy Day, Martin Luther King, Aung San Suu Kyi, Mairead Corrigan.

Modern travel and electronic media have awakened humanity to itself. We have access to stories and wisdom from every continent and every era of history. We have seen our planet from space, floating in a dynamic universe. We are slaves to neither ancient nor modern doctrine. We may see and think for ourselves. Anyone may study and learn from the Buddha or Jesus, without accepting or casting judgement on anyone else's legendary, mythological, or religious interpretation of these religious leaders. The lessons of the Buddha transcend Buddhism, and the teachings of Jesus transcend Christianity.

"The biggest obstacle to interfaith tolerance," the Dalai Lama has said, "is a bad relationship with one's own faith tradition." I am writing this book because I believe the Western world needs the authentic voice of Jesus, as much now as it did in the first century, and because I cannot tolerate the submarine *Corpus Christi* with its nuclear weapons, warmongers, and hucksters posing as that authentic voice. Being tolerant of religion means respecting religious experiences, not accepting the trivialization of those experiences, and much less the absolute violation of those experiences by those who command evil, make money, incite violence, or perpetrate abuse on innocent children in the name of religion.

This book surveys the more than 200 ancient documents that contribute to our understanding of Jesus and his real message. I rely on the research of scholars who have made this search their life's work. I have discovered one important characteristic of such scholars: The wisest appear to be the most humble. Those who genuinely care about humanity's history do not make absolute pronouncements or presume infallibility. History defies simple interpretations.

Reliable historians also make no significant distinction between so-called orthodox accounts and other written sources. Each source rests on its own credentials. Historians consider the earliest manuscripts, the presumed date that the lost originals might have been composed, the alleged witness, and the writers' biases. We will use these methods to examine historical questions such as where Jesus might have been born, his parentage, and the hometown of Mary Magdalene.

One surprise is that the earliest Christians were not Christians at all. Like Jesus, they were Jews, who did not necessarily consider their teacher a messiah. We will meet the poor, dispossessed Ebionites and the ascetic Nazoreans, who followed the teachings of Jesus before his memory became associated with complex cosmologies and divine expectations. We shall find that their own acts of compassion revealed his "presence" among them. The New Testament Greek word used to describe this "coming" of Jesus is *parousia*, meaning a felt presence of a great person. Citizens of twelfth-century Assisi may have felt the presence of Jesus as they witnessed the life of Francis. I felt such a presence in the living grace of my grandmother.

The coming of Jesus that my sister and I celebrated, by ritually opening tiny doors on the Advent calendar, would not have indicated the physical arrival of Jesus to his earliest followers, but rather the presence of his grace in their own actions. As Matthew Fox explains, "The name of Jesus is being used to accumulate wealth and political power. But in the end, God is Love. And love, not power, will have the last word." Or so we may hope.

· I ·

WITNESS

We can, at the present day, scarcely imagine the long agony
in which the historical view of the life of Jesus came to birth.

ALBERT SCHWEITZER, *THE QUEST FOR*
THE HISTORICAL JESUS, 1909

Only about thirty papyrus manuscripts and fragments prior
to the fourth century attest to the words and deeds of Jesus.
Today, paleographers (scholars who study ancient documents)
generally believe the oldest manuscript evidence of a New Testament story is a famous little scrap of papyrus, about the size of a
cash-register receipt, called "P52," held by the Rylands Library in
Manchester, England. Text on both sides confirms the fragment
comes from a codex, or ancient book. Handwriting analysis links
the scribe to the era of Emperor Hadrian, 117 to 138 C.E., about
one hundred years after the time of Jesus. It measures about six
by nine centimetres and contains 110 legible Greek letters comprising twelve complete words and twenty partial words.

The earliest indication of Bible stories in the first three centuries after the life of Jesus is like so many islands disappearing into
the mist. P52 represents the last rock in the surf on the last islet.

Here, paleographers pore over the remnants of the physical trail as it disappears into the sea of time. The front side of P52 reveals the following roughly rendered in English:

> us Jew
> no one that the w
> id signify
> die ent
> rium P
> and say
> ew

Prior to this second-century scrap of papyrus, no physical written evidence attests to Jesus. Scholars have filled in the presumed missing letters and words to match a passage that appears in the *Gospel of John* 16:31, in which Jesus stands before Pilate:

> Pilate said to them, "Take him yourselves and judge him according to your law." The Jews replied, "We are not permitted to put anyone to death." This was to fulfill what Jesus had said when he indicated the kind of death he was to die. Then Pilate entered the headquarters again, summoned Jesus, and asked him, "Are you the King of the Jews?"

There appears to be a significant leap from fragment to gospel, but the words and letters fit well enough with later Greek manuscripts that most scholars are confident P52 parallels the passage in *John*. Beyond that, we cannot know what the remainder of the original codex contained. Scholars believe the Gospels, in some form, existed by this time, and archaeologists have excavated ancient sites looking for evidence of complete manuscripts.

THE EARLIEST BIBLE

In 1840, at the University of Leipzig, a twenty-five-year-old Bible scholar, Constantin von Tischendorf, grew frustrated in his attempts to translate the Greek New Testament. No two versions agreed, and Tischendorf recognized "many errors" in manuscripts resulting from centuries of copying. He suspected some editors had consciously made changes "as materially affect the meaning, and, what is worse still, did not shrink from cutting out a passage or inserting one."

Tischendorf set off on an expedition to discover authentic versions of the Greek Gospels. At the Bibliothèque Nationale in Paris he painstakingly restored a fifth-century manuscript that had been scrubbed clean in the twelfth century to be used as writing paper. The recovered text did not answer his questions, but his success earned him the patronage of the Saxon King Frederick Augustus II. In April 1844, Tischendorf embarked for Egypt, funded by the king, "to discover some precious remains of any manuscripts...which would carry us back to the early times of Christianity."

A month later, at the foot of Mount Sinai, in the library at the Monastery of St. Catherine, he found a basket filled with old parchments, goatskins inscribed in uncial Greek, all capitals, without word breaks or punctuation. On the spot, based on these clues, Tischendorf dated the documents between the fourth and eighth centuries. The librarian informed him that two other stacks of deteriorating manuscripts had been burned. Among the parchments, Tischendorf discovered an Old Testament, described in his memoirs as "one of the most ancient that I had ever seen." He asked to take the bundles with him, but his enthusiasm "aroused their suspicions." The monks let him take forty-three pages, and he encouraged them to take scrupulous care of the remainder.

Tischendorf returned to Paris, translated and published the recovered pages, and prepared for a second expedition to Egypt. In 1859, he returned to the monastery and discovered a complete Greek manuscript of the New Testament and most of the Old Testament. These manuscripts became known as *Codex Sinaiticus*, the oldest known complete copy of the Bible, dating from about 350 C.E.

There is a significant gap of three centuries from the execution of Jesus in about 30 C.E. to the tiny P52 remnant composed around 125 C.E., and finally to the earliest complete Bible manuscripts from 350 C.E. We may wonder how accurately the stories were preserved.

Some Bible scholars claim that the P52 fragment suggests the *Gospel of John* must have been written in the first century, allowing four or five decades for copies of the gospel to travel from its presumed place of origin in Syria or Ephesus, on the Aegean coast of Turkey, to Egypt, where the papyrus fragment was found. Three problems cast doubt on this interpretation.

First, the fragment P52 does not establish that the *Gospel of John* existed in full, even in the early second century, although some edition probably did. The fragment can attest only to the brief scene it conveys: A man appeared before the Roman prefect Pontius Pilate concerning conflicts with the Jewish establishment. Since the circumstances fit with later stories, we can presume this person is the same Jesus (in Hebrew, *Yeshua* or *Yahushua*, meaning a "saviour" from God) who appears in those later documents, but we cannot assume, on the basis of this fragment, that later stories associated with this scene existed with it. Here, we have stumbled upon a salient characteristic of evidence about Jesus sayings, and we will encounter this problem repeatedly. Sayings and stories that appear in the Gospels exist in earlier versions. In such cases, an early fragment of a scene does not confirm the existence of an entire gospel that appears later in the record. Scholars generally believe an edition of the *John* Gospel existed by the second century, but the P52 fragment attests to nothing but itself.

Secondly, it does not take forty or fifty years for a manuscript copied in Ephesus or Syria to reach Egypt. In the first century, a boat journey from the Aegean coast, across the eastern Mediterranean to Egypt might have taken a week, perhaps two weeks with stops at the islands along the way, but not forty years. According to the Acts of the Apostles and Paul's First Letter to the Corinthians, the teacher Apollos from Alexandria travelled easily between Egypt and the Aegean, preaching his version of Jesus' message. People, stories, and documents circulated constantly throughout Mediterranean communities during the first century. Since this story of Jesus' trial originated in Jerusalem, closer to Alexandria than to Ephesus, and since sea and land travel from Palestine to Alexandria was common, one could fairly assume that the story from Jerusalem could reach Egypt as quickly as it might reach Syria to the north or Ephesus on the west coast of Asia Minor.

Thirdly, the *Gospel of John* was likely not composed in a single, complete first edition. Many scholars believe it first appeared in Syria as a list of miracles that were later incorporated into narratives. Text analysis can identify breaks in language or style, referred to by paleographers as "seams," identifying various editions. For example, the first eighteen verses of the *John* Gospel comprise a Semitic poem that resonates as a distinct voice, interspersed with earlier passages about John the Baptist. Likewise, a second closing, chapter 21, appears as a later addendum. We don't know who the first author or later editors were, or precisely when they composed portions of the Gospel prior to its appearance in full around 350 C.E. Furthermore, until the age of printing, in the fifteenth century, no two surviving copies of *John* are identical. Consequently, suggesting that the fragment implies an earlier gospel reverses the historian's logic and constitutes a retrofit, working backwards to presume an earlier event based on much later evidence.

As we follow the trail of stories from the voice of a living Jesus, across three centuries to the appearance of gospel manuscripts, we encounter missing pages, edited passages, conflicting accounts, and faulty translations. The tiny P52 fragment reveals the challenge scholars face when interpreting incomplete evidence.

FOR THIS I WAS BORN

In the scene in which Jesus appears before Pilate, a problem arises concerning the Greek word for "Jew." In the first century, northern Galilean Israelites and southern Judeans did not necessarily consider themselves aligned with one another, even though they shared aspects of the Jewish religion. First-century Galileans felt oppressed as Jews by Romans and as Israelites by the wealthier, urban Judeans. In the original Hebrew or Aramaic, "Jew" and "Judean" implied quite distinct meanings. *Yehuda*, the Jewish "people of god," refers to all Jews. *Yehudi* were residents of Judea, decendents of Yudah, the fourth son of Jacob, and historic enemies of the Israelites. However, the Greek word for "Jew," *Ioudaios*, confuses the two meanings.

Dr. K. C. Hansen, an expert in Hebrew, Aramaic, Ugaritic, Akkadian, and Greek, as well as modern languages, translates this word in most Bible passages as "Judeans," distinct from the northern Israelites, and specifically distinct from Jesus and his Galilean friends.

"Are you king of the Judeans?"

One could construe this question as referring to general, ethnic Jews, as with most English Bibles, but the shift in meaning is significant. Jesus, being a Jew, did not abhor Jews, but he may have stood in opposition to Judean priests who taxed the poor and enjoyed special privileges under the Romans. New Testament passages that portray all Jews as Jesus' antagonists indicate later Greek-speaking Christian language intended to disparage Jews, not the language of Galilean peasants and fishermen. Throughout our search for the message of Jesus, we will preserve this distinction.

The P52 papyrus depicts a simple Galilean peasant hauled before the most powerful politician in Judea. On the reverse side of the fragment, we discover the earliest known physical evidence of a quote attributed to Jesus. Here are the surviving words and letters in English:

> this been born
> rld that I bear
> s the true
> says to him
> and this
> to Y
> any

The "Y" suggests Yeshua, or Jesus. Scholars extrapolate these clues to parallel *John* 18:37–38. When asked to account for himself, Jesus exhibits earth-shaking personal power:

"So you are a king?" said Pilate.

"You're the one who says I am a King," responded Jesus. "This is why I was born and this is why I came into the world: to bear witness to the truth. Everyone who belongs to the truth can hear my voice."

"What is the truth?" asked Pilate. When he had said this, he again went out to the Judeans. "In my judgement there is no case against him," he told them.

We may wonder: Did Jesus really say this in a trial before Pilate? Many scholars doubt these represent his actual words, and for good reason. We would not expect accounts written six decades or more after the events to contain extensive verbatim transcriptions of such a trial. The *Gospel of John* includes long homilies attributed to Jesus that are almost certainly the work of the author. In this passage, however, the words resonate with the culture-crashing courage we associate with Jesus. When confronted with life or death at the hands of a tyrant and a mob, this vulnerable, human Jesus coolly deflects adulation, and offers up modest dignity in its place.

By simply bearing witness to the truth, Jesus — whether historically or mythically — exposes for history the cowardliness and duplicity of his tormentors. The statement, allegedly from Jesus, suggests a leader who stood up to power and possessed a sublime wit. This response also suggests the ideal attitude — "witness the truth" — with which to launch an investigation into that person's authentic teachings.

TENDER YOUTH AND SERVANT MAIDS

In the year 112 C.E., near the time that a Greek-speaking scribe composed the P52 fragment, the Italian governor of Bithynia on the Black Sea, Gaius Plinius Secundus, wrote to Roman Emperor Trajan seeking advice. Plinius — known to history as Pliny the Younger, poet, senator, and friend to historian Tacitus — had found among the citizenry a messiah cult whose believers had been accused of inciting rebellion.

During the second century around the Mediterranean, failing to make supplications upon demand to the Roman gods and emperor could bring charges of sedition, punishable by death. Nevertheless, the emperor upheld certain legal standards. Prisoners could not be executed on hearsay, for example, so Pliny ordered the accused brought into his court to make supplications to the emperor's image before his eyes. Those who obeyed faced a second test, requiring them to curse "Christus" (Latin for the Greek *Christos* or "the anointed one"), whom they worshipped as a messiah. Some did so, were interrogated, and released. Following Roman law, Pliny executed those who refused to honour the emperor's gods. Troubled by the frequent executions, he wrote to Trajan:

> Nor are my doubts small, whether there be not a distinction to be made between the ages and whether tender youth ought to have the same punishment as strong men?

Executing children apparently bothered his conscience. He also wondered if being a "Christian, without any crimes besides," should result in punishment. Pliny's description of the group as "Christian" represents the earliest known use of this term, although it allegedly was also used about the same time by a church elder in Antioch. Pliny reported the Christian custom of meeting before sunrise on a set day each week, when they would share a common meal, sing a hymn "to Christus, as a god," and take an oath promising to commit no crime against their fellow citizens, "no theft, or pilfering, or adultery."

Perhaps in fear that Trajan might doubt his resolve, Pliny assured the emperor that he had interrogated those who refused to recant, finding it "necessary to inquire by torments...which I did of two servant maids, called Deaconesses, but discovered no more than that they were addicted to a bad and extravagant superstition."

In a return letter, Trajan ignores the question of "tender youth" but replies that Pliny has judged well. "These people are not to be sought out," he commands, "but if accused and convicted, they are to be punished." The miscreants may have appeared innocuous to the emperor, but for one final observation that Pliny shared with his patron: "There are many of every age, of every rank," and "this superstition is spread like a contagion."

Pliny does not mention Jesus—the Latin *Iesus*—but only Christus. Although other messianic leaders and movements flourished during the Roman era, we might presume from our twenty-first-century perspective that the Christians in Bithynia in the year 112 considered their messiah to be Jesus. Nevertheless, eighty years after the death of Jesus, Pliny does not mention him by name and appears to know nothing about him.

Searching outside Christian texts for early—pre-fourth-century—evidence of Jesus yields precious few accounts. The Jewish Talmud—sixty-three tractates of written law, commentary, and dialogues written after the destruction of Jerusalem in 70 C.E.— offers virtually nothing about Jesus. The Babylonian version of the Talmud mentions one "Yeshu" in a passage about proper procedures for a stoning.

> On the eve of the Passover Yeshu was hanged....a herald went forth and cried, "He is going forth to be stoned because he has practiced sorcery and enticed Israel to apostasy."

The full passage suggests this Yeshu held some political connection with authorities and had five disciples, Matthai, Nakai, Nezer, Buni, and Todah. These details clearly don't match the Christian Jesus. John P. Meier sums up the evidence in *A Marginal Jew: Rethinking the Historical Jesus*: "In the earliest rabbinic sources, there is no clear or even probable reference to Jesus of Nazareth."

In 1947, an itinerant goat herder discovered the first of the Dead Sea Scrolls in a cave near the ancient monastic community of Qumran, east of Jerusalem. To date, some 870 scrolls have been recovered from eleven caves. The scrolls have been attributed to the Essene sect, although this remains uncertain. Some experts believe that both John the Baptist and Jesus were Essenes, but this also remains unconfirmed, and the scrolls offer no such evidence. The authors composed most of these manuscripts during the two centuries before, during, and after the life of Jesus. They contain not a single reference to Yeshua, a Galilean teacher.

The Roman historian Tacitus, Pliny's colleague, provides the earliest unambiguous secular reference to Christus as a historical person in Judea. Although Tacitus reveals an anti-Christian bias, he reports that Nero unfairly prosecuted Christians to deflect accusations that he had set Rome's notorious fire in 64 C.E.:

> ...to suppress the rumour, he falsely charged with guilt, and punished Christians, who were hated for their enormities. Christus, the founder of the name, was put to death by Pontius Pilate, procurator of Judea in the reign of Tiberius; but the pernicious superstition, repressed for a time, broke out again not only through Judea, where the mischief originated, but through the city of Rome also, where all things hideous and shameful from every part of the world find their centre and become popular.

To set the record straight, Pilate was a prefect, or governor, not a procurator. Tacitus generally is a reliable historian, although his flippant dismissal of the "pernicious superstition" tarnishes his credibility. In this case, however, his bias suggests that the information is reliable. It appears unlikely that Tacitus would invent this episode to defend a group he loathed. The passage in his *Annals* from 115 C.E. confirms that Christians existed in Rome in the second century and that they believed in a Christus, who had been executed by Pontius Pilate in Judea.

We must be careful about reading into such accounts more than they offer. Historians insist on a commitment to absolute objectivity, a commitment, in fact, to witness the truth. From Pliny and Tacitus we hear nothing about the person of Jesus, and only that a messiah movement existed in the early second century, linked to a Christus in Judea. Thus far, we have not yet found a single secular reference to associate this person with the name Jesus, from the Greek Iēsous, or Hebrew Yeshua.

The Jewish historian Flavius Josephus, writing in about 90 C.E., appears to have made such a reference. Two short passages, in Books 18 and 20 of *The Jewish Antiquities*, written in Greek, mention Iēsous, but remain highly controversial.

A WISE MAN

Josephus was born to an aristocratic, priestly family in Jerusalem in 37 C.E. "By my mother," he claims in his autobiography, "I am of royal blood." He served as a general in the Jewish rebellions against Rome, which he recounts in *Jewish Wars*. He is reliable regarding most events, but he clearly favours the Jewish elite against the peasantry, coddles the Roman autocracy, exalts himself, and covers his own tracks. He took three wives, including a captured slave girl, in violation of Jewish law, which he later claims he did under direct orders from the future emperor, Vespasian. Josephus wrote his histories in the comfort of Vespasian's court in Rome, and later under the protection of Vespasian's sons Titus and Domitian, between 71 and 94 C.E. His writings reveal his loyalties.

> Domitian...augmented his respects to me; for he punished those Jews that were my accusers....He also made that country I had in Judea tax free, which is a mark of the greatest honor to him who has it; nay, Domitia, the wife of Caesar, continued to do me kindnesses.

He took the name Flavius in honour of his Roman patrons. He has little good to say about Jewish peasants, messianic leaders, or rebel outlaws, except for his acknowledgement that John the Baptist was a "good man." He blames peasant rebels for the demise of Jerusalem, and his Roman leaders do no wrong, make no mistakes, and prove justified in their worst atrocities.

Josephus's credibility wavers as he describes his own military prowess, his brilliant strategies, and the devotion of his subordinates. He fashions grandiose scenes about himself in the third person, including his miraculous escape from Jewish assassins — "the swords were just at his throat" — that play like a scene from a modern Hollywood thriller. His surrender to Vespasian comes across as downright self-serving, particularly when he justifies his duplicity among Jewish compatriots and his miraculous survival and prosperity at the hands of the Roman enemy.

In the year 70, Josephus accompanied Roman commanders during their assault on Jerusalem. His accounts extol Rome's efficiency and her generals' grandeur as the streets of Jerusalem literally ran with blood. The Jews, his own people, he suggests, deserved their fate because they followed rebel leaders. Josephus shifts from Roman apologist to defender of the Jewish aristocracy in different versions of certain incidents. He renders the historical scenes brilliantly, but one must read between the lines to separate the writer's pandering from authentic history. Nevertheless, Josephus provides an eye-popping glimpse into first-century Palestine, for which historians remain grateful.

In chapter 18 of *Antiquities*, recounting the era when Jesus might have been known in Judea, Josephus tells how the prefect Pontius Pilate sent troops from Caesarea into Jerusalem by the dead of night, carrying ensigns embossed with images of Emperor Tiberius. At daybreak, the Jews stood horrified at the violation of their law regarding idols, and rightfully suspicious that Pilate intended to abolish Jewish religious authority. Protesters marched to Caesarea on the coast and petitioned Pilate, who sent assassins among the crowd to selectively execute troublemakers. The Jews — men, women, and children — prostrated themselves on the ground and offered their lives en masse. Pilate, explains Josephus, "was deeply affected" by the gesture and relented. Later, however, he recovered from his queasiness, sent soldiers to execute "a great number...And thus put an end to this great sedition."

We witness here the patrician's fluency from both sides of his mouth, but the historical scene rings true. Following this story in *Antiquities*, we find what may be history's earliest independent record of the name Jesus, the Greek Iēsous.

> About this time there lived Iēsous, a wise man, if indeed one ought to call him a man. For he was one who performed surprising deeds and was a teacher of such people as accept the truth gladly. He won over many Jews and many of the Greeks. He was the Messiah. And when, upon the accusation of the principal men among us, Pilate had condemned him to a cross, those who had first come to love him did not cease. He appeared to them spending a third day restored to life, for the prophets of God had foretold these things and a thousand other marvels about him. And the tribe of the Christians, so called after him, has still to this day not disappeared.

For centuries, scholars have cogitated over this and a later passage recounting the execution of James, "the brother of Jesus, who was called Christ." These passages are found in all the surviving manuscripts, so some historians believe these are authentic Josephus accounts. Nevertheless, the Jesus passages in Josephus remain controversial for three fundamental reasons. First of all, scholars have no extant manuscript of the text before the Middle Ages, by which time Christian editing of historical documents was well underway. Secondly, although ancient secular and religious authors mention Josephus, no commentator mentions the Jesus references prior to the fourth-century Church historian Eusebius. Finally, to some scholars, the language in this passage sounds not like an aristocratic Jewish priest, Josephus, writing for Roman patrons, but rather like the voice of a later Christian theologian. Since this reference represents the only secular pre-fourth-century written evidence of a Jesus in Palestine corresponding to the New Testament Jesus, a great deal of historical relevance remains attached to the conclusion.

AN ELUSIVE JESUS

The evidence that the voice in this passage is not Josephus hinges on statements such as "He was the Messiah" and "a third day." In the historical record, these doctrines arrive as purely Christian ideas, and nowhere else does Josephus speak as a Christian. As an aristocratic Jew, he ridicules messianic heroes such as Judas the Galilean and Theudas the magician, and wastes little ink on peasants, except to blame Israel's troubles with Rome on the resistance leaders, whom he depicts as "deceivers" and "enchanters."

In the Hebrew scriptures, the Christian Old Testament, we find thirty-eight references to messiahs — MSYH, pronounced, roughly, as "moshe-ach"— meaning "anointed one." Each reference points to a particular anointing or specific role: David as messiah of the God of Jacob, King Saul as messiah of Yahweh, and even the Persian King Cyrus as a messiah of the Judeans. The Jewish tradition did not name a single messiah as redeemer of all humankind. This claim would have appeared puzzling to first-century Jews, subversive to Roman rulers, and not something Josephus would toss off without some elucidation.

By comparison, he used three long paragraphs to describe John the Baptist and his historic influence on the Herod family, but makes no reference to Jesus with the Baptist. In a story that follows the Jesus reference, Josephus goes into far greater detail about the intrigues of a freedwoman who bribes the priests of Isis than he does over the world-shaking appearance of a universal saviour. If Josephus actually had said that this Jesus was the Messiah, as a point of historical fact that he believed to be true, he would typically have explained himself to his Jewish readers and Roman patrons. We might fairly expect one of his 10,000-word historical tours de force describing the events of the saviour's life and impact on society.

There are further complications. Church historian Eusebius quotes variations of Josephus's reference to Jesus, suggesting that several rewrites existed. In the mid-third century, orthodox church scholar Origen wrote a lengthy book critiquing the Platonist Celsus, who accused Christians of abandoning reason for blind faith. Origen uses every historical reference available to bolster his position, but explicitly states that Josephus did not acknowledge Jesus. Furthermore, no other pre-fourth-century church writer — not Ignatius, Irenaeus, Tertullian, or any other — draws upon Josephus to support his claims regarding Jesus. For many historians since the sixteenth century, this does not add up. In the seventeenth century, the Bishop of Norwich, Richard Montague, acknowledged that the passage was probably a later Christian addition.

Soon after Roman Emperor Constantine adopted Christianity in 313, the Josephus passage first appears in the historical record, from Eusebius, Bishop of Caesarea, who enjoyed the patronage of Constantine and wrote the first ecclesiastical history for the emperor. When Constantine convened the Council of Nicaea in 325 to establish the doctrines of the Roman state religion, Eusebius played a key role, providing the historical background and writing the first draft of the now-famous Nicene Creed that Catholics learn to recite in childhood, as I did. Nineteenth-century Swiss historian Jakob Burckhardt called Eusebius "the first thoroughly dishonest historian of antiquity." He was not the first, but Eusebius inserted events into history that have no corroboration. Some observers believe he invented the two passages in Josephus, and then quoted them in his history.

In 1963, Josephus historian and translator Louis H. Feldman, at Yeshiva University in New York, proposed a third possibility, suggesting that Josephus may indeed have mentioned Jesus as the victim of Pilate and as the brother of James, but that later Christian writers inserted segments, such as "He was the Messiah." This view is now commonly held. When scholars delete the presumed Christian inserts, they arrive at a possible Josephus reference that may be close to this:

> About this time there lived Jesus, a wise man, a teacher who performed surprising deeds. He won over many Jews and Greeks. Pilate had condemned him to a cross. Those who had first come to love him did not cease, and the tribe of the Christians, so called after him, to this day, has not disappeared.

Most scholars remain impartial, conducting objective textual forensics without promoting a theological position. In such circles, the authenticity of these passages remains inconclusive, although modern scholarship tends to doubt the "Christian" phrases as original. The Josephus testimony of Jesus may be authentic, partially authentic, or entirely counterfeit. If one holds to a preconceived notion of how history should be, the choice may seem simple. For the genuinely curious, certainty remains elusive.

After reviewing the secular references to Jesus in the first three centuries following his death, we are left with this: From Pliny's account we learn that a group of believers were called Christians after Christus, the messiah they worshipped as a god. The Christians met on a fixed day of the week before sunrise, sang, vowed to live an ethical life, and shared a common meal. Women served the congregation as deaconesses, the movement flourished, and some Christians would not recant their beliefs, even under torture. Almost concurrently, Tacitus links Christus to an execution under Pilate in Judea, consistent with the papyrus fragment P52. Josephus may, or may not, link this execution to a Iēsous, who was considered by some to be a messiah.

Among first- and second-century historians who do not mention Jesus at all, we may count Plutarch, Livy, Seneca, Philo, Judaeus, Dio Chrysostom, and dozens of others. We may feel shocked that we possess so little from early secular historians about Jesus, and that we learn absolutely nothing from these scant references about the actual teachings of Jesus. We might presume that his words and deeds inspired the communal meal and ethical lifestyle observed by Pliny, but we do not gain from the early historians a single quote to aid in our quest for the authentic teachings of Jesus.

A HISTORICAL JESUS

Josephus describes an incident, about thirty years after the time of Jesus, involving another Jesus, or Yeshua, son of Ananias, who railed against the Temple priests in Jerusalem, provoked Jewish authorities, claimed to hear divine voices, and inspired tales among the populace about his supernatural origins. Roman governor Albinus had Yeshua Ananias arrested, flogged, and released. Some historians believe that this Yeshua served as a model for at least some later narratives about Yeshua the Nazarene.

Certain scholars — G. A. Wells in *The Jesus Myth*, Robert M. Price, and others — believe the Jesus stories are a composite and doubt that the biblical Jesus existed as a single, knowable historic figure. This remains a minority view, but cannot be discounted out of hand. Dr. William R. Inge, former Dean of St. Paul's Cathedral in London, when asked to write a life history of Jesus, conceded, "there are no materials for a life of Christ."

Eighty years after Hermann Reimarus launched the quest for the historical Jesus, David Friedrich Strauss published *The Life of Jesus Critically Examined*, in which he attempted to distinguish mythology from history. Strauss pointed out that the mythologizing of heroes does not imply that the hero never existed. On the contrary, Strauss believed that the scattered praise for Jesus in different contexts suggests that he did exist.

Meanwhile, in America, Thomas Jefferson, an advocate of religious tolerance and separating politics from religion, took his scissors to the Bible to extract "the gold from the dross." He wrote to the first U.S. Surgeon General, Dr. Benjamin Rush, explaining:

> Fragments only...come to us mutilated, misstated, and often unintelligible...disfigured by the corruptions of schismatizing followers...perverting the simple doctrines he taught, by engrafting on them the mysticisms of a Grecian sophist, frittering them into subtleties, and obscuring them with jargon.

To lawyer and diplomat William Short, Jefferson wrote:

> I find many passages of fine imagination, correct morality, and of the most lovely benevolence; and others, again, of so much ignorance, so much absurdity, so much untruth, charlatanism and imposture, as to pronounce it impossible that such contradictions should have proceeded from the same Being.

Jefferson describes what he believed were the authentic Jesus teachings as "the most beautiful morsel of morality which has been given to us by man...universal philanthropy...gathering all into one family under the bonds of love, charity, peace, common wants and common aids." Finally, Jefferson described his summary of the historical Jesus:

> Among the Jews, Jesus appeared. His parentage was obscure; his condition poor; his education null; his natural endowments great; his life correct and innocent: he was meek, benevolent, patient, firm, disinterested, and of the sublimest eloquence.

Jefferson died in 1826. His handbook, *The Life and Morals of Jesus of Nazareth*, first appeared in print in 1904. Two years later, Albert Schweitzer published *The Quest for the Historical Jesus*. Schweitzer agreed that Jesus' ethics required extraction from later doctrine. As he searched the record, Schweitzer concluded that the Gospels created a messiah of faith fashioned from scarce historical reports, merged with the religious experiences of Jesus' followers, and embellished with the religious ideas and narratives of the age in which they were written.

Schweitzer, however, realized that even in his time, Church leaders were not yet prepared to accept the upheaval in church history that would follow from making a clear distinction between a historical Jesus, whom any student of history could study, and the Messiah of Christian faith. Unwilling to confront the Church, he let the historical question rest, took up medicine, and spent the remainder of his life living the teachings as he understood them: by healing impoverished African villagers at his hospital in Lambaréné, Gabon. His humanitarian efforts earned him the 1952 Nobel Peace Prize and the admiration of the world.

Since Schweitzer, hundreds of devoted scholars have taken up the search for historic evidence regarding Jesus. Modern research reveals that Jesus probably did exist, even though independent historical sources are rare and later writers borrowed or created certain stories.

In dating these texts, researchers must juggle two sets of dates: first, the era when the manuscripts were copied, and secondly, the presumed date that an original "autograph" version may have been composed. The earliest actual manuscript fragments known, all those before 200 C.E., provide glimpses of stories that appear later in the Gospels of *Mark*, *Thomas*, *Mary*, and *John*. The earliest presumed accounts of Jesus include arrest and crucifixion stories, lists of miracles, and sayings recorded in the earliest edition of the *Thomas* Gospel and the presumed "lost source," used by the authors of *Matthew* and *Luke*.

Meanwhile, the earliest unambiguous references to Iēsous appear in the letters of the classically educated Jew Saul of Tarsus, who signed his long epistles with the Greek name Paulos, or Paul. Paul remains a controversial figure, reviled by some, adored by others, and confusing to historians. Although his letters do not speak directly about the life of Jesus, they provide important information in the search for his authentic teachings.

·2·

SAUL OF TARSUS

> Christians must distinguish between Jesus and Paul.
>
> MATTHEW FOX, *A NEW REFORMATION*, 2005

In first-century Israel and Judea, street-corner alms tables provided peasant meeting places, makeshift synagogues, where radical ideas often circulated among the destitute and their defenders. Early Jesus followers shared common meals, as we heard from Pliny. The practice appears to have been extended into the community in the form of free food distributed at these alms tables. This led to trouble, as the authorities tolerated generosity, but not subversive sermons.

According to the New Testament Acts of the Apostles, following the death of Jesus, Jerusalem's high priest, Annas, arrests several Jesus disciples, hauls them before the aristocratic Sadducee priests, and charges them with proclaiming a resurrection of the dead. Allegedly spared from execution by Gamaliel, grandson of famed Torah scholar Hillel, the apostles are flogged, banned from speaking in public, and released.

In response to the risks of public proselytizing, the twelve disciples call a meeting to explain: "It is not right that we should neglect the word of God in order to wait on tables." They ask the congregation to name "seven men of good standing" who will oversee the public giving and teaching, the dangerous front line of the movement. One of these chosen seven is the saintly Stephen, of Greek heritage, who proves courageous, eloquent, and astonishingly well-educated. When temple guards arrest Stephen at the alms table for blasphemy and drag him before the high priest, he closes a long, moving account of Jewish history by turning the indictment back upon his accusers. He charges the priests with killing "the Righteous One" and betraying Torah law. The outburst earns him a death sentence, as the story goes, and the temple elite escort him into the street to stone him. As Stephen, Christendom's first official martyr, forgives his attackers with his last breath, a young Pharisee, Saul, stands among the mob, keeps watch over the cloaks of stone-throwers, and nods his approval.

THE MYSTERIOUS SAUL

Historians consider Acts, written in the 90s, an anonymous work that freely mixes history with legend. Like the Gospels, this work is "good news" and religious advocacy, not necessarily history. Church fathers ascribed the work to Luke, in the late first century, but we know nothing of the author. Nevertheless, this passage serves to introduce to history Saul of Tarsus, the young cloak-holder, who led persecutions against Jesus devotees and later became known as Saint Paul. No historical record corroborates him outside church documents and Paul's own famous letters.

In one possible exception, Josephus mentions a Saul who violently persecutes Jewish peasants, hobnobs with powerful men in Judea, appears related to Herodian rulers, and participates in scenes paralleled in Acts. The parallels suggest to some scholars that this could be the Paul of Acts or perhaps the model from which later writers devised certain scenes. In Paul's letter to the Romans, he mentions a kinsman named Herodian, which corroborates the

Josephus story about Paul, suggesting a well-connected, wealthy Jew and active enemy of the Jewish peasant revolt.

Since we cannot confirm any of Paul's history, a great deal of academic debate swirls around him. Scholars such as Donald H. Akenson in *Saint Saul* depict Paul as a fallible but sincere advocate for the legacy of Jesus, challenging Roman authority with a radically new kingdom of God. Other scholars depict Paul as similar to Josephus's conniving and self-serving Saul. If so, some believe he may have actively subverted the peasant rebellion by co-opting its most celebrated spiritual leader. Was Paul a saint, an infiltrator, or a loyal proselytizer? We don't know. We cannot confirm that Josephus is talking about Saul of Tarsus, and no other pre-fourth-century historian outside the Roman Church mentions him.

We are left with ecclesiastical records concerning Paul, but even among the patriarchs, no references exist until the second century. None of the Gospels — of *Mark*, *Matthew*, *Luke*, *John*, *Thomas*, *Mary*, *Philip*, or others — reveal any knowledge of Paul or his letters. Around the year 150, Polycarp of Smyrna (modern Izmir, on the west coast of Turkey), allegedly wrote to the Philippians and mentioned an earlier writer: "Paul...when among you, accurately and steadfastly taught the word of truth in the presence of those who were then alive. And when absent from you, he wrote you a letter." This reference to Paul, which has been historically disputed, appears a century after his death.

A hundred years is a long time, especially in first-century oral culture. For us, in the twenty-first century, a hundred-year-old story would come from the era of Einstein, Picasso, and Helen Keller. Such stories now can be preserved in print and electronic media, but we possess no such record from the first century. As we trace evidence about Paul to the events the stories describe, we leap many decades in an oral culture, when few but the wealthy travelled, read, or wrote letters.

Two millennia have passed since the era of Paul and Jesus, papyrus documents existed in Egypt two millennia earlier, and writing existed in China and India two millennia before that. In such great sweeps of history, a lifetime represents a fleeting moment. When we compress history to see the bigger picture, we must be careful not to squeeze out the life. Mediterranean culture changed dramatically between 50 and 150 C.E., as Jews dispersed from Jerusalem, Gentile Christianity took root, and the Roman Empire reached its apogee.

About fifty years after Polycarp, around 200 C.E., a scribe composed a "Prayer of the Apostle Paul," and added it to the end of a Gnostic tractate. This acolyte's prayer, Paul's own letters, Acts, and the Polycarp letter comprise the only early evidence concerning Saul of Tarsus. The paucity of historical references to Paul remains something of a mystery. Nevertheless, Paul probably existed and wrote seven authentic letters, of which we have third-century copies.

THE JERUSALEM DEAL

Two episodes from Paul's authentic letters link us to known historical events. In his Second Letter to the Corinthians, he mentions King Aretas IV of Nabatea taking control over Damascus, which would be approximately 38 C.E., and which links to the history of John the Baptist. In Paul's letters to congregations in Rome and Galatia, he mentions the 45 C.E. famine in Judea, for the relief of which he is raising money. The Acts of the Apostles portrays Paul as a Greek-speaking, worldly Jew from Tarsus, in the Roman province of Cilicia, on the coast of what is now southern Turkey. If this story is accurate, and Paul's letters do not confirm it, his father was a successful merchant and tent-maker, and a Roman citizen, a privilege of landowners that accrued to Paul. As a youth he travelled from Tarsus to Jerusalem, likely by boat along the Levant coast, a week's sailing, as opposed to four weeks over 200 leagues of scorching Roman roads.

He may have studied with Torah scholar Gamaliel in Jerusalem, joined the traditional and strict Pharisees, and accompanied temple authorities to execute blasphemers. If we believe he is Josephus's Saul, he was a privileged scoundrel known for extortion and violence against defenceless victims. Acts does not give details of his persecutions of Jesus followers, but stoning the condemned and taking their property would be typical. The followers of Jesus lived in constant fear of exposure and punishment by law enforcers such as Paul.

As the story goes, on his way to Damascus, Paul experienced a visitation by Jesus, changed his ways, and became an advocate for the movement he had once persecuted. Perhaps Paul experienced a legitimate epiphany, but a historical problem stems from three contradictory versions in Acts and his letters. In the first version in Acts, Paul hears a sound, sees a light, falls, is blinded, and talks to the apparition, who tells him, "I am Jesus, whom you are persecuting." The men with him hear the sound but do not see anything. In the second version, the men see but do not hear, and the apparition says, "I am Jesus the Nazorean." There is also a difference in the purpose of the letters he carries to Damascus. They are letters of introduction to the synagogue in one case, and in the second version, letters of damning evidence from Jesus followers to unnamed colleagues. In the third version, the apparition adds instructions to Paul to preach to the Gentiles for the forgiveness of sins. Curiously, the storyteller does not bother to reconcile these inconsistencies.

Even more curious are Paul's references to this event. In his Letter to the Galatians, he claims, "God...set me apart before I was born," and in his Second Letter to the Corinthians, he claims he was "caught up to the third heaven...into paradise and heard things that are not to be told, that no mortal is permitted to repeat." Whatever happened to Paul, he embellished it later. He returned to Jerusalem to tell the Jesus disciples that he had mended his

ways and was now one of them, an apostle, sent by God to deliver
the message of Jesus.

He was not, as we might imagine, well received, and he ended
up in the Syrian city of Antioch, where he met a Cyprian landowner and Jesus devotee, Barnabas, and his cousin John Mark.
Barnabas became Paul's only real friend and supporter. Antioch,
now Antakya in modern Turkey, was a fortified Roman garrison,
650 kilometres north of Jerusalem. A century later, Antioch could
claim to be the centre of Christianity, but in 50 C.E., the Jesus congregation there represented a distant outpost. King Herod had
built a colonnaded boulevard through Antioch, flanked by elegant
porticos. Citizens worshipped at the gold-panelled Temple of Jupiter and attended Roman theatres and baths. The super-rich lived
south of the city, in villas among gardens, near the Daphne spring,
site of the nymph's escape from Apollo. Worldly urban Jews in
Antioch remained loyal to their Roman overlords. Jewish families,
like Paul's, who had served the Romans, earned citizenship. Most
Galileans and Judeans would have considered them compromised.

A crisis developed when news reached Jerusalem that Paul had
accepted Gentile recruits and abandoned Torah laws regarding
circumcision and diet. The Jerusalem group summoned Paul to a
conference, at which they allegedly cut a deal. The timing of this
meeting remains vague. We possess no evidence of a contract, and
we rely entirely on Paul's testimony that he met three followers of
Jesus: James, the brother; Peter, a leader; and John, an apostle.
Paul tells us no more about these men, except that they served as
"pillars" of the Jesus community in Jerusalem. Josephus mentions
the execution of James in 62 C.E., which may be an authentic historical event. The *Thomas* Gospel has Jesus naming his brother
"James the Righteous" as his successor. The Gospel of Hebrews
suggests that the community held James in high esteem, and he
may have served as a leader among the Ebionites.

Acts and Paul's letters describe the Jerusalem deal with Peter and James, indicating that it allowed Paul to proselytize the Jesus message to Gentiles and waived the circumcision requirement on two conditions: that his congregations honour the idolatry and dietary laws, and that he collect money for the poor. In modern terms, this amounts to a franchise granted from the head of the Jesus congregation, Peter, and the head of Jesus' family, James, to the newcomer, Paul, a well-connected urban Jew with a storied and violent past. Not surprisingly, this arrangement fails to settle the conflict.

According to Paul's account, none of the parties actually live up to the agreement. Paul relaxes the dietary laws in Antioch; Peter arrives and appears to go along with him, but changes his mind when James shows up. In Galatians, Paul attacks Peter for betrayal: "I opposed him to his face." Paul may have painted this scene to make himself appear blameless and Peter duplicitous, but why, we might ask, does Paul consistently attract conflict? Did he possess an irascible personality? We cannot doubt that a movement to expand beyond the founding group in Jerusalem would meet resistance. Indeed, within the first decades after Jesus' death, followers clashed repeatedly over control of his legacy. Paul appears to be central in most of these conflicts.

Paul's world-changing mission around the Aegean begins inauspiciously, when he clashes with his devoted colleague and advocate, Barnabas, over his decision to ditch Barnabas's cousin John Mark. Paul claims that Mark had not carried his weight on their previous voyage to Galatia, and had deserted them in Perga, on the south coast of Asia Minor. John Mark had allegedly sailed back to Jerusalem, and Paul no longer considered him an ally.

When Paul refuses to take John Mark, Barnabas backs his cousin and never again works with Paul. This breakup appears excessive, since the two had been inseparable spiritual colleagues for years. Barnabas had been the first to believe Paul's story about seeing Jesus. He introduced Paul to the Antioch group, and vouched for him when others doubted. Furthermore, according to Acts, they both thoroughly believed that the audible voice of the Holy Spirit had decreed their mission together. Why, one might wonder, could they not resolve a dispute over Barnabas's cousin Mark? What were Paul and Mark fighting about? And what did their conflict have to do with the teachings of Jesus?

THE LONER

Several early sects of Jewish Jesus followers compiled sayings or wrote gospels that did not survive the purge by Roman Church authorities, so we know them only through their Christian detractors. Two such sects, the Nazoreans and the Ebionites, will reappear throughout our quest for the Jesus sayings. The name Nazoreans (or Nazarenes) likely does not refer to a town of Nazareth. Outside gospel stories, there exists no evidence for a town of Nazareth before the third century C.E. The Gospel evidence suggests the title Jesus the Nazorean, not Jesus from Nazareth. The Hebrew root *nazar* means to abstain, set apart, or consecrate. The Nazoreans likely were an ascetic sect "set apart" in their religious purity. The Nazoreans practised asceticism and pure living, and we will revisit them throughout our journey.

The Ebionites took their name from the Hebrew word *ebyon*, meaning "poor." Just as the Inuit have many words for snow, early Hebrew tribes employed many words to describe the nuances of poverty, including the *ebionim* and *anawim* of Jewish tradition, the poor ones and outcasts. Nomadic descendents of mixed-heritage *habiru* likely became the early proto-Hebrews, and the prophet Micah honours the "small clans" of the countryside. Dispossessed peasants living on the edge of survival comprised the audience for the historic Jesus. The Ebionites and Nazoreans were rural peasants, not elite, urban Jews. Most of them were not literate. These peasants faced repression, poverty, and debilitating disease. They flocked to teachers such as John the Baptist and Jesus for comfort, healing, and a message of hope. Their ancestors had survived Assyrian, Persian, and Greek overlords. They now suffered under Roman legions and local collaborators.

Nineteenth-century German theologian Ferdinand Christian Baur believed that Paul's mission and letters expound a precise antithesis to these poor Jewish Jesus followers, the Ebionites, Nazoreans, and the Jerusalem group headed by Peter and James. Baur maintained that the New Testament Acts of the Apostles represents a later effort by the Church to reconcile this contradiction between the peasant followers represented by Peter and literate urbanites represented by Paul. British Bible scholar Michael Goulder agrees, and suggests that the Jerusalem and Paul wings of the Yeshua movement competed throughout the Mediterranean world. Modern scholars tend to accept Baur's thesis of competing factions, but expand the number to include Ebionites, Nazoreans, ascetic Essenes, Gnostics, Greek Cynics, mystic healers, congregations associated with Matthew and Luke, "Markan" and "Johannine" communities, a possible Barnabas group responsible for a guide to community behaviour, devout Jewish followers known as Talmidim ha-Yeshua, and a mystical wing of Galileans that may have included the disciples Thomas and Mary Magdalene.

This conflict among factions shines some light on the clash between Paul, Barnabas, and John Mark. Although these people lived in circumstances far different from ours, they possessed familiar instincts and needs. Real people experience familial, spiritual, and class conflicts. The Jerusalem leader Peter quarrelled not only with Paul but also with Mary and others. These characters were human. We've mythologized them, but they struggled with very real resentments, insecurities, fears, and desires.

Among the rivalries, we find in Acts that Peter claims God had selected *him*, not Paul, for the mission to Gentiles. Later, one Demetrius apparently leaves Paul in protest and joins the Jerusalem group. A disciple named Alexander abandons Paul over unknown issues, and Paul complains bitterly about "false teachers." In the second century, Church father Irenaeus records that the Ebionites rejected Paul: "The Ebionites use only that Gospel according to Matthew and repudiate the Apostle Paul, calling him an apostate from the Law."

Paul admits that he sometimes expresses his own point of view. To his loyalists in Corinth he declares, "I give my opinion as one who by the Lord's mercy is trustworthy." To bolster his arguments, Paul paraphrases sayings from the Jesus tradition. Sometimes he appears to get it wrong. In *Mark*, *Thomas*, and elsewhere, Jesus compares true disciples to children. In Paul's First Letter to the Corinthians, he flips this around. "I put away childish things," he says. "Do not be children in your thinking...be adults." He then sets out a list of rules, including his pronouncement "Let your women keep silent in the church." Many scholars believe this decree against women is a later addition by Church patriarchs, since it appears in different places in manuscripts and always slightly out of context. In any case, it has nothing to do with the teachings of Jesus. According to Albert Schweitzer, "the Gospel of Paul is different from the Gospel of Jesus...the Greek, the Catholic, and the Protestant theologies all contain the Gospel of Paul in a form which does not continue the Gospel of Jesus, but displaces it."

The scholars who believe Paul remained faithful to the radical message of Jesus point out that calling Jesus a son of God defied Roman imperial authority. Many ancient schools — Pythagoreans, Mithras worshippers, and the followers of Socrates — openly called their leader son of God, so we know this notion could survive Roman scrutiny. On the other hand, Baur believed, "the apostle

Paul appears in his Epistles to be...indifferent to the historical facts of the life of Jesus." Thomas Jefferson called Paul "the first corrupter of the teachings of Jesus." If such judgements seem too harsh, they are not without foundation.

Paul appears in the record as a loner. Though born Jewish, he displayed no loyalty to Jewish customs. He broke away from the Jerusalem group and poor Ebionites to set up in Antioch among sophisticated, Greek-speaking Jews and Gentiles. Even there he clashed with John Mark, and, finally, his most loyal supporter, Barnabas. Paul struck out on his own, picking up companions he could control, preaching his exclusive interpretation of the Jesus story, and clashing with competitors around the Aegean. He suffered from a chronic "thorn in the flesh," variously interpreted as malaria, epilepsy, or a debilitating eye infection, ophthalmia, that may explain his experiences of blindness. The only extant description of Paul survives in "The Acts of Paul and Thecla," a popular second-century legend recorded in Greek and Coptic manuscripts, depicting his travels through Iconium, northwest of Tarsus, in central Asia Minor. As the story goes, the virgin Thecla is enraptured by Paul's discourse on abstinence and virginity, forsakes her fiancée, and follows Paul. The narrator tells us: "He was a man of moderate stature, with scanty hair, crooked legs, blue eyes, large knit brows, and a long nose; at times he looked like a man, and at other times he appeared as an angel."

IĒSOUS CHRISTOS

The earliest physical evidence of Paul's letters exists in fragments from about 220 C.E., copied on papyrus 160 years after Paul disappears from the Church record in Acts, holding audience with Roman and Jewish leaders in his Italian residence. The anthology includes portions of six authentic letters and three likely forgeries attributed to Paul. In *Saint Saul*, Donald Akenson lists seven authentic letters, one each to the Thessalonians, Romans, Galatians, and Philippians, one to slave owner Philemon, and two to the church in Corinth. He lists Hebrews, Titus, and the two Timothy letters as certain forgeries, and Ephesians, Colossians, and a second letter to the Thessalonians as likely forgeries. However, if we want to know what Paul says about the life and teachings of Jesus, we may ignore the doubtful letters for a simple reason: Paul says very little about the life and teachings of Jesus, and the forgeries — attacking heresy, proclaiming doctrine, and establishing Church authority — add nothing. To gather information about Jesus from Paul, we may focus on four authentic letters: 1 Thessalonians, 1 Corinthians, Galatians, and Romans.

Paul wrote unusually long letters compared to the thousands of recovered first-century letters, which tend to average well under 100 words. Paul's letters run over a thousand words, and his longest, to the Romans, is 7,000 words, three times longer than the longest letter by Cicero, laureate of Rome's golden age. Scholars describe these extensive, polemical letters as "epistles," surpassing private correspondence to serve as public records regarding theology and community behaviour.

The Epistle to the Thessalonians, possibly Paul's first letter, written about 50 C.E., replies to doubts regarding his character. Paul recounts his sacrifices and assures the congregation that his appeal "does not spring from deceit or impure motives." He describes himself as "upright, and blameless," and furthermore, "approved by God." He does not attribute any teachings to Jesus, does not quote Jesus, and tells the readers nothing of his life except that Jesus was "killed" by the "Jews." Paul promises that Jesus will return soon to rescue them "from the wrath that is coming." Otherwise, nothing here helps us know what Jesus taught his followers, but Paul delivers a restrained yet historic bombshell in the first verse. The letter, he claims, is written in the name of God and "the

Lord Jesus Christ," *Kyrioi Iēsous Christos*. This is history's earliest reference to Jesus as a messiah.

The Greek Iēsous is a transliteration of the common Aramaic name that we render in English letters as Yeshua or Yahushua. The "Y" sound indicates the Jewish God, YHVH, and *shua* is deliverance; thus Yeshua means "God's deliverance," or simply, "saviour." Greek masculine names never end in a vowel sound, so Yeshua became Iēsous. Fifth-century Latin scribes transliterated the Greek to Iesus, which was common for one thousand years, until 1526, when William Tyndale's English Bible first employed the Germanic-English "J" to give Jesus, pronounced "Hay-soos," later "Jay-soos," and eventually the Americanized "Jee-zuz." The *Gospel of Philip*, written between 150 and 250 C.E. in Syria, refers to Jesus as Yeshua Christos Nazorean, and explains that "Nazorean is he who reveals what is hidden."

These three names will appear frequently among the various Jesus congregations as Yeshua ha-Nazir and other variations. We may use Yeshua and Jesus interchangeably, but when I use Yeshua in this book, I imply the historical figure, a poor Galilean, who inspired devotion and left behind a treasure of sayings.

The tradition of joining Christos to Jesus perhaps began in Antioch among Greek-speaking Jews such as Paul. Christos derives from the Greek *chrism*, oil, and means "anointed with oil." As we saw in the previous chapter, the anointed heroes of Jewish history were rebel leaders and kings. The Aramaic *meshichah*, anointed, became the Greek *messias*, our messiah. When scribes translated Jewish scriptures into Greek during the centuries before Jesus, they fashioned a noun from "anointed" and thus formed "Christos" to mean "the anointed one."

Early peasant Jewish followers of Jesus, particularly the Ebionites, were not necessarily Christians. That is, they did not consider Jesus a messiah. The poor Ebionites and Nazoreans admired Jesus as their founder and teacher. They considered his spirit among them not as a physical resurrection but as the *parousia*, the "presence" of Jesus evoked through their own righteous actions in the world. Many other peasant Jewish factions, however, did believe in messiahs.

Five influential messiahs besides Jesus enter the historic record between 4 B.C.E. and 70 C.E.: Judas of Galilee; Simon, a rebel slave in Perea; Athronges, a Judean shepherd; Menahem, the grandson of Judas; and Simon bar Giora. From humble beginnings, bar Giora became a military leader and defender of Jerusalem. He achieved minor guerrilla victories and finally surrendered to the Romans on the Temple Mount, dressed in purple robes, declaring himself "King of the Jews," a career arc patterned after the archetypal Jewish messiah, King David.

The addition of Jesus to the list of messiahs may not appear earth-shaking, but Paul added important nuances: His Iēsous Christos was destined to return from death to save the faithful, and Paul actively expanded the ranks of faithful to include Gentiles, that is, everybody. Whatever his faults, no one can deny him this historic role. Looking back from the twenty-first century, we know how events played out, but at the time, Paul's proclamation incited controversy among Jesus followers.

Paul chides his colleagues in Corinth for saying, "'I follow Paul,' or 'I follow Apollos' or 'I follow Cephas' or 'I follow Christ.' Has Christ been divided?" Yes, in fact, the legacy of Jesus was acutely divided. Rival followers scrambled to claim authority over his story. Paul reveals in Corinthians, "some among you say that there is no resurrection," a statement foreshadowing conflicts 300 years later in Nicaea, and 1,200 years later in southern France. Not surprisingly, Paul's affinity for controversy eventually attracted complaints about money.

Paul reveals little or nothing about his finances, but he certainly was not among the poor peasants. As a Roman citizen, and perhaps

as a landowner in Tarsus, he paid taxes. He travelled by boat whenever he wished, and in the 60s, according to Acts, he lived two years
in an Italian villa "at his own expense." He had agreed to raise
money for the Jerusalem poor, but doubts about his financial integrity become evident through his defence against such charges. "Who
tends a flock and does not get any milk?" he appeals to the Corinthians. "Do we not have a right to our food and drink?...Whoever
threshes should thresh in hope of a share in the crop." Paul insists
he has given up such claims to teach for free, but some followers in
Corinth remained unconvinced. Later in this same letter he writes:

> Concerning the collection for the saints: you should follow
> the directions I gave to the churches of Galatia. On the first
> day of every week each of you is to put aside and save what-
> ever extra you earn, so that collections need not be taken
> when I visit. And when I arrive, I will send any whom you
> approve with letters to take your gift to Jerusalem. If it seems
> advisable that I should go also, they will accompany me.

One could interpret these passages as Paul bending over backwards to assure the Corinth congregation that he can be trusted
with money. However, if the members agreed with that assessment,
his earnest pleas would not be necessary. Perhaps his accusers
were simply jealous or paranoid. Perhaps they failed to appreciate
that some of the crop must go to the threshers. Meanwhile, in spite
of his clashes with Peter, James, and Barnabas, Paul repeatedly
claims to be working on their behalf. "I am going to Jerusalem in a
ministry to the saints," he writes to the Roman congregation, "for
Macedonia and Achaia agreed to share their resources with the
poor among the saints." Clearly, money changed hands and Paul
served as bagman. He indeed escorts the money to Jerusalem, but
we never hear of Paul actually handing over the cash. In the record

of Jesus' mission, as we shall see, he touched money only once, and with complete contempt. To be generous to Paul, we might say, in modern terms, he simply took the Jesus movement to the next level and helped to organize their fundraising.

In his Letter to the Corinthians, Paul reminds those who say he is "not an apostle" that he has "seen Jesus Christ." He sounds almost gloomy as he confides to his loyalists, "If I am not an apostle to others, at least I am to you."

Paul accuses the Galatian congregation of "deserting" him by "turning to another gospel," and then insists, "there isn't another gospel, but there are some who are confusing you." Paul complains of "false brothers" spying on him. The battle for the legacy of Jesus appears well underway. "You have heard no doubt," Paul admits to the Galatians, "I violently persecuted the church." One might doubt that Paul would bring this embarrassment up, unless he could not avoid it, and we might assume from Paul's violent background and his urgent defence that a significant number of Jesus followers did not trust him. However, Paul does not forsake us, and offers pearls, if not volumes, about the figure he calls Iēsous Christos.

PAUL'S JESUS

In Paul's version, Jesus, after being "killed by Jews," rises on the third day, appears to Peter ("Cephas"), then to the twelve, later to over 500 brothers and sisters, to James, and, "last of all," to Paul. These brief scenes, plus the Last Supper, comprise Paul's account of the original Jesus followers. He does not mention Mary Magdalene, identified as the author of her own gospel. He mentions neither Thomas, Philip, Matthew, nor any others. Since none of the gospel writers mentions Paul, we may assume there were at least two virtually distinct, occasionally clashing, wings of the movement. Since most early Jesus followers were illiterate, we possess no certain record before Paul.

Throughout his letters, Paul paraphrases Jesus sayings that correspond with other sources, but does not, with one exception, attribute the aphorisms to Jesus. Paul's stirring song to love in Corinthians—"love is patient; love is kind"—reflects his own highest vision and literary skills while improvising on a central tenet from Jesus. We will find that his advice to "eat whatever is set before you" echoes instructions from Jesus. In his epistle to the Roman followers he counsels, "Bless those who persecute you." *Matthew* and *Luke* both attribute "love your enemies" to Jesus in the popular Sermon on the Mount, and most scholars agree that Jesus likely said this, although it also appears in records of common wisdom.

The sayings about loving one's enemy in *Matthew* 5:43 ("pray for your persecutors") and *Luke* 6:27–36 ("do favors for those who hate you") show how independent authors created unique versions of an aphorism handed down through an oral tradition by autonomous communities. Likewise, Paul paraphrases the love saying with his own panache and purpose. Rather than quote Jesus, Paul borrows ideas and melds them with his own. In Romans, at the end of his discourse on loving one's enemies, Paul proclaims: "Let every person be subject to the governing authorities...those authorities have been instituted by God...those who resist will incur judgement. For rulers are not a terror to good conduct, but to bad." This passage leads some scholars to question Paul's motives. He leaps from loving one's enemies to promoting Roman authority in the name of God. At moments such as this, he sounds more like the collaborating Josephus than the culture-crashing Jesus.

Only once in his letters does Paul directly quote Jesus. In his Letter to the Corinthians he introduces to history the Christian Last Supper. Elements of this story—particularly the covenant sworn in blood—are found in the Jewish scriptures, Jeremiah, Zechariah, and Exodus. Paul names his source for this story as "the Lord," possibly during the visitation on the road to Damascus, although he does not specify. The Gospels of *Mark*, *Matthew*, and *Luke* also recount this scene. *Mark*'s version is widely considered the earliest independent account after Paul's; *Matthew* may have copied *Mark*'s story; and *Luke*'s version, with a decidedly different monologue, represents a third tradition of this famous meal.

Although the Last Supper is treated as a Passover meal, there are no traditional symbolic dishes such as bitter herbs or common liturgy that would be associated with Jewish Passover. Such anomalies lead scholars to believe the meal is a later Roman Christian revision of an authentic meal story. In *The Essential Jesus*, John Dominic Crossan demonstrates that the earliest known images of Jesus — frescoes and stone carvings from the second and third centuries — depict him and the disciples at a communal meal of bread and fish, not bread and wine. Bread and fish reflect the common sharing and feeding of multitudes familiar in the Jesus traditions. Greek-speaking Christians in Antioch later called this meal the "Eucharist" — literally "thanksgiving." Nevertheless, we may reach closer to the meal tradition of Jesus in the images of bread and fish than in the ritual of bread and wine. In Paul's version, the wine appears as a link to the blood covenant of Moses in Exodus, and to the future humble king portrayed in Zechariah. The story also reveals deeper roots.

Some historians point out that Paul may have been influenced by the cult of the god Mithras. According to Greek historian Plutarch, Tarsus, Paul's hometown, served as a centre of Mediterranean Mithraism. Roman society had absorbed and transformed the rites from Persia, where the prophet Zarathustra had predicted a messiah appearing at the end of time to triumph over evil. Followers considered Mithras a son of God, part of a holy trinity, the "light of the world," and born of a virgin three days after the winter solstice, attended by gift-bearing shepherds. Before ascending to heaven, Mithras held a last supper with his twelve disciples, during which they ate bread and drank wine, symbolizing the body and blood of Mithras. A hundred years after Paul's account, Christian writer Justin Martyr, in his *First Apology* to the Roman Senate, blames "wicked devils" for having slipped the Last Supper into ancient Mithraic literature. Many scholars believe Paul simply borrowed this story from Mithraic lore and inserted Jesus in the role of Mithras. The wine ritual connects ancient Persian and Jewish history to a Roman future in the Mediterranean.

The fragments of history recovered from Jewish and Christian records yield few certainties, but sharing a communal meal had become an early signature rite among Jesus followers. Nothing concurrent collaborates Paul's version of this meal, the only instance in which Paul quotes Jesus: "This is my body, which is for you. Do this in memory of me.... This cup is the new covenant in my blood. Do this, as often as you drink it, in memory of me."

In his own voice, Paul counsels the reader that, by re-enacting this scene, "you proclaim the Lord's death until he comes." The arc of Paul's story has taken us — and the communal meal — from the alms table of Stephen, as an expression of public sharing inspired by Jesus, to Paul's promise of an anointed messiah, who will return to claim authority over the world. This, Paul promises, will bring about the kingdom of God on earth. In the first century, Roman governors might interpret this doctrine as seditious, especially among Gentiles. Paul appears to place himself at risk by suggesting a divine king other than the Roman emperor, and he reports many instances of his own arrest and imprisonment. In every such case, however, he describes a clever or miraculous escape.

PAUL'S KINGDOM

Paul tells his audience that the returning Christos will bring about the end of earthly rule and deliver the kingdom, but he does not reveal what Jesus says the kingdom is. For that we must rely on

other witnesses. Paul does associate the kingdom with relinquish-
ing pleasures of the flesh. He tells the Corinthians, "flesh and
blood can't inherit the Kingdom of God." To the wayward followers in Galatia he sets out his path to the kingdom: Avoid "works of
the flesh...fornication, impurity, licentiousness, idolatry, sor-
cery...quarrels, dissensions, factions...drunkenness, carousing,
and things like these." Paul's prescription for the spiritual life may
possess merit, but he does not claim that Jesus advocated this doctrine. On the contrary, Jesus allegedly caroused with sinners, ate
and drank liberally, and consorted with women in public.

Akenson, who believes "Saint Saul" provides an important early
source for Jesus, allows, "Saul has his own way of understanding
the life of the historical Yeshua." University English teacher and part-
time Bible scholar Michael Turton believes Akenson understates
the case, and that "Paul's letters are basically silent on the historical
Jesus." In *The Gospel According to Jesus*, author Stephen Mitchell
claims, "The narrow-minded, fire-breathing, self-tormenting
Saul...wasn't even interested in Jesus; just in his own idea of the
Christ."

Many scholars believe Paul got at least part of the Jesus message
right. Others suggest he was a corrupter, or suspect him as an agent
for the dark side. Pamela M. Eisenbaum offers a unique perspective
as both a practising Jew and Professor of Christian Origins at the
Iliff School of Theology in Colorado. "From a Jewish perspective,"
she notes that Paul is viewed as "a self-hating Jew, and a master
manipulator of others....From a feminist perspective, Paul is an
ally of Christian conservatives who wish to keep women in a subor-
dinate position." Nevertheless, Eisenbaum believes, "Paul was a
committed, well-intentioned Jew, even if the subsequent uses of his
teachings were abominable where Jews and women are concerned."
Paul continues to provoke debate, but none deny that he proved to
be one of the most influential written voices in human history.

Jesus, as far as we know, never wrote a word. His audience and most followers were illiterate peasant outcasts, fishers, and farmers. Writing had existed for millennia, but generally among the elite. The earliest evidence of papyrus dates to about 3000 B.C.E., during the Egyptian First Dynasty, and the word means "belongs to the house," that is, to the ruling aristocracy. By the first century, papyrus had become a highly valued commodity shipped throughout the Mediterranean from Byblos, north of Tyre on the Levant coast. Thus, Byblos papyrus became known simply as *byblos*, and a papyrus book became a *byblios*, the root of the English words "bibliography" and "bible." Jewish factions in this era clashed over written and oral traditions.

The Jewish book of Ezekiel marks a critical point in human history, when divine truth became associated with the written word. The prophet Ezekiel claims God handed him a "written scroll" implying the ultimate word of God. By the first century, the elite Sadducees represented written law, whereas middle-class Pharisees promoted traditional oral interpretations of law, albeit elite law, not peasant convention. The land-based peasants embraced still older oral traditions, alienated from both factions of the Jewish Temple. Pharisees, Sadducees, Essenes, and educated, landed Jews such as Paul may have kept written records, but peasant Galileans, messianic rebels, and poor urban Judeans conducted their lives and business by word of mouth. Some marginally literate peasants — perhaps a real Thomas or Peter — wrote letters or compiled lists of sayings.

Just as air travel, television, and the Internet have shaped our era, first-century culture experienced an information explosion of its own. The first-century information highway moved at the speed of a Bactrian camel on the trade routes, or of a ship crossing the Mediterranean, but it moved. Writing practices crept down the social ladder to the middle classes. Historians estimate literacy in the Roman Empire to be about 10 to 15 percent of the general population, less than 5 percent of the rural poor, and perhaps a few percent in the Galilean countryside. In patriarchal Palestine, women comprised only a tiny portion of these literate citizens. The battle between Paul and other Jesus followers echoed, in part, a battle between the peasant oral culture and the middle-class literate culture supported by elite patrons. By writing his doctrines and ideas, Paul secured his version of the Jesus legacy for later Church writers. Most of Paul's writing defends his reputation, proclaims doctrine, and formulates community rules. Certain passages, such as his ode to love, reflect pure poetic brilliance, and some passages paraphrase Jesus, but Paul's revelations about Jesus remain theological, with oblique clues about the teacher from Galilee.

Saul of Tarsus remains an elusive, controversial figure, and the historical record cannot confirm whether he was a saint, rogue, Roman collaborator, well-intentioned intellectual, or a fabrication of later writers. Nevertheless, the body of letters provides one version of the early transformation from an oral Jesus movement into written doctrine. Paul's doctrine would become a cornerstone of later Christianity.

In summary, Paul gives Jesus the title of Christ and names his chief followers as James the brother, Peter the "rock," and John the disciple. He tells us that Jesus held a final communal meal, during which he promised a new covenant with God. He recounts that Jesus was betrayed by "the Jews," crucified, and buried, and that he rose on the third day, appearing to the disciples and finally to Paul. He paraphrases some sayings from common Jesus traditions — do good to all, we reap what we sow, love your enemies — but does not attribute these sayings to Jesus. He occasionally twists a saying to his own purposes — obey authorities, be an adult — and tells his readers that Jesus will return to establish the Kingdom of God.

The idea of a future kingdom for a deity's chosen people can be traced back eight centuries to early Persian and Jewish beliefs about overcoming the oppression of invading empires. Paul adds that belief in this kingdom brings rewards in heaven.

In the first century, the ancient vision of a promised kingdom for the righteous reappears in the revolutionary desert movement led by John the Baptist. Roman and Jewish authorities considered John's movement subversive. Rome's vast empire left them with sparse defences along the border lands in the Levant, where they nervously faced a Parthian empire to the northeast and Nabatean warlords to the southeast. Jewish rebels threatened independence in Israel and Judea. Rome responded to open sedition with mass crucifixions to terrorize the populace. Into this hair-trigger political environment, during the reign of Emperor Tiberius and under the local rule of Tetrarch Herod Antipas in the first century, along the Jordan River, John the Baptist and Jesus step into recorded history.

DOWN BY THE RIVER

By John's time the only place in the country where Jews could legally offer sacrifices was Jerusalem, and its services were expensive. To introduce into this situation a new, inexpensive, generally available, divinely authorized rite, effective for the remission of all sins, was John's great invention.

MORTON SMITH, *THE SECRET GOSPEL*, 1973

Princess Salome clutches a silver tray but turns from the severed head wistfully. Her lips are tightly closed, perhaps betraying a life adrift in a moral sea beyond her comprehension. A matron in the shadows touches the girl's shoulder but averts her eyes and appears to offer little help. A rugged young jailer delivers the head almost stoically, but not quite. Some misgiving haunts him as well. The dead desert mystic, mouth falling open as if to speak, appears animated, while the three living characters seem lost in private soul-searching. A chilling self-doubt hangs in the air.

This seventeenth-century painting by Michelangelo Caravaggio depicts the final scene from the Gospel story of John the Baptist. The four traditional Gospels do not always agree, but a composite biblical version of John and Jesus begins with John baptizing followers at the Jordan River. During Jesus' baptism, the Holy Spirit in the form of a dove descends upon him, and a voice from heaven declares him the son of God. Jesus picks his first disciples from among John's followers and begins his mission.

In the meantime, John is arrested by Herod Antipas (son of Herod "the Great"). Later, during Antipas's birthday banquet, his alluring stepdaughter Salome entertains the revellers with a dance. The performance so overwhelms Antipas that he offers Salome a wish. She consults her mother and then asks for the head of John the Baptist. According to the biblical story, Antipas admires John, feels troubled about the execution, but is compelled by his promise.

What can we make of this story? Is it accurate? Does it reflect history? The desert Baptist had allegedly made a public mockery of King Herod Antipas, and here begins the most famous story in the Western world: the life and message of John's protege, known to us as Jesus the Nazarene.

THE BIBLICAL BAPTISM

In a 2007 book, *Jesus of Nazareth*, the Catholic Pope offered his interpretation of the historical Jesus and John. The author signs his book "Joseph Ratzinger/Benedict xvi," as both common historian and pope. He assures readers that the book is "not a magisterial act"—that is, not a papal edict—but rather a "personal search." Ratzinger discards a pope's presumed infallibility and grants that "everyone is free to disagree with me." The concession honours academic protocol by inviting scholars to treat his conclusions as they would those of any colleague.

Since scholars describe their method of research, Ratzinger explains his: "Above all...I trust the Gospels," by which he means the four canonical Gospels, *Matthew, Mark, Luke,* and *John.* While acknowledging "modern exegesis," the analysis of manuscripts, Ratzinger views "the Jesus of the Gospels as the real Jesus." He argues that "this figure is much more logical...than the reconstructions we have had to confront in recent decades," by which he means the academic search for a historical Jesus.

Ratzinger concludes that John's historical role is "the announcement that one greater than John is to come." He appeals to Old Testament passages that "envisage a saving intervention of God." That intervention, of course, is portrayed in Christian literature as the arrival of Jesus on earth. Ratzinger also bases his assessment on the *Gospel of John* 1:6–15, beginning with these passages about John the Baptist:

> There appeared a man, sent from God, named John....He was not the light; he only came to testify to the light. (John 1:6)

> John testified..."This is the one I spoke of when I said: 'He who is to come after me ranks ahead of me because he came before me.'" (John 1:15)

Already, in these first lines, scholars face tremendous textual difficulties and historical uncertainties. Scholars have parsed the Greek manuscripts for centuries, and there exists a modern doctoral dissertation, or several, on every word. The *Gospel of John* is the latest of the four orthodox Gospels, written in about 90 C.E. It is not considered a historical work, but rather an ecclesiastical affirmation of faith. We will examine this Gospel in later chapters, but for now, keep in mind two points:

First, take care not to confuse the Johns and to distinguish texts from authors and their subjects. The testimony about Jesus is allegedly that of John the Baptist, a historical figure, whose life is well documented in secular accounts. The authorship of the *John* Gospel remains unknown, variously attributed to fisherman-disciple John the son of Zebedee; a later Church elder; or the "beloved disciple" mentioned in the Gospel. Other possible authors have been suggested, but it is most likely that a Greek-speaking Jewish school of disciples composed a first edition of this Gospel in Syria, fifty to seventy years after the death of Jesus. The earliest evidence of the name *The Gospel According to John* appears about a century later. Throughout this book, we will distinguish between text, author, and subject. To help keep this clear, when I reference a text, not an author or subject, I use the popular titles in italics: *John*.

Secondly, the lines from *John* quoted above are embedded in fourteen verses of a Semitic hymn that opens the gospel in a distinctive voice and style, suggesting a later edition. The sections that introduce the Baptist appear older, and many scholars believe that verse 1:6 above represents the original opening of this Gospel. Different hands have added the poetic prologue to *John*, the final chapter, and other passages, perhaps in the second century. Without resolving these issues now, we will note that when scholars interpret such verses, they employ this sort of textual analysis.

Joseph Ratzinger, as historian, does not discuss these issues in his book, but accepts traditional interpretations of *John* as history. Jewish historian Josephus, writing about the same time as the *John* author, mentions the Baptist, but says nothing about his presumed role as herald of someone greater, and nothing about Jesus appearing with John. As a historian, one might expect Ratzinger to at least mention Josephus's dissenting view, as well as the textual uncertainties, but he ignores all of this.

Finally, Ratzinger depicts the baptism as a sacrificial atonement, whereby "Jesus loaded the burden of all mankind's guilt upon his shoulders." Ratzinger acknowledges, "All of this will have to wait for Christian baptismal theology to be worked out explicitly." In other words, Ratzinger concedes, the first-century historical record does not confirm this interpretation "worked out" by later Christian writers. To be fair, he announced at the beginning that his conclusions would match orthodox doctrine.

Géza Vermes, a Hungarian-born Oxford historian, and one of the first scholars to examine the Dead Sea Scrolls, gives Ratzinger poor marks for an "absence of stringent linguistic, literary, and historical analysis of the Gospels." Vermes contributed to the quest for a historically accurate Jesus with his 1973 book, *Jesus the Jew*, placing Jesus in a genuine first-century Jewish context. He criticizes Ratzinger's book as "a haphazard mixture of life and doctrine." Historians, as Vermes points out, cannot cherry-pick passages that support their thesis, but must also reference texts that contradict their conclusions. The historian must, in other words, be prepared to discover something new and unexpected.

Serious historians also take care not to retrofit later ideas into the events they seek to explain. When Ratzinger declares that the Baptist's "whole mission" is directed toward announcing Jesus, we are reading later "Christian baptismal theology," as he admits, placed back into the life of the desert mystic John. We will experience such pitfalls of historical inquiry throughout our search. Historians typically avoid reading into accounts more than they offer. In the language of text scholarship, this is the difference between "exegesis," drawing meaning *from* historical manuscripts, and "eisegesis," reading meaning *into* a text.

In searching for the genuine teachings of Jesus, we begin with John the Baptist for three reasons. First, we will find that Jesus' message both borrows from and diverges from John's message. Secondly, the meeting of John and Jesus is the first story contained in all the Gospel accounts. The Gospels of *Mark* and *John* — and the newly discovered Gospels of *Thomas*, *Mary*, *Philip*, Hebrews, Ebionites, and others — do not contain birth or infancy stories about Jesus. Neither do early versions of the *Luke* and *Matthew* Gospels. The verifiable historical record of Jesus begins with his appearance as a disciple of the popular ascetic John. Finally, secular historians and other religious traditions attest to certain elements of the Baptist's story. Josephus, born a generation after Jesus, and both Tacitus and Suetonius establish the Herodian aristocrats in the historic record. Josephus links the Herods' history to John the Baptist, and this provides at least a tenuous link to Bible stories and the characters we wish to know about here: Jesus, Mary Magdalene, and the Galilean peasants who resisted Rome's authority in the dry hills along the Jordan River.

GREATER THAN JOHN

Matthew depicts John the Baptist as Jewish prophet Elijah reborn. However, in *John*, the Baptist assures the priests that he is *not* the prophet Elijah. Rather, he is "a voice crying out in the wilderness," announcing the coming of someone greater. In *Matthew*, the Baptist recognizes Jesus, in *John* he does not, and in *Luke*, the Baptist had already recognized Jesus as the messiah and "leapt for joy" while they both awaited birth in their mothers' wombs. Clearly, the *Luke* story records later mythologizing, but there is another problem: the *John* Gospel leaves out the baptism of Jesus altogether. *John* 1:32–34 simply says: "John testified: 'I have seen the Spirit descending as a dove from the sky; and it hovered above him.... I have seen this, and I have testified: this is the Son of God.'"

Why does the *John* author remove Jesus' baptism? The answer to this question will inform our understanding of this critical history. We do not possess a secular account of the baptism, but nine evangelical accounts attest that John baptized Jesus. These nine accounts appear to be copies of three original, independent versions found in *Mark*, the Gospel of the Hebrews, and a letter attributed to second-century Christian theologian Ignatius. Scholars generally believe that five other Gospels borrowed and revised the brief account in *Mark*, which is considered the earliest canonical account. The Gospels of *Matthew*, *Luke*, *John*, Nazoreans, and Ebionites presumably borrow the story from *Mark*, but add explanations to deal with what Crossan calls, respectfully, "theological damage control." The evangelists faced a dilemma: If John baptized Jesus, does that imply John is superior to Jesus? Furthermore, does it mean that Jesus was a sinner who needed purifying? We hear a resounding no from all these accounts, but witness the evolution of the story. Here is the *Mark* original:

> At that time, Jesus came from Nazareth in Galilee and was baptized by John in the Jordan. As Jesus was coming up out of the water, he saw heaven being torn open and the Spirit descending on him like a dove. A voice came from heaven: "You are my Son…"

In the Gospel of the Hebrews, a second original and independent version, possibly written in Alexandria sometime after the *Mark* version, Jesus' mother suggests going to John for baptism, but Jesus balks:

> "How have I sinned? Why should I go and get baptized by him? Only if I don't know what I am talking about…"
> (Hebrews 2:2)

But the story implies that he goes, because

> When the Lord came up from the water, the whole fountain of the holy spirit came down on him and rested on him. It said: "My Son, I waited for you in all the prophets…"
> (Hebrews 3:3)

Text scholars believe these two accounts represent the earliest independent record of Jesus being baptized by John. Already, in the Hebrews account, we witness the author's attempt to tell the

story in such a way that the problem is solved: Jesus implies he is
not a sinner and needs no purification. Scholars believe the *Luke*
and *Matthew* authors copied from *Mark*, but notice the changes:

> Then Jesus came from Galilee to John at the Jordan, to be
> baptized by him. John tried to stop him, saying, "I need to
> be baptized by you, and yet you come to me?" Jesus
> answered him, "Let it be for now; for this is the proper way
> for us to fulfill all righteousness." Then John consented.
> (Matthew 3:13–15)

The author of *Matthew* improves on the defence of Jesus by
having the Baptist himself reject the idea that he is superior to
Jesus. *Matthew* has Jesus explain that his purpose is to fulfill "righteousness," implying both common propriety and Jewish prophecy.
For comparison, observe how two other early Jewish sects of Jesus
followers, the Nazoreans and the Ebionites, dealt with the issues.
The Gospel of the Nazoreans copies the Hebrews story and the Ebionites borrow the *Matthew* version, but with a significant twist:

> When the people were baptized, Jesus also came and got
> baptized by John. As he came up out of the water, the skies
> opened and he saw the holy spirit in the form of a dove com-
> ing down and entering him. And there was a voice from the
> sky that said, "You are my favoured son." (Ebionites 2)

The Ebionites borrow the *Matthew* version, but with Jesus as
"favoured son," implying he is not the only child of God. Each
account reflects the understanding of evangelizing communities
that thrived some fifty to 100 years after the time of Jesus. After
the *Mark* original, later authors make a special effort to clarify
that Jesus was more important than John. This tells us that John

was important to Jews during this period; otherwise, why bother linking Jesus to him at all, much less exalting Jesus above him?

Finally, listen to how this progression is recalled in the letter attributed to Ignatius, second-century Bishop of Antioch, writing to a congregation in Smyrna on the coast of Turkey:

> I have observed that you are perfected in an immoveable faith... being fully persuaded with respect to our Lord, that He was truly of the seed of David according to the flesh, and the Son of God according to the will and power of God; that He was truly born of a virgin, was baptized by John, in order that all righteousness might be fulfilled by Him.

We can now trace the evolution of this story about John and Jesus. Josephus mentions no relationship between the two and treats John as the more significant historical figure. Gospel writers likely in Syria (*Mark*) and Egypt (*Hebrews*) claim John baptized Jesus, but Hebrews adds qualifying passages that depict Jesus as more significant. The qualifying stories evolve through the communities that produced the Gospels of *Matthew*, *Luke*, Nazoreans, and Ebionites, until Jesus appears irrefutably more important than John and represents the fulfillment of Jewish prophecies. These authors also borrow symbols from common Middle Eastern stories, such as the dove, depicting a new beginning, used by the Sumerians in the epic of King Gilgamesh and by Jewish writers in the story of Noah. Finally, *John*, the last canonical gospel, drops the baptism altogether, keeps the qualifiers, and depicts the Baptist in the role of witness to Jesus' special status. By the end of the second century, 150 years after the events, the exalted status of Jesus is presented by Ignatius as an orthodox doctrine of faith.

This story demonstrates how historical events become woven with cultural metaphor. We might be able to discern individual strands, but we may also pause and marvel at the fabric itself, the patterns of history and mythology as they merge in humanity's stories. Notice also that we do not have to take the actual words and sentences as history, but rather we find clues in the motifs that run through the stories. These recurring themes — resisting authority, helping the poor, sin and righteousness — not literal words, are the jewels historians look for when analyzing such traditions. The memory of these events is shaped to portray evolving religious beliefs and shifting social conditions.

AT THE JORDAN RIVER

Josephus is our most reliable source for the Baptist's story, but his point of view changes. He speaks, by turns, as a Jewish aristocrat, a Roman apologist, and a fantasy writer spinning his own daring deeds. History is written by the victors, the elite, obviously by the literate, usually by males, and often by those who are loyal to the status quo of their age. Written history, in other words, almost always reflects the conventions of a culture and its sanctioned voices. Ironically, an author's biases may help historians discover historical truth. Josephus, who claimed royal Hasmonean blood, provides stark, believable details about the private lives of the ruling classes and generally dismisses rebellious peasants, but in his *Jewish Antiquities*, written in about 90 C.E., Josephus appears to harbour a tender respect for John the Baptist:

Now some Jews thought that the destruction of Herod's army [by Aretas] came from God, and that very justly, as punishment of what he did against John, called the Baptist: for Herod slew him, a good man, who commanded the Jews to exercise virtue, both as to righteousness towards one another and piety towards God, and so to come to baptism so that the washing would be acceptable...not in order to absolve some sins, but for the purification of the body; supposing still that the soul was thoroughly purified beforehand by righteousness.

The passage is loaded with nuance and history. Josephus rarely ventures this close to sympathy for peasant values. His disdain for Herod Antipas appears to contradict his typical fawning over aristocrats, until we understand that certain elements of the Jerusalem elite, particularly Hasmoneans, considered the Herods to be plebeian outsiders from Idumea, not devout Jews, and not real royalty. Still, we may wonder why Josephus, a loyal aristocrat, would support a common mystic like John. One answer is that exhalting John embellishes his snub of the Herods. He provides another hint in his biography. Josephus, born a generation after Jesus and John, reports investigating "several sects" of Jewish religious schools, begining at the age of sixteen. He describes studying with Sadducee lawyers, Pharisee scholars, ascetic Essenes, and finally a wandering desert master, Banus, who

...used no other clothing than what grew upon trees, and had no other food than what grew of its own accord, and bathed himself in cold water frequently, both night and day, to purify himself, I imitated him in those things, and continued with him three years.

Given Josephus's tendency to exaggerate his exploits, we might guess he spent less than three years with a wandering ascetic, but perhaps he did as he claims. The account gains some credibility because it helps explain Josephus's deference for the desert baptizer, John. This analysis reflects the historians' "criterion of embarrassment." Josephus, the reasoning goes, would not go out of his way to praise a peasant such as John unless both the accounts of both Banus and John were true.

Note also that Josephus takes a particular interest in settling the debate regarding John's ritual "washing." The English "baptism" derives from Greek *baptô*, "to dip." Was John dipping disciples in the Jordan River for purification of the body, as Josephus claims, or for the atonement of sins, as the New Testament Gospels claim? Or both? Josephus asserts that the washing only took place after a deeper spiritual purity had been achieved by "righteousness," that is, by acts of compassion in the living community.

In Jerusalem, Temple priests enjoyed a monopoly on forgiving sins, and Josephus appears to absolve John from any possible charge of claiming such authority, by insisting that his baptism is *not* "to absolve some sins." However, Josephus may protest too much here. John's mission in the desert arose in direct competition with priests in the Jerusalem Temple. The poor outcasts who followed John could not afford the fees associated with a sanctioned Temple purification, so John offered a complimentary service at the Jordan River, effectively breaking the priests' monopoly. Josephus's strident denial may betray an intention to sanitize John for the author's elite Roman and Jewish audiences. Josephus may have felt sympathy for the popular teacher, but only as a pious "good man," not as a political threat to the status quo. We may trust the Gospel accounts on this point: John forgave sins without a permit.

Along the banks of the river, four significant issues converged: purity, forgiving sins, confronting authority, and doing good deeds for others. These concerns circulated as popular topics in the cultural environment into which John and Jesus emerged. Simple good deeds may go unnoticed by the political authorities, but breaking the priests' monopoly and drawing crowds put John on a collision course with Herod Antipas.

SALOME AND HERODIAS

The Herods were a tightly knit family. Jewish peasants might have whispered "incestuous" behind their backs. The powerful patriarchs shared a fondness for their young nieces, or even the daughters of their nieces. Their alliances, betrayals, marriages, and peccadilloes remain hopelessly confusing, and the Herod family tree becomes a family web strewn with more than a few abandoned wives, bastard sons, and inconvenient corpses. Meanwhile, the young aspiring heirs enjoyed holidays in Rome, where they curried imperial patronage.

The Herodian women, abused and traded like chattels, were not powerless, for one very important reason: They represented the matrilineal bloodline of Jewish royalty. Earlier, in 37 B.C.E., Idumean warlord Herod ("the Great") helped the Romans depose the Jewish Hasmonean family and thereby won Rome's blessing as "King of the Jews." To consolidate his power, Herod divorced his Samaritan wife Malthace, married Hasmonean teenager Mariamne, and then methodically executed her relatives. He dispatched Mariamne herself at the age of twenty-five, but her granddaughter, Herodias, would exert royal influence and appear in biblical stories. Herod went through ten wives and countless concubines, leaving fifteen recorded children, including the notorious Herod Antipas, who clashed with our desert baptizer, John, and allegedly met the prisoner Jesus face to face in Jerusalem.

The story of the Baptist's execution begins when the married Antipas takes a fancy to his niece, Herodias, who is married to his half-brother Herod Philip. To gain the princess as his own, Antipas plots to divorce his wife, who uncovers the scheme and flees to her father, Nabataean King Aretas IV, in the desert southeast of Judea. Aretas, dishonoured by the treatment of his daughter, assembles his army, marches north, and defeats Antipas. This much, at least, the secular historical record supports. In the Bible stories, however, sometime before Aretas arrives for battle, Herod Antipas holds his now famous birthday banquet.

In *Mark* and *Matthew*, Salome, Herodias's daughter by Philip, dances for the assembled men and orders up the head of the Baptist as a prize, but only after consulting with her mother. Herodias allegedly resented John for publicly denouncing her scandalous divorce from Philip and her marriage to Antipas. Is this tale of retribution history or legend? Did Herodias barter her daughter to Antipas and his cronies in exchange for revenge against John? Did Antipas bend to the will of Herodias?

Historians must analyze the available accounts to sift bias or wishful reporting from reality. Two important tools help them to identify authentic events: corroboration and convergence. Hearing the same story from two or more reliable, corroborating witnesses, as in a courtroom, helps to verify an event. Convergence occurs when independent reports complement each other by confirming similar or logically sequential events from different perspectives.

PREVENTING MISCHIEF

According to Bible stories, Antipas only carried out the execution of John on the wish of Herodias, his wife, delivered through Salome, his compelling young stepdaughter. In the *Mark* account, we are told:

> Herod had sent and seized John, and bound him in prison for the sake of Herodias, his brother Philip's wife because he had married her. For John had told Herod, "It is not lawful for you to have your brother's wife." And Herodias held a grudge against him, and wanted to kill him. But she could not, for Herod feared John, knowing that he was a righteous and holy man, and kept him safe.

Compare this with Josephus, who mentions no birthday banquet, dance, or request for John's head from Herodias or Salome. Rather,

> Herod [Antipas], who feared that the great influence John had over the people might provide him the power and inclination to raise a rebellion — for they seemed ready to do anything he should advise — thought it best to put him to death, to prevent any mischief.

What do we learn from these passages? First, John drew a crowd, presumably by his inspired teachings and free atonement. And secondly, John's ability to attract and arouse crowds threatened insurrection, providing ample motivation for Antipas to execute him. John's location, in the desert, east of the Jordan River, heightens the political theatre. Crossing the Jordan, purifying oneself, and returning to Judea from the wilderness — a re-enactment of the legendary Jewish arrival into the promised land — reflected Jewish prophecy regarding the new kingdom. Herod Antipas would not have missed the seditious symbolism. He wanted to be king of the Jews like his father, not a mere "tetrarch" sharing quarter-power with his half-brothers, and he knew that his Roman patrons expected him to demonstrate absolute control. Make no mistake: Antipas would not hesitate to execute a potential troublemaker.

For parallels to our modern world, compare Josephus's explanation, to prevent mischief, with Chinese dictator Deng Xiaoping's warning to democracy advocates that "every possible means will be adopted to eliminate any turmoil." Or consider the infamous 1968 memo from FBI director J. Edgar Hoover, who urged his agents to "prevent the rise of a black 'messiah' who would unify and electrify the militant black nationalist movement." In both cases, the instruction is not to arrest lawbreakers, but rather to terminate any hope of a popular leader's rising up and unifying the underclass.

Blaming Salome and Herodias for John's murder probably represents later, patriarchal fiction designed to absolve Antipas. Notice the similarity with the Gospel depictions of Pilate as a reluctant executioner. By virtue of the historians' criterion of convergence with the known cultural milieu, Josephus appears trustworthy here: John drew a rebellious crowd and lost his head for it.

Dating the execution of John is difficult. Other points of known history, such as the battle with Aretas IV and the arrival of Syrian general Vitellius in Judea, intersect with the Baptist's story and suggest to historians that the death of John occurred in about 36 C.E. But that won't work with Bible stories that place John before Jesus in the late 20s. Recall that Josephus does not associate Jesus with the Baptist. Some arguments can be made for an earlier date for John the Baptist, but the historical convergence is not yet working. So the question remains: Did Jesus really know John?

We don't know exactly when the Baptist lived. Historians place him sometime between 23 C.E., the earliest possible date that Herodias could have married Antipas, and 36 C.E., when his nephew Agrippa met Tiberius in Rome, a year before the emperor died. Mythologically, we don't need to know. The stories tell us about the clash between wealthy overlords and starving peasants who longed for justice and believed their God would deliver it. Those poor outcasts flocked to holy men, such as John or Jesus, who might purify their souls with a mere word or a dip in the river.

IMPENDING CATACLYSM

Albert Schweitzer struggled with the question of whether or not Jesus believed that the coming kingdom of God implied the end of the world. Schweitzer concluded that Jesus did believe this, and therefore interpreted his teachings as an "interim ethic" awaiting a final divine judgement. Later scholars took up Schweitzer's question regarding this cataclysmic "last event," in Greek *eschaton*, and here the Jesus story crosses inexorably with John's.

Historians trace the eschatological world-transformation tradition back at least eight centuries before John and Jesus, to Persian and Jewish beliefs about the succession of empires. Persians believed that after the Assyrian, Median, old Persian, and Greek empires, a "saviour king" would rule the earth on behalf of their single god, Ahura Mazda. Over time, these ideas about a new divine kingdom became "apocalyptic," meaning that their god would initiate the final events. The Jewish version predicted an empire of Jews serving the god of Moses. However, these expectations proved wrong, since the next empire arrived with neither a Persian nor a Jewish saviour, but rather with the thundering boots of Roman legions. Persians and Jews grudgingly postponed their respective apocalypses.

By the time of John and Jesus, belief in a final cataclysm initiated by God, on behalf of God's believers, was a common expectation in Judea and Israel. We would find nothing unusual if both John and Jesus shared this expectation. But history warns us to take nothing for granted. We have seen that historians employ rules of evidence and consistent methods to avoid bias, especially their own preconceptions. We have considered the rules of corroboration and convergence. Text scholars also give extra weight to the earliest texts by carefully dating manuscripts and by identifying later editing within manuscripts. Text scholars, or "exegetes," call this rule "chronological priority," and refer to later editing as "redaction."

Texts contain internal evidence, including papyrus or parchment quality, inks, binding styles, letter styles, handwriting, words used, punctuation, and historic references. For example, a soot-based ink on papyrus rolls using all capital Greek letters could place a manuscript in the first or second century. Certain idioms might place it earlier or later in that period. An iron sulphide nutgall ink on a bound codex (book style) would place a manuscript in the third to sixth centuries.

However, such manuscripts might be copied from earlier texts. Within a document, as with the *John* introduction, certain sections may be older than others. Sections of manuscripts, when compared with others, often reveal almost verbatim passages that scholars usually interpret as being dependent upon each other or on a common source from an earlier period. Religious historian Karen L. King describes five indicators of literary dependence: similar language style, organization, narrative setting, verbatim word-for-word passages, and citation formulas such as "so it was written."

Scholars use all these clues to identify the earliest stages of evidence about Jesus, portions of existing gospels believed to have originated between 30 and 60 C.E. We identify portions of gospels because each collection reveals identifiable layers, representing an original text and a later redaction. Scholars place in this earliest period sections from the Gospels of *Thomas*, *Luke*, and *Matthew*, the authentic letters of Paul, Hebrews (the Egyptian narrative, not the New Testament letter), Egerton (another Egyptian gospel), and fragments found at Fayyum and Oxyrhynchus in the central Nile Valley. Many scholars further believe that accounts of miracles and the execution of Jesus existed in written text before 60 C.E. All of this occurred before any narrative gospels had appeared.

Certain verses in *Luke* and *Matthew* suggest that these authors copied from *Mark*, one reason historians consider *Mark* the earliest canonical Gospel. Other parallel verses in *Luke* and *Matthew* suggest they also copied from another early source that may have appeared in writing by the 50s, likely in Galilee. These nearly verbatim verses contain no arrest, execution, or resurrection, and reveal parallels to *Thomas* and Hebrews. Scholars believe these verses reflect the earliest written layer of the Gospels. Here, then, is

the story of John the Baptist in its most likely original form, composed during the first decades after the death of their teacher:

> John appeared in the countryside, along the Jordan River.
>
> He said to the crowds coming to be baptized: "You chil-
> dren of vipers! Who warned you to flee from the impending
> doom? You had better start bearing fruit worthy of your
> repentance. Don't tell yourselves: 'We have Abraham as our
> forefather!' For I tell you: God can produce children for
> Abraham from these very stones! Even now, the axe is aimed
> at the root of the trees. So every tree not bearing good fruit
> is felled and thrown on the fire."
>
> "I baptize you in water, but one to come after me is more
> powerful than I, whose sandals I am not worthy to remove.
> He will baptize you in holy spirit and fire. His pitchfork is
> in his hand, and he will clear his threshing floor and gather
> the wheat into his granary, but the chaff he will burn on a
> fire that can never be put out."

At the earliest stage of written memory, we find John's apocalyptic vision, "the impending doom," and his emphasis on public
acts, "bearing fruit." We learn that his baptism in the river implied
atonement, "repentance," and that his audience considered themselves descendents of Abraham. We also learn that this community
believed John announced someone "more powerful," who would
separate righteous people of god, "the wheat," from their unrighteous enemies, "the chaff." Both author and audience hope for and
believe in an imminent impending rescue from poverty and oppression by a messenger from their god. We know from the context that
this community believed Jesus was that liberating messenger.

In a later second-century text, the *Secret Book of James*, attributed to the brother of Jesus, James asks "the saviour" how they

should prophesy or predict the future. Jesus exposes the lack of understanding in the question:

> "Don't you know that the head of prophecy was cut off with John?...When you know what 'head' means, and that prophecy issues from the head, then understand the meaning of 'its head was removed.'"

By the second century, the execution of John had become a metaphor about the end of Jewish prophetic tradition and a new vision of the longed-for kingdom. Few text scholars believe this passage represents a direct quote from Jesus, but it shows how communities of followers came to view their saviour. And in this we again witness history, John losing his head, mixed with metaphor, a new covenant with God. Like a typical sage, this Jesus leaves the answer unexplained. The disciple must figure it out. Later, however, Jesus offers a hint to James: "...unless you receive this [kingdom] through knowledge, you will not be able to find it."

LIKE A CHILD

The early, pre-Gospel Jesus followers also told a story of the spirit leading Jesus into the wilderness, where he allegedly encounters Satan. Academic opinion splits on whether or not Jesus predicted a cataclysmic end as did John, but if he did, he returns from his private contemplations in the desert with a somewhat revised plan: Accept your poverty, and give away anything that you have to others who ask. In such verses, Jesus refers to his audience as "the poor... the hungry...the weeping," and he encourages them with the message that their poverty brings them closer to righteousness. This, then, signals the beginning of a radical new message: Don't just purify yourself and wait around for God to save you; rather, act now on behalf of others. God takes care of you. You take care of others. That is the kingdom of God.

Notice that Jesus appears to weigh in on the very issues raised by John's mission: purity, atonement, authority, and kind acts. He shifts the emphasis and cuts to the mundane chase of poverty and survival: Help your neighbours. Jesus then departs from the Jordan River wilderness and returns to the villages of Galilee. He rejects purity rituals and dietary rules, and he takes up eating and drinking with tax collectors and sinners. Compared to the ascetic John, he appears almost self-indulgent.

However, the record reveals method in his radical style and distinctive voice. The *Thomas* Gospel, which appeared, at least in part, between 30 and 60 C.E., only mentions John the Baptist once:

> Jesus said, "From Adam to John the Baptist, among those born of women, no one is so much greater than John the Baptist that his eyes should not be averted. But I have said that whoever among you becomes a child will recognize the kingdom and will become greater than John."

Here, the break with the Baptist appears explicit. Jesus honours his mentor John, and does not deny the apocalypse of Jewish tradition, but neither does he emphasize it. Jesus tells his audience to avoid religious pretensions and to emulate a child, innocent and natural. Lucky are the poor to be near the kingdom. We shall find that Jesus turns his disciples' attention to "righteousness," to compassion here and now.

If the single, dubious historical reference in Josephus and Paul's own letters were all we had, we would know almost nothing about the life, deeds, and teachings of Jesus. Fortunately, other followers recorded events and sayings during the first three decades after the death of Jesus, before the earliest gospels appeared. Some of this material remained lost to history and could be inferred only through documented attacks by later writers and evidence implicit in the known gospels. However, in the late nineteenth century, ancient documents began appearing on the European antiquities market that led archaeologists on a search for the lost sayings of Jesus.

·4·

CHILD IN THE KINGDOM

All the world religions insist that no spirituality is valid
unless it results in practical compassion.

KAREN ARMSTRONG, *THE BATTLE FOR GOD*, 2000

In the sixteenth century, the German monk Martin Luther
denounced papal corruption by writing ninety-five arguments
against selling indulgences, or pardons for sins, and nailing his
complaints to a church door in Wittenberg, Germany. Luther's
reform movement broke the Vatican's monopoly on Jesus, but did
not reform the selection of gospels or policies of the Inquisition.
During the next two centuries, independent churches spread
throughout northern Europe. These churches forged alliances
with local oligarchs, confiscated Jewish property, burned synagogues, and exterminated pagans. In the eighteenth century, Bible
scholar Jean Leclerc fled Geneva to avoid reprisals for claiming
that Jesus had taught his disciples to take responsibility for their
own salvation, independent of religious authorities. He survived
in the safety of Amsterdam, and in 1716 published *Historia Ecclesiastica*, introducing a radical idea: Gospel writers must have used
earlier sources.

A generation later, Leclerc's method of comparing texts inspired German academic Johann Griesbach to published parallel passages of *Matthew, Mark,* and *Luke* side by side as a research tool. Griesbach emphasized two important facts. First, the *Gospel of John* did not share Jesus sayings or deeds with the other three. The *John* author depicts Jesus delivering long Paulist homilies on theology and declaring himself the only link to God. The *John* author recasts the Jesus narrative, locates Jesus' confrontation with money-changers at the beginning of his mission, places the anointing of Jesus in Bethany with Judas present, and depicts other scenes in contradiction to *Mark, Matthew,* and *Luke.* The *John* Gospel almost appears as a separate religion.

Secondly, Griesbach noticed that certain passages from *Mark, Matthew,* and *Luke* share nearly verbatim narrative and dialogue. These parallels raise questions regarding which Gospel came first and who copied from whom. Where the Gospels diverge, questions remain regarding which conflicting account appears accurate. The solution to this problem impacts our understanding of what Jesus actually might have said.

Bible scholars refer to these three similar Gospels — *Mark, Matthew,* and *Luke* — as "synoptic" (literally "seen together"), and the uncertainty about their origins and sequence as the "synoptic problem." Solving this problem launched an academic hunt for the Bible authors' sources.

THE SOURCE

Scholars soon suspected that the *Gospel of Mark,* not *Matthew,* likely came first and served as a source for the later two. In the fourth century, Church historian Eusebius cited a second-century patriarch, Papias, in naming *Matthew* as the first Gospel, and this became Church custom. However, scholars since the 1830s have discovered good reasons to doubt Eusebius's academic rigour.

Matthew and *Luke* often disagree about the sequence of events in the life of Jesus, but generally follow Mark's chronology when they do agree, suggesting that they both used *Mark* as a reference. *Mark's* language appears earlier and closer to Aramaic. For example, the account of Jesus healing a child in Gerasenes (Mark 5:41) identifies a "little girl" by the Aramaic word *talitha*. *Luke* and *Matthew* appear to fix up or simplify confusing syntax in *Mark's* more primitive style, and scholars doubt the *Mark* author would copy a simple construction by making it more convoluted. *Mark* also omits scenes, parables, and sayings that he likely would have included had he known the *Matthew* or *Luke* accounts. In the end, most scholars today place *Mark* first, likely composed between 70 and 80 C.E.

Some 200 verses common to *Luke* and *Matthew* are not copied from *Mark,* but are so nearly verbatim that they cannot be explained by coincidence or oral tradition. Scholars believe the *Luke* and *Matthew* authors lifted these passages from a common source. Imagine you are a schoolteacher and two students submit essays with verbatim passages. You trace some of the common passages to a textbook, but conclude they copied the other passages either from each other or from some unknown source. This is precisely the case with the Gospels of *Luke* and *Matthew*. However, since the two Gospels occasionally contradict each other — in the birth story and in the scene at the tomb, for example — it does not appear likely that one copied the other. Historians conclude that some written source, earlier than *Mark*, must have existed.

In 1801, the Englishman Herbert Marsh named the mysterious source after the Hebrew letter *beth*. Later, German Johannes Weiss labelled the lost collection "Q," signifying the German *Quelle*, meaning "source." This name stuck. The Q sayings may have appeared in writing by the 50s, likely in Galilee.

Researchers began to identify "seams" in manuscripts, characterized by shifts in handwriting style, voice, form, message, motif, or projected audience. Obvious seams may include all of these shifts. Recall the seams in the opening of the *John* Gospel, mixing early stories of the Baptist with later poetic cosmologies. An example from Jewish scriptures appears in the Book of Isaiah. The first thirty-nine chapters were written prior to the exile of the Jews to Babylon in the sixth century B.C.E., but later chapters mention Persian King Cyrus, and so must have been written after the exile, marking a distinctive seam in the text, revealing later editing.

Such seams identify the lost Q passages, but scholars dug even deeper, uncovering seams within the Q material to reveal various layers. For example, in chapter 10 of *Luke* — dispersed in chapters 9, 10, and 11 in *Matthew* — the two Gospels repeat verbatim lines such as "Although the crop is good, still there are few to harvest it." Both authors present Jesus telling his disciples to carry no purse or knapsack and to wear no sandals. However, at *Luke* 10:12–15 (*Matthew* 10 and 11), Jesus suddenly begins chastising Sodom, Gomorrah, and Galilean peasants. No longer do we find parallels to *Thomas* or *Mark*, but rather parallels to Jewish prophets Isaiah and Ezekiel. The message shifts from instructions about modest behaviour to a diatribe against pagans, threatening them with eternity in hell. This is a seam in the text, a clear break in the language, tone, and message.

Later, in *Luke* 10:21–22, Jesus declares, "My Father has turned everything over to me." This sounds startling. Up to this point, Jesus has consistently told his disciples — in the records of *Mark* and *Thomas,* and in earlier Q material — to find the kingdom by looking within and helping others. Jesus has consistently deflected attention from himself and appeared humble. Now, he abruptly reverses these instructions, his modest demeanour falls away, and he makes himself the one and only link to God, similar to passages in the *John* Gospel. Historians regard this as another seam, reflecting a third group of Jesus followers.

Text scholars now recognize three layers, possibly from differ-ent locations as well as different times. The first, now called Q1, records simple aphorisms and instructions from Jesus. A second layer, Q2, introduces a future apocalyptic judgement against the rivals of a community committed to Jewish law. A final stage, likely added after the 70 C.E. Roman–Jewish war, introduces Jesus as a messiah and reflects a community in despair that the apocalyptic kingdom has not yet arrived.

Not all observers believe a sayings source Q existed as a manu-script. E. P. Sanders of Duke University and British Bible scholar Michael Goulder believe that *Luke* copied *Matthew*, accounting for the matching verses. However, the diverging infancy accounts and other inconsistencies would likely be reconciled if *Luke* had copied *Matthew*. Since the nineteenth century, most independent Bible scholars believe a source document such as Q existed. One does not have to believe, however, that Q was a single written document to appreciate its significance. The term "Q" may simply indicate these 200 nearly identical passages embedded in *Luke* and *Matthew*. The painstaking textual research has peeled back layers of memory, composition, and revision, bringing us closer to the actual words of Jesus, devoid of narrative and embellishment:

I am telling you, love your enemies; bless those who curse you.
Give to anyone who asks.
Every tree is known by its fruits.

This textual research led nineteenth-century German scholars to establish four necessary steps to understanding the authentic message of Jesus: (1) Set myth apart from history. (2) Distinguish the *John* Gospel from the three synoptic Gospels. (3) Recognize that the *Mark* Gospel came first. And (4) analyze the Q verses in *Matthew* and *Luke*. Since no manuscript of these early sayings

existed, the "lost Gospel" became the Holy Grail of biblical archaeology. The quest for Q would produce some real-life action heroes
and yield an unexpected surprise.

Most records of ancient writers — Plato, Aristotle, Tacitus,
Sophocles — survive only in medieval copies. Papyrus deterio-
rates in damp conditions, and the classical sites in Italy and Greece
yield few original records. However, a generation after Constantin
von Tischendorf returned from Egypt with ancient Greek parchments bearing the earliest known copies of the Bible, the dry
Egyptian deserts began to yield even more ancient papyri, which
found their way to European dealers and changed the face of
scholarly enquiry.

TREASURE AMONG THE TAX RECEIPTS

In 1888, British antiquity students Bernard Grenfell and Arthur
Hunt met at Queen's College, Oxford, climbed the Tyrolean alps
together, and dreamed of treasures buried in Egyptian graves.
Grenfell was a brilliant, hyperactive, impetuous dreamer, full of
wild hunches. His friend Hunt shared his enthusiasms, but seasoned them with academic rigour. Funded by the Egypt Exploration
Society of London, the two followed a trail of stories about papyrus
documents appearing in obscure way stations along desert trade
routes. The young men approached as closely as real life allows to
the fictional archaeologist Indiana Jones. From Alexandria, they
travelled 300 kilometres south to the Bahr Yusuf branch of the
Nile, which empties into an inland sea. There, they came upon a
small, dusty town on an east–west caravan path at the edge of
Egypt's great Western Desert. In their first report home, Grenfell
and Hunt described "a few squalid huts" in a town known to the
locals as Behneseh. Here, Egyptian peasants had discovered papyri
fragments that they sold to European collectors.

Behneseh was the Arabic town of El Bahnasa, site of ancient Egyptian Per-medjed, where a local fish deity purportedly ate the penis of Osiris after his brother Seth dismembered his body and threw the parts into the nearby river. Egyptian merchants had created a prosperous capital, shipping dates, olives, and wine to western oases and cities along the Nile. They erected temples to Osiris, Amun, and Isis. After Alexander conquered Egypt in 332 B.C.E., the Greeks combined their gods with local gods, creating Amun-Zeus and Isis-Hera. The invaders eventually erected temples to the purely Greek gods Demeter, Dionysius, and Apollo. By the first century, Greek builders had encircled the city with three miles of walls and adorned it with colonnaded streets and a theatre for 11,000 spectators.

The Greeks called the town Oxyrhynchus, "sharp snout," after the famous fish, but by the time Grenfell and Hunt arrived, the golden age of Oxyrhynchus had long since passed. A few colonnades survived along the dusty streets, but the archaeologists were not attracted to public squares and temples. Acting on local rumours and one of Grenfell's impulsive hunches, the two friends established their headquarters on the outskirts of town, where centuries of garbage lay under the sand. There, they began a systematic excavation of the ancient Oxyrhynchus rubbish heap.

At a few shillings per worker per week, they hired thirty foremen and a hundred diggers. Down they went through the sand, delicately lifting papyrus scraps from centuries of rubble and trash. They soon found a cache of records about everyday Egyptian life from 250 B.C.E. to 700 C.E. They discovered private letters, shopping lists, tax returns, risqué novels, government decrees, and divorce proceedings. They learned about an eight-year-old slave boy who fell from a window to his death, and a merchant who sent 4,000 narcissi to a friend's wedding. "We engaged two men to make tin boxes for storing the papyri," wrote Grenfell, "but for the next ten weeks they could hardly keep pace with us."

In the end, they recovered some 50,000 documents in Greek, Latin, Hebrew, Egyptian, Coptic, Syriac, and Arabic script. Among the household items, they discovered classical literature, a critique of Plato, plays of Aeschylus, and a chapter of Virgil's *Aeneid*. These discoveries rank among the most significant in history, but the jewel of Oxyrhynchus appeared on the back of a discarded and deteriorating survey record. Here, in ancient Greek script, Grenfell and Hunt found a cryptic, broken message: "These are the...sayings...the living Jesus spoke...also Thomas. And he said '...of these sayings will not taste...Those who...should not stop...they find.'"

The stunned archaeologists felt certain they had uncovered the long lost, and fervently anticipated, source of Jesus sayings. They eventually found three separate manuscripts, dated between 150 and 250 C.E., comprising twenty axioms attributed to Jesus, some with parallels in the New Testament canon, including several Q verses, and others previously unknown. The fragments contain no narrative, miracles, arrest, or execution story. The oldest of the three papyri appears within a few decades after the P52 fragment that describes the trial before Pilate, in which Jesus states he came into the world to witness the truth. An Oxyrhynchus fragment, POxy1, quotes Jesus regarding what he actually witnessed:

> Jesus says, "I took my stand in the midst of the world, and I appeared to them in flesh. I found them all drunk, and I did not find any of them thirsty. My soul aches for the children of humanity, because they are blind in their hearts and [do not] see."

Grenfell and Hunt returned to London and published a pamphlet called *Logia Iēsou*, *Sayings of Jesus*, which they described to their patrons and colleagues as the "Lost Gospel." Newspapers proclaimed the discovery, academics hotly disputed its significance, and some observers dismissed the fragmentary gospel as a heretical anomaly. However, several parallels to the Q verses from *Luke* and *Matthew* lent credibility to the claim that these sayings would prove authentic.

A LIGHT WITHIN

The Logia Iēsou of Oxyrhynchus represents the earliest known collection of Jesus sayings, some in fragments, others more or less complete. Six of the axioms correspond to similar lines, though spoken in different circumstances, in *Luke* and *Matthew*. Two sayings appear only in *Matthew*, one parallels a *John* passage, and five others correspond to *Mark*. The remaining six Oxyrhynchus sayings were previously unknown when published. Scholars hypothesized that they belonged to another early, independent Jesus tradition.

Grenfell, Hunt, and others, however, underestimated one important clue. The first line had mentioned Thomas, but with little context to understand the significance of the reference. The identity of this sayings collection would remain a mystery for forty-five years, until an Egyptian farmer near the village of Nag Hammadi, 350 kilometres south of Oxyrhynchus, discovered thirteen leather-bound books in a cave, including the *Gospel of Thomas*. The sayings matched the Oxyrhynchus renderings with slight variations, and scholars realized that Grenfell and Hunt had actually unearthed sections from an earlier Greek version of the *Gospel of Thomas*, which contains 114 sayings attributed to Jesus.

The discovery was not the missing Q collection, but it echoed Q and revealed an entirely fresh tradition from the first decades of the movement. Just as scholars had used the *Gospel of John* to fill in missing portions of the P52 fragment, scholars used the *Thomas* Gospel to fill in lacunae in the Oxyrhynchus sayings. The six axioms that correspond to the Q source became prime candidates as authentic Jesus sayings. They are presented here with their numerical identification from the complete *Gospel of Thomas*, translated by Stephen Patterson and Marvin Meyer:

2. Jesus said, "Those who seek should not stop seeking until they find."

24. ...He said to them, "Anyone here with two good ears had better listen. There is a light within a person of light, and it shines on the whole world. If it does not shine, it is dark.

26. Jesus said, "You see the sliver in your friend's eye, but you don't see the timber in your own eye. When you take the timber from your own eye, then you will see well enough to remove the sliver from your friend's eye."

33. Jesus said, "What you will hear in your ear, in the other ear proclaim from your rooftops. After all, no one lights a lamp and puts it under a basket, nor does one put it in a hidden place. Rather, one puts it on a lampstand so that all who come and go will see its light."

36. Jesus said, "Do not fret, from morning to evening and from evening to morning about what you are going to wear."

39. Jesus said, "The Pharisees and the scholars have taken the keys of knowledge and have hidden them. They have not entered nor have they allowed those who want to enter to do so. As for you, be as sly as snakes and as simple as doves."

One might want to savour this opportunity to contemplate first-century hearts and minds working through the mysteries of life with such grace and inscrutability. The *logia* reverberate with common sense, but slip the grasp like a mist. Did the recorder get this right? How does one proclaim from an ear? Is this a mistake? Can we be simultaneously sly and simple? These keys? They hid them where? Why didn't they go in? How do we get the keys?

The *Matthew* author places the first two sayings in the Sermon on the Mount, and the author of *Luke* presents them in an ambiguous setting as Jesus approaches Jerusalem. To link sayings to a presumed historical speaker, exegetes employ a triage method. First, certain sayings are borrowed from the past or from common lore attested widely in the culture at the time. "Those with ears should listen," is an example. However, we must keep in mind Jesus may have said such things and applied common wisdom to his circumstances. The second type of saying arrives in reverse from the future, reflecting the phrasing of a later writer or editor. Plato slips his ideas onto the lips of Socrates. Paul slips his ideas around the name of Jesus. Jesus almost certainly did not say these words imputed by future writers. Other sayings, the third type, sound unique and original, and they converge so well with the time and circumstances that they become candidates for authenticity.

"You don't see the stick in your own eye" might be something one would hear from one's mother or wise uncle. "Don't worry about what you'll wear" may sound common, but since Jesus spoke to the poor, advising them not to worry carried a radical, empowering edge. "Be sly as snakes and simple a doves" signals an original style, and this recognizable creativity is a mark of authenticity.

The historian's "criterion of discontinuity" identifies the signature twist on a common theme, the way the artist Georgia O'Keeffe painted desert flowers or jazz musician Miles Davis played Chicago blues. The discontinuity shifts a larger cultural convention, breaks apart the paradigm, smashes taboos, and makes something new from commonly available material. If someone two millennia from now found shreds of six O'Keeffe paintings, they might reasonably place them in our century and from one artistic hand. So it is with the sayings of Jesus, especially those widely attested in the early records. Although the Oxyrhynchus and Nag Hammadi discoveries did not reveal the lost Q Gospel, they confirmed that sayings collections existed prior to the known Gospels, a transitional stage between oral storytelling and later written narratives or theological pronouncements. We will discover that the *Thomas* anthology shares some thirty-seven sayings, in variant versions, with the Q collection. In this sense, archaeologists had discovered about a third of the presumed lost Gospel.

This historical process from event, through memory and popular story, to sayings collections and gospels written on papyrus, unfolded over two centuries. Jesus may have spoken often about looking inside oneself, mending one's own mistakes, and finding the light within. These teachings were passed on initially through whispers and gossip. At some point, perhaps twenty or thirty years after his death, followers collected sayings in written anthologies, likely in Aramaic, Syriac, or Greek. None of these original documents survive today. Over a period of another twenty to thirty years, scribes copied and circulated written accounts, and eventually translated them into Greek and Coptic versions, as we see in the sayings from the *Thomas* collection. Meanwhile, the authors of *Mark*, *Luke*, and *Matthew* placed these sayings into narrative settings: Jesus walking down a road, standing on a hillside, or sitting in a public square.

There exists no evidence to conclude precisely which words or narrative contexts actually go back to the historical Jesus. We possess no chronicler's notebooks or autograph editions. The author of the *Thomas* anthology writes, "These are the secret sayings that the living Jesus spoke and Didymos Judas Thomas recorded," making this the only Gospel or collection that explicitly names a compiler. None of the New Testament authors identify themselves or their sources. Nevertheless, in the century since the Logia Iēsou appeared in print, most scholars have come to believe that certain Oxyrhynchus sayings reflect core lessons from Jesus, including the six sayings above. These axioms, taken with their counterparts in the canonical Gospels, suggest that if Jesus walked the earth and taught a way to spiritual awareness, he likely taught this:

> Seek and you will find.
> Look within. There is a light within, seek that light.
> When you find it, share it with the world.
> Before you judge others, look at yourself and attend to your own shortcomings.
> Don't worry about your clothes or comforts.

And he added this caution:

> Religious leaders don't necessarily practise what they preach or point the way to real spiritual understanding. Be cautious. Stay simple.

These lines from the Logia Iēsou represent the earliest known testament to sayings directly attributed to Jesus, the Jewish peasant teacher Yeshua. They all appear among the independent Q tradition, but interestingly not in *Mark*. Scholars would identify thirty-one additional *Thomas* sayings that match the *Matthew/Luke* Q sayings, and some of these appear in *Mark*, implying they are the core sayings of Jesus. Recall that we cannot retrieve precise word sequences from such records, since styles conflict, but rather we may discover the essential human experience behind the words. These themes — modesty, trust, seeking and finding a light within, speaking out, and wariness with leaders — will resurface regularly.

IN FRONT OF YOUR FACE

Throughout antiquity, scribes copied freely from oral and written sources without acknowledgement. Our modern disdain for plagiarism did not prevail in the first century, when followers of sages paid close attention to a teacher's witticisms and twists on common wisdom. Acolytes liberally attributed sayings to teachers they had never met, and even to legendary founders. Authors retrofitted their narratives to agree with later doctrine or earlier prophecy and they placed their own heroes into leading roles in borrowed legends.

Rulers such as King Cyrus, 500 years before the Roman–Galilean troubles, imposed their mythologies on colonized cultures such as the Jews of Palestine, but cleverly, by writing themselves into the subjugated people's history. In *The Pagan Christ*, Tom Harpur describes how Egyptian ideas — a single male God, a divinely endowed priesthood, avatars, eternal life — came to be embedded in Persian and Christian theology. We've already seen how Paul shaped Jesus sayings and perhaps applied Zoroastrian Mithras stories to his doctrine of the new covenant.

Palaeologists and exegetes use these borrowed references to trace the age, authorship, and provenance of ancient documents and the ideas they contain. We know, for example, that the golden rule existed in virtually every ancient culture from the Hittites to the Huns. A child in Galilee in the reign of Tiberius may have heard the axiom as motherly advice or perhaps from Hillel, who, legend claimed, could recite the entire Torah while standing on one leg. When pressed to perform the feat by young students, he would lift a foot and say: "What you do not want done to you, do not do to your neighbour. That is the entire Torah. All the rest is commentary."

The saying appears Hillel-style in *Thomas* 6, attributed to Jesus: "Don't do what you hate," but with a distinctive positive twist in *Mark* and *Matthew*: "Love your neighbour as yourself." If Jesus said this, he borrowed it from his culture and shaped it into a positive form to fit his message.

Before it dawned on anyone that Jesus might himself be a god, his message would have been heard by his poor peasant audience as encouragement from a sage, offering relief from the burden of state and temple taxes, landlords, natural disasters, and the absolute subjugation of Roman rule. The themes of the Logia Iēsou, which we now know as sections from the *Gospel of Thomas*, reflect this context. They are themes of finding spiritual hope in a life of meagre subsistence.

"Look within" appears consistently among the earliest and most widely attested axioms of Jesus. *Thomas* 5 parallels *Mark* 4:22 and expands this idea to seeing the world clearly: "Know what is in front of your face and what is hidden from you will be disclosed to you. For there is nothing hidden that won't be revealed."

Socrates and the Buddha voiced the theme of looking within, but Jesus offers a distinctive twist. "What is hidden will be revealed" speaks to mystery traditions and the hope of promised redeemers, albeit Jesus turns the quest back to the listener. Furthermore, in the Oxyrhynchus *logia*, Jesus exhorts his followers to act on what they learn from their inner witnessing, not to judge others, but to speak out. In *Thomas* 33, Jesus says, "What you will hear...proclaim from your rooftops."

The Oxyrhynchus fragments provide another theme evident among the earliest and most reliable sources of Jesus sayings: "Don't worry" about what you will wear or eat. This theme assures the poor and dispossessed that God cares for them as much as for the lilies or sparrows. However, the Jesus of the *Thomas* sayings also issues a warning to be wary of those who claim to be God's intermediaries:

Look inside and trust God, but don't trust those who trade in God's name. Be "gentle as doves," but "sly as snakes." Additional Oxyrhynchus *logia* include sayings about spirit and matter, fasting, not tasting death, being naked without shame, intoxicated humanity, and a cryptic axiom about lions and humans. Some of these sayings correspond to Gnostic ideas and to the *Gospel of Mary*, another source of cryptic sayings.

Today, we possess the complete *Thomas* anthology because an unknown monk in the fourth century possessed the wit and courage to conceal them in a jar and bury them in the desert hillside. The books survived a violent Roman purge and book burning, and remained in their tomb until the twentieth century, when a poor Egyptian farmer went searching for garden soil.

COPS AND OUTLAWS

In the spring of 1945, a farmer, Muhammad Ali al-Samman, was digging in the hills on the eastern bank of the Nile, looking for *sabakh*, nitrogen-rich soil to use as fertilizer, when he bore into a cave and inadvertently uncovered a sealed, one-metre-tall, red clay jar. Ali broke open the jar and found a cache of leather-bound papyrus books, or codices. He took the books home and left them in his kitchen, where his mother apparently used some pages as fire starter. He traded others to local speculators for oranges and cigarettes. Meanwhile, Ali and his brothers carried out a revenge killing against a man they believed had murdered their father. When police investigated the murder, Ali hid the codices. He gave one to a Coptic cleric, who sent it to Cairo for an appraisal. Egyptian authorities caught wind of the rare codex and claimed it for the Coptic Museum.

Ali then traded the rest of the books on the black market, some through a one-eyed outlaw, Bahij Ali, who sold them to Cairo antique dealers. Most of these went through an Italian collector to the Coptic Museum. One codex may have been traded to three successive dealers, all of whom disappeared mysteriously. Police found the body of one, Alfredo Malardi, at the bottom of an alpine lake. Later alleged owners of the manuscript, Thomas Malko and Peter Volder, simply disappeared along with the codex, which — if it actually exists — has never been recovered.

A Cairo antique dealer, Albert Eid, smuggled one book to a safety deposit box in Belgium, and upon Eid's death, Dutch scholar Gilles Quispel acquired it for the C. J. Jung Foundation in Zurich. No one — not even Ali, who found them, and who did not reveal his story for thirty years — knows how many books or pages may have been lost to fire or wayward dealers. The Coptic Museum now holds the entire surviving collection of twelve books, numbered I through XII. The remnants of a thirteenth book appeared tucked inside codex VI, likely placed there when buried.

These books now comprise the famous Nag Hammadi Library, fifty-two Coptic tractates from diverse and overlapping traditions, many from early Jesus followers. The *Thomas* manuscript comprises one of the fifty-two separate works. In 1956, Dr. Gilles Quispel carried a photocopy of the *Thomas* sayings from Cairo to Utrecht, Netherlands, and a year later, French scholar Henri-Charles Puech recognized within it the earlier Greek Logia Iēsou.

Among the aphorisms from *Thomas* that match the "lost" Q sayings, twelve also match sayings or themes in *Mark*. Thirty-five *Thomas* sayings are unique, not appearing in any synoptic Gospel or in *Mary*, *John*, or *Philip*. Some verses parallel Jewish scripture, common lore, and so-called Gnostic theologies. The earliest layers of *Thomas* may have appeared in Syrian script, sometime between 30 and 60 C.E., before or concurrent with the letters of Paul, the Q verses, or any other known Jesus tradition.

We will encounter the 114 *Thomas* sayings throughout this book, but first we will look at what *Thomas* has to say about our unfinished business with a spiritual kingdom, promised in Jewish scripture, predicted by John the Baptist, and announced by Paul. Paul tells us little about this kingdom, except that material preoccupations won't get us there. He does not quote Jesus on the subject. *Thomas*, however, quotes Jesus eighteen times on the nature of the kingdom of God. These sayings represent the earliest, most widely attested description, allegedly in the words of Jesus, about a divine kingdom.

BASILEIA

Once we have a historical record regarding the kingdom taught by Jesus, the next obstacle is the word itself. The Aramaic word Jesus likely used, *malkutha*, does not imply a territory, but rather sovereignty itself. Greek translators used *basileia*, which we translate as "kingdom," "reign," "realm," "empire," and so forth. The Greek word derives from *baino*, "to walk," which became *basis*, "a foot," and eventually the foundation of something. Rulers, presuming they made up the foundation of society, called royal power *basileia*, the "foundation."

The King James English edition of the Bible translated *basileia tou theou* as "kingdom of God," which has become commonly used. Some modern scholars reject "kingdom" because it implies inherited, patriarchal monarchies. The Jesus Seminar, after much hand-wringing among some 200 scholars, came up with "God's imperial rule" and "God's domain." The scholarship is precise, but the poetry feels wrong. "God's imperial rule" never sounds right to my ear, and does not resonate like the voice of a first-century peasant. "Kingdom of God" works just fine, since we easily hear "kingdom" in its mythic context as a better, more just, more enlightened world. The term can also simply imply a more enlightened awareness.

The eighteen kingdom references in *Thomas* refer to a kingdom of God, a kingdom of heaven, or, in two cases, "a new world" and "places of my father." Thirteen of these appear in *Mark, Matthew,* and *Luke*. Scholars generally agree that these axioms comprise the core message that Jesus offered about a spiritual kingdom.

Jesus did not need to explain Jewish traditions to his Galilean neighbours. His listeners would know that Jewish scriptures use "kingdom" to describe the historical reigns of David and Saul as well as a future realm ruled by a righteous Jewish king on behalf of God, for the benefit of God's people. In some prophetic Jewish traditions, including that of John the Baptist, God would initiate the future kingdom with an apocalyptic judgement. Jesus, however, takes a 180-degree turn here and proposes a radical understanding of the divine kingdom.

We have seen that the first hint Jesus provides about a kingdom is to look for the light within. The third *Thomas* saying quotes Jesus warning, "If your leaders say to you, 'Look the kingdom is in the sky,' then the birds of the sky will precede you." Jesus brings his disciples back to earth and insists that the kingdom is "inside you and outside you." Look inside and look around in front of your eyes. The kingdom is not far away in time and space, but rather available to each person and at any time. This saying reflects Jesus' consistent advice to look within for spiritual truth. The saying demonstrates that Jesus reversed certain Jewish traditions, such as Proverbs 3:5, that instruct readers to trust in God and "do not rely on your own insight." Jesus flips this around: Look within. Know yourself. Then, look around in front of you. Be aware in the here and now.

Even so, Jesus offers no guaranteed, pro forma kingdom, but rather speaks in metaphors and parables to stimulate the disciple's own awareness. The kingdom is like a shepherd with a lost sheep, a buried treasure, a pearl among a shipment of cargo, a woman spilling grain from a broken jar, the leaven in bread dough, or a tiny mustard seed. Some of these metaphors remain quite obscure, others more obvious, but they all challenge first-century conventions by removing the spiritual realm from a distant heaven or future time and fixing the disciple's focus on the world at hand.

We won't always be able to wrap the parables or sayings of Jesus in obvious categories — love, generosity, trust — but may find ourselves facing obscure meanings. One ambiguous allegory from *Thomas* has the kingdom compared to a woman walking along the road with a jar of meal. There is a crack in the jar, the meal slowly spills out on the road, but the woman does not notice until she is home. This story parodies a traditional story about Elijah in Kings, in which a poor woman makes a cake for Elijah with her last flour, but the jar is not emptied as she uses the flour: A miracle occurs with a gift of food from God. Jesus reverses the image for his audience. The kingdom is something small and unnoticed — a crack in a jar — rather than something grand and dramatic. Such images reveal a core Jesus message about the nature of spiritual awareness. This idea comes into full blossom in the metaphors of the leaven and mustard seed that we find in a core group of sayings.

MOVING MOUNTAINS

The *Thomas* collection, the Q verses, and the *Gospel of Mark* comprise the three earliest substantial records of Jesus sayings. We might wonder: Do any sayings appear in all three early records? Yes, there are nine if one is counting close word matches, and twelve if one includes similar themes. Think of these as the "*Thomas–Q–Mark*" core sayings. They will resurface throughout our investigation. Here are the nine similar sayings in their *Thomas* form and number:

> *The hidden is revealed*: "Know what is in front of your face, and what is hidden from you will be disclosed to you. For there is nothing hidden that will not be revealed." [Thomas 5]

His disciples asked him, "Do you want us to fast? How should we pray? Should we give to charity? What diet should we observe?" [The answer is given in "Fruits of action" below, but the *Thomas* collection follows this with Jesus saying] "Don't lie, and don't do what you hate, because all things are disclosed before heaven. After all, there is nothing hidden that will not be revealed." (Thomas 6)

Fruits of action: "If you fast, you will bring sin upon yourselves, and if you pray, you will be condemned, and if you give to charity, you will harm your spirits. When you go into any region and walk about in the countryside, when people take you in, eat what they serve you and heal the sick among them. After all, what goes into your mouth will not defile you; rather, it's what comes out of your mouth that will defile you." [Thomas 14] "Grapes are not harvested from thorn trees, nor are figs from thistles, for they yield no fruit. Good persons produce good from what they've stored up; bad persons produce evil from the wickedness they've stored up in their hearts, and say evil things." (Thomas 45)

Mustard seed: "Heaven's kingdom is like...a mustard seed, the smallest of all seeds, but when it falls on prepared soil, it produces a large plant and becomes a shelter for birds of the sky." (Thomas 20)

Light and lamp: "What you will hear in your ear, in the other ear proclaim from your rooftops. After all, no one lights a lamp and puts it under a basket, nor does one put it in a hidden place. Rather, one puts it on a lampstand so that all who come and go will see its light." (Thomas 33)

Rich get richer, poor are deprived: "Whoever has something in hand will be given more, and whoever has nothing will be deprived of even the little they have." (Thomas 41)

Kingdom in knowledge, not in a place: Jesus said, "If your leaders say to you, 'Look, the kingdom is in the sky,' then the birds of the sky will precede you. If they say to you, 'It is in the sea,' then the fish will precede you. Rather, the kingdom is within you and it is outside you. When you know yourselves, then you will be known, and you will understand that you are children of the living Father." (Thomas 3)

Last shall be first: " ... Many of the first will be last, and will become a single one." (Thomas 4; the *Matthew* version [20:16] may be the original: "The last will be first and the first last," without the qualifying "many.")

Unity from duality, move mountains: "When you make the two into one, you will become children of Adam, and when you say, 'Mountain, move from here!' it will move." (Thomas 106)

Entering a strong person's house: "One can't enter a strong person's house and take it by force without tying his hands. Then one can loot his house." (Thomas 35)

Variants of these nine axioms appear in all three earliest written accounts of what Jesus said: *Thomas*, Q, and *Mark*. They comprise at least part of the core Jesus message. Conclusions are not that simple, from the academic point of view, but you may set these in a special list of authentic sayings. Jesus probably articulated some version of all these ideas. Compare these with the six Logia Iēsou from the earliest Greek *Thomas* anthology that matched the Q sayings:

Seek and find.

There is a light inside.

Share that light with the world.

Before you judge, notice the stick in your own eye.

Don't fret about your clothes.

The Pharisees took the keys to knowledge. Be sly as a snake,
gentle as a dove.

Sharing the light inside is the same in both cases. Seeking and
finding is the active version of the hidden being revealed. "The
poor get poorer" contradicts "Don't worry about your clothes," but
observe the subtlety. Dualistic thinking is the problem, not the
solution. "Don't worry about your clothes," "The poor get deprived
even more," and "Blessed are the poor" all work together to suggest
that the disciple drop material concerns for the real work. Namely,

Produce good from what you have stored up in your heart.
Don't follow the priests and Pharisees, who puff themselves
up with religious pretensions but never enter the kingdom.
Don't worry about dietary laws. Eat what you're served.
Don't just follow convention (or lists of rules!). Think for
yourself. Find your own light. Don't just give to charity, fast,
pray to gain merit, or act as if you are spiritual. Give to whoever asks. Build up good in your own heart, through every
action, every day, every moment.

The final four cryptic sayings above — the kingdom in knowledge, first will be last, moving mountains, and entering a strong
man's house — point to the inner struggle of the seeker. Do you
want to enter the kingdom? Look inside, not into the sky. When
you no longer separate spirit from matter, you will be in the kingdom. When you make the two into one, inside like the outside,

male like female, then you will become divinely human and can move mountains. Not "faith" but self-knowledge will move mountains, because such knowledge dispels duality and reveals unity. Spirit and matter are one. Mountains merge with mist. The kingdom is like a tiny mustard seed. Watch out. It can grow into something useful. If you have two good ears, you'd better listen.

A LITTLE SOMETHING FOR EVERYONE

The divine kingdom is compared to a mustard seed in *Thomas*, *Mark*, *Matthew*, and *Luke*. *Mark* turns this into a parable, making it the only Jesus parable confirmed by these three earliest independent sources. Most scholars consider the seed saying to rest at the heart of the Jesus message and the *Thomas* version to most closely represent the voice of the Galilean: "The kingdom is like a mustard seed. It's the smallest of all seeds, but when it falls on prepared soil, it produces a large plant and becomes a shelter for birds of the sky."

The small, modest thing grows into something useful, but not necessarily something grand and dramatic. The image appears to parody a common Jewish reference from the books of Ezekiel and Daniel, about a tiny sprig growing to become a giant "noble cedar" with roots that spread across the earth, branches reaching to heaven, fruit for all, and shelter for animals and birds.

Jesus pokes a little fun at the venerable image of the cedar, substituting the wild mustard plant, an ordinary weed known to invade farmers' fields. The *Matthew* and *Luke* authors, perhaps influenced by the scriptures, have the mustard seed growing into a tree. The author of *Mark*, sounding uneasy with the modest image, claims the mustard plant is the "biggest" of garden shrubs, but *Thomas* preserves the botanically correct and likely authentic version: a common wild mustard plant. The image satirizes religious pretension with a counterculture sense of humour. For Jesus, spiritual awareness is not something to boast about. It starts with the smallest seed, invades highly structured society like a weed, and provides protection for innocent creatures. As we assemble Jesus' most likely original oral teachings, we can start here, with the lowly mustard seed.

Judging by the crowds Jesus attracted, his scandalous spoofs enjoyed some popular approval. Perhaps, however, he met with more than a few blank stares, so he expands this idea through his parables. He compares the kingdom to the tiny pinch of yeast that permeates the entire mass of dough. The simple, one-sentence version in *Matthew* and *Luke* may represent the closest to the oral teaching: "The kingdom of heaven is like yeast, which a woman took and concealed in three measures of flour until it was all leavened."

This metaphor would sound provocative to a first-century Jewish audience. They would consider yeast a symbol of corruption and would remove all traces of yeast from their homes during Passover, thus the unleavened bread. Jesus compares the kingdom to this negative symbol, leaven, which is "concealed" in flour, by a woman no less, and invisibly works its magic throughout the dough. The use of "three measures" — approximately fifty pounds — of dough appears to satirize a Genesis story about Sarah, who used three measures of choice flour to bake cakes for heavenly messengers visiting her famous husband, Abraham. For Jesus, the spiritual kingdom is like the yeast in the flour, not like those exalted visitors.

Linguists and historians agree that these two metaphors, the mustard seed and leaven, capture the pithy, provocative language of the Galilean teacher. According to the 200-plus critical scholars of the Jesus Seminar — following peer review, rules of evidence, corroboration, and internal evidence of language and style — the leaven saying "transmits the voice of Jesus as clearly as any ancient record can." Other parables, comparing the kingdom to a pearl found in a large shipment of goods, a hidden treasure, or a lost sheep, likely reflect Jesus sayings, and confirm the image of spirituality as a small thing with profound meaning.

Recall that upon John the Baptist's execution by Herod Antipas, Jesus appears as the popular heir of this movement, and he honours John as the greatest teacher of Jewish history, but adds, "Whichever one of you becomes a child will recognize the kingdom and will become greater than John."

Can this be right? John's the greatest of all Jewish prophets, but if we become as a child and achieve the kingdom, we're greater? One can almost see the folks in the back of the crowd screwing up their mouths and glancing sideways at the spies running off to tell their masters. Here, we witness the unambiguous break that Jesus makes, not only with John, but also with Jewish orthodoxy. For Jesus, the divine kingdom is not a future apocalypse and final judgement. The kingdom is here, now, inside you and all around you, like a tiny seed growing, like an innocent child. These related ideas from Jesus shift the kingdom from future hope to present action.

In *Thomas* 22, Jesus compares the kingdom to nursing babies. When Jesus sees infants and mothers, he tells his disciples, "These nursing babies are like those who enter the kingdom." In the *Mark* version, disciples try to stop children from bothering Jesus, but the teacher intercedes: "Let the little children come to me; don't stop them. After all, the kingdom belongs to such as these." As we recall, Paul of Tarsus takes the opposite point of view in his Letter to the Corinthians: "Put away childish things...be adults." What qualities of children does Jesus emphasize? He doesn't. Figure it out yourself: innocence, love, dependence, modesty, vulnerability? Finally, in *Thomas* saying 113, repeated in *Matthew*, Jesus sums up his message. The kingdom, he says, "will not come by watching for it. It will not be said, 'Look here!' or 'Look, there!' Rather, the father's kingdom is spread out upon the earth, and people don't see it."

The kingdom is available to those who are like children in modesty and naturalness. Ernest Renan wrote in his 1972 book, *The Life of Jesus*:

Jesus understood...the official world of his time would by
no means adopt his kingdom....Leaving the world, with
its hard heart and narrow prejudices on one side, he turned
towards the simple....The kingdom of God was made — 1st,
for children, and those who resemble them; 2nd, for the
outcasts of this world...3rd, for heretics and schismatics,
publicans, Samaritans, and Pagans.

According to Elaine Pagels, in her landmark 1979 book, *The
Gnostic Gospels*, the Jesus we meet in the *Thomas* Gospel "rejects
as naïve...the idea that the Kingdom of God is an actual event
expected in history." Pagels believes the kingdom "symbolizes a
state of transformed consciousness." This transformation, Jesus
implies in the parables, is available to us anywhere, anytime.

In the parable of the wedding feast, found in *Thomas*, *Luke*, and
Matthew, the proud elite members of society are too busy to attend,
so the master of the house sends his servants into the street to
"bring back whomever you find." Nowhere does Jesus talk about a
future apocalyptic kingdom. "Blessed are the poor," he says, "for
to you belongs heaven's kingdom." In *The Historical Jesus*, Crossan
gracefully sums this up as the "Kingdom of Nobodies," society's
outcasts.

This is why the poor are fortunate. They remain undistracted
by the comforts of wealth. According to those who first recorded
the oral traditions of Jesus, he said entering the kingdom is difficult
for the wealthy and powerful, but not impossible. It is easier for a
camel to pass through the eye of a needle than for the rich to enter
this kingdom, but only because the rich are preoccupied by their
pleasures and power. Paul may not have been wrong that attachment to gratification of the flesh distracts us from the kingdom, yet
Jesus points more to power and arrogance, pomposity and pretension, as obstacles to the kingdom.

The *Thomas* Gospel represents a counterpoint to Paul. Whereas Paul creates doctrine and rarely quotes Jesus, *Thomas* avoids doctrine and quotes Jesus exclusively. This split illustrates the vital difference between descriptive and prescriptive speech. The best storytellers, historians, teachers, and journalists describe what they witness, tell what they heard, and quote real people. This is descriptive speech, echoing events, conditions, and observations. As the great Greek historian Thucydides put it, "History is philosophy obtained from evidence." Prescriptive speech is philosophy by opinion or belief. It is imposed upon us by the overbearing parent, the television evangelist, or the political dictator. Do this, as I say, don't ask questions, here is your prescription for life. Just follow the rules. That is prescriptive speech. Keep this in mind as we walk this path. Be sly as a snake.

The kingdom arrives for those who remain humble and pay attention to the world around them. This is the kingdom discovered by Francis of Assisi, and I believe it is the kingdom my grandmother knew. This is the kingdom of social innovators such as Black Elk, Rosa Parks, or Gandhi, who wrote: "My experience tells me that the Kingdom of God is within us.... If, therefore, we wait for the Kingdom to come as something coming from the outside, we shall be sadly mistaken."

Indeed, this is the kingdom of the Ebionites and other early Jesus followers, who told stories about Yeshua the Galilean, distributed free food to the destitute, and gave society's outcasts comfort in the here and now. Those who heard this message became his true disciples.

·5·

INTO THE TOWNS

> Bread and debt were, quite simply, the two most immediate
> problems facing the Galilean peasant, day laborer and non-
> elite urbanite. Alleviation of these two anxieties were the
> most obvious benefits of God's reign.
>
> JOHN KLOPPENBORG, "ALMS, DEBT, AND DIVORCE,"
> *TORONTO JOURNAL OF THEOLOGY*, 1990

Common sense tells us that Jesus was not a Christian; he was a
Jew, but even this remains too simple. A peasant family in
Galilee during the reign of Emperor Tiberius might share blood
and customs with neighbouring Canaanites, Samaritans, Phoenicians, Assyrians, and Aramaeans. The Galilean Jews spoke Aramaic
more commonly than Hebrew. Both were Semitic languages
related to Canaanite, Babylonian, and Arabic.

The name Galilee meant "nations district," a place of ethnically
mixed semi-nomadic *habiru* descendants, caravan travellers, tent-
dwellers, wanderers, and vagrants with Hittite and Mitanni blood
from the north. Although repeatedly conquered, northern Israelites preserved a tradition of independence from foreign overlords,
including their Judean relatives to the south. Both Israelites and
Judeans considered the other compromised. Judeans objected to

Israelite intermarriage, and Israelites accused Judeans of collaborating with Persians and Romans. Yes, Jesus was a Jew, but in Galilee, he would have grown up among ethnically mixed neighbours, and may have possessed mixed blood himself. He rejected Jewish convention and consorted with outcasts.

Although trade routes passing from Damascus to the coast brought diverse and worldly people through Galilee, the region stood remote from the centres of power. Secluded caves and treacherous terrain provided cover for rebels, bandits, and renegade messiahs. Greek cities east of the Jordan infused Galilean culture with ideas gleaned from both East and West. The Judaism of Jesus would appear to us quite distinct from modern Judaism or Judaism practised at the temple in Jerusalem, several days' walk from the rolling hills of Galilee.

AM HA-ARETZ

Because Galileans' agriculture thrived on natural rainfall, their farming proved more durable, if less grand, than the irrigated city states of Mesopotamia to the east. Canaanite peasants endured successive invasions by Egyptians from the south and by Hittites, Mitanni, Assyrians, and Aramaeans from the north. The Habiru absorbed stories, rituals, and deities from their neighbours. Remnants of those stories echo in the deeds and sayings of Jesus.

Early Hebrew clans — according to Genesis accounts of Joshua, Isaac, Jacob, and Rachel — worshipped many gods. Evidence of Jewish polytheism appears on archaeological artifacts and in the books of Exodus, Psalms, Kings, and Ezekiel. During the Jewish kingdoms of Saul, David, and Solomon, peasants worshipped the goddess Asherah, often in alliance with the Jewish god YHVH, leaving behind some forty references in the Old Testament.

After the glory days of Solomon, about a thousand years before Jesus, the Jewish world split between Judah and Israel, weakening both. Babylonians captured Judean slaves seven centuries before Jesus, but most peasant Jews in Galilee remained on the land and continued to mix freely with other tribes. When King Cyrus defeated Babylon, he allowed captured Jews to return to Judea and to practise their religion, albeit modified to place Cyrus in a role of honour. Persian overlords typically coerced client states such as Israel to abandon fertility deities for a single, infallible, male god similar to the Persian deity.

Just as Josephus wrote Jewish history for his Roman patrons, the post-exile scriptures record Jewish history with deference to Cyrus and the Persians. The Jewish Book of Isaiah names Cyrus as God's anointed one, the only case in Jewish history of a Gentile messiah. The Book of Ezra denounces the Israelites who had remained on the land during the exile and had "taken strange wives" from among the Canaanites and Hittites. These books emphasize purity and launch a campaign to rid the land of mixed races. The Book of Ezra instructs the Judeans: "Separate yourselves from the people of the land."

This centuries-old Jewish family feud between politically connected "people of the book" and poor, culturally mixed "people of the land" continued into the time of Jesus. Our modern term "pagan" literally means "a country peasant." The single male god was an urban, military, royal idea. In the countryside, indigenous peasants worshipped fertility deities and divine nature, practised religious tolerance, and followed the custom of *derech eretz*, making the world right through good manners or common decency.

According to E. P. Sanders in *Jesus and Judaism*, "The sayings material, viewed as a whole, is not what we would expect of a prophet of Jewish restoration. It is not focused on the nation of Israel.... when collective terms are used they do not imply 'all Israel.'" Rather, Sanders points out, Jesus speaks of the "little flock," the "poor," and the "sinners." Jesus rose from and addressed the people of the land.

The mixed culture of Galilee, independent of Judea, provides context for Jesus' warnings about duplicitous Pharisees and his instructions to love one's neighbours. Jesus rejected temple puritanism for commonsensical ethics. Galilean farming communities in the first century lived on the edge of starvation, taxed into absolute poverty by three levels of government: the temple in Jerusalem, Herodian overlords, and the Roman state. Poverty, malnutrition, and unchecked infections led to pandemics of blindness and leprosy. The peasants clung to scarce promises of salvation from itinerant healers, redeemers, messiahs, and rebels. Josephus tells of multitudes following messiahs to the desert, only to be rounded up and slaughtered by Roman soldiers. Rome and the Herods did not tolerate assemblies of potential troublemakers. Into this political powder keg walks Jewish peasant Yeshua ha-Nazorean, barefoot, humble, outcast, but thoroughly unintimidated.

TESTIMONY OF EUSEBIUS

Among the roughly thirty pre-fourth-century papyrus fragments attesting to Jesus' words and deeds, none are original records. According to Helmut Koester, a professor at Harvard Divinity School,

> What happens as an oral tradition arises about an historical event or an historical person is that, strangely enough, the first oral tradition is not an attempt to remember exactly what happened, but is rather a return into the symbols of the tradition that could explain an event. Therefore, one has to imagine that legend and myth and hymn and prayer are the vehicles in which oral traditions develop....the telling of the story is anchored in the worship life of the community.

The closest glimpse we get to this oral tradition comes from the initial layers of the earliest known accounts: *Thomas*, Q, *Mark*, the Egerton and Hebrews Gospels, and various fragments from Fayyum and Oxyrhynchus in Egypt. Most scholars believe the four New Testament gospels were composed after the Roman destruction of Jerusalem in 70 C.E., *Mark* first, and *John* two decades later. The names of these New Testament Gospels, however, do not appear until the fourth century, recorded by Eusebius, although, to make this more complex, he cites earlier sources difficult to corroborate. Eusebius credits Papias from the second century with naming Mark as a Gospel writer. This Mark may refer to the cousin of Barnabas, John Mark from Cyprus, who clashed with Paul in Antioch and then fled to Jerusalem. However, we possess no other evidence that supports this conjecture. The *Mark* Gospel grew popular during the second century in Syria, Galilee, Alexandria, and eventually in Rome, but not among the Aegean churches in Greece and Asia Minor.

Eusebius also credits Papias with naming Matthew as the author of the popular gospel. Eusebius asserts a Hebrew original of *Matthew*, but idioms and language use show that the author composed the text in Greek, with Aramaic influences, probably around 80 C.E., in Roman-dominated Palestine for a predominantly Jewish audience.

Eusebius applies the name "John" to the fourth gospel, citing Irenaeus, who allegedly heard this from Polycarp in Smyrna, but no evidence from Irenaeus or Polycarp substantiates these claims. Eusebius, composing Church history for his patron, Emperor Constantine, cannot be counted on as a reliable source without corroboration. A Greek first edition of *John* likely adopted miracle stories from Syria in the late first century, and a nearly final text may have appeared thereafter in Ephesus, on the Aegean coast. Early use of the *John* Gospel is almost exclusively found around Ephesus and Antioch in Syria, centres of Paul's influence. We can appreciate the *Gospel According to John* as a magnificent example of second-century Greek literature, but it offers precious little in our search for the authentic message of Jesus. Only one line from *John* parallels anything from *Thomas, Mark, Luke,* and *Matthew.* Quoting a saying from the authentic Jesus, *John* 4:43 states, "A prophet gets no respect in his own home country."

The earliest extant document that claims Luke as the author of a gospel is a seventh-century Latin fragment, possibly from an earlier Greek original, called the Muratorian fragment. Paul's Letter to Philemon identifies Luke as a physician, but some researchers doubt that the author of the *Luke* Gospel could have been a physician, and no evidence prior to the seventh century links Paul's Luke to the manuscript. The Gospel is addressed to Theophilus ("friend of God"), presumably the author's patron. The *Luke* Gospel appears in Corinth on the Greek mainland and across the Aegean in Ephesus, likely around 80–100 C.E. The author, like the others, remains unknown.

When we refer to *Mark* and the others, we employ the Church convention adopted by Eusebius in the fourth century, without implying an identifiable person in the historical record. Likewise, when we speak of the Q sayings, we refer to the common *Luke* and *Matthew* verses, whether or not Q existed in a single written document. Each Gospel as we know it today represents a late stage in a three-centuries-long tradition resulting in the oldest surviving Greek versions. Mistakes in later Latin and English translations tack on another 1,500 years of redaction.

The *Thomas* Gospel presents a special case as the only gospel that cites its source in the text. Both the Greek and Coptic manuscripts attribute the sayings to Jesus as recorded by Didymos Judas Thomas, presumably a disciple of Jesus. The name Judas, or Yudah, appears frequently during this era, and both the Greek Didymos and the Aramaic Thomas (Teoma) mean "twin." Some historians speculate that Thomas might be a twin brother of Jesus, but no evidence establishes this. Some analysts suggest the term "twin" represents a metaphor about the disciple who most closely approached Jesus in understanding. *Thomas* saying 13 recounts a scene in which Jesus pulls Thomas aside to deliver secret teachings, which the author does not reveal.

In the end, we know nothing specific about the authors of any gospels. We rely on clues such as corroboration, chronology, convergence, and originality to identify the authentic voice of Jesus. The earliest testimony — the *Thomas*, Q, and *Mark* sayings — reflect a cryptic, radical Jesus who defies convention and places spiritual responsibility squarely on the shoulders of his followers. The Q material, however, goes beyond this to reveal the simple instructions Jesus gave to followers and his witty retorts to his critics. Like Gandhi in the twentieth century, Jesus arrived on the first-century scene with a spirited and brilliant new approach to facing down an imperial master.

LET THE DEAD BURY THEIR DEAD

The so-called Q1 layer of axioms opens with Jesus assuring a crowd that the divine kingdom belongs to the poor, the hungry, and the grieving. Decades later, *Matthew* and *Luke* incorporated this into the Sermon on the Mount. The Q sayings expand on this description of Jesus' audience, describing those who might become a disciple. Scholars citing Q sayings generally use the verse chronology from *Luke*, since that Gospel appears to preserve the most likely original sequence. The list below depicts the earliest known description of the disciples by Jesus:

The poor, hungry, and grieving (Q/Luke 6:20–26)
Those who have no home (Q/Luke 9:57–58)
Those who demonstrate understanding through the fruits of
their actions (Q/Luke 6:43–45)

Anyone who seeks and asks god for help (Q/Luke 11:9–13)
Anyone in the streets, the crippled and blind (Q/Luke 14:21)
Anyone with two good ears who will listen (Q/Luke 14:35)
Those in conflict with their family (Q/Luke 14:26)

Most of these descriptions sound reasonable, but the last say-ing sounds shocking. Scholars and general readers struggle over the scandalous language of Jesus in *Luke*: "If any come to me and do not hate their own father and mother and wife and children and brothers and sisters — yes, even their own life — they cannot be my disciples."

What? Jesus, who taught that one should love one's enemies, suggests his disciples must hate their own families? This idea is par-alleled in *Thomas*, but *Matthew* softens the impact by saying, "Those who love their father and mother more than me are not worthy of me." On the criterion of embarrassment — since no evangelist would invent this — most independent Bible scholars believe the shocking version in *Luke* reflects the authentic Jesus.

Stephen Mitchell, in the *Gospel According to Jesus*, suggests that Jesus harboured a grudge regarding his family, as reflected in other scenes in which he rejects, and is rejected by, his mother, siblings, and hometown community. Mitchell suggests Jesus may have resented being treated as an illegitimate son and had not yet made peace with his family. Nobel Prize–winning author José Saramago, in *The Gospel According to Jesus Christ*, also depicts this tension between Jesus and his mother.

The Jesus Seminar explanation suggests that this disturbing axiom reflects a break with conventional filial relationships and does not necessarily advocate hatred. In Jewish Palestine and through-out the Mediterranean, family loyalty held tremendous power over individual choices. Society had become almost entirely patriarchal, from the one male god to king to family father. The Bible story of

Abraham and Isaac states that a father should kill his son on God's apparent command. Jewish law in Deuteronomy instructs a father to kill any member of the family who might suggest, "Let us go worship other gods." We cannot be certain about Jesus' original language or meaning, so his rejection of family loyalty stands on its own as an example of his radical rejection of conventional thinking.

The other descriptions of disciples, however, sound sensible and have parallels in the *Thomas* sayings. Jesus primarily addresses society's outcasts, the poor *ebionim* and *anawim*. Recall that early Hebrew language employed some twenty words and idioms to describe the poor. They were known as *dal*, "the weak"; *yarash*, "the dispossessed"; or sometimes simply *rash*, those "left out."

For aspirants not among the destitute, however, Jesus also offered hope. The divine kingdom exists for everyone, for those who seek, who ask for help, and finally for anyone "with two good ears" who will listen. The popular lore about "two good ears" makes an important point that Jesus repeats often. Although the divine kingdom exists for everyone, it does not arrive as a free gift. A disciple must listen, seek, and make an effort. Attaining the kingdom is not impossible for those born into comfort, but difficult, requiring a special effort. The destitute peasants enjoy a head start because they remain free from the trappings of wealth and power.

For all disciples, rich or poor, Jesus insists that listening and seeking are only the beginning. The Q sayings make a second critical leap. Jesus insists that a person who listens to him, a person who looks within and finds the kingdom, but who fails to act, is like one who "builds a house on sand" (in *Matthew*) or "on ground without a foundation" (in *Luke*). Near Eastern philosophers in the first century commonly used the metaphor of a house with or without a foundation, so Jesus or his followers likely borrowed this image to emphasize a core principle of his teaching: The proof of understanding is in action.

Jesus emphasized simple compassion and generosity, and the communal meal represents the earliest manifestation of this instruction to transform spiritual insight into action. This emphasis on action both recalls Aristotle and predicts modern existential psychology: To be and to act precede any presumed human "essence." We are what we do. The simple message — remain humble, worry about your own shortcomings before you judge others, and give to those in need — could occupy a follower for a lifetime, but Jesus adds more.

First of all, Jesus asks his disciples to commit now and commit fully. No waiting. No half-measures. *Matthew* sets this instruction to commit fully in Peter's house in Capernaum. *Luke* sets the scene along a road in Samaria. A disciple promises to follow Jesus, but only after he returns home to bury his father, and Jesus responds: "Let the dead bury their dead."

Again, this shocking statement, found in the early Q sayings, flips the convention of family responsibility on its head. In proper Jewish society, according to the laws in Leviticus, only a high priest could be excused from the filial duty of burying a parent. Jesus reverses the convention and implies that those who know themselves and practise generosity are the true priests of virtue. Furthermore, Jesus insists that introspection and compassion are not pursuits to delay until later. Act now and do not make excuses about the demands of life. Commit to the divine kingdom now and everything else follows. Worldly duties may exist, but a true disciple acts on these duties from the spirit of compassion, not from convention. This may remind us of the Zen Buddhist saying, "Magical power, marvellous action! Chopping wood, carrying water." Before a seeker fully awakens, he or she performs worldly tasks. After one awakens, in the Buddhist tradition, one might perform the same tasks, but those actions are transformed from habit to consciously chosen effort. This is "karma yoga" in Buddhist and Hindu terminology, mindfulness in action.

Jesus suggests that a just, egalitarian society, the kingdom of God, could appear on earth through the ethical actions of ordinary citizens. In the sayings preserved by these communities, Jesus instructs disciples to commit fully, forget convention, and model life on the demands of this divine kingdom.

BEHAVIOUR IN THE KINGDOM

Jesus followers in Galilee referred to their practices as "the way" or "the way of Yeshua." Followers of the Nazorean tradition believed that they represented the true disciples or "keepers of the Way." References to "the Way" appear in Jewish Kabbalah mysticism and Gnostic wisdom schools. In the Acts of the Apostles, Paul proclaims, "I worship the God of our fathers as a follower of the Way." Groups such as the Ebionites did not consider Jesus a divine being, but believed they manifested his "presence" through compassionate acts. Sources vary, but we can summarize the earliest description of "Yeshua's Way" as follows:

Look within and out into the world.
Commit fully, now.
Remain humble.
Don't worry about your comfort.
Act on your knowledge.

And how should one behave in the new kingdom?

Speak out, teach others.
Be generous.
Be merciful.

Heal the sick.
Love everybody, not just family and friends.
And announce the divine kingdom.
Otherwise, avoid rules and the rulers who enforce them.

In the last chapter, we examined core Jesus sayings that appear similar in *Thomas, Mark,* and Q. In addition, certain themes, not necessarily actual words, appear in these three sources. Among these themes is Jesus' mission instructions to his closest followers. The synoptic accounts provide four different lists of instructions, one version each in *Mark* and *Matthew,* and two in *Luke,* which copied both the *Mark* and Q versions. Some of these instructions appear in the *Thomas* sayings. The synoptic versions specify instructions regarding clothes, money, and action in the community. The variations reveal how quickly early Jesus groups diverged, but they agree that Jesus sent disciples into the towns; that he instructed them to carry no bag, no money, and no change of clothes; and that he charged them to heal the sick. The accounts agree that Jesus instructed disciples, upon entering a new town, to remain in the first house that accepted them rather than look around for better lodging.

Most of these core instructions appear to be authentic directives from Jesus: Disciples take a vow of humility and rely on grateful strangers to take them in. They visit towns and heal those who suffer ailments. Since the towns in Galilee remained culturally mixed, most Jesus followers maintained the inclusive philosophy of Jesus. The *Matthew* Gospel, however, disagrees on this point, as the author explicitly instructs followers in the voice of Jesus, "Go nowhere among foreigners and enter no town of the Samaritans, but go rather to the lost sheep of the house of Israel." Since Jesus welcomed sinners and pagans, and excluded no one, this injunction in *Matthew* sounds inconsistent. Accounts in *Luke* have Jesus specifically leading disciples through Samaria as well as the pagan lands in Tyre and Sidon. Here, the *Matthew* Gospel diverges, and we likely witness Jesus followers expressing their own point of view.

The community that created the *Matthew* account remained localized along the inland Jordan River corridor during the first century, even after the devastation of Jerusalem in 70 C.E. The *Matthew* Gospel does not appear among early Syrian, Egyptian, Greek, Galatian, or Roman Jesus followers. Isolation in Palestine, and the sanction against foreigners, indicates that the community behind the *Matthew* Gospel adhered to Jewish purity laws, at least until the mid-second century. The mention of "lost sheep of Israel" suggests an original community from Galilee that may have regarded the southern Judeans as foreigners, albeit potential allies who might be encouraged back into their Israelite tradition. The instructions in *Thomas*, a more cosmopolitan tradition reaching into Egypt, show a slightly different emphasis:

> When you go into any region and walk about the country-
> side, when people receive you, eat what they set before you,
> and heal the sick among them. After all, what goes into
> your mouth will not defile you; what comes out of your
> mouth will defile you.

Mark includes this saying about defilement in a different con-text, after a visit from Pharisees, and uses it to question Jewish dietary laws. *Thomas* applies the saying to instructions in the vil-lages, among the people, granting more value to the acceptance of local hospitality than adherence to religious convention.

The different uses of a single saying reveal diverging commu-nities applying the teachings from Jesus to their own particular concerns. One must read between the lines, around the narrative, and behind the metaphors to find the authentic voice of Jesus. These sayings — about food and defilement, or the warning to be as wise as snakes — likely issue from Jesus, because they appear in independent sources applied to different contexts, indicating that they circulated as oral memories. Far from subtracting from the Jesus story, the diverse use of sayings points to a dynamic, natural process in which communities of real people applied wisdom from an extraordinary teacher to the challenges of their lives.

A LABOURER'S WAGES

We should not be surprised, then, that the subject of money soon creeps into the record of the Jesus followers, as we witnessed in Paul's pleadings to the Corinthians. The famous story of the coin and the emperor provides some insight into Jesus' relationship with money. Many text scholars rank the terse version in *Thomas* closest to the original. *Thomas* gives no details of who asks the question about paying taxes:

> They showed Jesus a gold coin and said to him, "The Roman emperor's people demand taxes from us." He said to them, "Give the emperor what belongs to the emperor; give God what belongs to God.

Thomas adds, "and give me what is mine," considered a later addition. In *Mark*, "Pharisees and Herodians" ask the question and hand Jesus the coin, but this detail may reflect that author's viewpoint. *Mark* also has Jesus pointing out that the coin displays the emperor's image, perhaps so readers would not miss the message. In all cases, the pithy repartee from Jesus rings true, and most text scholars consider this among the sayings most likely to be authentic. The Galilean teacher deftly deflects the question, turns the issue around, and makes it clear that the kingdom has nothing to do with money. Note that the visitors, whether they are wily doubters in the crowd or plotting Pharisees, must show Jesus a coin. This detail confirms that Jesus would not likely have a coin with him.

Not all followers took this injunction against carrying money seriously. In *Luke*'s second version of instructions to disciples, after the command to stay at the first house they enter, "eating and drinking whatever they provide," the author tacks on, "for workers deserve their wages." Nowhere else does Jesus suggest disciples should expect wages, and this passage sounds like a revision by the author of *Luke*. It is possible that the writer intended only food from hosts, not money, but the term "wages" does not come from Jesus, and may reflect controversy over the acceptability of taking payment in Corinth and Ephesus, where the *Luke* Gospel originated.

By the beginning of the second century C.E., when Acts and the *Luke* Gospel began circulating, conflicting congregations promoted their own champions and their own interpretations of Jesus' message. Some of the various ideas could easily coexist, but other ideas and beliefs are mutually exclusive. Either Jesus said the kingdom is available to everyone, spread out over the earth in the here and now, or he said, as the *John* Gospel has it, that he alone represents access to a future kingdom. Either Jesus said disciples should carry no money or he said they could take wages for their work. Jesus never calls food "wages." One cannot have it both ways, and the Jesus communities clashed over these issues.

The *Mark* Gospel diverges from others when Jesus specifically tells the disciples to wear sandals and carry a staff. The Jesus of *Matthew* and *Luke* pointedly tells them *not* to wear sandals or carry a staff. Where *Luke* copies the *Mark* version, it reverses *Mark* on the staff and avoids mentioning sandals. We might wonder why Jesus or anyone else would care if a disciple carried a staff on the road. However, in the first century, carrying a staff could imply important links to ancient scripture and to schools of popular philosophy.

In a practical sense, carrying a staff implied a traveller's aid and protection against highway bandits. However, if one had no possessions, then one had no need of protection from robbers. Symbolically, the staff could reflect an image of the people's shepherd or suggest healing power. In the Second Book of Kings (4:29), for example, the prophet Elisha instructs his servant to take his staff on the road, visit the family of a deceased child, and "lay my staff on the face of the child" to heal him. If the staff symbolized healing to Jesus, why would he prohibit a staff as *Matthew* and *Luke* suggest? However, there existed popular philosophical reasons why a staff, sandals, and knapsack might be important and controversial to first-century Jesus followers and even to Jesus himself. Such rules set one school of philosophy apart from its rivals, with monumental consequences. These seemingly trivial distinctions among communities of Jesus followers reveal the distinctive twist Jesus gave to a life of compassion.

THE DOGS OF PHILOSOPHY

According to the Roman historian Cicero, before setting out to conquer the known world in 336 B.C.E., the great Macedonian king Alexander stopped in Corinth. There he visited the ascetic sage Diogenes, who lived in a large ceramic tub on the outskirts of town, in the company of animals and social outcasts. The philosopher's detractors called him "the dog," *kyon* in Greek. Diogenes gleefully adopted the slur, and his followers thereafter called themselves *kyonos*, Latin *cynici*, or Cynics. Diogenes had renounced worldly comforts and, according to legend, relinquished his last possession, a wooden bowl, after witnessing a peasant boy drinking from cupped hands. Barefooted and in rags, he wandered the marketplace, holding a lantern in broad daylight, insisting that he was "looking for an honest man." He mocked the rich and powerful, and his admirers considered him the heir of Socrates, and the wisest man in Greece. Apparently the future ruler of the Western world wanted to confer with the eccentric sage.

According to Cicero, writing in 45 B.C.E., Diogenes had boasted that he surpassed even Alexander's rival, King Darius of Persia, because he desired nothing, while the king could never get enough to satisfy himself. Alexander, twenty years old, approached Diogenes in all his military glory, casting a shadow over the humble home of the philosopher. Cicero does not record what advice Alexander may have sought or received, but when he asked if he could do anything for Diogenes, the sage replied: "Just at present, I wish that you would stand a little out of the line between me and the sun."

Diogenes, like Jesus, left no writings behind, but the legends of his life expose the contradictions of power. Who is more satisfied, the one who desires nothing or the one who desires to control the world? A huge territory makes for weak borders. Imperialism makes the empire poor. Those addicted to material status must work their whole lives to stockpile possessions. Cynics after Diogenes, down to the time of Jesus, made a name for themselves by poking fun at elite society. They wore no sandals and only a modest tunic. They carried no change of clothes. They did not engage in gossip or salute strangers on the road with frivolous greetings, just as *Luke* claims Jesus instructed his disciples. However, Cynics specifically carried a staff, symbolizing their itinerant lifestyle, and they carried a knapsack of belongings, representing their self-sufficiency. In a later letter attributed to Diogenes, the sage reportedly writes to the Pythagorean philosopher Hicetas:

Do not be upset, Father, that I am called a dog and wear a double, coarse cloak, carry a knapsack over my shoulders, and have a staff in my hand…living as I do, not in conformity with popular opinion but according to nature, free under Zeus.

By the time of Jesus, Cynics had spread throughout the Mediterranean, and a popular school of Cynics existed in Gadara, only a day's walk east from Galilee, across the Jordan River. Travellers in the region would make a point of visiting Gadara to bathe in the hot springs associated with the Greek deity Eros. According to the New Testament Gospels, Jesus visited Gadara at least once. *Mark* tells of Jesus healing three deaf-and-mute outcasts there, and *Matthew* depicts Jesus driving demons from two tomb-dwelling madmen outside Gadara, sending the demons into a herd of pigs. The pigs rush from a cliff into the sea, presumably the Sea of Galilee.

Since we know virtually nothing about the details of Jesus' youth, we cannot know if he had visited Gadara regularly, bathed in its hot springs, and met Cynics there. We don't know if wandering Cynics passed through Nazareth, or if he met them on the road. However, a young man in Galilee, interested in social conditions, could hardly have remained ignorant of the itinerant Cynic satirists known for street theatrics that mocked the overlords. Stories circulated about Menippus from Gadara, who mocked himself by casting critics into his stories, saying "that Cynic dog, Menippus," with his "oriental felt cap" and wearing "a lion's skin."

Menippus's animal skin suggests the attire attributed to John the Baptist, who assembled his multitudes east of the Jordan River in the wilderness, where renegades, prophets, messiahs, and rebels attempted to elude Roman soldiers. The Oriental cap could be from Arabia, Persia, or the Far East, and hints at the cross-cultural world of the Levant. Middle Eastern philosophers in the time of Jesus enjoyed access not only to hats from the East, but also to stories and wisdom arriving from India and China with the trade caravans.

Likewise, Mediterranean philosophers travelled east. Some people believe Jesus may have travelled east as a young man, and it is possible, but it would not be necessary to travel far to hear and absorb Eastern ideas. The Levant had become a melting pot of worldly philosophy, and Gadara remained a centre of free discourse.

Cynic poet Meleager lived in Gadara a hundred years before Jesus, and some of his writings survive, including this epigraph for his tomb, mixing Aramaic, Arabic, Phoenician, and Greek languages: "Tread softly, Stranger, over the sacred dead…If you are a Syrian, I say to you 'Salam!' if a Phoenician —'Naidios!'— and if Greek — 'Chaire!' and you return me the same."

Salam, of course, is "peace," *shalom* in Hebrew. The poet gives voice to the spirit of tolerance among tribes and cultures in the northern Levant. A century later, these lines are echoed in Jesus' instructions to disciples found in the Q sayings (Luke 10:5): "Whenever you enter a house, first say, 'Peace to this house.'"

Jesus and the Cynics offered an unpretentious teaching, humble in both style and message, that encouraged the poor and hungry while exposing the hypocrisy of the privileged. A Greek historian of philosophy, Dio Chrysostom, who never mentions Jesus, praised Diogenes and followed his example, "mixing with herdsmen and hunters, genuine people with their simple and straightforward life-style." Just as Jesus points to inner awareness and avoiding written law, a Diogenes disciple, Crates, proclaimed, "Law is a fine thing, but not as good as philosophy…it is better to do something willingly rather than under compulsion." The Cynic Epictetus, who lived a generation after Jesus, wrote, "God is within, and your genius is within."

Many of these sayings and idioms existed as features of the common oral culture. Epictetus, writing about the fruits of philosophy, echoes Jesus' metaphor of the mustard seed: "The seed has to be buried deep for a time, hidden away and allowed to grow slowly, so it can come to maturity." The Stoic philosopher Seneca — a contemporary of Jesus who also ran afoul of the Roman emperor — repeats the idea that goodness appears as the fruit of action: "Who would be surprised at finding no apples on the brambles in the wood, or be astonished because thorns and briars are not covered in useful fruits?" Both Cynics and Jesus urge their followers to speak out: "If the opportunity offers," wrote Epictetus, "the Cynic must speak up on the public platform like Socrates."

Because of the similarities in style, language, and message, some historians have suggested that Jesus was, in fact, a Cynic sage. It is not possible to know if Cynic ideas directly influenced Jesus, or if his mission simply reflected a similar response to oppressive social conditions. Nevertheless, a wandering ascetic in a modest tunic, carrying no money, mocking priests and emperors, and claiming a kingdom for outcasts, would have appeared to first-century observers as a Cynic-style sage. Yet, even if Jesus adopted Cynic motifs and techniques, his message and mission reveal that he differentiated himself from a purely itinerant Cynic philosopher.

TOSSING THE KNAPSACK AND STAFF

Cynics challenged the status quo, not with political revolution, but with satirical wit. The rhetorical twist became a standard Cynic ploy. When confronted with an accusation — of being a "dog," or being impure or foolish — the Cynic never denied the charge, but rather twisted the meaning to expose the hypocrisy of the accuser. For example, when reproached for entering "unclean places," Diogenes allegedly responded, "the sun enters privies without becoming defiled." His teacher, Antisthenes, when accused of consorting with bad company, replied, "Physicians attend to their patients without catching a fever." The Cynic's trick was to agree with, rather than deny, accusations, but then to shine a new light on the issue by shifting the metaphor. Yes, Diogenes would admit,

I go into unclean places, but am I not then like the sun? Yes, Antisthenes, would admit, I consort with outcasts, but am I not like a doctor attending to the sick? Cynics and their followers took great pride in besting their opponents in these rhetorical games.

We witness these techniques in the authentic Jesus sayings, two of which virtually parallel the sayings by Diogenes and Antisthenes. According to *Mark* and *Luke*, when Pharisees accused Jesus of hanging around with tax collectors and sinners, he responded, "Since when do the healthy need a doctor? It is the sick who do." In a scene uncovered in Oxyrhynchus by Grenfell and Hunt, a fragment called Oxy 840, Pharisees confront Jesus for entering the Temple without performing a ritual bath. Jesus acknowledges this, but chides the Pharisees for "washing the outer layer of skin," as do prostitutes in making themselves desirable. "My disciples and I," says Jesus, "have washed in waters of eternal life." Like the Cynics, Jesus exposes the emptiness of convention and ritual, not by denying his transgressions, but by twisting the meaning to demonstrate a deeper purpose.

We'll never know if Jesus came up with these sayings himself, but the message and style display a remarkable resemblance to popular Cynic philosophers of his age. Epictetus, writing almost concurrently with the authors of the New Testament Gospels, tells his disciples, "Know yourself," and offers guidance in "The Way of a Cynic":

How is it possible that a man who has nothing...can pass a life that flows easily? See, God has sent you a man to show you that it is possible. Look at me, who exists without a city, without a house, without possessions...but only the earth and heavens, and one poor cloak. And what do I need? Am I not without sorrow? Am I not without fear? Am I not free?...Who, when he sees me, does not think that he sees his king and master?"...while [a Cynic] is being flogged he must love the men who flog him...what to a Cynic is Caesar, or a Proconsul, or anyone other than He who has sent him into the world, and whom he serves, that is, Zeus?...his body he has himself given for anyone to use as he sees fit....Where will you find me a Cynic's friend?...He must share with him his sceptre and kingdom.

If we substitute "disciple" for "Cynic" and "God" for "Zeus," this passage could easily be the voice of Jesus. The ideas — know yourself, love those who rebuke you, accept poverty, seek freedom, and discover a divine kingdom — parallel the earliest recorded message of Jesus. Epictetus's leap from poverty to divine freedom parallels the career of Jesus, the Jewish King David, and the later messiah Simon bar Giora.

Each of these radical social critics responded to injustice with a divine kingdom that could stand against power, wealth, and oppression. According to F. Gerald Downing, author of *Cynics and Christian Origins*, "It's not really an opposition to civilization, but a correction, just as Taoism in China is a correction to Confucianism.... In India, Shiva plays a comparable role in a trinity, alongside Brahma and Vishnu." Likewise, this correction of society parallels the Jewish idea of *derech eretz*, the "way of the land," making the world right with common decency. History does not always allow us to know who influenced whom. Perhaps these cultural parallels reflect common responses to similar pressures.

Beyond claiming that Jesus was a Jew, a Cynic, an Essene, or a messiah, if we want to know what Jesus actually taught, we may benefit by avoiding simple explanations. This caution also avoids what philosophers call the "nominal fallacy," thinking we understand something because we have named it. Witness instead the variety of first-century influences — Egyptian, Persian, Greek,

Roman, Jewish, and Cynic—upon the peasants as they respond to being excluded from wealth, power, and patronage. We could say that Jesus was a Galilean, Israelite, peasant, outcast, revolutionary, Cynic, Essene, mystic, Gnostic wisdom teacher. Even so, we probably missed some influences.

Nevertheless, Jesus was unique. In spite of the influences he may have encountered, he undoubtedly brings something new to the story of humanity. Here we return to the knapsack and the staff. Cynics needed nothing from the world and wandered independently with their possessions in a knapsack, carrying a staff as the sceptre of their kingdom. For the Cynic, the staff and knapsack identified them as itinerant, self-sufficient philosophers and social critics.

The followers of Jesus took a different course. Like the Cynics, they challenged the status quo and adopted poverty and humility as outward symbols of a new, divine kingdom. However, the Jesus followers promoted communal sharing, not individual self-sufficiency. They travelled, reached out to others, created groups wherever they went, shared meals, and cared for the infirm. Whereas the Cynics grew from an urban, Greek, intellectual world and practised individual satire, the followers of Jesus grew from a rural, Jewish, peasant world and practised community reform. They remained people of the land, diverse, practical, and willing to change the world in the here and now. Jesus' call to action implied more than mocking the pretensions of the rich, but rather, curing the ills of the poor.

COMMON DECENCY

Throughout the first century, after Jesus' death, groups of followers formed distinct traditions. "For the first forty years," writes New Testament scholar Burton Mack, "we are able to identify at least seven different streams within the Jesus movement, though there may have been many more." We have met some of these, the Ebionites, Nazoreans, communities associated with the canonical

Gospel writers, and the Jerusalem group headed by Jesus' brother James and the apostle Peter. Paul's group in Antioch eschewed circumcision and dietary laws, and Paul visited congregations in Corinth, Ephesus, Galatia, and elsewhere. A competing faction in Corinth apparently followed Apollos from Alexandria. The *Mark* tradition also appears to have split into distinct congregations in Galilee and Alexandria.

We possess manuscripts of anthologies, gospels, infancy stories, dialogues, letters, epistles, community rules, and scraps of lore from Oxyrhynchus, Nag Hammadi, and Akhmim in Egypt. Such diversity attests to Jesus' impact as well as his personal charisma. He moulded worldly ideas into a new message about self-reflection, communal sharing, generosity, and healing, appropriate to the circumstances in first-century Galilee.

In searching for the authentic sayings of Jesus, we have pushed back through time to locate the earliest records. There we find Josephus's stories of the Baptist, Paul's letters, the *Thomas* and Q sayings collections, accounts of the trial of Jesus, scenes from *Mark*, and so forth. Before we move on, we might summarize what these early records suggest that Jesus taught. The following sayings are paraphrased and grouped by related topics. These ideas all occur in the record before we have any confirmation of narrative gospels:

Seek the truth.
There is a light within; look and you will find it.
Know yourself.
When you find the light within, share it with the world.

A divine kingdom is within you and all around you.
Speak out, teach others about this kingdom.
This kingdom is like a small seed that grows.

It is like leaven in bread, a tiny force that affects everything.
Observe the world before you, here and now.

Commit fully, now.
Act on your knowledge.
Your understanding is revealed in the fruits of your actions.

Be generous and merciful.
Share what you have with others.
Help the poor, hungry, and grieving, and those who have no
    home.
Don't worry about your own comforts.
Your poverty and sadness bring you closer to the divine
    kingdom.

Remain humble; don't exalt yourself.
Don't judge others, but rather improve yourself.
Be as a child, open, curious, authentic, and modest.
Love your enemies and those who rebuke you.

Otherwise, avoid rules and follow the truth you discover
    yourself.
Act from awareness, not habit or convention.
Don't blindly repeat rituals.
Don't trust those with spiritual pretensions.
Question those who presume to speak for God.

If you have two good ears, listen to what I am telling you.

This mission implies a world-shattering agenda for social
upheaval: common decency on a grand scale. Francis of Assisi
took these instructions literally and attempted to live by them.

We cannot say the same for his contemporary, Innocent III. As we witness people who attempt to live by such precepts — Gandhi, Mother Teresa, Albert Schweitzer, Aung San Suu Kyi — we marvel, even as we notice their feet of clay, that such compassionate and courageous people could actually walk the earth.

Jesus also displays a cryptic wit that encourages followers to wake up from their habitual thinking and see the world as new at every moment. A story appears in *Mark* about Jesus meeting a Phoenician woman from Syria in the pagan community of Tyre, on the coast north of Galilee. The writers of *Mark* likely knew this story from common lore and set Jesus in the role of an itinerant sage. The story presents the cultural shift that Jesus proposed, cast in the style of a Cynic's retort. Jesus appears to be exhausted from his travels, seeking peace and quiet in a foreign land, away from the admiring crowds, when a desperate woman seeks him out, falls at his feet, and begs him to drive a demon from her daughter, who is home in bed. Jesus initially sends her away, saying, "Let the children be fed first, for it isn't good to take food from children's mouths and throw it to the dogs." If the story ended here, one might think that Jesus was putting her off to get rid of her, or simply advocating that she care for her child as any mother would. However, the woman resists and says to Jesus, "But sir, even dogs under the table get to eat scraps from children." Jesus, impressed by the woman's clever reply, says, "For that retort, be on your way, the demon has come out from your daughter."

Two important details enliven this story. First, the tale provides the only case, apocryphal or not, in which someone appears to best Jesus in the Cynic's game of verbal repartee. The woman's cleverness snaps Jesus from his complacency. He acknowledges her rhetorical triumph, and confirms that her daughter is healed, which, upon returning home, she discovers is true. Secondly, the story demonstrates the respect that Jesus and his followers held for women, giving them equal footing with men, a radical notion in first-century Palestine. The Cynics also dismissed patriarchal traditions. The Cynic Crates wrote that "Women are not by nature inferior to men." Jesus' contemporary Musonius Rufus wrote: "Would it ever be proper for...only men, to give careful consideration to the issue of living their lives well?" Jesus accepted women as disciples and may have chosen Mary Magdalene for certain special teachings. Sadly, the historical record of Jesus — not to mention the rest of recorded history — suffers a severe lack of the feminine voice.

The Roman Church would later purge virtually all traces of women disciples from the story of Jesus. Perhaps because they could not make Mary Magdalene disappear, they slandered her reputation. Fortunately, at the end of the nineteenth century, a mysterious Coptic papyrus codex appeared on the antiquities market in Cairo, allegedly from the ancient Egyptian city of Akhmim. Grenfell and Hunt had found earlier Greek fragments of this manuscript in Oxyrhynchus. Suddenly, after nearly two millennia of suppression, the feminine voice of the Jesus tradition emerged. Once again scholars had to revise their understanding of the Galilean's message.

·6·

THE MAGDALENE

These first Christians had no New Testament, no Nicene Creed or Apostles Creed, no commonly established church order or chain of authority, no church buildings, and indeed no single understanding of Jesus.... such contentious issues as whether the resurrection was physical or spiritual were stimulating theological conversations and causing rifts within and among Christian groups. By the time of the Gospel of Mary, these discussions were becoming increasingly nuanced and more polarized.

KAREN KING, *THE GOSPEL OF MARY OF MAGDALA*, 2003

In January 1896, while Grenfell and Hunt struck south along the Nile toward Oxyrhynchus, a German Egyptologist, Dr. Carl Reinhardt, poked through antiquities markets in Cairo and came across an ancient leather-bound papyrus book. Reinhardt recognized the Coptic letters and dated the codex to the fourth or fifth century C.E. The Egyptian dealer claimed a peasant had discovered the book, wrapped in feathers and hidden in a wall niche, in the town of Akhmim, 200 miles south of Cairo. Except for some missing pages, the papyrus appeared in good condition, suggesting that if the dealer's story proved true, the book had been stashed in the wall recently, since the pages would not have survived 1,500 years in the open air. More likely, Reinhardt surmised, the codex had been looted from an ancient burial site. He negotiated a price and purchased the manuscript.

Upon his return to Berlin, Reinhardt deposited the codex with the Egyptian Museum, which assigned to it the reference title "Papyrus Berolinensis 8502." Carl Schmidt from the Royal Prussian Academy of Sciences confirmed a fifth-century date and determined that the book contained three previously unknown accounts of Jesus teachings: the *Apocryphon of John*, the *Sophia of Jesus Christ*, and the *Gospel of Mary*. The text had been drafted in Sahidic Coptic script, from southern Egypt near Akhmim. The collection is now popularly known as the "Akhmim codex." Its original 1,500-year burial site will never be known.

The Coptic language originated as a translation tool in Egypt during the period of Greek authority. After Alexander's audience with Diogenes, he set out to dominate the world, first sacking a Persian outpost in Syria, and then marching south through the Levant into Egypt. In 332 B.C.E., at the age of twenty-four, he captured the delta seaport capital of Rhacotis and renamed it Alexandria. Greek-speaking kings ruled Egypt thereafter for three centuries.

During this Greek period, scholars wrote Egyptian words with Greek letters and devised new letters to account for Egyptian sounds and words. The new script became known as Coptic, after the Coptos region of the southern Nile. Coptic literature blossomed here during the first century, when Jesus followers arrived, and congregations devoted to Mary Magdalene flourished in monasteries in the dry hills along the great river of life.

By 1912, Carl Schmidt had prepared a translation of the *Gospel of Mary* for publication in Germany, but a ruptured water pipe at a Leipzig print shop destroyed the first edition. The First World War stalled the project, and Schmidt passed away in 1938. Meanwhile, the Oxyrhynchus site provided two second-century Greek fragments of the *Mary* Gospel, composed 300 years before the Coptic version. Editor Walter Till updated the translations based on the Greek fragments, and the *Gospel of Mary* appeared in print in 1955. The world at last gained access to the voice of the one woman closest to Jesus the Nazorean: Mary Magdalene.

SEED OF HUMANITY

Early writers portray Mary Magdalene as a favoured disciple who enjoyed a special bond with Jesus. Some observers conclude that Jesus and Mary were sexual partners, perhaps married, and that the famous wedding at Cana, during which Jesus allegedly changes water to wine, depicts the union of Jesus and Mary Magdalene. This interpretation remains possible, but speculative; no evidence confirms such a relationship. Still, Mary enjoyed a special rapport with Jesus. The *Gospel of Philip*, damaged and lacking some words, offers these clues:

> Mary Magdalene...loved her more than all the disciples, and used to kiss her often on.... The rest of the disciples...said to him "Why do you love her more than all of us?" The Savior answered and said to them, "Why do I not love you like her? When a blind man and one who sees are both together in darkness, they are no different from one another. When the light comes, then one who sees will see the light, and one who is blind will remain in darkness."

Because of the gaps in the *Philip* manuscript, we do not know where Jesus kissed Mary. Many translators assume he kissed her "on the mouth," but we cannot know and do not need to know. He kissed her often, loved her, and spoke highly of her ability to see the truth. The passage implies that her eyes were already open when Jesus met her. The gospels of *Mary* and *Philip* revere the Magdalene among disciples, and honour her loyalty and depth of understanding.

The popular modern stories of a Mary–Jesus bloodline, connected to French kings, hidden parchments, and secret societies, remains completely fictional, based on counterfeit documents forged by con artist Pierre Plantard and slipped into the French Bibliothèque Nationale. The irony in the "Holy Blood" hoax is that the real story is far more remarkable. Here we might witness in our own time how mythologies are born and used to speak to the culture that contrived them. The modern Mary bloodline myth is presented as a revival of the feminine in religion, but it may actually undermine a genuine revival of women's rightful place in religious history. A patriarchal church indeed suppressed goddess worship, and Mary Magdalene's role among the apostles, but fabricating a spurious history may not help restore these traditions. Mary Magdalene, on the other hand, deserves to be taken seriously.

A Greek-speaking author likely composed the *Gospel of Mary* in the early second century, possibly in Egypt, not long after the gospels of *Luke* and *John* appeared around the Aegean. A cult of Mary likely existed in Galilee and Egypt after the execution of Jesus, and she may have travelled to both Ethiopia and France. The synoptic gospel writers do not always agree on the women travelling with Jesus, but they consistently name one female disciple: Mary Magdalene.

Few treatises from the first three centuries speak with the voice of a woman. A notable exception is the alluring devotional poem "Thunder: Perfect Mind," discovered at Nag Hammadi, south of Akhmim, and likely composed in the second or third century:

For I am the first and the last.
I am the honored one and the scorned one

I am the whore and the holy one
I am the wife and the virgin...
...I am cast out upon the earth

This work provides a valuable woman's voice, assumes a union of opposites, reveals parallels with the Indian Bhagavad-Gita, and contains certain sayings attributed to Jesus:

What is inside you is what is outside of you.

The poem also parallels some ideas found in the *Gospel of Mary*:

I prepare the bread and my mind within.
I am the mind
I am the knowledge of my inquiry

Since later patriarchs obscured and purged the feminine perspective, the *Mary* Gospel requires special consideration. The extant collection in Greek and Coptic lacks six pages at the beginning, which scholars label chapter 1, and four subsequent missing pages, called chapter 8. The contents of these sections remain unknown. Biblical archaeologists rank finding them, along with finding the presumed Q anthology, at the top of their most-wanted list.

Mary likely refers to a living, historical person. The *Gospel of Mary* records the beliefs of her followers, a Mary congregation in Syria or Egypt during the second century. The account also shines new light on the teachings of both Mary and Jesus. Whereas the *Gospel of Thomas* offers Jesus sayings with almost no dialogue, the *Gospel of Mary* relies on dialogue among the disciples. The discussion opens with at least five disciples — Peter, Andrew, Matthew, Levi, and Mary — conversing with "the Saviour." Scholars accept that this is Jesus, although the manuscript does not explicitly name him. Most scholars believe he represents a resurrected Jesus, since the disciples discuss his persecution. *Mary*'s Jesus voices familiar refrains in a fresh language. "Peace be with you," Jesus greets the disciples. "Acquire my peace within yourselves." He then advises them: "Be on guard lest someone deceives you by saying 'Look over here!' or 'Look over there!' For the seed of true humanity exists within you. Follow it. Those who search for it will find it."

These instructions converge with the *Thomas, Mark*, and Q accounts. *Mary*'s Jesus repeats the common refrain "Anyone with two good ears should listen," but adds: "Anyone with a mind should think!" These slight shifts in language will prove significant and show how different congregations remembered similar sayings. While the message remains consistent, the language reflects this particular congregation, apparently concerned with personal safety, the source of sin, and the fate of matter.

BODY AND SOUL

The surviving manuscript opens with a popular debate about the nature of matter and the body's fate after death. A disciple asks Jesus, "Will matter then be utterly destroyed or not?" Jesus replies: "Every nature, every modeled form, every creature, exists in and with each other. They will dissolve again into their own proper root."

The saying recognizes an interdependence among living things, similar to Buddhist and Taoist philosophy. The Chinese *Tao Te Ching*, written about 500 years before the time of Jesus, says similarly, "The great Tao flows everywhere...All things derive life from it...and all things return to it." In the *Mary* version, Jesus urges the disciples to be content and "be encouraged in the presence of the different forms of nature." The passage expands on the instruction of Jesus to "look at what is in front of your face," alerting the disciples to take comfort in the myriad forms that nature assumes.

Plato and his followers had presumed a soul separate from matter and treated the body as a corruption of pure spirit. This belief prevailed in the first centuries of the common era, but Greek naturalists such as Thales, Pythagoras, and Aristotle taught the counter-idea that spirit is present everywhere in nature. They found divinity evident in celestial cycles, geometric laws, and the perfect numbers associated with musical harmony. This naturalist unity appears in the *Gospel of Philip*, written in Syria about a century after the *Gospel of Mary*:

Light and darkness, life and death, right and left, are brothers of one another. It is not possible to separate them from each other.

This sounds like the unification of opposites described in "Thunder: Perfect Mind," Aristotle, and the Taoists. Jesus expresses this notion that spirit rests everywhere in nature in *Thomas* saying 77:

Split a piece of wood; I am there. Lift up the stone, and you will find me there.

And Jesus says in *Thomas* 29:

If the flesh came into being because of the spirit, that is a wonder, but if spirit came into being because of the body, that is a wonder of wonders. Yet I marvel at how this great wealth has come to dwell in this poverty.

This "wealth" is spirit, and the poverty refers to the body. But Jesus, typically, flips first-century beliefs on their head by suggesting that spirit may come from the flesh, not flesh from spirit. If this is the case, the disciple Peter wonders in the *Mary* dialogue, if the body is not the source of corruption, what is? He asks Jesus, "What is the sin of the world?" Jesus replies:

> There is no such thing as sin…rather you yourselves produce
> sin when you act according to the nature of adultery…good
> came among you as the essence of every nature.

Thus, we hear that just as action, not ritual, creates righteousness, so action also creates sin. When we act within our nature, Jesus says, we embody the good. When we act against nature, we create evil. Is the body sinful? Jesus critiques the question itself because it reveals the erroneous split between nature and spirit. The divine kingdom appears here on earth as the fruit of natural and common decency.

In the *Mary* dialogues, we hear a congregation placing Jesus among the beliefs and challenges of their practical lives. When *Mary*'s Jesus sends the disciples out to preach, he instructs them:

> Do not lay down any rule beyond what I ordained for you,
> nor promulgate law like the lawgiver, lest it dominate you.

This passage presents new language addressing a familiar warning to avoid laws and lawmakers. Resolve your conflicts among yourselves. Don't make laws. In this regard, the *Mary* Gospel feels consistent with all we've read in the earliest known records of what Jesus did and said. The Jesus in *Mary*'s gospel, however, adds that a group's own laws will "dominate" its members, perhaps implying that those laws will themselves become a source of passion and distraction. This discussion reflects the authentic crisis these early-second-century congregations faced as church organizations formulated rules, often in conflict with each other, as evident in Paul's clash with groups in Jerusalem and Corinth.

A VISION

After his warning to avoid making laws, Jesus departs, and a discussion among the disciples begins. They are fearful about going out to preach. They had witnessed — even if from a safe distance — the humiliation and crucifixion of their teacher. James, the brother, might have felt vulnerable. Peter had a wife, and presumably a family. No one wanted to be the next victim. If the authorities "didn't spare him," an unnamed disciple asks, "how will they spare us?" Mary has remained silent during these opening scenes, but here the author introduces to history, in a capacity other than asking a question or serving Jesus, the voice of Mary Magdalene:

> Do not weep and be distressed nor let your hearts be irresolute. For his grace will be with you all and will shelter you. Rather, praise his greatness, for he has joined us together and made us true human beings.

Hearing Mary's encouragement, the disciples forget their fears and discuss the teachings. We find out that Mary may have received certain esoteric teachings privately, as did Thomas, and that she understood certain teachings more accurately than other disciples. Peter asks her: "Sister, we know that the Savior loved you more than any other woman. Tell us the words of the Savior that you know, but which we haven't heard." Mary responds: "I saw the Lord in a vision."

This represents important testimony. Mary does not report that Jesus came to her in flesh and blood, nor as a ghost or spirit, but in a vision. Likewise, the *Sophia of Jesus Christ*, written about the same time as the *Mary* Gospel, claims that the seven female and twelve male disciples witnessed a vision of Jesus, "not in his previous form," but as an "invisible spirit." These texts reveal an ongoing discussion among Jesus followers about whether such appearances were physical or spiritual.

Recall that the Greek New Testament word for the appearance of Jesus in the community is *parousia*, meaning a "presence," or "visitation." *Mark*, the earliest gospel, does not mention a physical coming of Jesus and specifically says in chapter 13, "if anyone says to you at that time, 'Look! Here is the Messiah...do not believe it." Like *Thomas*, the Ebionites, and the earliest Greek manuscripts of *Mark*, the *Mary* author does not mention a physical resurrection, but rather an experience of sensing the presence of the teacher. Mary asks the vision of Jesus, "how does a person who sees a vision see it — with the soul or with the spirit?" Jesus answers:

The seer does not see with the soul or with the spirit, but with the mind, which exists between these two.

If Mary understood a special teaching, this is our best clue. Jesus points to the mind, the active intelligence of the disciple, and applauds Mary for her persistence:

Congratulations to you for not wavering at seeing me. For where the mind is, there is the treasure.

In the dualistic beliefs of the time, the human soul "fell" to earth, but the spirit pushed upward, toward the heavens. The mind, however, exists here and now, among the living. In the *Mary* passage, Jesus describes the mind as a bridge linking the physical and the spiritual. Understand, and the duality disappears.

The mind in these passages does not imply the physical brain, but awareness itself. This awakened mind reflects a popular Greek Stoic belief in the *pneuma*, a native intelligence in all living things. The image parallels the Buddhist Dhammapada: "All things are preceded by the mind, led by the mind, created by the mind....A mind beyond judgements watches and understands."

After this, Mary describes a soul's journey through the heavenly realms, presumably as told to her by Jesus. The soul departs from an encounter with "Desire" and takes up a dialogue with a "third power, which is called Ignorance." The soul of Jesus defeats ignorance by pointing out that it has "recognized that the universe is to be dissolved." Seven powers interrogate the soul during its journey, attempting to keep it bound to the lower realms. Finally the soul announces:

> What binds me has been slain, what surrounds me has been destroyed, my desire has been brought to an end, and my ignorance has died.... I was set loose from a world... and from the chain of forgetfulness that exists in time.

This language reverberates with worldly wisdom, matching the Buddha's description of his enlightenment: "I have awakened. I have severed the ties that bind me to the world." In Buddhism an enlightened one has "slain" fear, desire, and ignorance. Likewise, the first three powers the soul must face, according to the report by Mary, are "Darkness... Desire... Ignorance."

The final statement by the soul, "set loose... from the chain of forgetfulness that exists in time," parallels a scene from the Sanskrit epic the Ramayana, in which the supreme God, Brahma, sends Time to remind King Rama of his divine origin: "I send Time to remind you. Return to yourself."

These parallels do not establish that Hindu or Buddhist ideas had reached the Levant and influenced Jesus or his followers, but such an influence is possible. Buddhist and Vedic ideas appear throughout Babylonian, Essene, and other ancient Near Eastern wisdom. The parallels might also be explained as independent spiritual insights that inspired similar expressions. The historical record does not confirm lines of influence regarding these ideas, but we may marvel at the similarity of language used to describe the release of the spirit from ignorance. The *Gospel of Mary* insists that the material world is not evil, but rather attachment to fear, desire, and ignorance create evil, ideas discussed from China to Athens.

WHAT ARE YOU THINKING?

"Thunder: Perfect Mind" also reconciles dualities: "I am the whore and the holy one.... I am peace, I am war." This poem, the *Mary* Gospel, and *Philip* demonstrate that certain communities of Jesus followers embraced unity in nature, treated the human mind as a source of spiritual insight, honoured women's voices, treated Jesus as a teacher of wisdom, and considered his appearance to devotees as a "presence," not a physical resurrection. We might understand why later church authorities attempted to silence these voices and eradicate these beliefs that hand spiritual responsibility directly to the seeker.

Still, the *Mary* Gospel does not always agree with other congregations of Jesus followers around the Mediterranean. *Mary* closes with a debate likely heard within these communities, when Andrew rises to challenge Mary's interpretation, saying, "I for one do not believe the Saviour said these things, because these teachings sound different from his thought." Andrew's brother Peter then questions Mary's credibility: "Did the Savior speak privately with a woman and not openly so we all could hear? Surely he didn't imply she is more worthy than us." Mary weeps and says: "Peter, my brother, what are you imagining? Do you think I made this up secretly by myself or that I am telling lies about the Saviour?"

Levi leaps to Mary's defence and chastises Peter:

Peter, you have always been hot-tempered and quick to show anger. And you are doing that now by interrogating the woman as if you are her adversary. If the Saviour considered her worthy, who are you to disregard her? For he knew her completely and loved her devotedly. Instead, we should be ashamed and, once we clothe ourselves with perfect humanity, we should do what we were commanded. We should announce the good news as the Saviour commanded, and not be laying down any rules or making laws.

The *Gospel of Mary* shows that some male followers struggled with the idea that a woman would understand the teachings of Jesus better than they did. Accounts of a confrontation between Mary and Peter appear in the *Gospel of Thomas*, the second-century *Gospel of the Egyptians*, and the third-century *Pistis Sophia* ("faith wisdom"). These dialogues with Jesus mention both Mary and a Salome (not the dancing Herodian princess) as disciples, and reflect sexual tension among second-century congregations of Jesus followers. The multiple accounts of the conflict between Mary and Peter suggest a real event, perhaps a merging of several events.

In the introduction to the *Gospel of Mary* text in *The Nag Hammadi Library*, Karen King writes,

Peter and Andrew represent orthodox positions that deny the validity of esoteric revelation and reject the authority of women to teach. The Gospel of Mary attacks both of these positions head-on through its portrayal of Mary Magdalene. She is the Saviour's beloved, possessed of knowledge and teaching superior to that of the public apostolic tradition. Her superiority is based on vision and private revelation and is demonstrated in her capacity to strengthen the wavering disciples and turn them toward the Good.

Following his defence of Mary, Levi sets the example by going into the streets to teach the message of Jesus. Thus ends the *Gospel of Mary*, an account by the "apostle to the apostles," a favoured disciple, and first witness to the empty tomb of Jesus. This short manuscript represents a tour de force of second-century cosmological debate, helping clarify the authentic teachings of Jesus and the dynamic discussions those teachings inspired.

The familiar sayings from Jesus found in the *Gospel of Mary* suggest that the author drew accounts from the earliest layers of oral tradition. The more complex ideas may reflect Mary Magdalene's actual interpretation or the concerns of a congregation devoted to her in Egyptian desert sanctuaries. Although the historical record tells us little about the person or life of Mary Magdalene, we glimpse her history from the sparse and sometimes contradictory evidence.

MIRIAM

The first Mary, or Miriam, in the Bible, the sister of Moses, appears with a tambourine on the shore of the Red Sea, leading a dance to celebrate their escape from Egypt. The origin of the name remains uncertain, but it may have originated in Egypt from *mry*, meaning "beloved." *Mry-amun* meant "beloved of Amun," an epithet adopted by Egyptian royalty. In Farsi, an *am* suffix is possessive, so *Mryam* could mean "my beloved." The *yam* ending is also a Semitic word for "sea," so the Hebrew or Aramaic *Miryam* could mean "beloved of the sea."

Its origin remains a mystery, but the name Miriam is common in ancient Hebrew literature. The New Testament mentions seven women called Miriam and two others presumed in certain traditions to be Miriam, or Mary: Mary Magdalene; Jesus' mother; Mary Salome, possibly a sister or aunt of Jesus; Mary Cleophas, possibly an aunt of Jesus; Mary of Bethany, sister of Martha and Lazarus; Mary the mother of John and James Zebedee; and the "other Mary" mentioned in *Matthew*. An unnamed woman anoints Jesus' feet in *Luke*, and is later associated with Mary Magdalene. Finally, to make matters more complex, the alleged adulteress from the *Gospel of John*, saved and pardoned by Jesus, is later confused with Mary Magdalene.

Paul, in his letters, never mentions Mary Magdalene, not surprisingly, since he reveals almost nothing about the life of Jesus. Although he praises his women helpers and couriers, he specifically forbids women from speaking in his churches. If Paul knew about Mary Magdalene, he ignored her. His letters mention Peter, James, John, and Barnabas as disciples, but nothing of the famed Magdalene.

The *Gospel of Thomas* names six disciples: Thomas, Peter, Matthew, James the Just (Jesus' brother), and two women: Salome and Mary. Mary asks Jesus, "What are your disciples like?" to which he answers, "They are like little children living in a field that is not theirs."

The Q verses name no disciples. Rather, Jesus speaks to the Devil, to crowds, a Roman officer, and Jewish elders, and to "this generation." Disciples who ask questions are identified only as "someone." Thus, records from the first four decades after the life of Jesus, and prior to the destruction of Jerusalem in 70 C.E., name seven disciples who knew Jesus and travelled with him: Thomas, Matthew, Peter, John, Jesus' brother James, Salome, and Mary.

The tradition of twelve male disciples first appears in a church handbook from northern Palestine, the *Didache*, and in the canonical Gospels written after 70 C.E. The *Sophia of Jesus Christ*, discovered with the *Thomas* Gospel, mentions twelve male disciples but also counts seven women. The second-century Apocalypse of James, a dialogue between Jesus and his brother, mentions "seven women who have been your disciples" and specifically credits Mary and Salome with more advanced understanding than the male disciples.

The New Testament Gospels disagree about the women who travelled with Jesus, except that they all name Mary Magdalene. The discrepancies may prove impossible to resolve, but the consistent presence of Mary remains certain. She appears as the loyal disciple, one who never cowers before the ferocity of Rome, accompanies Jesus' mother at the death of her son, and arrives first at the tomb to anoint the fallen leader of their movement. However, the author of *Luke* asserts that Mary and other women travelling with Jesus are all reformed sinners:

> Some women who had been healed of evil spirits and infirmities: Mary, called Magdalene, from whom seven demons had gone out; Joanna, the wife of Chuza, Herod's steward; and Susanna, and many others, who provided for them out of their means.

Luke, written in about 90 C.E., links the female companions of Jesus to wealthy patrons in Herod's court, which sounds unlikely, and he presumes that Mary had been exorcised of precisely seven demons. This account, for which we have no previous evidence, appears to originate with the *Luke* author. The *Mark* Gospel mentions seven demons in relation to Mary at the tomb, but Bible scholars today recognize this verse as a later addition based on the *Luke* story. The *Oxford Annotated Bible, New Revised Standard Version*, provides this note regarding this addition to *Mark*:

> Nothing is certainly known either about how this Gospel originally ended or about the origin of vv. 9–20, which, because of the textual evidence as well as stylistic differences

from the rest of the Gospel, cannot have been part of the original text of Mark.

These suspect *Mark* verses do not appear in the two earliest known copies of the New Testament, *Codex Sinaiticus* and *Codex Vaticanus*, both from the fourth century. Early manuscripts of the *Mark* Gospel end at 16:8, after Mary Magdalene, Salome, and Mary the mother of James visit the empty tomb and hear from an unidentified young man that Jesus "has been raised." Although he instructs them to tell the other disciples to go to Galilee, where Jesus will meet them, the three women flee in fear and say "nothing to anyone." Again we face a great deal of mystery. Perhaps the author of *Mark* ended his account here because he possessed no record of what happened to Jesus. We have to take the original ending of *Mark* at face value: The women left the tomb and said nothing. The *Luke* author, writing a few decades later, begins the tradition of slagging Mary Magdalene.

SORTING OUT THE MARYS

At the end of the sixth century, Catholic Pope Gregory claimed that the "seven devils" associated with Mary referred to "all the vices." Gregory claimed Mary "used unguent to perfume her flesh in forbidden acts…coveted with earthly eyes…held God in contempt," and committed other "crimes" for which she spent the rest of her life in repentance. The Pope called her a "sinner," and Church gossip thereafter branded her as a prostitute reformed by Jesus.

According to Elaine Pagels, "in its earliest years the Christian movement showed a remarkable openness toward women." Second-century followers of Carpocrates in Alexandria, for example, credited their teachings to Mary, Martha, and Salome. Marcion, who researched the historical Jesus, appointed women as priests. Valentinus in Egypt supported women prophets and healers. Early

Jesus followers included women and practised healing that later Christians considered heretical magic. Morton Smith, ancient history professor at Columbia University, suggests that the campaign against Mary Magdalene reflects the transition of the Jesus movement from peasant communal groups sharing food and comfort to upper-class Christians with patronage connections to Rome. At the end of the second century, Church patriarch Tertullian mocked a deaconess in North Africa as "that viper" and insisted, "It is not permitted for a woman to speak in the church."

"The pattern is a common one," writes Jane Schaberg in *The Resurrection of Mary Magdalene*, "the powerful woman disempowered, remembered as a whore." Historian John William Draper notes that Pope Gregory wielded power on a par with European royalty, outlawed the study of classical literature, expelled mathematicians from Rome, destroyed popular temples, and torched the Palatine library, one of the greatest depositories of ancient knowledge. In eighteenth-century London, Archdeacon John Jortin criticized Gregory as "an ambitious, insolent prelate...patronizing ignorance."

The negative images of Mary also echo older, patriarchal problems. In *Hebrew Myths*, Robert Graves and Raphael Patai recall that the first woman, co-created with Adam, is Lilith, who considers herself equal to Adam and objects to lying beneath him during sexual intercourse. When Adam insists, Lilith departs. She later appears in the Book of Isaiah as a demon who lives with wild animals. The more submissive Eve takes her place as Adam's mate, and allegedly corrupts all humanity forever. This clash of female images persists throughout the Bible.

In Genesis, Abraham has sex with both his wife, Sarah, and her Egyptian slave Hagar, who gives birth to a first son, Ishmael. When Sarah later gives birth to Isaac, she insists that Hagar and Ishmael be sent away. The women in these stories — Lilith and Eve, Hagar and Sarah — represent images of women created by men in a thoroughly patriarchal setting, woman depicted as either respectable wife or sexual object, Madonna or whore. This split reflects a male problem, not a female problem. No role existed in this world for a powerful woman, so the male stories reduce strong-willed Lilith to a child-killing demon and Hagar to an outcast, and later reduce Mary Magdalene to a "sinner." Modern popular stories transform Mary from a prostitute into the wife of Jesus, still defined by her man, but her identity transcends both these images.

Mary's gospel depicts her as a "worthy" disciple, much loved by Jesus. She is likely the woman who anointed Jesus, recorded in all four canonical Gospels. *Mark* sets the story in Bethany at the home of Simon the leper, where an unnamed woman with an alabaster jar of oil anoints Jesus on the head. Bystanders complain about the waste of valuable oil, but Jesus honours the woman. "Wherever the good news is announced in the world, what she has done will be told in memory of her." If this woman is Mary Magdalene, *Mark* does not say. *Matthew* copies the *Mark* version almost verbatim.

Luke divides the story into two settings, one at a Pharisee's home in Galilee, where a "sinner" shows up weeping, anoints Jesus' feet with her tears, wipes his feet with her hair, and anoints him with ointment from an alabaster jar. The Pharisee registers disgust that Jesus would let this reprobate touch him, but Jesus responds with a parable about two debtors. The one who owes more appreciates forgiveness more, so likewise this sinful woman appreciates Jesus more than the Pharisee. The second *Luke* version is set in Bethany, with Mary sitting at Jesus' feet while her sister Martha does the housework. When Martha objects, Jesus defends Mary's loyalty. Common elements in the *Mark* and *Luke* accounts include an unnamed woman anointer, an alabaster jar of ointment, an indignant observer, Jesus defending the woman, and the name Simon: a leper in *Mark*, a Pharisee in *Luke*.

The author of *John* sets the anointing in Bethany at the home of siblings Lazarus, Mary, and Martha, with Judas Iscariot complaining about the wasted oil. The author also adds some invective against Jews deserting Judaism. The similarities among the accounts suggest that a story circulated orally and that an anointing of Jesus by a woman likely took place. Where the stories diverge, we cannot know who might be recording actual history. Was Mary Magdalene Mary of Bethany? Is the Magdalene from Magdala in Galilee or from Bethany in Judea? Karen King doubts that these two Marys are the same person, but Margaret Starbird, in *Mary Magdalene: Bride in Exile*, suggests they are the same person and that the Magdalene is indeed the anointer. Other writers suggest that the Magdalene anointed Jesus, whether or not she was a sister of Martha.

By first-century conventions, a woman who anointed the feet of a man and wiped them with her hair would be considered guilty of a scandalous public display. However, no evidence suggests the Magdalene was unchaste. The record suggests, rather, that during the early decades after the death of Jesus, stories circulated that a woman, possibly named Mary, ritually anointed Jesus, and that her familiarity with the Galilean teacher offended some members of polite society. Since Jesus appears to have openly accepted women as disciples and frequently offended polite society, none of this can strike us as odd.

In 1969, responding to the weight of evidence, the Catholic Church issued a magisterium officially acknowledging that no scriptural evidence supported Gregory's slander against Mary Magdalene. Nevertheless, in 1995, Pope John Paul II formally prohibited the discussion of women priests, basing his opinion on "the example recorded in the Sacred Scriptures of Christ choosing his Apostles only from among men." On the contrary, as we have seen, evidence from the first four decades after the death of Jesus places Mary and Salome among seven named disciples.

Many scholars consider *Mark*'s unadorned description of Mary the most reliable report in the orthodox canon. It represents the single known narrative portrayal of Mary prior to *Luke*'s "sinner" version. The author of *Mark* introduces Mary Magdalene at the crucifixion of Jesus:

> There were also women looking on from afar, among whom were Mary Magdalene, and Mary the mother of James the younger and of Joses, and Salome, who, when he was in Galilee, followed him, and ministered to him.

Mark leaves Mary departing from the tomb, keeping silent about what she had just witnessed. Thomas knew her and put a question to Jesus on her lips. Her name appears in accounts from Syria to Egypt, where her story endured among communities along the Nile River. Sometime early in the second century, a Greek-speaking scribe in Alexandria recorded her dialogues with Jesus and the disciples, the *Gospel of Mary*. Later, her story picks up in Aksum (modern Ethiopia) and in southern France.

In spite of uncertainties regarding Mary Magdalene, we sense a woman of confidence, leadership, and loyalty. She stands by her friends, scandalizes society with brash devotion to a social reformer, accompanies the condemned man's mother at her darkest hour, and oversees his burial for the protection of his spirit. She is loyal and courageous, the companion who exerts an influence deeper than words spoken or written.

Mary remains the archetypal strong woman, powerful in her own right, and an embodiment of wisdom. She also represents the struggle such a peasant woman might face in a society dominated by patriarchy and class privilege. But to first-century peasants, the enduring images of Mary — the alabaster, the tears, the courage —

echoed deep memories of Anath, the sower of seeds, who restored fertility each spring, and her mother, Asherah, Queen of Heaven.

VENUS IN THE SPRING

The earliest known female images from around the Mediterranean are limestone and terracotta figurines of plump women with exaggerated breasts, including the famous Venus of Willendorf from about 25,000 B.C.E. and the Venus of Laussel, who prominently holds a horn. Historian of feminine religion Cynthia Eller warns against projecting modern gender identity onto these ancient images and societies. The historical record, Eller notes, does not indicate a matriarchal age of peace, but rather an era of gender balance reflected in ancient mythologies of "primal couples."

Historian Rosemary Ruether reports that archaeologists "have found no societies with exclusively female leadership." Rather, the evidence reveals divisions of labour that included armed male protection and hunting and female gathering and cultivating. The robust figurines of women consistently appear in association with food storage and eventually agriculture. Ruether believes they reflect the power of fecundity and natural abundance. Women gatherers likely learned to scatter seeds and grow food before their hunting male companions. Since women also gave birth, they watched over the cycles and mysteries of life.

Ancient cosmologies reflect earthly society, so goddesses and gods emerge together, sharing divine duties: An and Ki in Sumeria, for example, and primal forces yin and yang in China. However, society's male protectors eventually became military commanders, then hereditary kings, and a patriarchal structure did indeed displace gender-balanced human society. New warrior gods replicated human warrior kings. In Babylon, the male god Marduk defeats the goddess Tiamat and splits her body open to make heaven and earth. From this point on in human history, we find images that portray women and material existence as flawed.

In Sumer, the goddess Inanna fought back to become king-maker on earth. Her story reveals the human transition from nomadic to agricultural society. Inanna's brother urges her to marry the shepherd Dumuzi, but she insists he become a farmer. She descends into the underworld, then forces Dumuzi to take her place during the winter. Dumuzi periodically returns to earth, helping Inanna sow the fields, restoring life.

Inanna's kingmaker powers depict a very real phenomenon of our earth's place in the cosmos. Inanna — Venus, the morning and evening star — leads the equinox sun into the sky, and it is here that she chooses a celestial king. When people today talk about the Age of Aquarius arriving, they refer to genuine movements of stars and planets, well-known to our ancestors. In about 23,800 B.C.E., the vernal equinox sunrise appeared as it does today, about halfway between the constellations of Pisces and Aquarius. Slowly, over generations, Venus and the rising sun moved through the constellations: Aquarius, Capricorn, Sagittarius, Scorpio, Libra, Virgo, and Leo in about 10,000 B.C.E., at the dawn of human agriculture.

Modern astronomers and astrologists know this movement of the stars as the "precession of the equinox," a 25,800-year wobble in the earth's rotation that shifts our view of the heavens slightly each year. Venus led the sun into Cancer in about 8000 B.C.E., when the earliest stages of Stonehenge appeared. She had moved into Gemini by 6000 B.C.E., and Neolithic Saxons devised solar and lunar observatories to track these movements. Since the queen of heaven led the rising sun into the sky, she was seen as kingmaker. In about 4450 B.C.E., Inanna chose Taurus, and bull deities enter the human record.

Two millennia before Jesus and Mary, Venus chose Aries, the ram, and shepherd kings appeared throughout the Middle East, Mithras was depicted slaying the bull, Vedic and Mesoamerican calendars recorded the event, and a flurry of activity refined Stonehenge. Greek naturalist Hipparchus provided the earliest surviving scientific description of the equinox cycle and Plato called it the "Great Year."

In about 135 B.C.E., Venus abandoned Aries and took up with Pisces, the fish god, who now controlled the spring planting. This reign of Pisces over grain is portrayed in second- and thirty-century catacombs from Rome to Alexandria, some depicting Jesus healing the infirm and sharing meals of bread and fish. The shepherd kings of Jewish history still wielded influence, but the future would favour the fish deities. The peasants in the field were fully aware that a great shift in heavenly powers was upon them.

ANATH AND TAMMUZ

The images associated with Jesus and the Magdalene remain inexorably linked to these spring equinox celebrations. Venus, the Sumerian Inanna, became Isis in Egypt, Ishtar in Akkadia, and Asherah in Canaan. In the Middle Ages, Ishtar became Eostre, the Anglo-Saxon goddess of spring and source of our term "Easter." The modern resurrection celebration preserves Ishtar's symbols of nature: spring flowers, eggs, rabbits, and the green and white of Catholic Easter vestments.

Semitic tribes in Canaan worshiped Asherah at forest shrines. Jewish scriptures associated her with their god YHVH. Asherah often appears with signs of the zodiac — rams, bulls, twins, crabs, and lions — recalling Venus leading the sun through the constellations. She wears a necklace of acorns, a symbol of food, life, and nature. The Phoenicians believed she watched over flocks of sheep, and during the first century, northern Israelites associated Asherah with the tree of life and with a flock of devotees. Her ancient symbols — the horn, breasts, womb, fertility — remain alive in the stories of the Magdalene.

Asherah sometimes appeared with a heifer's head and two crescent horns resembling the waxing and waning crescent moons, and with a halo of moonlight around her head. The moon's light was symbolized by the diffused surface of alabaster stone, so her statues are commonly carved from alabaster. Thus, we find the alabaster jar carried by the woman who anointed Jesus.

Women of Canaan and Israel traditionally made sacrifices to Asherah. They might simply pour out part of a drink onto the ground as an offering or burn perfumed incense at her shrines. Peasant women would set out "Asherah's tables" near town gates or at crossroads on the new moon to feed poor passing strangers. This practice, sharing Asherah's bounty, likely influenced the communal meal adopted by Jesus and his followers.

In Canaan, ancient Inanna and Dumuzi became Asherah and Tammuz. Asherah's daughter Anath resurrected life each spring with the body of her deceased brother/lover Tammuz. The fourth Jewish month, in early summer, takes his name, Tammuz. A spring ritual associated with Anath and Tammuz involved the annual day of atonement, either for personal transgressions or for the people's failure to uphold divine law. In northern Israel, the tribe of Joseph celebrated this day of atonement by assimilating the rites of Tammuz, whereby a messiah dies and returns. The ritualized atonement created the tradition of a "scapegoat," piling the sins of the community onto a poor goat and running it into the desert. As self-medication against the torments of unspeakable regrets, the ritual probably worked well. In some cases, the scapegoat would be replaced by a human victim in the role of Tammuz, the "suffering servant" of the people.

The rites included a ritual humiliation and death of a king chosen by the people's queen. A peasant Canaanite version involved a local honoured young woman choosing a king, who is mocked with a crown of brambles, a rag robe, and a reed sceptre called the "grain of Tammuz." Peasants at a spring fair might stage such events as a humorous farce at the expense of some vainglorious young man. The event could also take a cruel turn, being exploited to settle an old score, punish a scoundrel, or simply enjoy a day of vindictive fun at the expense of some unfortunate prisoner. Over the hundreds of years and thousands of performances of the ritual, these and many more uses likely occurred, and people talked about the funniest or cruellest for generations.

The sceptre of grain that Tammuz holds as he is humiliated represents the death and restoration of life. The ritual king Tammuz—or Attis, Osiris, or Baal—must die, because through death, life is restored. In the Greek version, Dionysus is hung on a cross. In the *John* Gospel we hear an echo of the grain of Tammuz: "The hour is come, that the Son of man should be glorified. Truly, I say unto you, unless a grain of wheat falls to the earth and dies, it remains alone; but if it dies, it bears fruit."

Because of the similarities between the humiliation ritual of Tammuz and the mocking and crucifixion of Jesus, a first-century peasant observer might easily merge the two stories. The historian Arnold Toynbee suggested that Roman soldiers imposed the ritual on Jesus to mock both their prisoner and Jewish peasants who conducted such rites. Some scholars since the eighteenth century have suggested that the story of the mocking and execution of Jesus was adapted by *Mark* from these popular legends. We cannot know precisely which ritual stories may have merged with history in the four decades between his death and *Mark*'s account. However, the Magdalene remains the one person, other than the victim's mother, that all accounts place at the humiliation and execution of Jesus. We may now begin to glimpse the role of Mary in the life, teachings, and later stories about Jesus the Nazorean.

THE MAGDALENE

In 327 C.E., Emperor Constantine's mother, Helena, toured Palestine on a goodwill mission. Her powerful son had adopted Christianity, established Church doctrine, launched a campaign to eradicate alleged heretics, and recently murdered his wife and son. In Palestine, Helena visited local royalty and promoted the new imperial religion. She purportedly discovered the birthplace and cross of Jesus, albeit three centuries after his lifetime, and the hometown of Mary Magdalene, allegedly Magdala on the Sea of Galilee. Constantine's court historian Eusebius recorded these discoveries in the *Onomasticon*, a list of biblical sites, including the town Magdala, from Aramaic *mgdl*, meaning "tower." A nagging problem with this story remains: There exists no first-century evidence of such a town, including the gospel accounts of *Mark* and *Matthew*.

Mark's Gospel calls the region Dalmanutha. The earliest Greek manuscripts of *Matthew* refer to a lakeside town of Magadan, for which we have no explanation, and which does not refer to Mary. Copyists after Eusebius in the fourth century wrote Magadan as "Magdala," to conform with Eusebius and the emperor's mother. Modern translations use the original names from *Mark* and *Matthew*: Dalmanutha and Magadan.

Josephus, in about 70 C.E., refers to the site on the western shore of the lake, but he calls the town Taricheae, a Greek reference to the famous salted fish that the village shipped throughout the Mediterranean. He describes a town of 40,000 inhabitants, "full of materials for shipbuilding, and with many artisans." He provides the Aramaic name of the lake, Gennesareth, but gives no Aramaic name for Taricheae. The first-century Greek geographer Strabo calls the town Taricheae, as do Roman naturalist Pliny the

Elder, historian Suetonius, and Roman records spanning 200 years. These accounts mention Aramaic names, but none mentions Magdala.

The Book of Joshua tells of the Israelite Nephtali tribe acquiring the land of Migdal-El, or tower of El, around Lake Gennesareth (Sea of Galilee). The earliest references to towns known as Magdala appear in third-century Talmud manuscripts, including Magdal Nunayya, "tower of the fish," which some historians equate with Taricheae. Possibly, in the second or third century, Taricheae became Magdala Nunayya, but the record provides nothing to equate a first-century town on the Sea of Galilee with the name Magdala.

Other problems persist with the epithet "the Magdalene." If Mary Magdalene is the sister of Martha in Bethany, then she's not from Galilee at all. The Catholic Church once insisted the Magdalene was Mary of Bethany, but changed its position in 1969. Karen King, translator of the *Mary* Gospel, doubts the Bethany link and believes a town called Magdala may have existed in the first century. Margaret Starbird doubts a first-century Magdala town, places the anointing in Bethany, and links the Magdalene to the sister of Martha. She and other scholars believe the evidence suggests that "Magdalene" represents a title, not a hometown.

The same question remained unanswered regarding "Nazorean." It is entirely possible that both "Nazorean" and "Magdalene" are titles and have nothing whatsoever to do with towns. Jerome, who translated the Bible into Latin at the opening of the fifth century, believed the term Magdalene reflected Mary's stature as a disciple, that she appeared "as a tower"— a title, not a hometown.

Mary's peasant contemporaries would hear the term Magdalene with a particular reference to their history. In about 730 B.C.E., Assyrian armies overran Israel and Judea, forcing the peasantry into servitude. Noble Jewish prophets such as Isaiah responded by encouraging the humbled nation with predictions of a new kingdom to come. One voice, however, rises in the Jewish scriptures, not from a noble such as Isaiah, but from a commoner, Micah, near the village of Moresheth in the hill country southwest of Jerusalem. Micah, the peasant prophet, blames Israel's troubles on the Jewish people's transgressions against their neighbours. Specifically, he scolds elite temple prophets who "give oracles for money," priests who "teach for a price," and leaders who "build Zion with blood."

Micah prophesies that the glory of Israel will return not through war, but with a peasant shepherd king who will bring peace. He delivers the famous line "They shall beat their swords into plowshares," and he promises that this king of Israel will not be born in Jerusalem, but among the "little clans," in the birthplace of David, in Bethlehem of Ephrathah.

Micah grieves for the peasants treading their fields under the Assyrian yoke, suffering hunger and subjugation. "Siege is laid against us," he calls out, lamenting Assyrian atrocities. However, Micah foresees salvation not from warrior kings but rather from the "outcasts" living modestly by planting and harvesting God's abundance on earth. A day will come, promises Micah, when "they shall sit under their own vines and under their fig trees, and no one shall make them afraid." He calls out to the "hill" of Zion, the earthly daughter of Israel, and perhaps to a very real daughter of his family: "Now why do you cry aloud? Is there no king in you?...And you, O tower of the flock, hill of daughter Zion, to you it shall come, the former dominion shall come."

The Hebrew and Aramaic idiom for "tower of the flock" is the *magdal-eder,* her people's queen. Her tower is the hill overlooking the entire valley, from which she sees everyone and acts as the people's protector. She chooses a king who assists her in restoring life and defending the people. The Greek *h Magdalhnh,* "the Magdalene," may indeed represent this title *magdal-eder,* the tower of the flock.

A strong, independent woman called the Magdalene would almost certainly evoke this image among orthodox Judeans such as Micah's little clans, and among northern Israelite communities in rural Galilee, where the *magdal-eder* could appear almost indistinguishable from Anath, daughter of Asherah. The Jewish prophet Ezekiel recounts visiting "the Lord's house, and behold, there sat women weeping for Tammuz." To the author of Ezekiel, such worship amounted to an abomination, but to the women, their weeping replicated the goddess's lament upon Tammuz's descent into the underworld, from which Anath would bring him back. The rite of weeping honoured death, atonement, and the rebirth of a nation.

Similarly, the Magdalene weeps for Jesus. The *John* Gospel reports, "They said to her, 'Woman, why do you weep?' She replied, 'Because they have taken away my Lord, and I know not where they have laid him.'" Whatever the author intended, this passage would have reflected to first-century peasants the women weeping for Tammuz.

Tammuz, the god-man, is born of a virgin, dies, and is resurrected. The Anath and Tammuz legends include the unity of male and female, a tree of knowledge, anointing a shepherd king, alabaster signifying the goddess, a mock crown and sceptre, resurrection of a sacrificial king, a promised future kingdom, and women's communal meals for the poor. We recognize all of these details in the Jesus story. As we have come to expect with Jesus and Mary, they add a distinctive twist.

Historian Rosemary Ruether suggests that ancient pagan religions honoured nature and wisdom but lacked a visible "social justice tradition," perhaps because it was not necessary. She credits the example of Jesus and Mary Magdalene with adding the idea of worldly justice through spiritually inspired action. Jesus and the Magdalene shock the status quo and change the balance of power. They give the poor and dispossessed hope for a better future. Jesus accepts women equally, as he accepts everyone equally, correcting the gender and class bias of conventional society. Ruether believes the Jesus and Mary relationship represents a united male–female spirituality that "calls us to repent of power over others and to reclaim power within and power with one another."

According to Elaine Pagels, the *Gospel of Mary* depicts Mary Magdalene as "the one favoured with visions and insight that far surpass Peter's." The second-century *Dialogue of the Saviour* expands earlier sayings collections into a discussion between Jesus and the disciples, similar to the *Mary* Gospel. *Dialogue of the Saviour* mentions only three disciples — Matthew, Judas, and Mary — and praises Mary as the "woman who knew the All." In addition to the canonical Gospels, at least seven independent texts written during the first three centuries after Jesus place Mary as a favoured disciple.

History is chaotic. We don't know which of these images a community honoured when they said "the Magdalene" or "the Nazorean." To investigate the history of the first century is to discover that any and all of these images could, and probably did, occur to various tellers and hearers of these stories. Just as peasants in Tyre or Gadara may have taken Jesus for a Cynic sage, peasants in all of Israel, Judah, and beyond might have taken the bold woman with him as the *magdal-eder*, the tower of the people, and this may indeed explain her title, Magdalene. Even if Mary did come from a town of Magdala, this would have enhanced her image as the tower of her flock. To our great fortune, she apparently told her story and scribes in Egypt recorded it. We may thank her nameless devotees, who buried this manuscript in the dry hills along the Nile River, for the good news that the library of human knowledge still possesses the *Gospel of Mary*.

·7·

KINGDOM OF DECENCY

> In his ethical code there is a sublimity, distinctiveness and originality…If ever the day should come and this ethical code be stripped of its wrappings of miracles and mysticism, the Book of the Ethics of Jesus will be one of the choicest treasures of the literature of Israel for all time.
>
> JOSEPH KLAUSNER, *JESUS OF NAZARETH*, 1922

When my three sons were young, we lived in a rural island community, where jobs and resources were scarce and people practised both self-reliance and common generosity. Most people knew how to preserve food and fix their own plumbing, but if one didn't, a neighbour would help. I don't wish to romanticize rural life; our community faced the usual social challenges, and disputes often raged into feuds. Nevertheless, if a tree fell on someone's house, neighbours pitched in to make repairs. When our youngest son, Liam, faced an emergency with the onset of a sudden life-threatening illness, phones rang throughout the island, and the entire community, including those with whom we had disagreements, drove their vehicles to the school soccer pitch in the middle of the night and lit the field with their headlights so a helicopter could land and whisk him off the island and into a hospital. Kindness exists everywhere, in city and country, but in small communities, where people still rely on each other directly, these qualities endure naturally. Written codes of ethics are an urban invention.

When we moved to the city some years later, we happened to live near a liquor store where the homeless returned empty bottles for a meagre income. In a rural community, many are poor, but no one is destitute. Homelessness is also an invention of the city, and my middle son, Jonah, eight years old, had never seen men and women with their worldly goods in shopping carts or paper bags. Whenever we walked to school or the store, he would give a quarter or something from his modest allowance to each person who asked. We had neither encouraged him to do this nor discouraged him. His benevolence was his own. He became known among the homeless, and well liked. One day as we passed by, a familiar man looked up at Jonah, looked at me, shrugged, and did not approach us. His restraint suggests the multiplying power of compassion, and it touched me as deeply as my son's generosity.

One day, Jonah told me, "Dad, I have a problem." His problem, he explained, almost in tears, was this: "There are too many people in Vancouver with no money." Our son's goodwill seems to have been natural, perhaps reinforced by his childhood rural experience, but still instinctive, not calculated. He was not following a code to tithe, attempting to impress anyone, or trying to earn school credits for volunteering in the community. He simply gave to those who asked. About a month later, a girl in our city was murdered. Police found that half a dozen people had heard screams but had not responded. The contrast between my son's behaviour and this apparent callousness raises the question: How do people lose the natural instinct for compassion? This question also seemed to come up with Jesus and his friends.

THEIR HEARTS ARE DISTANT

The historical record of ancient Palestine tells us a great deal about Herodian royals and Roman glories but provides only rare glimpses of common reformers attempting to balance the social equation. Still, we have evidence of citizens prostrating themselves before Pilate in Caesarea, women setting up food tables in rural Canaan, the Cynic Menippus mocking complacent society in Gadara, rebels hiding in Galilean caves, the warrior messiah Simon bar Giora wrapped in his purple cape facing down Romans in Jerusalem, and the familiar New Testament reformers John the Baptist, Mary Magdalene, and Jesus the Nazorean drawing crowds and irritating authorities. The poor ones were not powerless.

Historians point out that original versions of gospels likely appear earlier than the oldest extant manuscripts, so they track two sets of dates: (1) the approximate date of the oldest surviving manuscript, and (2) the presumed date that scholars believe an earlier first edition was composed. For example, history's oldest manuscript fragment depicting Jesus appears a century after his life, around 125 C.E., matching a story from the *John* Gospel. However, based on language style, scholars believe an original *John* Gospel appeared between 90 and 120 C.E. During this same period, historians placed the Gospel of *Mary* and the Apocalypse of James; an epistle attributed to Barnabas; letters by the first Christian patriarchs, Ignatius in Antioch, Polycarp in Smyrna, and Clement in Rome; and writings from rival movements led by Valentinus in North Africa, Marcion on the Black Sea, and the Ebionites east of the Jordan River.

As we push back in time to the previous decades, 80–100 C.E., the gospels of *Matthew* and *Luke* appeared, along with the *Dialogue of the Saviour*; the *Gospel of Peter*; the Egerton Gospel, an independent narrative of Jesus; and a New Testament letter, attributed to Jesus' brother James, defending the poor against statements by Paul that allegedly favoured the upper classes. Within fifty years after the life of Jesus, the movement in his name had already splintered along class lines, and between Paul's doctrine of faith and Jesus' message of self-reflection and social action.

Still earlier, during the Jewish revolt and the fall of Jerusalem, from 60 to 80 C.E., historians place the Gospel of the Egyptians, a dialogue based on the *Thomas* sayings; the original *Gospel of Mark*, ending with Mary Magdalene fleeing the tomb of Jesus; and a story from the fragment Oxyrhynchus 840, in which Jesus debates Pharisees about washing "the outer layer of skin" while ignoring inner righteousness. At this time, a Christian acolyte wrote the Letter to the Colossians, later attributed to Paul, preaching faith in the messiah and denouncing ascetic practices, Jewish traditions, and Gnostic teachings. Thus we see that, even within thirty years after the life of Jesus, congregations of followers clashed over his legacy.

Finally, if we claw back through the record to the very earliest evidence of Jesus' teachings, we find precious few accounts from the first three decades after his life, from 30 to 60 C.E. The authentic letters by Paul appear in the 50s. These attest to the existence of Jesus and several disciples, and announce Jesus as the messiah. The Gospel of the Hebrews, known only through later citations, appears to have been composed in Egypt in about 50–60 C.E. This gospel depicts the divine pre-existence of Jesus, his life, and sayings, portraying his post-death appearance as the incarnation of divine wisdom, the goddess Sophia.

Three short fragments, known as Papyrus Egerton, appeared in Syria in the mid-first century. Egerton depicts Jesus talking to lawmakers about Moses, healing a leper, and scolding hypocrites who "honour me with their lips, but their hearts are far distant." These lines, taken almost verbatim from the Book of Isaiah, are later repeated in the *Matthew* Gospel. Here we reach as close as the evidence takes us to the survivors of the Jesus movement, and already we hear of hypocrisy and conflict.

The first layer of *Thomas* and the Q axioms had appeared by the 50s, around the Jordan River in Galilee, possibly linked to the lake-front town of Tiberias. We have seen that the parallel sayings in *Thomas, Mark, Luke,* and *Matthew* suggest a core Jesus message that we might summarize as: Find your inner light, share it with the world, give to others, eschew wealth, shun violence, avoid rules, and heal the sick. This mission appears as a public program for the dispossessed and a counterforce to social conflict. A tragic irony of history is that such programs alarm the privileged, who may inter-pret public compassion as insurrection. Rome and its terrorized local administrators met the generosity of Jesus with brute force.

Our earliest physical evidence of a Jesus story, the P52 frag-ment, depicts the trial of Jesus before Pilate. We should not be surprised that the violent story of his execution travelled quickly among peasant communities.

THE PASSION

The narrative versions of the story disagree on details of the execu-tion. *Mark* and *John* do not agree about the day Jesus was put to death, placing it either on (in *Mark*) or before (*John*) Passover. There is no trial before the Jewish Sanhedrin in *John. Mark*'s Jesus dies in agony, mocked by soldiers, whereas *John*'s Jesus dies in full control, fulfilling scriptures from Psalms and Job with his last breath: "Since Jesus knew that the course of events had come to an end, so the scripture would come true, he said, 'I'm thirsty.'" These contradictions in later accounts do not suggest that the events behind the stories are fictional. Narratives of the arrest, mockery, and execution of Jesus existed early in the first century, providing a folklore source for the later gospel accounts. Pieces of the story cir-culated independently, evolving with each storyteller.

Shifting details are exactly what we would expect in stories told orally in the villages of Judea and Galilee. The tiny Fayyum fragment discovered in Egypt, possibly copied from a mid-first-century original, portrays the disciple Peter assuring Jesus that he will not deny him. Jesus answers, "Before the cock crows twice, you will deny me three times." The *Mark* version agrees that the cock crows twice. *Matthew, Luke,* and *John* tell a version in which the cock crows only once. Whether a cock crowed once or twice, Jesus appears to have warned Peter in the dead of night that he would deny knowing his teacher before morning.

Crucifixion, a torture considered beneath the dignity of the upper classes, inflicted an excruciating death on its lower-class victims. Soldiers crucified poor miscreants regularly as a deterrent to public uprisings. Perhaps Jesus persuaded Peter to live to fight another day, or perhaps the cock-crowing stories came from folktales. No Roman record mentions the execution, but since Jesus appears to have rallied masses and provoked authorities, he became a target for public reprisal, and his execution appears in the Christian gospel record as a not unusual event.

In the 1990s, Marion L. Soards, New Testament professor at the Louisville Seminary in the United States, collated the work of thirty-four historians to determine the most probable sequence of events leading to the execution of Jesus. Father Raymond E. Brown, a member of the Pontifical Biblical Commission, used Soards's research in his book *The Death of the Messiah from Gethsemane to the Grave*, a massive review of virtually every academic theory ever proposed regarding Jesus' death.

Brown and Soards conclude that the Gospel Passion narratives echo stories that circulated orally prior to the *Mark* Gospel. *Matthew* and *Luke* borrowed the *Mark* story and embellished it with folkloric tradition. The narrative in *John* appears independent of the synoptic Gospels, but familiar with folk traditions. The events believed to be authentic by more than 70 percent of the scholars examined by Soards all appear in *Mark* chapters 14 and 15. These are the facts they agree on:

Sometime during the reign of Roman Emperor Tiberius, about 30 C.E., Roman soldiers arrested a person named, in Greek, Iēsous, in Aramaic, Yeshua, or in modern English, Jesus.

Someone who called him "Rabbi" betrayed Jesus to the Romans. The betrayer may have been Judas, although this name likely reflects a later fiction designed to indict the Jews.

The soldiers led Jesus before the chief priests and elders in the Jewish community, who had apparently collaborated in the arrest.

During the march to the execution site, Roman soldiers forced a bystander, Simon from Cyrene, in North Africa, to carry the cross. The *Mark* account specifically mentions that this Cyrenian is the father of Alexander and Rufus, so the author may have conferred with these sons as a source for his story. (Imagine a scene forty years after the famous execution: "Yes, my father was there. The soldiers made him carry the cross.")

The Roman soldiers brought Jesus to a place known as Golgotha, or "Skull Place," and crucified him.

The soldiers cast lots for the rights to his garments.

These events comprise the core story. If one believes the crucifixion of Jesus occurred as a historical event, these represent the elements of the story most likely to be true. Everything else is much more speculative. If we expand our criteria to include details that half of the thirty-four scholars believe to be accurate, then we can add:

Someone at the arrest drew a sword to defend Jesus.

Jesus appeared before Pilate but answered nothing.

Pilate released the bandit Barabbas to the crowd.

Soldiers mocked Jesus as King of the Jews.

They dressed him with a purple robe, crown of thorns, and
a reed.

Bystanders mocked Jesus as a failed destroyer of the Temple.

Others mocked Jesus on the cross, saying, "save yourself."

He was crucified with two bandits.

Someone gave him wine with myrrh, a sedative.

Someone gave him vinegar, which would ease his thirst.

He cried out to a god, "Eloi, Eloi."

He called to the prophet, "Lo, Elijah."

Jesus was a messiah.

A young man followed Jesus, lost his linen cloth, and fled naked.

The elements in this second group are more uncertain. We might recognize the mocking stories as a version of the Anath and Tammuz atonement rituals. The scenes depicting Jesus calling out to God, and soldiers gambling for his clothes, come almost verbatim from the Jewish Psalms. The final detail, regarding a young man with a linen cloth, remains a mysterious element of the Jesus story. This person may correspond to the young man Mary met in the tomb, a young man Jesus raised from the dead in Bethany, the disciple "loved by Jesus," or a young man mentioned in a "more spiritual" version of *Mark* from a second-century letter, or he may be a later invention. If this young man existed, he reportedly received special teachings from Jesus, as did Mary Magdalene, but his identity remains obscure. Did a favoured disciple run away naked?

In 1886, French archaeologist Urbain Bouriant discovered what might be the earliest Passion account, in the *Gospel of Peter*, from a monk's grave at Akhmim, Egypt. Scholars knew of this gospel because at the end of the second century, Serapion, a Bishop of Antioch, denounced it for giving the impression that the resurrected Jesus was not a physical body but rather a "vision," as described in the *Mary* Gospel.

Whereas some historians believe *Mark* represents the earliest version of the Passion story, Arthur J. Dewey from Xavier University writes in *The Complete Gospels*, "the original stage of Peter may well be the earliest passion story in the gospel tradition." The first-century gospel parallels the original *Mark* version, ending with Mary Magdalene seeing a handsome youth in the tomb and fleeing in fear without telling anyone. According to Dewey, "almost every sentence of the passion narrative of Peter appears to be composed out of references and allusions to the psalms and prophets." He suggests that the original story "was shaped by the Jewish tradition of the suffering righteous one." This story describes a virtuous Jewish leader provoking authorities, who accuse him of blasphemy, condemn him, and ritually mock him in death. In the end, the righteous one is vindicated and exalted in heaven. This, Dewey believes, is the model for the Jesus Passion story.

We witness here an apparently authentic event embellished over time in typical folkloric fashion. Many details presumed true today do not appear in historical records. None of the Gospels, for example, mentions nails being used in the Crucifixion, a conjecture, possibly true, added centuries later. Raymond Brown describes four stages in the evolution of this Passion story. In the first stage, accounts depict Jesus upsetting convention and criticizing Temple priests, leading to his arrest by Roman soldiers, abuse, and execution. At this stage, Jesus appears as a wise teacher with many followers, targeted for execution by the authorities, similar to John the Baptist or Yeshua Ananias.

In the second stage, after the destruction of Jerusalem in 70 C.E., writers began to link Jesus to Old Testament prophecies such as the suffering servant of Isaiah. Brown believes these gospel writers "dramatized" the events and "simplified" the motives of Jesus' enemies, representing neither wholesale invention nor literal history, but rather typical mythic storytelling.

According to Brown, these later authors grew "soft on the Romans" and blamed the Judeans for Jesus' death, a twist that began with expatriate Jews such as Paul. Later, ex-pagan Christians blamed all Jews for the death of Jesus, reflecting widespread anti-Jewish sentiment in Europe. Allen D. Callahan, New Testament professor at Harvard Divinity School, believes Jewish collaboration is overstated. "He was causing trouble. He constituted a security risk and he was dealt with the way the Romans always deal with security risks in the provinces," Callahan believes. "It was a Roman job, there's no mistake about that."

Countless innocent victims suffered a similar fate, yet in the dusty streets of Sepphoris, Gadara, Capernaum, Antioch, and Alexandria, this particular story endured, attracted followers, and grew archetypal. The earliest narrative accounts of this peasant wise man from Galilee attest to his brutal murder, the sort of dramatic event people would remember. However, the Jesus story attracted embellishment because people admired the Galilean's personal example and his ethical teachings.

COMMON WISDOM

Among the treasures discovered by Grenfell and Hunt at Oxyrhynchus is a small, mutilated papyrus fragment from the third century, with twenty-four readable lines. It depicts Pharisees confronting Jesus. The fragment, known as Oxy 1224, represents a literary style midway between the simple sayings found in *Thomas* and the dialogues in *Mary*. Scholars date a presumed original from the mid-first century. According to this manuscript, the Pharisees "were angry that he reclined in the midst of sinners.

But when Jesus heard, he said, 'Those who are healthy have no need of a physician.'" This common Cynic proverb appears in *Mark*, *Matthew*, and *Luke*.

The reverse side of this fragment offers another quote, presumably from Jesus: "...and pray for your enemies." This, too, reflects a common theme. It appears in the Akkadian Council of Wisdom 2,000 years earlier: "Do not return evil to your enemy"; in a first-century pagan prayer, "May I wish for all men's happiness"; in the Buddhist Dhammapada: "Only love dispels hate"; and in the Taoist proverb: "Return love for hatred." The Jesus version appears in the three synoptic Gospels.

In the Oxy 1224 fragment, as in *Mary*, Jesus approaches an unnamed disciple "in a vision," asking, "Why are you discouraged?" The disciple asks, "What then did you renounce? What is the new doctrine that they say you teach, or what is the new baptism that you proclaim?" We do not get to hear the answer in this fragment, as the reply breaks off. Nevertheless, this is the right question: What did Jesus say that was new? We will have to seek elsewhere for the answer.

To begin, we must identify the cases in which authors have placed common sayings on the lips of Jesus. If Jesus did repeat these popular proverbs and prophecies, he borrowed them from his environment. We have already noted that the golden rule attributed to Jesus was used by Torah sage Hillel during Jesus' youth, and by Buddhists, Zoroastrians, Hindus, Greek philosophers, and Confucius, in 500 B.C.E.

Giving a barren fig tree a chance to bear fruit, attributed to Jesus by *Luke*, echoes a common folk metaphor about giving a young student or seeker a chance to thrive. Likewise, sowing seeds that fall on rocks or good soil — attributed to Jesus by *Thomas*, *Mark*, *Matthew*, and *Luke* — represents a common harvest metaphor used to explain why some succeed where others fail.

Typical of common lore ascribed to Jesus are the sayings about the old and new: a new patch sewn to old cloth, new and old wine, and so forth, appear in *Thomas*, *Mark*, *Matthew*, and *Luke*. All four versions of the "old and new" sayings were common proverbs. The *Luke* author confirms this by having Jesus add, "as they say."

Other sayings attributed to Jesus arrive not from the past, but from the future. We know that Jesus was a Jew, not a Christian, so when gospel authors place later Christian doctrine on his lips, scholars doubt its authenticity. Paul begins the written Christian tradition, linking the Christos to Jewish prophecies in his Letter to the Corinthians, claiming the messiah died and "rose up on the third day according to the scriptures." The *Mark* author shows that he is familiar with this tradition when he quotes Jesus explaining that he is "destined" to suffer, die, and rise up after three days. Both these passages appear as retrofits, Paul inserting his messiah story into Jewish literature, and *Mark* attributing Jewish scripture to Jesus. Robert W. Funk, the late Guggenheim and Fulbright scholar of New Testament Greek language, explained, "Sayings and parables expressed in 'Christian' language are the creation of the evangelists or their Christian predecessors."

Some quotes ascribed to Jesus reflect knowledge of later events. In *Mark*, Jesus describes the effects of war and beatings in synagogues that suggest knowledge of what Josephus later wrote and of the destruction of Jerusalem. These quotes appear to be creations by the author, looking back to Jesus through the war of 66–70 C.E. Occasionally, scholars notice that Jesus quotes Jewish scripture, but with Greek words and phrases from the Septuagint, the Greek version of the Bible. Such quotes are almost certainly the creations of later Greek writers. Similarly, when Jesus is quoted speaking without a human witness, such as in his dialogues with the Devil in the wilderness or his private prayers, scholars believe the authors created these passages. Long, thousand-word homilies in the *John*

Gospel are considered the work of the authors, since no earlier record corroborates such passages, composed sixty years after the events. The beautiful and uplifting quotations in *John* reflect the creative voice of the author.

Jesus repeated, revised, and renewed proverbs from his first-century environment. He advised disciples, "Know yourself," which is inscribed on the Apollo Temple's lintel at Delphi and attributed to Thales, Pythagoras, Socrates, and the mythical Greek poetess Phemonoe. Jesus appears to borrow sayings from Cynic sages, Stoic philosophers, and Asian traditions. Funk suggests that he "perhaps acquired his knowledge of common lore from itinerant philosophers who visited Galilee while he was growing up." Jesus appears as a self-educated peasant, interested in the wisdom of his world, clever enough to harness it for the benefit of his contemporaries, and perceptive enough to enhance it with his own insights.

THE ESSENCE

This search for an authentic Jesus message has followed the commonsensical rules of evidence used by historians, as well as by journalists and police detectives. First, we scrutinized the records for corroboration by the earliest independent sources. Secondly, we considered general historical convergence: Which sayings reflect social conditions of first-century Galilee and Judea? We have used other historical clues such as traces of Aramaic, and the criterion of embarrassment, which identifies ideas offensive to subsequent writers, and so not likely to have been invented. We identified passages that Jesus borrowed from ancient lore and later doctrines that gospel writers retroactively placed on his lips. Finally, we looked for the consistent, original voice of Jesus. Bear in mind that the earliest known manuscript of a sayings collection, the Logia Iēsou, included six sayings from *Thomas* that matched Q verses from *Matthew* and *Luke*:

Seek and you will find.
Seek the light within you.
Share your light with the world.
Before you judge others, notice the impediment in your own eye.
Don't worry about your clothes and comforts.
Beware religious authorities, who take the keys to knowledge
    but don't enter and don't let you enter. Be sly as a snake,
    gentle as a dove.

We can start here to define a core message. We also looked at the confluence of the Q verses with both the *Thomas* and *Mark* gospels. We found nine shared sayings and three additional shared themes:

The kingdom is like a mustard seed, small, but it grows
    naturally into something useful.
The kingdom is not in the sky, but here and now, found
    in self-knowledge.
What is hidden will be revealed.
Place your light on a lamppost; don't keep it hidden. Speak
    out. Help others.
What you put into your mouth does not defile or purify you,
    but what comes out does. Bring forth good fruits.
Make the two into one and move mountains.
The first will be last.
Those who have will get more. Those with nothing are
    deprived.
To enter a strong man's house, you must bind him first,
    and then enter.

The three common *Thomas–Q–Mark* themes are:

Ask and you will receive; seek and you will find.

Your sins are forgiven as you forgive others.

A disciple's mission: remain simple and humble, go to towns, share food, heal, give what you have, and tell people, "This is the kingdom."

We have seen that Jesus also repeated common wisdom sayings such as:

The golden rule: Treat others as you wish to be treated.

Love your enemies.

It is the sick who need a doctor, not the healthy.

Salt your knowledge with wisdom.

Whoever has two good ears should listen.

Jesus did and said much more, but these ideas form the core of his teachings. John Dominic Crossan developed a meticulous method of cataloguing Jesus themes or "complexes," not necessarily verbatim language, from the multiple texts. Crossan identified 522 shared subjects, such as the mustard seed, kingdom and children, mission and message, and so forth. Crossan ranked them based on chronology and the number of independent sources, and published his results in *The Historical Jesus*. Some themes are events, not proverbs or parables, and others reflect earlier or later ideas not attributable to Jesus. However, in addition to the ideas above, Crossan also ascribes to Jesus aphorisms and ideas such as

The kingdom is like leaven in bread.

Blessed are the poor, the sad, the persecuted.

Split wood, lift a stone, and I am there.

Prophets get no respect in their own homeland.

Hear or reject the messenger and the "one who sent me."

Foxes have holes; the son of Adam has nowhere to rest.

Let the dead bury the dead: Commit now.

The first shall be last.

Who tries to save one's life will lose it.

If slapped on the cheek, offer the other cheek.

The sower: seeds cast onto good and bad soil.

The Good Samaritan: Compassion makes one a neighbour, not authority or religion.

The coin: Give the emperor what belongs to the emperor; give to God what belongs to God.

Most of these themes, aphorisms, and parables likely appear within the first thirty years after the execution of Jesus, and can be traced to three or more independent sources, but not all. The Good Samaritan story, for example, appears only in *Luke*, some fifty years after the execution. Opinions vary among scholars about attributing such sayings to Jesus, although they fit seamlessly into his message.

To resolve these issues, Robert Funk invited thirty scholars to the Pacific School of Religion in Berkeley, California, in 1985, to address the Reimarus question: Which sayings did Jesus most likely originate? Funk died in 2005, but the Westar Institute continues to meet twice a year. The group, popularly known as the Jesus Seminar, includes more than 200 scholars from Europe, North America, Australia, New Zealand, and South Africa. They have published the results of their work in hundreds of academic papers and several popular books, including *The Five Gospels*, *The Complete Gospels*, and *John the Baptist and Jesus*.

These scholars do not pretend to be infallible, but they do provide rigorously informed opinions based on strict, published rules of evidence. The Westar Institute method traces parallel word sequences rather than themes, and focuses on the early and widely attested sayings. These scholars do not always agree, but their varied, independent opinions and methodologies provide some balance to help us arrive at the most likely history.

Among the highest-ranked items on the lists compiled by Westar's Jesus Seminar, we find the familiar sayings and themes outlined above. *Matthew* and *Luke* both place several of these sayings in the Sermon on the Mount. The authors of *Luke* and *Matthew* use the Q verses as a source for this sermon, although they select somewhat different items and add their own perspective. *Matthew*, for example, denounces sexual desire and pagans, and *Luke* censures the rich. Nevertheless, scholars place the essence of this sermon at the heart of Jesus' teachings. Both accounts of this sermon include the golden rule. Thus, we find the essential Jesus teachings wrapped neatly around this core ethical principle of ancient Judaism and worldly wisdom. Among the top ten items on the Jesus Seminar list of likely Jesus sayings, seven are found in the Sermon on the Mount:

Blessed are the poor.
Blessed are the hungry.
Give to anyone who asks.
If someone asks for your coat, give your shirt also.
If someone asks you to walk a mile, walk the second mile also.
If slapped on the cheek, offer the other cheek.
Love your enemies.

These seven lines alone comprise a radical social agenda. We've heard them so often, we may take them for granted, but imagine living by these precepts. Jesus encourages the poor and oppressed to give what they have and show compassion to their tormentors. *Thomas* quotes Jesus saying, "Good persons produce goodness from what they have stored up. Wicked people produce evil from the wickedness they've stored in their hearts." For Jesus, righteousness and sin are the fruits of personal action, not the result of rituals or convention. As self-reflection and humility form the core of Jesus' personal advice, non-aggression and generosity form the first planks of his social platform. *Thomas* adds: "If you have money, don't lend it at interest. Rather, give to someone from whom you won't get it back." This counsel to give without expectation of return is borrowed from Jewish tradition, but with a typical Jesus-style twist. The prophet Ezekiel says that a righteous man "does not... require a pledge for a loan." In the Book of Tobit, which contains moral folktales from diaspora Judaism, the dying father Tobit delivers a stirring lecture to his son: "Give some of your food to the hungry and some of your clothing to the naked. Give all your surplus as alms." Such advice is reminiscent of *derech eretz*, making the world right with common decency. Jesus adopts this tradition but adds to it. Whereas the dying Tobit tells his son, "Give none to sinners," Jesus pointedly seeks out sinners and excludes no one. Jesus expands the tradition with *unconditional* generosity.

The early Q sayings include this unequivocal duty: "Give to everyone who begs from you." Similar lessons in generosity appear in legends of Socrates, the Buddha, and Lao Tzu. Cynics relinquished possessions and mocked the pretensions of the wealthy, but they did not incite active social reform. Jesus did. This, then, begins to answer our lingering question: What did Jesus say that was new? Jesus turned spiritual philosophy into social action.

In the famous story of the Good Samaritan, a lawyer asks Jesus, "So, who is my neighbour?", at which point Jesus tells the story of a travelling Judean robbed, beaten, and left for dead beside the road. A Jewish priest and a Levite — representing established religion — pass by but ignore the victim. A Samaritan, typically considered a foreign enemy of Judeans, takes pity, cleans the man's wounds, and puts him up at an inn. Who is a neighbour? Jesus' subversive answer typically reversed conventional thinking. The neighbour is not

necessarily someone of the same culture, nationality, or religion —
and not someone with spiritual pretensions — but rather the person
who demonstrates compassion with action. This answer would
have sounded radical in first-century Judea, and remains a lesson
the world still appears to need 2,000 years later.

WHAT DID YOU SEE?

Jesus' unconditional generosity leads to the earliest actions by his
disciples, namely the communal sharing of food. Such giving
reflected a common peasant practice of sharing "Asherah's bounty"
at communal tables.

Only four stories appear in all four canonical Gospels — *Mark*,
Matthew, *Luke*, and *John* — the core events of the Jesus tradition:
the baptism by John, the anointing by a woman disciple, the Crucifixion, and the sharing of food with a hungry multitude. The
feeding story first appears in the *Gospel of Mark*, in two versions.
People follow Jesus into the countryside to witness his teaching and
to be healed. The followers number 5,000 men plus women and
children in the first version, and 4,000-plus in the second version.
The story outline remains similar in both cases.

It is late, the crowd is hungry, and Jesus feels compassion for
them. A disciple suggests sending the crowd away to find food, but
Jesus asks what they have available. The disciples come up with
some bread and fish, but not nearly enough to feed such a crowd.
Jesus asks the multitude to sit on the ground, gives a blessing over
the loaves and fishes, and distributes food to the crowd. Everyone
eats, they are satisfied, and there is food left over: twelve baskets in
the first story, seven in the second.

It is possible that a similar tale in the Book of Kings influenced
this New Testament story. Tales of Elijah and his attendant Elisha
represent a northern Galilean tradition that individuals can access
their god's power directly, independent of temple priests:

A man came from Baalshalishah, bringing the man of God
bread of the first fruits, twenty loaves of barley, and fresh
ears of grain in his sack. And Elisha said, "Give to the men,
that they may eat." But his servant said, "How am I to set
this before a hundred men?" So he repeated, "Give it to the
men, that they may eat, for thus says the Lord, 'They shall
eat and have some left.'"

It is possible that actual feeding of crowds by Jesus attracted
these scriptural allusions during oral transmission. In a separate
story that follows the second *Mark* version, the disciples complain
of having only one loaf of bread, and Jesus chastises them: "Why
are you talking about having no bread? Do you still not understand? Are your hearts hardened? Do you have eyes and fail to see?
Do you have ears and fail to hear?" See what? Hear what? Jesus
does not answer the riddle; he poses it. He prompts his disciples to
see what appears before their eyes and to hear what he has said.
What has he said? Be generous. Give whatever you have to others.
Give to everyone who begs from you. Don't worry about what you
will wear or what you will eat.

Jesus does not say or imply that through him a deity has turned
a few loaves and fishes into thousands of loaves and fishes, although
this represents a common interpretation of this story. Neither the
author of *Mark* nor those who copied his account in *Matthew* and
Luke claim that a few loaves became thousands. In *John*, Jesus does
not make this claim, although the author calls this event a "sign,"
meaning a divine miracle, and quotes "the people" who witnessed
it as saying, "This is indeed the prophet who is to come into the
world." Although the *John* author does not explicitly say so, he
implies that the answer to Jesus' riddle is that the disciples missed
seeing this sign, this miracle.

John's account accurately reflects that some people believed Jesus was the new Jewish messiah. These peasants would know receiving holy temple bread from a priest implied that David was the rightful king. *Mark*'s story compares the people to "sheep without a shepherd," invoking the shepherd king David, or his descendants. However, whether or not the *John* author is correct about the quotation or the sign, we still have not heard what happened. We have not answered Jesus' question. Our evidence tells us that Jesus spoke simply, literally, and immediately. What did you see? What did you hear?

MIRACLE OF GENEROSITY

The author of the *Mark* story emphasizes the numbers — five loaves, two fish, twelve or seven baskets of leftovers — and some interpretations seek meaning in these numbers. One explanation suggests the five loaves represent the five books of the Torah nourishing the Jewish people, but first-century Jews considered the Torah one book, not five, so this interpretation would have appeared later. It is possible that the twelve or seven baskets of leftovers refer to the twelve tribes of Israel and the seventh day of creation. Or perhaps they refer to the twelve disciples and the seven Christian dioceses that were "left over after Judaism," according to later Roman Church tradition. Such interpretations remain dependent on the beliefs of their presumed authors. However, "two fish" is an obvious symbol to peasant Galileans in the first century. Even if the two fish are taken literally, first-century listeners might read the story as divine confirmation of the new age, brought about by Venus and the equinox sun moving into association with Pisces, the fish. As we have seen, first-century peasants considered that the equinox stars were bound up with their survival. Their movements coincided with spring rites, atonement rituals, and Asherah's bounty set out on communal tables.

Between the two food stories in *Mark*, we find Jesus showing disdain for Pharisees who demand from him a sign to prove his powers. "Why does this generation insist on a sign? I swear, this generation will receive no sign." Thus, the only evidence regarding Jesus and a divine miracle in this story contradicts *John* and appears to explicitly reject the idea. Jesus says he is not here to perform miracles and prove himself to anyone. He's here to witness the truth, and he has asked his disciples to do the same.

Could this story recount a mundane miracle? Did the disciples miss seeing the obvious? Jesus has already asked them to see what is before their eyes. He has warned them: The divine kingdom is spread out over the world and you don't see it. The crowds were the poor, hungry, sick, and *anawim* "outcasts." Jesus blessed them for their low standing and told them poverty brought them closer to the truth of the divine kingdom on earth. Nevertheless, he told them to stop worrying about their comforts and to give what they had to their neighbours. Perhaps Jesus was asking his disciples to witness the power of this unconditional generosity.

The concept of loving one's neighbour poses a translation problem to scholars. The Greek *agape*, generally translated in English as "love," is more accurately translated as "sharing." Crossan and Reed explain that *agape*, sharing, is the New Testament equivalent of Old Testament "justice," meaning to share equitably what belongs to YHVH. To love one's neighbour is to share what you have with them. This sharing is the *derech eretz* of the people of the land, common peasant decency, the kindness of strangers, the Samaritan's deeds, or the instinct of an innocent boy to share what he has with the homeless. The *John* version adds an interesting detail that a generous youth provides the food to distribute, evoking the child in the kingdom, the natural generosity of innocence.

No matter how poor, dispossessed, and forgotten we are, Jesus appears to demonstrate that if we share what we have, there will be enough for everyone. Is this what the disciples failed to notice? The text does not say. We have to figure this out ourselves. Regardless of what symbols the storytellers attached to this incident, the story appears to be about sharing. The multitudes sit on the "green grass," so this is summer, when even the poor would have wild food to collect. Is it possible that 5,000 or 10,000 people, even poor people, wandered into the countryside without taking a single thing to eat? Did not some clever mother put bread or fruit in her bag? Did any of these 5,000 men think to bring water and a dried fish? Did Jesus set the example by giving away the modest loaves and fishes that he and his disciples had? Perhaps he did, and perhaps this gesture inspired others to share what they brought. The unadorned power of generosity may represent the most straightforward interpretation of this story. The miracle of sharing creates the kingdom here and now.

The earliest frescoes and stone relief images of Jesus reveal him at communal meals with bread and fish. The sharing of food appears as the first social act of his followers. Caring about another person's hunger is the kingdom spread out on the earth. Giving, however small the gift, multiplies the common bounty because it inspires others to generosity. The nod from the homeless man who wouldn't take advantage of a generous boy is the prolific power of compassion at work, the divine kingdom in front of our eyes. Sharing is the social justice platform of Jesus. Sharing is the miracle. It may well be the miracle that the disciples missed seeing. It may be the miracle we still miss seeing.

Keep in mind, the poor were outcasts. No one in authority cared about them. That someone as righteous and charismatic as Jesus cared might appear to them like a miracle. Of course, some of these dispossessed peasants flocked to see Jesus not for sermons or free food, but for another purpose. They came to be healed.

HEAL THE SICK

Ritual and magic constituted health treatment during the first century, and Jesus earned a reputation as a healer. According to New Testament scholar Stevan Davies, such healers were so ubiquitous that to say Jesus was a healer is "no more exciting than to say he was a carpenter." The point is taken — healers were common — but Jesus as a healer proves far more significant than his woodworking skills.

We find fewer witnesses to the healing stories of Jesus than to his sayings. Whereas five or six sources corroborate certain sayings, the miraculous healings generally appear in only one or sometimes two independent sources. The healing testimonies also reflect both scriptural symbology and later Church doctrine. Still, these accounts may reflect actual events. Jesus' instructions to disciples in *Thomas*, Q, and *Mark* confirm that sharing food and healing people formed the heart of his social mission. Whether we interpret these actions as simple generosity or divine miracle may depend on our beliefs, awareness of history, and concept of cosmology. Similarly, to understand how Jesus and his first-century contemporaries interpreted healing and feeding people, we need to understand their beliefs, awareness of history, and cosmology.

The record suggests that Jesus attracted people from across class divisions: outcasts, labourers, tax collectors, officials, Pharisees, and scholars. His disciples rise from the ranks of labourers and villagers, and the multitudes appear as poor *ebionim* who endured horrendous medical conditions, suffered from debilitating diseases, and came to Jesus for healing. These peasants likely credited disease to impurity, personal sins, or bad relations with their deities. An official or middle-class citizen in Jerusalem could pay for sacrifices at the Temple or hire a professional prophet to appeal to YHVH. The poor, however, were on their own. The poor's only medical help came from folk knowledge of botanical remedies, prayers, and rituals.

Wandering holy men performing healing rituals represented Galilean and rural traditions as opposed to Jerusalem temple traditions, although both represented the legacy of prophet-healers Elijah and Elisha. After Elisha, Hebrew scriptures cease recording prophecy, largely because Jerusalem Temple priests assumed this role. Nevertheless, independent healers thrived in Israel and Judea.

Josephus records the life of a Galilean prophet, Onias, or Honi in rabbinical literature, known for successfully appealing to YHVH a century before Jesus. In Honi's time, warring Jewish factions led by brothers John Hyrcanus II and Aristobulus II battled for control of the Jewish state. Supporters of Hyrcanus hauled Honi into their camp and insisted he intercede with the divine power against Aristobulus. Honi refused to take sides and asked his god for peace instead. Irate Judeans stoned him to death.

Similarly, in Jesus' time, a prophet who earned a reputation for healing people without fees, and who drew crowds of thousands, could expect censure from Temple priests and suppression from Roman authorities. According *Mark*, Pharisees resented the popularity of Jesus, and Tetrarch Herod Antipas worried that the upstart Galilean might be his nemesis, John the Baptist, reborn.

Certain gospel healing stories reveal their origin in the Septuagint, the Greek translation of Jewish scriptures, suggesting they emerged in later, Greek-speaking Christian communities. For example, the Bible story of Jesus healing a youth of Nain contains telltale signs of Greek translations from the Jewish Book of Kings. The Nain healing appears in *Luke*, apparently copied from a tale about Elijah. Both stories concern raising the dead son of a "widow" (*chera*) by a healer, who speaks to the boy and touches him. *Luke* employs the common Septuagint opening "And it came to pass" (*kai egeneto*) and ending "he gave him to his mother." In both stories, the son rises to speak and bystanders declare that the healer is a prophet. Finally, both stories take place at the "city gate" (*ton pylona tes poleos*). This last detail gives away the *Luke* author, because no wall or gate appears in the archaeological record of Nain, a small village in Galilee. Not only is the story lifted from Jewish scriptures, it is lifted specifically from the Greek translation by an author unfamiliar with Galilee.

Appealing to God was a common Jewish approach to healing, but battling devils is a feature of later Zoroastrian and Greek Christian interpretations. The Devil as a being only enters Jewish tradition after the influence of Cyrus and the Persians. The Old Testament Hebrew word *satan* is a common generic noun meaning "adversary," depicted as heaven's official accuser of sinful humans. This satan is mistranslated in later Greek versions as *ha diabolos,* "the Devil," meaning a specific evil being. The Devil opposing God reflects Zoroastrian and Greek dualism — evil earth versus perfect heaven — not ancient Hebrew scripture or peasant Jewish tradition. Later Christian Church patriarchs associate this Satan with the Serpent in Eden, and a post-biblical tradition associates Lucifer, the "light-bearer," with the Devil. This light-bearer is Venus rising in the east, Asherah, the Queen of Heaven, transformed into a male, and then into an evil demon. We cannot retrofit these ideas onto Jesus and his contemporaries, who did not necessarily believe that demons caused illness. Nowhere in the authentic sayings of Jesus does he speak to demons.

The *Luke* author claims Jesus drove seven demons from Mary Magdalene, and *Mark* reports that Jesus drove a demon from a howling madman in the hills of Decapolis, east of Galilee. *Mark* also depicts Jesus healing a man's withered hand in Capernaum on the Sabbath, in violation of Temple convention, further enraging Pharisees and Herodians, who "conspired to destroy him."

Soon thereafter, scholars from Jerusalem accuse Jesus of being in league with the Devil, to discredit his healings. "He has Beelzebul, and by the ruler of the demons he casts out demons."

Beelzebul is the Canaanite fertility deity Baal, recast by post-exile Jewish priests as the "prince of demons." In the Book of Kings, Elijah allegedly defeats the prophets of Baal in a showdown of magical powers on Mount Carmel. Elijah mocks the Baal priests as they fail to call fire down from heaven to ignite a bull offering, then he constructs a proper Jewish altar and has no difficulty calling down fire from YHVH, supposedly proving once and for all that the god of Moses is the one and only true god. Jewish convention thereafter turned Baal into the head demon. This culture clash resurfaces when Jerusalem scribes accuse Jesus of being in league with Baal.

Note, however, that Jesus does not rely on any obvious magic ritual, but rather heals on the authority of his own word. *Mark* reports that Jesus performed his first exorcism in Capernaum as "one who has authority, unlike the scribes." We hear the astonishment in the voices of bystanders asking one another, "What is this? A new kind of teaching with authority!" Even Jesus' family tries to restrain him because others have claimed, "He's out of his mind." In *Mark*'s Sermon on the Mount, Jesus introduces his core teachings with the Hebrew phrase *amen lego hymin*, meaning "*Truly*, I say to you." The word *amen* here, "truly," expresses his personal power.

This air of direct authority distinguishes Jesus from conventional priests, who mediated with God for a fee. Jesus appears more closely related to Jewish healer Amos, and to the Essene "teacher of righteousness" who did not charge fees or claim status as a prophet. In the healings found in *Mark*, *Matthew*, and *Luke*, Jesus does not speak for Elohim, or "the Father," but rather acts directly.

These disputes over healing powers reflect first-century social conflict and rebellion. Behind the metaphors, we'll find common human experiences: the rich with patronage connections and Temple priests with a religious monopoly lording over the outcasts, who have nothing and are desperate for food, healing, and some good news. These first-century peasants in Galilee came to believe that Jesus could heal their afflictions, and in some cases he probably did.

HOPE HEALS

We may view Galilean, Canaanite, and Phoenician peasants as uneducated by our standards, but in some respects their knowledge surpassed ours. The people of the land knew which constellation would rise with the sun and how many days until the next new moon. They tracked natural cycles and knew more than most moderns about natural cures. They knew that anise might ease a sore throat or a woman's cramps, that marjoram might relieve a headache or insomnia, and they knew where to find these healing plants. They also knew that faith healed.

Once, during a long walk on a deserted beach, philosopher, anthropologist, and ecologist David Abram told me stories about his travels through Sri Lanka, Indonesia, and the Philippines to learn how indigenous shamans use magic in healing. He later elaborated these observations in his book *The Spell of the Sensuous*. An accomplished magician, Abram observed that certain healers, such as the so-called "psychic healers" in the Philippines, used sleight-of-hand techniques to trick their patients, pretending, for example, to extract some bloody object from a person's body and fling it into a fire. We may call this primitive hocus-pocus, but Abram made two important observations: First, the healings often worked, and secondly, the magicians facilitated these healings by "altering perception."

Western medicine expresses the link between perception and health in scientific terms such as psychoneuro-immunology, psychoneuroendocrinology, psychosomatic illness, hypochondria, and the common placebo effect. Modern medicine is aware that mental perceptions ("psycho") trigger responses in the nervous system ("neuro"), which trigger responses in the immune system and release hormone messages to the body through the endocrine glands. What this adds up to is that a thought in the mind can influence a physical response in the body.

Modern medical science also acknowledges the sociological component of illness, symptoms, and healing. Purely physical disease caused by a virus or bacteria might be cured by purely physical treatment. However, the body's response to any treatment varies with the social and mental condition of the patient. The technical term for such connections is "biopsychosocial" treatment. Physicians sometimes use the term "illness" to emphasize the psychosocial aspects of symptoms and "disease" to emphasize the physical. Nevertheless, bodily systems, physical agents, mental states, and social conditions all contribute to a person's health, illness, and recovery. For example, in a trial led by spinal surgeon Dr. Jerome Schofferman, patients who suffered childhood sexual trauma had one-sixth the success in recovering from lumbar surgery than patients without that past trauma. Social conditions influence mental conditions, which in turn influence the body's reaction to disease and medical treatment.

The placebo effect describes the observed reaction of human patients to the belief that they have received a treatment. There remains a great deal of controversy about the mechanisms underlying such reactions, but the effect is well-known. Medical experiments for any new medicine must use a placebo group to show that the observed efficacy of the treatment is not a psychosomatic reaction to the patient's belief that he or she will improve. Thousands of studies confirm the effect. For example, trials in Ipswich, England, using salicylic acid to dissolve warts showed a 48 percent improvement in the placebo group, who only thought they had received treatment. The body can produce natural opiates, so placebos prove astonishingly effective in pain relief. A 30 to 40 percent improvement rate is common in placebo pain tests. A trial that showed penicillin V as 88 percent effective in relieving pain simultaneously found a 75 percent improvement with a placebo. A study published in the *American Journal of Psychiatry* showed that "about 80% of the therapeutic effect of anti-depressant medication is a placebo response."

We know now that social stress contributes to mental stress, which influences immune functions. Common stress-reduction techniques — yoga, meditation, hypnosis, or even watching humorous films — can improve a patient's speed and degree of recovery. Similarly, improving a patient's living conditions, or simply giving patients hope of a better life, can improve recovery rates.

We can only guess if Jesus, like most of his contemporaries, believed that certain diseases were caused by demon possession. He probably did. In the twenty-first century, we may trace epilepsy, a withered hand, or psychotic behaviour to causes other than demons, but if Jesus spoke to alleged demons as *Mark* records, we might assume he believed in their presence. Regardless of what Jesus, his patients, or we believe about his healings, they worked. We know from modern sociopsychoneurological science that if his patients believed he could heal them, some would be healed. If Jesus drew crowds of thousands, if they believed in his powers, and if he told them their ailments would improve, we know that hundreds, perhaps even thousands, might actually improve based on their belief alone. Faith heals, and for the person healed, it is 100 percent effective.

Mark describes a long list of miraculous healings in Galilee, Decapolis, Phoenicia, Samaria, and Judea. Few of these stories are corroborated. *Matthew* and *Luke* copy some healing stories from *Mark* that are not counted as independent sources. *John* borrows certain details from either *Mark* or a common source, but sets them in entirely different circumstances. Distinguishing history from the mythology among these accounts remains difficult, but bear in mind that the gospel writers and believers did not intend to separate history from mythology. The important point is that Jesus healed people.

A RADICAL CURE

The *Mark* Gospel depicts the first healing in Capernaum, on the Sea of Galilee. The significant detail in this story is, first of all, that his direct authority amazes people, and his fame spreads rapidly. Secondly, he violates Jewish law by healing on the Sabbath, attracting the attention of powerful enemies, namely Pharisees and Temple priests. Overwhelmed by crowds, Jesus seeks seclusion in the countryside, where he is less known. He heals a leper, insisting that he keep quiet about it, but the leper cannot contain his excitement, and crowds again besiege Jesus.

He takes refuge in a house, but the throng lowers a paralytic through the roof. Jesus says to the man, "Your sins are forgiven." His audience would consider sin a cause of illness, but prying scholars at the scene wonder who has given Jesus the authority to forgive sins. This leads to complaints that Jesus consorts with tax collectors and sinners, at which point Jesus borrows the Cynics' response about doctors healing the sick, not the healthy. Eventually, as we've seen, he is accused of being in league with demons.

We do not have to know precisely which techniques Jesus used — forgiving sins, applying spittle and mud, healing touch, or his own word — to see that his methods of healing people worked, appeared revolutionary, and attracted admirers and antagonists. Most importantly, Jesus' free healing broke the Temple's monopoly on divine power, just as Jewish rebels attempted to break Rome's monopoly on violence. On a grander scale, he provided hope in otherwise hopeless circumstances. Healing and feeding people, manifesting the divine kingdom here and now, were practices as seditious as storming the king's palace. Sharing food and healing gave some measure of social dignity to outcasts and comprised the core of the Galilean's nonviolent revolution.

David Abram points out that magic healing is the art of making something impossible happen, which startles people, causing them to shed their preconceptions. He calls it "the oldest craft there is." Shamans, healers, and sorcerers work with perception of both the individual and the group, and may experience the same sense of magic that the audience experiences. "Magic," observes Abram, "is a way of keeping the world alive and healthy, and of keeping humans in a healthy connection with the rest of the natural world." The magical healer is "the intermediary between the human community and the more-than-human." That more-than-human world may be perceived as a world of animals, animal spirits, deities, demons, gods, goddesses, or a powerful force that pervades the universe. The spell of the healer lifts people from drudgery and everyday perceptions, providing hope.

Nothing could be more radical in a state of severe repression than healing and feeding the poor. In 1975, Gerd Theissen, New Testament professor at Heidelberg University, called the political impact of Jesus "itinerant radicalism," suggesting that the very act of wandering the countryside giving freely to the poor made a political statement. Crossan calls this "unbrokered egalitarianism," and the term "unbrokered" touches the heart of the matter. Jesus did not ask the Temple priests for the authority to heal and he did not seek a patron to finance his charity. Jesus, like his mentor the Baptist, gave freely outside the matrix of patronage that dominated first-century Mediterranean societies. He appears to have taken one more radical step by encouraging his disciples to wander through towns and villages doing exactly what he was doing: healing people, encouraging them to share their meagre resources with their neighbours, and telling them, "The kingdom is here."

This Jesus matches Josephus's description of "a wise man who performed surprising deeds." In the second century, Roman governor Pliny notes that Christians met at sunrise, sang songs, lived an ethical life, and shared a common meal. These secular observations now appear accurate. The social program promoted by Jesus encouraged followers to act once they discovered the light inside themselves to share food and heal people. That program is the divine kingdom on earth.

Jesus lived and worked on the boundary between the magical, oral culture of Mediterranean peasants and the rational, literary culture that would dominate later centuries, including our own. This is not simply a boundary in time; it is a boundary in the very perception of time. Literary culture existed before Jewish scriptures, and magical, oral cultures still exist in the twenty-first century. Both types of culture offer survival skills and living values, but we now live almost entirely in a rational, literary world. The Hebrew language and the presumed written words of God played a significant role in this shift. The people of the book enriched cultural heritage but also relentlessly subjugated the people of the land. Literary culture transformed a cyclic understanding of time and nature into a linear or historical understanding of time and nature. The heirs of the people of the book, European culture, learned how to use reason, engineering, and violence to secure and harvest the resources in their environment. The people of the land kept themselves alive by finding a place in the cycles of nature, and they made the world right with common decency. The new social contract proposed by Jesus actually adopted an ancient social contract: Feed and heal each other. Nevertheless, in first-century Palestine, under layers of law and authority, simple, one-to-one responsibility for each other had become revolutionary. Jesus assumed authority—forgiving sins, healing without a licence—which defied the status quo. In his own time he may have been seen as a teacher, exorcist, wise man, Cynic philosopher, incarnation of Elijah, revolutionary, or deity. We should take note, however, of what Jesus appears to have said about himself.

· 8 ·

ON WHOSE AUTHORITY?

When goodness grows weak,
When evil increases,
I make myself a body.

KRISHNA, BHAGAVAD-GITA

John Izzo, a former Presbyterian minister, spent time visiting indigenous tribes in East Africa. One evening he found himself beside a fire listening to an elder in the Hadza tribe tell a creation story through a translator. In the story, a giant kills all the people of Africa except for a young woman and a young man, who emerges from a honey tree. They flee the giant and renew the human race. Near the climax of the tale, as the storyteller described a "blue snake," the assembled elders broke off into frenzied debate. The translator explained that some of the elders insisted the snake was either white or yellow, not blue. The discussion about the snake persisted for some time before the teller shrugged and spoke to the translator, who explained to the visitors, "He says he's telling the story. It's blue."

Oral legend, we understand, treats historical events as pliable *mythos*. We do not need to know if the cock crowed once or twice to understand that the threat of state reprisals could terrorize a person to the point of denying his friend, as Peter allegedly did.

World literature allows us to glimpse human choices and perceptions through myth. However, literature also reflects bias, prejudice, and opportunism. We've witnessed how even a reliable historian such as Josephus might embellish events to shore up his own reputation. We have seen how various traditions might cherry-pick stories from the folk record to support a particular point of view. We have seen that writing fixes a story into static, sometimes completely spurious, history.

Oral storytelling may, on the other hand, serve the truth in other ways. As the childhood game of "telephone" teaches us, stories shift in the telling, lip to ear, even without obvious bias. However, since stories fluctuate in the oral process, the more outrageous, biased, or self-serving adaptations get left behind, leaving a nucleus of valuable human experience. In this sense, oral history may preserve certain core truths about authentic history better than semi-factual, but prejudiced, written history.

We might appreciate, then, the threads and gaps in transmission from the voice of a wandering Galilean to us. His teachings passed to casual listeners and close devotees, and then spiralled through public discourse spanning several decades, before any of the earliest sayings anthologies were compiled in Greek. Some 200 various records likely existed by the end of the second century, when editors began to copy and assemble manuscript collections reflecting their own circumstances and beliefs. We have seen that conflict naturally arose as congregation leaders revised and added to the canon, often replacing undesirable passages with their own interpretations. Certain congregations linked their Jesus canon to the ancient Hebrew scriptures, translated into Greek as the Septuagint, and later into Latin as the Christian Old Testament.

Historians find nothing unusual about this evolution. A similar process gave rise to most literature of ancient human civilization, from the Ramayana in India to the epic of Gilgamesh in Sumer. The very act of writing changed human storytelling and memory between 500 B.C.E. and 500 C.E., a pivotal transition for humanity. Oral culture had preserved peasant sensibilities and ethics. Simple lists of sayings from popular sages might preserve remnants of that peasant perspective, but narrative writing evolved primarily among royalty and aristocrats, a version of history painted by those in power. In contrast, a cry of hope for the dispossessed would register as a radical message during most eras of history.

HUMILITY AND INTEGRITY

Consider the parable of the unforgiving slave: A master intends to sell a slave and his family to recover a debt that the slave cannot repay. The slave begs for mercy and the master forgives the obligation. However, the slave then accosts another slave, who owes him money, and has him imprisoned for failure to pay. When the master hears this, he rescinds his clemency and punishes the ingrate.

Although only *Matthew* attributes this story to Jesus, some scholars believe it goes back to Jesus because it echoes his provocative style and bolsters his message of humility. The author of *Matthew* construes the parable to mean that God will punish those who do not forgive their neighbours. This emphasis on punishment provides an example of a later bias. The *Matthew* author hears the parable as a warning to beware retribution from a punitive God.

The lesson in the tale, however, is not that God will punish sinners but that disciples should *not* punish presumed sinners. Jesus has already instructed his disciples not to draft laws, rebuke others, or demand allegiance, but rather to serve, to behave as children, and to go among the people as sheep among wolves. Punishment was an entitlement of the privileged. Jesus, however, taught unconditional forgiveness. The parable's message is not to fear punishment but rather to be kind to others. Forgive others as you are forgiven.

Humility and integrity appear as motifs throughout the Jesus sayings and parables. Recall the warning in the Logia Iēsou from Oxyrhynchus, to "take the timber from your own eye" before presuming to "remove the sliver from your friend's eye." Jesus consistently reminds his disciples to improve themselves and refrain from judging others. In *Mary*, *Luke*, and *Matthew*, Jesus counsels his disciples, "Do not pass judgement on others." The *Mary* Gospel defines sin as acting against one's nature, that is, contrary to one's authentic self. Sin is a violation of personal integrity, not written law.

Ask a child about life, Jesus says. The first shall be last, the last shall be first. Those who exalt themselves will be humbled. Jesus remains unambiguous about this. The proverb found in *Thomas* and *Matthew*, to "not let the left hand know what the right hand is doing," is a directive to give without boasting or expecting return. To the blessed poor and hungry, *Matthew* adds the meek or gentle (Greek *praeis*). *Matthew* uses this word as Jesus enters Jerusalem, assuring the "daughter of Zion" that her "king comes to you in modesty."

As we have seen, Jesus reserves his harshest criticism for those who display religious pretensions. He delivers his only severe rebuke to priests, Pharisees, and scholars who flaunt their authority and demand special privilege. Such warnings appear in all the earliest collections of sayings. *Mark* puts it this way:

Look out for the scholars who like to parade around in long robes, and insist on being addressed properly in the marketplaces, and prefer important seats in the synagogues and the best couches at banquets. They are the ones who prey on widows and their families and recite long prayers just to put on airs.

Jesus does not resort to subtlety here, but rather confronts hypocrites head on. His attack on scribes, or scholars, reflects the schism between the people of the land and the people of the book. Speakers in the oral tradition appear to mistrust the writers and lawmakers, who freeze ethics in language and distort the message by design. Recall from the Logia Iēsou that Jesus criticized Pharisees and scholars who "take the keys of knowledge" but "do not enter."

Luke directs a similar accusation against "law makers," and *Matthew* against "Pharisees and imposters." These denunciations converge consistently with Jesus' instructions to give with modesty, make no laws, look within, and be aware of your own shortcomings. As with the story of the Good Samaritan, Jesus implies that correct morality comes from self-awareness and social awareness, not from institutions, laws, and authority. The Pharisees and scholars, he says, are preoccupied with convention ("washing the outside") and with prestige ("important seats in the synagogue"), and are therefore distracted from the truth.

Jesus warns first and foremost against spiritual conceit. A similar lesson appears in the legend of the Buddha's enlightenment. Mara, the Vedic deity of love and death, attempts to distract the Buddha, as he sits in meditation. Mara summons his forces — rain, burning coals, and sandstorms — to distract the Buddha. When that fails, he sends his daughters — Desire, Discontent, and Passion — but they fail also. Then Mara sends the heavy guns — Ego, Skepticism, and Self-righteousness. None is able to distract the Buddha. Finally, Mara sends his last daughter: Spiritual Pride.

Although this did not work on the Buddha, later Buddhism warns that spiritual self-importance picks off many practitioners. Buddhism teaches that spiritual awareness is "nothing special," and that the most advanced state of awareness is "ordinary mind." Jesus delivers virtually the same warning to beware of religious pretensions. Stay gentle as doves.

Consistently, Jesus advises disciples to prove their knowledge through action, specifically healing and sharing food. He deflects honour and recognition, draws listeners' attention back to themselves, and makes himself out to be nothing special. The *Mark* Gospel records Jesus asking, "Why do you call me good? No one is good except for God." Luke and the Egerton Gospel have Jesus saying, "Why do you call me 'Master, master,' and not do what I tell you?" Jesus does not want praise or "lip service," but action.

I AM THAT ONE

We can assume that the best authority on Jesus is Jesus, and we'll find widely corroborated evidence in the earliest accounts from *Mark*, *Thomas*, and the Q verses, in which he refers to himself directly or obliquely:

Mark 1:38: Jesus leads his disciples to "neighbouring villages" to "speak there" because "that is what I came to do."

Mark 2:8–18: Jesus heals a paralytic, and the author (not Jesus) explains that on earth, "The Son of Adam has authority to forgive sins." When Jesus is denounced for associating with sinners, he delivers the Cynic retort, "Since when do the healthy need a doctor?" Finally, Jesus says: "The Son of Adam [a human, possibly a reference to himself] lords it over the Sabbath." Jesus appears here as a healer, Cynic philosopher, and social rebel.

Mark 4:3–8: Jesus tells the parable of the sower and the seeds that fall on good or bad soil. He implies, perhaps, that he is such a sower, that is, a teacher.

Mark 6:3–4: An onlooker refers to Jesus as "a carpenter... Mary's son." He notices their resentment and says: "No prophet goes without honour, except in their hometown."

There is nothing unusual here. Jesus is a teacher, a sage, a healer, a prophet, and a bit of a troublemaker regarding Jewish tradition. In the Q verses, Jesus refers to himself as "your teacher, not your judge," and claims he came to "set the earth on fire," which we take metaphorically, as a reference to the radical message of his teachings.

Mark tells a story of Jesus on the northern road to Philippi, as Jesus asks his followers: "What are people saying about me?" Unnamed disciples tell Jesus that people say he is John the Baptist, Elijah, or "one of the prophets." Peter adds, "You are the anointed one." *Matthew* copies *Mark*, but adds a reference to "the Son of God." *Luke* copies *Mark*, but has Jesus refer to himself as the "Son of Adam." The story of Jesus asking what people say about him may portray a historical incident also independently attested in *Thomas*, who does not copy *Mark*.

In *Thomas* 13, Jesus asks his disciples, "Compare me to something and tell me what I am like." Peter compares Jesus to "a just angel." Matthew calls him "a wise philosopher." Thomas says, "Teacher, my mouth is utterly unable to say what you are like." Among these three, Jesus praises Thomas, and adds, "I am not your teacher. Because you have drunk, you have become intoxicated from the bubbling spring that I have tended."

Thomas appears to have achieved the enlightened awareness of his teacher Jesus, intoxicated from the same spring of self-knowledge. The saying demonstrates that certain congregations believed Jesus made no claims about divinity but rather tended the spring of knowledge. Recall that *Thomas* quotes Jesus saying, "Split a piece of wood; I am there," and *Mary* locates spirit in nature. For the seeker who discovers his or her own light and awareness, the world lights up and the spring of knowledge appears everywhere.

The earliest Greek layer of *Thomas* opens saying 30 with the line: "Where there are three, they are without God, and where there is only one, I say I am with that one." This "only one" is the unification of opposites that we have consistently heard about. Jesus describes a state of being in which dualities evaporate, revealing unity. In the divine kingdom, "male and female are one." In Greek *Thomas* 29, we heard Jesus flip first-century cosmology around, suggesting, "...if spirit came into being because of the body, that is a wonder of wonders." Jesus leaves the question open: Did spirit arise in matter? Certain communities of the Jesus movement — including those that produced the gospels of *Thomas*, *Mary*, and *Philip* — reflect this naturalist tradition, shared by Greek philosophers Thales and Pythagoras and by Eastern sages Lao Tzu and the Buddha.

In the later, Coptic version of *Thomas*, the "piece of wood" saying has been attached to *Thomas* 77: "I am all. From me all came forth." This sounds as if Jesus is exalting himself, which contradicts the humility he has otherwise advocated and displayed. This is likely a Coptic revision, similar to redactions found in many later manuscripts about Jesus. Only in the *Gospel of John* does Jesus unequivocally exalt himself: "I am the light of the world... I am the way, the truth, and the life," and so forth. The "I am" proclamation does not exist in Hebrew. It is considered blasphemous, since only God is associated with "I am." This construction replicates a common Greek figure of speech (*ego eimi*) spoken by gods. The quotes appear in long, 200- to 300-word passages attributed to Jesus, composed more than sixty years after his life, and not considered by historians to represent Jesus quotes. Virtually all independent Bible scholars concur that the "I am" passages reflect the language of the author, not the voice of Jesus.

In *John*, most modern Bibles have the Baptist referring to Jesus as "the Son of God." However, all early manuscripts, including *Codex Sinaiticus*, do not read "Son of God" but rather "God's chosen one." Likewise, many modern Bibles open *Mark* 1:1 with "The

beginning of the good news of Jesus Christ, Son of God." The
Oxford Annotated Bible notes, "other ancient authorities lack 'the
son of God.'" Indeed, *Sinaiticus* and the third-century Church
theologian Origen omit the phrase "Son of God" in this passage
from *Mark*. Thus, "Son of God" represents a critically important
revision made 300 years after the death of Jesus, when scribes
edited the original Gospels.

In Jewish tradition, all humans are considered "children of God,"
and pure, faithful Jews might be seen as "chosen" children of God,
signifying religious responsibility, not necessarily elevated status.
Egyptian, Persian, Greek, and Roman stories identify numerous
sons and daughters of gods taking human form, many born of virgins, who suffer, die, and are reborn. Sons of god include Osiris
and Horus in Egypt, Krishna and Rama in India, Mithras in Babylon, Beddru in Japan, Hercules, Dionysus, Orpheus, Hermes,
Tammuz, and many others. Followers of historical figures such as
Pythagoras and Socrates honoured them as sons of god. Similarily,
Roman emperors after Augustus took the title *divi filius*, "son of
god." No self-respecting religion or school of philosophy in the second or third century would fail to claim that their founder was a son
of god, so we will find nothing unusual in this claim by peasant
followers or Church patriarchs regarding Jesus.

Jesus, however, does not use "son of God" to describe himself.
He consistently avoids exalting himself, eschews special recognition,
and uses metaphors to point to the quality of his personal experience. People called Jesus many things, but he avoided titles and
usually described himself as a "son of Adam" (often translated as
"son of Man"), meaning a child of humanity or simply a human.

FOXES AND HUMANITY

Greek scribes correctly translated the Hebrew phrase "son of Adam"
as son of *anthropos*, or human, distinct from deities. The Hebrew

word *adam* means a flushed or ruddy complexion, and became the common word for human. Maryanne Cline Horowitz explains, "The Hebrew term *adam* stands for the generic species of humanity which is composed of men and women." A Jewish peasant would commonly understand "son of Adam" as a human in a modest role, submissive to the deities. This usage appears in Job 25:5–6, depicting unrighteous humanity before God: "If even the moon is not bright and the stars are not pure in his sight, how much less a mortal, who is a maggot, and a human being [son of Adam], who is a worm."

Job, facing ruin, struggled to justify evil in a world created by God. Urged by his friends to confess whatever sins may have alienated him from God's grace, he stumbles between cynicism and hope. Job is the suffering son of Adam, a troubled mortal straining to survive. Psalms takes a more elevated view of the human condition. In verses 8:3–6, the sons of Adam appear blessed:

Our Lord, our sovereign...What are human beings, that you are mindful of them, or sons of Adam that you care for them? Yet, you made them a little lower than God and crowned them with glory and honour.

Here, "sons of Adam" are favoured by God and given dominion over life on earth. This idea appears common in the first century: Humanity occupies a place below deities and angels, but above the beasts. This cosmology rejects the naturalist view of Aristotle that divinity can be found in all things. Here, nature appears lowly, God high, humanity in between.

Finally, the Book of Daniel uses "son of Adam" to identify a specific human arriving to act as God's agent on earth. The Judean king selects Daniel as a court scholar, but he is among those captured and taken to Babylon. When Babylonian King Nebuchadnezzar's soothsayers fail to interpret the king's dreams, Daniel succeeds by predicting the future "fourth kingdom," ruled by Jews on behalf of El Elyon, "the Most High." The king, overwhelmed with gratitude, agrees that Daniel's El Elyon is the "God of Gods." Later, jealous adversaries have Daniel tossed into the lions' den for worshipping El. As the story goes, angels calm the lions, Daniel survives, and the new King Darius accepts El's supremacy. All of this leads to Daniel's recounting his own vision of the coming kingdom:

> I saw one like a son of Adam, coming on heaven's clouds.
> He came to the Ancient of Days and was presented before
> him. And dominion and glory and rule were given to him,
> that all peoples, nations, and languages should serve him.

In this passage, "like a son of Adam," means "one like a human," arriving on clouds. Centuries later, the *Mark* author uses this description from Daniel in a scene outside Jerusalem, depicting Jesus warning disciples not to expect a messiah but rather to expect "the son of Adam coming on the clouds."

The *Mark* passage does not identify Jesus as this "son of Adam," and it is not corroborated in other New Testament Gospels. According to Robert Funk, "It is the opinion of most scholars that *Mark* intends v.26 ('the son of Adam will come on the Clouds') as an oracle addressed to his own readers and not as something Jesus addressed to his disciples decades earlier." The *Mark* author goes on to "swear" that "this generation certainly won't pass into oblivion before all these things take place," a promise that later Church authorities had to rescind.

The *Mark* author had claimed earlier, "The Son of Adam has the authority to forgive sins," authority otherwise reserved for temple priests. A few lines later, the *Mark* author quotes Jesus in a passage that many scholars believe reflects the actual language of the Galilean: "The Sabbath day was created for humanity [Adam], not humanity for the Sabbath. So, the son of Adam even rules over the Sabbath day."

This saying, copied by *Matthew* and *Luke*, fits seamlessly into Jesus' apparent campaign to reverse convention. Jesus insists that secular and religious rules should serve people, not that people should serve the rules. Here, the "son of Adam" implies simple humanity, the struggling Job or the impoverished *ebionim*. The Sabbath is a time for people to rest and enjoy the sanctity of the world.

This brings us to the one "son of Adam" passage in the entire New Testament that is corroborated in two sources — in *Thomas* and Q — thus representing the most likely authentic and earliest known saying by Jesus regarding this phrase: "Foxes have their dens and birds have their nests, but the son of Adam has no place to rest his head."

The impoverished crowd knew that they had no Sabbath day of rest free from the struggle to survive. Slight variations occur among the three versions, indicating to scholars that the saying circulated orally and picked up nuances. Greek text scholars correctly translate "son of Adam" in this passage as "human being." Jesus appears to intend an oblique reference to himself as a simple human.

Once again, Jesus overturns conventional thinking. He places the son of Adam, the human, including himself, below the animals. To first-century Galileans and Judeans, this suggestion would seem shocking, but to itinerant sages from the East, this passage might sound similar to a proverb from the Buddha, found in the Dhammapada:

Those who awaken never rest in one place. Like swans rising from the lake, they leave their house and home.

Similarily, from Lao Tzu's *Tao Te Ching*:

Like a newborn babe before it learns to smile, I am alone,
without a place to go.

The feminine voice from "Thunder: Perfect Mind" echoes this humble status:

I am cast out upon the earth ...
Among those who are disgraced and in the least places.

The fox has a den and the birds have nests. Jesus and his disciples have abandoned even that. They remain wandering teachers
and healers with no home, no comforts, no day off, nowhere to
even rest their heads. They rely on the kindness of strangers. They
encourage the poor, heal the infirm, and inspire communal sharing. In this capacity, Jesus appears similar to John the Baptist,
Josephus's ascetic Banus, a Taoist or Buddhist monk, or Cynic
sage. He appears not to emulate a Galilean revolutionary, a Judean
rabbi, or a messiah king. Jesus, as a child of humanity, finds his
place in the natural world and will not even exalt himself above
the animals.

ONE GOD

In *Thomas*, Jesus generally refers to God as "Abba," meaning
"Father." In the Q verses, Jesus refers to God as "Father," or "El
Elyon," the "most high El." *Mark*'s Jesus refers to "Father" and to
"Eloi," meaning "my El." We have heard that when Jesus forgave
sins he did so on his own authority. Given these clues, we might
wonder what Jesus believed about deities. To understand this, we
must look briefly into the traditions he likely learned as a youth in
a Jewish culture, specifically a northern Israelite culture that had
adopted the Canaanite god El, as distinct from the Jewish YHVH.

Some historians suggest that Judaism, and specifically Moses, introduced monotheism to human culture, but the idea of an exclusive male god in heaven emerged naturally, as exclusive male kings gained power on earth. In about 1350 B.C.E. in Egypt, Akhenaten outlawed rival deities, executed their priests, and declared Aten the one and only God of the universe. On earth, Akhenaten assumed Aten's absolute power. His priesthood enjoyed a religious monopoly and exploited peasants with impunity.

Akhenaten died in about 1336 B.C.E., but the single, exclusive male god endured and served the vanity of other human kings. In northern Persia, the hermit Zoroaster claimed that the god Ahura Mazda had visited him on his mountain and had proclaimed himself the one and only God. This suited the Median kings in Persia, who embraced the deity and installed a priestly monopoly of their own.

Meanwhile, Semitic tribes had moved from the Arabian desert into Negev, south of the Dead Sea. Some of these tribes pushed north into Canaan, where they adopted the Canaanite god El and became "defenders" of El, the "Israelites." Their southern relatives occupied the Negev and Sinai, where some fell captive to Egyptian kings. Exodus 1:8–15 recalls the experiences of these southern Semitic slaves, likely during the reign of Pharaoh Seti I (c. 1294–1279 B.C.E.).

Typically, Exodus utilizes popular legend to glorify its hero, Moses. In infancy, Moses is allegedly cast adrift in a basket on the river and rescued by a princess, a sequence borrowed from tales of the Akkadian King Sargon a millennium earlier. Egyptian records do not record a mass escape of Israelites — 6,000 men, plus women, children, and herds of livestock — nor the demise of Pharaoh's army, which supposedly pursued them. Nevertheless, some Semitic slaves escaped and fled across the Sinai back into the Negev and Canaan. By the time Persian King Cyrus had overrun the Middle East, six centuries before Jesus, their god Ahura Mazda had assumed a militant and vengeful nature in alliance with Cyrus. Thereafter, Judeans in Jerusalem adopted the idea of a single, all-powerful deity.

The northern, mixed tribes understood divine beings differently. Jesus' use of "El Elyon" echoes the ancient Israelite and Canaanite "most high" god El, who presided over an assembly of deities with his consort, Asherah. The earliest records of El, from Ugarit on the northern coast of Syria, refer to *abū adami*, father of humans. In first-century Galilee, Jesus applied the common expression "god the father" to his understanding of a generous, merciful god for the poor and dispossessed, one that was not necessarily intended as a single, one-and-only deity.

CONVERGING GODS

The opening line of Genesis invokes "Elohim," a feminine plural form of El that remains ambiguous. The nun who taught me Catholic catechism explained, "Elohim is another name for God," but it's not quite that simple. The plural *im* could imply a grammatical "plural of majesty," indicating greatness, but not in all cases. In Psalm 82, El stands before his council and "judges among the elohim," clearly multiple deities. In Genesis 1:26, Elohim says, "Let *us* make humankind in *our* image," speaking to an assembly of deities.

In Genesis, Abraham accepts the original Jewish covenant with God, who tells him, "I am El-Shaddai," traditionally translated as "God Almighty." The northern Semites absorbed this aspect of God from the Canaanites. The Hebrew Shaddai could derive from *shadad*, to destroy, or from the Akkadian *shadû*, meaning "mountain-dweller." The idea of a destroyer from the mountain may reflect the common earthquakes of northern Syria. Cultural interpretations of this name likely shifted over time.

Later in Genesis, Abraham's grandson Jacob, the father of Israel in Canaan, lies dying in Egypt before his twelve sons. Jacob

chastises and praises his sons and proclaims their inheritance.
Finally, he speaks to his youngest and favourite son, born of Rachel,
the tender-hearted and wise Joseph. Jacob calls Joseph "a fruitful
bough by a spring," and says that his arms were made strong

> ... by the Aveer ["mighty one"] of Jacob, by the name of the
> Shepherd, the Rock of Israel, by El of your father, who will
> help you, by Shaddai, who will bless you with blessings of
> heaven above, blessings of the deep that lies beneath, bless-
> ings of the breasts and of the womb.

This passage does not suggest that these divine protectors are
one and the same. Shaddai appears distinct, as a god of abundance
represented by the breast and womb. Jewish scribes who translated
the Torah into Greek rendered "Shaddai" as *ikanos*, meaning
"ample" or "all-sufficient," implying something that has ripened,
and linked to the Hebrew *shadayim*, "breasts." This deity appears
consistent with the Genesis El-Shaddai, who promised Abraham, "I
will make you exceedingly fruitful." These divine protectors of
Jacob do not include the one and only god of Moses yet to come.

While northern Israelites consorted with Canaanites, the
Semitic slaves in Egypt sought freedom. When Moses scales Mount
Horeb in the Exodus account and asks God his name, the deity
replies, "I am I am." This god instructs Moses to tell his people, "*I
am* has sent me to you," and identifies himself to Moses as "the god
of your ancestors." We possess no conclusive origin for the Hebrew
YHVH that indicates this god. Some scholars link the name "I am"
to a first-person form of the Hebrew verb *HYH*, "to be." Historians
believe that the semi-nomadic Jews crossing the Sinai from Egypt
after 1250 B.C.E. brought the name YHVH with them, as it first sur-
faces in pantheistic Jewish settings.

An inscription on an eighth-century B.C.E. pottery shard from the Negev records: "I have blessed you by YHVH Shomron and his Asherah." A burial cave inscription near Hebron invokes "YHVH and his Asherah." Both inscriptions associate the Jewish god with the Canaanite queen of heaven. Here, we witness two distinct lines of tradition merging in Jewish histories: northern Semitic farmers, influenced by Akkadian and Canaanite culture, and southern nomadic ex-slaves who had escaped from Egypt.

The northern Israelites honoured their ancestor Abraham and worshipped El, Elohim, Asherah, Shaddai, and other deities. The southern Israelites honoured their ancestor Moses and worshipped the single god, YHVH. The authors of Genesis and Exodus fuse the two traditions by linking Abraham, through the genealogy of Isaac and Jacob, to Joseph and then linking Joseph to Moses in Egypt. God informs Moses that he had once revealed himself to Abraham as El Shaddai, but now reveals himself as YHVH. The two traditions are neatly stitched together. Two Semitic groups and multiple gods become a single, unified story, with a single, unified god, presumably displacing Ahura Mazda, Aten, and all other pretenders to the throne of heaven.

Over centuries, the Canaanite El assumes various roles as warrior, father, head of an assembly of deities, and consort of Asherah. In human stories, these deities related to each other as spouses, family members, allies, and antagonists, sharing duties, powers, and names. The shifts in perceptions about deities occurred over millennia, and a first-century peasant in Galilee would adhere to some, not necessarily all, of these traditions. It is not obvious, then, if Jesus considered the "Father" or "Most High God" to be an exclusive god. One would not typically say "Most High" except in reference to lesser deities. Nevertheless, Jesus appears to believe in a merciful, fatherly god who would look after the poor.

ABBA

Jesus' audience in Galilee would hear "Elohim" and "Father" in the evolving context of their mixed heritage. These peasants believed in Asherah, El, Anath, Baal, and local fertility gods and goddesses, regardless of what priests in Jerusalem believed, or what modern observers might believe. If we think of first-century Judaism as purely monotheistic, we will miss a great deal of the action.

Jesus warned his listeners not to worry about their comforts, that "Abba," God the Father, would provide, but he does not elaborate about that god. In *Mark*, Jesus cries out in Aramaic to Eloi, "my El," asking, "Why have you forsaken me?" This line comes from the Old Testament Psalms 22:1. Would a dying man in agony quote poetry? Maybe. But earlier in this scene, *Mark* borrows another passage from the same chapter of Psalms, the casting of lots for the suffering king's garments. Perhaps the author of *Mark* had Psalms open on his desk as he composed this scene. *Luke* has the dying Jesus saying, "Father, into your hands I entrust my spirit," from Psalms 31:5, and *John* tells a different version, with Jesus saying, "I'm thirsty," from Psalms 69, and "It's all over," from the Book of Job.

Jesus may have said some or all of these things, but, as we have observed, the disparity of accounts indicates that the authors freely borrowed scriptural quotes and attributed them to Jesus. We cannot necessarily know, therefore, what Jesus believed about the nature of the god El, whom he called "father," because his likely authentic comments on the subject remain scarce and obscure.

In *Thomas* 83, Jesus tells his disciples that within them exists "the image of the Father's light," and, in saying 69, he says that the persecuted are blessed, because they "have come to know the Father." Otherwise, the *Thomas* sayings focus on action in the world and tell us little about God the "father" or any other deity.

The Lord's Prayer probably mixes authentic words and ideas of Jesus with later redaction and invention. *Mark* and *John* do not include this prayer to God, and *Luke* and *Matthew* write slightly different versions, probably revised from their source, the Q sayings. For example, *Matthew* probably added the references, not found in *Luke*, to heaven and to evil. Text scholars differ on what came from Jesus, but the earliest edition of Q likely reads something like this:

Father, your name is holy
Deliver to us your kingdom
Provide us with the bread we need each day
Forgive our debts, as we have forgiven those in debt to us

Jesus likely said something like this, referring to God with the familiar "Abba," while also acknowledging that God's name is hallowed. This may suggest he believed the Judean prohibition against speaking the name of their god, but we might imagine that if Jesus intended the one and only deity YHVH, he would have said so.

The prayer asks that the kingdom of God come. This appears to contradict Jesus' statement that the kingdom already exists within, here and now, so the idea could reflect the apocalyptic beliefs of later followers. However, the request that God bring forth the kingdom may indicate a plea for God's assistance in experiencing the kingdom within, as described by Jesus. Finally, the followers ask for their daily food, which Jesus has assured them Abba would provide, and absolution from their debts, accompanied by the promise that they have forgiven others.

What we learn about Jesus' idea of god in this prayer is that a sacred god, like a compassionate parent, will provide necessities, help the honest seeker find the kingdom, and forgive shortcomings, especially for those who do likewise. The prayer presents a simple and exquisite concept of god, makes modest requests for help, does not presume to know the workings of heaven or the intentions of the deities, and does not presume that God considers the speaker to be anyone special. This prayer, therefore, remains consistent with the other early evidence of Jesus' humility.

Given this long history of shifting deities and empires, we are now able to see how the simple teacher Jesus might be interpreted by his contemporaries, regardless of what he intended. Some poor peasants might regard him as little more than a free meal or an encouraging word. Others might identify Jesus as a peasant shepherd king, as a descendant of King David, a messiah, prophet, healer, or rebel leader. Jesus the Nazorean and Mary Magdalene could be identified with Tammuz and Anath. The spring equinox sun had shifted from Aries into Pisces, and some observers might have identified Jesus with the new spring god, Pisces, the fish, and indeed some did, as we shall see in the next chapter.

Jesus could not necessarily control his story, even when he was alive. Once he was dead, his story fell upon many ears, was repeated by many lips, each harbouring personal, religious, and political perceptions of their own. Jesus wrote nothing and established no organization beyond a circle of devotees with simple instructions. Jesus offered, to whomever would listen, his advice, his encouragement, the healing power of faith, and his accrued wisdom.

MURDERERS AND THIEVES

Not all of Jesus' aphorisms or parables are easily interpreted, and in some cases, this may be the point. The sheer mystery of the obscure sayings tells us something about what Jesus was up to. Cryptic proverbs allow the listener to project one's own deep conflicts onto the story. Authentic wisdom is not a rulebook but rather a tool that helps individuals navigate through the world.

For example, when Jesus compares the kingdom to a child or a woman with a cracked jar, these metaphors sound intentionally enigmatic, without elucidation. When he announces in *Thomas* that he "found humanity intoxicated, but none thirsty," each listener is left to consider how he or she might be intoxicated yet thirsty. Like the Cynics or Taoists, Jesus does not explain, but rather provokes the listener to think and feel the meaning. In *Thomas* and *Luke*, we find a cryptic saying that suggests social as well as inner conflict:

I have cast fire upon the world, and see, I am guarding it until it blazes. (Thomas 10)

I came to set fire upon the earth; and how I wish it were already ablaze. (Luke 12:49)

The double attestation, early appearance, and the abrupt, provocative language suggest that this saying came from Jesus and circulated orally. *Luke* sets this saying after two stories expressing the idea that Jesus will return, "when you least expect it." This interpretation reflects the *Luke* author, writing five decades after Jesus for congregations troubled by the fact that the promised imminent return had been postponed. *Thomas*, typically, leaves the saying to stand on its own. Jesus appears conscious of the cultural upheaval his mission represented, but is not specific about the "fire" that will follow. We are left with the irony that Jesus' message of neighbourly love and self-knowledge should result in conflict, but history confirms that this is the case. Another saying that modifies the peaceful image of Jesus appears among the nine core sayings attested by *Mark*, *Thomas*, and Q: "One can't enter a strong person's house and take it by force without first tying his hands. Then one can loot his house."

Scholars believe this saying existed in the oral record and originated with Jesus. But why would Jesus use such a violent metaphor of binding someone and robbing their home? All three synoptic Gospels attribute this saying to Jesus after he is accused of exorcising demons with the power of Beelzebul. One might interpret this, therefore, to mean that before an exorcist can drive a demon from a sick person, he or she must first overpower the king of demons. The problem with this interpretation is that nowhere else does Jesus speak about a battle against a devil. The reference to Beelzebul comes from others, specifically scholars from Jerusalem, who accuse him of being in league with the Devil. As we observed in the last chapter, battling "the Devil" represents Persian, Greek, post-exile urban Jewish, and later Christian traditions, not the tradition of first-century Jewish peasants. Rather, we might interpret this battle with a strong person by considering the lines from *Mary*: "What binds me has been slain...my desire has been brought to an end, and my ignorance has died."

Jesus illuminated the struggle that each person faces within. Our biggest enemies are pride, fear, desire, and ignorance. The desperate ego is the giant that each person must slay, and perhaps this is the strong person that one must bind before discovering the divine kingdom. In Hindu terms, this reflects slaying the ego to achieve the *atman*, or god within. Never in the early, authentic sayings of Jesus does he blame problems on demons. Even more disturbing than looting the strong man's house is *Thomas* saying 98:

Jesus said, "The Father's kingdom is like a person who wanted to kill someone powerful. While still at home he drew his sword and thrust it into the wall to find out whether his hand would go in. Then he killed the powerful one."

Although this saying appears only in *Thomas*, some scholars believe the scandalous language suggests it may be authentic. No later community of Jesus followers would likely attribute this to their teacher unless he had actually said it. If so, then Jesus fully intends to shock his listeners. Does this metaphor suggest one must enter one's "own house," or "look within" before one undertakes an action in the world? Possibly so. Before we take action in the world, we should look within, thrust our sharp sword into our own wall.

As long as we are on a spree of looting and killing, we should also look at the parable of the leased vineyard, appearing in the three synoptic Gospels and in *Thomas*. A landowner rents his vineyard to tenant farmers, but when he sends his slaves to collect his share, the farmers beat them severely. Finally, the landowner sends his son, but the farmers, knowing he is the heir to the property, kill him.

Until the discovery of the *Thomas* anthology at Nag Hammadi in 1945, most independent scholars considered this parable to be the work of later Christian communities, since it was used as an allegory for developing their doctrines. The *Matthew* adaptation borrows images of the vineyard from Isaiah and portrays the farmers killing the slaves and dragging the son outside the vineyard. Finally, *Matthew* promises that the farmers will be punished, places a passage from Psalms on Jesus' lips, and interprets the story to mean that the kingdom will be seized from those who abuse it, and given to the righteous. The emerging Christian congregations naturally assumed that they were the new tenants, that God had forsaken Israel and given the kingdom to them. The added images come from the author.

The discovery of the *Thomas* version changed academic opinion about this parable because it appears without the allegorical interpretations. The *Thomas* version leaves the parable to stand on its own and demands that the listener figure out the meaning. Wealthy landlords in the first century commonly took advantage of poor tenant farmers. Jesus generally sympathizes with the poor, but does not appear to take sides in this story. Rather, he simply recounts the events. Perhaps this story shows that land should belong to the people who actually work it, and allegorically that the kingdom belongs to those who practise good acts in the world.

If we view these parables and aphorisms as allegories of our inner struggle, rather than taking them literally, they assume more significant and useful meanings. In keeping with *Mary*'s declaration, "What binds me has been slain," we might interpret these violent images as the conflict within. Perhaps our pride or our ego is the landlord that must be overcome. The teachings of Jesus are descriptive, not prescriptive; he witnesses the truth and describes what he sees, but he does not proclaim complex doctrines or extensive rules of conduct. His listeners are left to contemplate the meaning on their own.

SALT

One of the more cryptic metaphors found in the New Testament refers to salt that has lost its salty qualities. The ancient world valued salt highly as a food preservative, necessary for survival in the desert, and so valuable it served as currency along the Silk Road.

In the Old Testament books Numbers and Chronicles, YHVH describes his promises to the Jewish people as "a covenant of salt." In Leviticus, the Mosaic god insists that all meat offerings confirm this covenant by including an offering of salt. Since salt served as a common preservative, the metaphor may express the preservation of God's covenant. Other Old Testament books — Exodus, Ezekiel, and Kings II — refer to salt as both preservative and purifying agent. In this context, Jesus could be warning disciples to preserve the purity of their lessons. However, there appears to be more going on. The three versions of the saying attributed to Jesus display significant differences:

> Salt is good, but if salt becomes bland, how can you renew it? Maintain salt among yourselves and be at peace with one another. (Mark 9:50)

> You are the salt of the earth; but if salt has lost its taste, how shall its saltiness be restored? It is no longer good for anything except to be thrown out and trodden under foot. (Matthew 5:13)

> Salt is good. But if salt loses its taste, how will it be renewed? It is not fit for the soil or the manure pile. It just gets thrown away. (Luke 14:34)

Mark sets the saying in Capernaum, on the Sea of Galilee, and adds the conclusion about being at peace. *Matthew* sets the saying in the Sermon on the Mount, and adds the line about the "salt of the earth." *Luke* sets the saying on the road into Jerusalem and adds the reference to soil and a manure pile. The added elements suggest inventions of the authors. The core saying — "Salt is good, but if salt becomes bland, how will you renew it?" — likely came from Jesus. Here, again, we are able to witness the evolution of an idea as it is passed down by word of mouth and eventually written down. This saying defies simple explanation, especially since the original context has been lost.

The *Mark* setting in Capernaum, with Jesus speaking to the disciples, may be the earliest version. Jesus alludes to the fires of hell that never burn out, where "everyone there will be salted with fire." *Mark* lifts the inextinguishable fire from Isaiah in the Old Testament, and uses "salted with fire" as a device to introduce the salt saying. The author does not suggest that bland or contaminated salt is useless, but rather, "Have salt in yourselves, and be at peace with one another," suggesting the metaphor of salt as a preservative of a disciple's inner peace.

The *Luke* version describes salt that has lost its taste. Salt (sodium chloride) is an extremely stable compound that does not deteriorate or lose its taste, so the saying most likely refers to salt that has been contaminated, in which case it is useless and according to *Luke*, unfit for either soil or the dunghill. Salt could also be present with gypsum and manure in a common fertilizer. "Salt" in this case would be unfit for consumption, but could be considered an additive to soil, ironically, since too much will kill plants. Perhaps this explains why *Luke* says this salt is not fit for soil. Therefore, Jesus might be telling his disciples to safeguard the purity of the teachings. The *Matthew* author may have invented the "salt of the earth" introduction, possibly meaning "the preservation of the earth" or, as we shall see, the "wisdom of the earth."

In the ancient world — Vedic, Persian, and Egyptian traditions — salt became a metaphor for wisdom. Later, the rabbinical Jewish and the Roman Catholic traditions also used salt as an image of wisdom, or Sophia. According to the *Catholic Dictionary*, "Salt, exorcized and blessed, is put on the tongue of the candidate at Baptism as a symbol of wisdom and incorruption." The *Gospel of Philip*, composed in Syria in the third century, portrays congregations of Jesus followers using salt in offerings to represent wisdom: "The apostles said to the disciples, 'May our entire offering obtain salt.' They called Sophia [wisdom] 'salt.' Without it, no offering is acceptable."

Since Jesus rebuked the Pharisees for their religious pretensions, he may have used the salt saying to warn disciples about knowledge that lacks wisdom. Just as salt accents the flavour of food, wisdom seasons knowledge. One may appear to understand

a truth but still may not "taste" it. Socrates had warned of presumed knowledge that lacked wisdom. Anyone today might
witness the consequences of knowledge that lacks wisdom, such as
advances in technology that lead to environmental catastrophe or
horrific violence. Clearly, at times, our knowledge lacks wisdom.

The Sanskrit holy books, the Vedas, were compiled from oral
traditions, before, during, and after the life of Jesus. The Yajur-
Veda, or Veda of Holy Rites and Ritual, describes the importance
of salt in the preparation of ground for a sacred fire. Yama, who is
mentioned in the passage, is the Vedic god of justice and death,
allegedly the first mortal human to ascend through the astral
realms to heaven after death:

> He who...piles up the fire is piling it for Yama...he piles
> the fire on a place freed from death...verily he smites away
> any impurity in it; he sprinkles water on, for atonement...
> He puts down salt; salt is the nourishment and the propa-
> gating; verily he piles the fire in nourishment, in propagation,
> and also in concord; for the salt is the concord of cattle. Sky
> and earth were once together. Separating they said, 'Let us
> share together what is worthy of sacrifice.' What of yonder
> [sky] was worthy of sacrifice, it placed in this [earth], that
> became salt...when he puts down the salt he should think
> of yonder...(Yajur-Veda, Book 5, Part 2, v. 2.1)

We find, in this single passage, virtually all the metaphors for
salt that we find in both Jewish and Christian texts: spiritual
knowledge, an association with fire and earth, purity, atonement,
nourishment, propagation, concord (peace), and the proper method
of sacrifice to a deity. The salt saying from Jesus is not necessarily
dependent upon the Vedic tradition, but notice that these ideas,
allegories, and symbols appear universal.

Still, the saying remains obscure. Jesus does not spoon-feed his disciples, or us, with explanations of his parables and aphorisms. Like Socrates, the Buddha, and Lao Tzu before him, Jesus allows mystery and contradiction to enrich his teachings. Like a Zen koan —"What's the sound of one hand clapping?"— the cryptic sayings of Jesus invite the listeners to look within for answers, to overcome preconceptions, and reach a deeper understanding of their world.

We are left to ponder the meaning of salt that has lost its saltiness and to appreciate this invigorating openness of the teachings. Again, Jesus is descriptive, not prescriptive. Jesus stimulates; he does not dictate. Knowledge must be seasoned with wisdom.

WISDOM EAST AND WEST

"Taoist and Christian waters flow down from the same mountains and have their origin in the same eternal snows," writes Benedictine brother David Steindl-Rast. "If we know what they want to convey we will find it…in the deepest meaning of our own term Common Sense…. This is precisely what both Lao Tzu and Jesus point out to us…. Nothing holds greater promise for the future because nothing is more subversive."

This subversive common sense of Steindl-Rast is the common decency of the Jewish peasants who would make the world right with generosity and caring. Jesus surely offered original ideas, but he also taught what Aldous Huxley called "perennial wisdom": giving, sharing, healing others, remaining humble, and looking inside oneself. This is the divine kingdom that Jesus insists is "spread out over the world," available to anyone. We have seen that the Jesus teachings parallel Vedic texts, Cynic philosophers, and sayings of the Buddha and Lao Tzu. We should not be surprised. Jesus did not claim to possess a monopoly on the truth. Later Church patriarchs did make such claims, but not Jesus.

Ideas moved freely between the Mediterranean and the Indus Valley, yet even without direct influence, Jesus may have arrived at insights similar to those of the Buddha and Lao Tzu and used similar language to explain them. Gautama Buddha lived in northern India five centuries before Jesus, and, unlike Jesus, he reportedly grew up in a wealthy royal family. Nevertheless, legends of his life closely parallel stories of Jesus. Angels announce his supernatural conception to a chaste mother, saying, "A mighty son will be born to you." Wise men attend his birth, a demon tempts him, poor sinners flock to hear his teachings, he feeds multitudes with a few small cakes, heals the sick, walks on water, and tells his disciples that their efforts could move mountains. Some of the parallels among their sayings appear uncanny:

Your Father in heaven...sends rain on both the just and the unjust. — Jesus (Matthew 5:45)

The great cloud rains down on all whether their nature is superior or inferior. — the Buddha (White Lotus Sutra [Saddharmapundarika] 5)

Be wary of phoney prophets who come in sheep's clothing; inside they are voracious wolves. — Jesus (Matthew 7:15; Mark 13:22)

Matted hair, family, or caste do not make a master...you sit on a deerskin. What folly! When inside you are ragged with lust. — the Buddha (Dhammapada 26)

What goes into your mouth won't defile you; what comes out of your mouth will. — Jesus (Thomas 14; Mark 7:15; Q; Matthew 15:11; Luke 10:8)

Theft, deception, adultery: this is defilement; not the eating
of meat. — Buddha Kassapa (Sutta Nipata 242)

Jesus warns his listeners, "Don't acquire possessions here on
earth, where moths and insects eat away and where thieves break
in and steal it," and he encourages them to store up their treasures
in heaven through good action. Likewise, the Buddhist book of
short lessons, Khuddakapatha, explains:

> A person stashes a fund away, deep underground... but no
> matter how well it is stored... it won't always serve one's
> needs... water serpents make off with it, spirits steal it, or
> hateful heirs run off with it.... But when a person has laid
> aside a well-stored fund of generosity, virtue, restraint, and
> self control... that is a well-stored fund.

Similar to the small but influential kingdom described by Jesus,
the Buddha compares the accomplished master to "water on the leaf
of a lotus flower, or a mustard seed on the point of a needle." For
both Jesus and the Buddha, one should treat sacredness as something modest, not to be put on display like a great achievement.

Lao Tzu, a mysterious, legendary sage of ancient China who
may have lived about the same time as the Buddha, calls the divine
kingdom "the Tao," meaning "the Way." In his only collection of
proverbs, the *Tao Te Ching*, he says, "The Tao flows everywhere....
It has no aim; it is very small.... It does not show greatness, and is
therefore truly great." Like Jesus, Lao Tzu compares the disciple
who realizes the Tao, or the divine kingdom, to a child. "Can you be
as a newborn babe?" he asks. "Ever true and unswerving, become
as a little child once more." The great Tao that flows everywhere
"fulfills its purpose silently and makes no claim." These three great

sages — Lao Tzu, Gautama Buddha, and Yeshua — the most influential teachers of the ancient world, are still admired by millions of people today. All three discovered that the true spiritual life is a modest thing, not the realm of braggarts who dress the part and presume to speak on behalf of God.

> Those who exalt themselves will be humbled, those who humble themselves will be exalted. — Jesus (Matthew 23:12)

> The sage stays behind, therefore he is ahead. — Lao Tzu (*Tao Te Ching* 7)

They teach love, even toward one's enemies.

> "Love your enemies, help those who hate you." — Jesus (Luke 6:27; Matthew 5:44)

> "Live in joy, and in love, even among those who hate." — the Buddha (Dhammapada 15)

> I am good to those who are good, and also I am good to those who are not good. — Lao Tzu (*Tao Te Ching* 49)

Jesus, the Buddha, and Lao Tzu taught that spiritual understanding manifests as action in the world. They encouraged kindness, compassion, and generosity.

> Give to everyone who asks. — Jesus (Luke 6:27)

> Generosity overcomes meanness... Give whatever you can. — the Buddha (Dhammapada 17)

The more one gives to others, the greater one's abundance.—
Lao Tzu (*Tao Te Ching* 81)

Understandably, some observers have suggested that Buddhist
or Taoist ideas influenced Jesus, and that may be so, but perhaps, as
David Steindl-Rast suggested, these three streams of wisdom simply flowed down from the same heights and were glimpsed through
personal effort, insight, and awareness. No one owns these ideas.
Neither the Buddha nor Lao Tzu nor Jesus claimed to own them.
Nor did they profess to have originated them. Generosity represents common sense available to anyone. Neighbourly love and
self-reflection represent perennial wisdom. Ideas such as these
moved freely through first-century culture, just as they move
freely through twenty-first-century culture.

Jesus, then, appears to be exactly what he claimed to be: a son
of Adam, a human, who wandered the countryside without even a
place to rest his head. He did not exalt himself, not even above the
animals. He did not claim to speak on behalf of God or represent
the only source of divine wisdom. He rarely spoke of God, whom
he called "Abba," father, or spoke of the Canaanite El or Elohim.
He told his disciples not to worry about God but to care for their
neighbours. And he did not claim to possess a monopoly on the
truth. We are about to see, however, that others would make such
claims in his name. Once Rome had defeated Jerusalem and controlled Palestine, written narrative gospels about Jesus appeared
around the Mediterranean, with new interpretations regarding
his message. Here, we turn to our final questions: How did the
message of Jesus get confused or misrepresented? And what relevance does his real message offer us in the twenty-first century?

·9·

BATTLE FOR THE LEGACY

As the brethren desired me to write epistles, I wrote. But apostles óf the devil have filled these epistles with tares, cutting out some things and adding others.... No wonder, then, if some have dared to change even the word of the Lord.

BISHOP DIONYSIUS OF CORINTH, C. 170 C.E.

We cannot overestimate the horror wrought by Rome's obliteration of Jerusalem in 70 C.E., its impact upon world history, and how this devastation changed the way people remembered and applied the teachings of Jesus. The Roman army under Titus crushed every fortified Jewish town in its path. Soldiers dashed children on stones and hoisted them on spear points. They raped women and hanged them to die with their husbands and fathers. Surviving peasants fled into the remote hills.

According to Josephus, Galilee and Judea had seethed with rebellion, reprisals, tyranny, and betrayal throughout the life of Jesus and during the four decades thereafter. The Roman army remained strong but not invincible. Germanic tribes had stopped Roman advances at the Danube and the Rhine, the Picts held their line at the Firth of Clyde, and Jewish leaders dreamed of booting the Romans, and their collaborators, from Palestine.

Jesus had grown up in this environment of resistance and rebellion. When Herod died in 4 B.C.E., his son Archelaus slaughtered thousands of Judean rebels who had swarmed the Temple compound in anticipation of a revolt. Elite Pharisees and Sadducees abandoned the rebels and curried royal favour. The purist Essenes, opposed to both the rebels and the collaborators, fled to the wilderness. In the north, during the time of Jesus' youth, Judas the Galilean launched a "fourth philosophy," preaching liberty through insurrection.

By 66 C.E., Judas's grandson Menahem had assembled a gang of rebels, taken the southern stronghold of Masada, pilfered Herod Agrippa's armoury, and returned to Jerusalem with a Jewish brigade, intent on repelling the Romans. The high priest, Eleazar, offered tacit support by allowing the Jewish clergy to cancel sacrifices to the Romans. However, Eleazar, loyal to his Roman patrons, lost his nerve and had Menahem executed. The fight was on. By Passover in the year 70, the Roman army had surrounded Jerusalem. They cut off food supplies, felled trees for timber, built battering rams and siege towers, and began the methodical destruction of the city's massive walls.

THE SCATTERED ISRAELITES

Inside the besieged city, Passover pilgrims and other innocents huddled in makeshift tents, appealing to their god to intervene or send the promised king. Hundred-pound stones from ballistas rained down, smashing tents, rock walls, and roofs. For three months, the people, some driven to cannibalism and madness, slowly starved. Jewish soldiers and bands of renegades raided homes for food. Bodies littered the streets. Outside the walls, Roman soldiers whipped and crucified captured defenders. Josephus, now among the Romans, pleaded with the Judeans to surrender, and reportedly received a recycled ballista stone to the head for his trouble. Once inside, the Roman army slew all Jewish soldiers, infants, the aged, and infirm citizens. More than half a million were slaughtered. They sold able-bodied survivors as slaves to work in Egyptian mines, Roman brothels, and provincial theatres, where they would perish "by the sword and wild beast."

The nineteenth-century British Baptist C. H. Spurgeon described the destruction of Jerusalem as "more terrible than anything that the world has ever witnessed, either before or since." Spurgeon overlooked the European empires' decimation of indigenous populations in Africa and America, and had not witnessed the horrors of two world wars, but he is correct that the siege of Jerusalem ranks among humanity's darkest episodes. For added insult, Roman soldiers desecrated the Temple with idols. Vespasian built massive victory arches in Italy and struck coins inscribed with the words *Iudaea capta*, "Judea captured." The Romans banned Jews from the region, built a temple to Jupiter on the site, and renamed the city Aelia Capitolina, after Emperor Hadrian's family.

The annihilation of Jewish Jerusalem changed the ethos of the entire Mediterranean world. Jewish culture almost perished. Northern Israelites faded back into familiar agrarian ways with their Phoenician and Canaanite neighbours. The "little clans" kept their heads low and survived. Josephus reports that a few of the "nobility," like him, "went over to the Romans" and saved their lives. Jewish scholar Johanan ben Zakkai survived and opened an academy at Jabneh on the coast, south of modern Tel Aviv, where rabbis began to compile the Talmud commentaries on Jewish law and history. We have seen that these commentaries contain nothing about a Galilean sage Jesus.

The only possible secular record of Jesus is found in the Josephus reference discussed in chapter 1, which many historians consider a later forgery, identifying Iēsous as a wise man who performed amazing deeds, and whose brother James was executed. Pliny,

242 THE JESUS SAYINGS

writing in 112, identifies a messianic group of "Christians" who led ethical lives and included women deacons in their growing movement. About the same time, Tacitus identifies a group who follow "Christus," a person executed in Judea by Pontius Pilate. Nothing here tells us what people believed this person did or said.

A few Jewish stragglers in the hills clung to a faint hope of a kingdom led by the promised messiah. Some believed that Jesus — Yeshua the Nazorean, executed by Pilate — would return as this king. Others remembered Jesus as a wise and courageous hero. Groups such as the Ebionites appear to have followed Jesus' simple instructions, avoiding religious pretensions, sharing food, helping their neighbours, and seeking wisdom. These peasant followers experienced Jesus' presence by living simply and righteously. They accepted anyone, men, women, Samaritans, sinners, tax collectors, and nomads. Like the Essenes, they rejected violence, even toward their enemies.

Similar communities of Jesus followers flourished in Galilean villages, in Alexandria, along the Nile, in Pella east of the Jordan, in Antioch, Damascus, and Edessa, at the headwaters of the Euphrates River. Their records suggest that these communities preserved oral teachings of Jesus and eventually produced written inventories of his sayings, including the *Thomas* and Q collections.

Several generations of Jesus followers had come and gone by the time the earliest gospels appear in the record, so we cannot easily know how faithfully the tellers preserved the narrative events. We know from Paul's letters that widespread conflict had erupted regarding interpretations of sayings, women's role, money, and authority. Paul's and other records show that the disputes included the nature of God, the divinity of Jesus, and the Resurrection.

Jesus appears to have foreseen how power could corrupt the best of human nature, and he warned his followers against rules, doctrines, and spiritual pride. Even so, within a few decades after his death, Jesus' legacy had been, in Paul's words, "divided." After the fall of Jerusalem, throughout the second and third centuries, new writers claimed authority over the interpretation of Jesus' message. These "Church fathers," as they were later called — Clement, Ignatius, Polycarp, Irenaeus, Papias — remain extremely obscure. Some certainly are fictitious, and most are attested only by the later, fourth-century imperial court scholar Eusebius. To understand what Jesus said, we must also know what he did not say. We will follow the evolution of his message as interpreted by writers who attach their own philosophies and political interests to Jesus. The bickering and posturing soon intensified into full-scale denunciations and purges.

THE PHOENIX

A dispute in Corinth prompted a letter from the Church in Rome, attributed to a presumed Roman bishop, Clement, in the year 96 C.E., although no evidence confirms that Clement actually existed. The earliest reference to Clement is a fifth-century romance novel about "Clemens," a cousin of Emperor Domitian, later identified as a pope, a role that did not yet exist in the first century. Alfred Loisy, a French Catholic priest and historian, proposed in the nineteenth century that a Roman elder likely wrote the "Clement" letter in about 135 C.E. The author reveals that the dispute in Corinth involved money or compensation. Presbyters, or elders, who once appeared "satisfied with the provisions of Christ" now demanded more. The letter also reveals a deeper conflict over authority to speak for Jesus.

The Roman author quotes Jesus, saying, "Show mercy, that you may be shown mercy...as you give, so you shall receive; as you judge, so you shall be judged." This passage echoes the Sermon on the Mount. The variation of language indicates that these stories had been transmitted orally and emerged in later written documents. The letter encourages humility in Jesus' name. "For it is to the humble-minded that Christ belongs," the author writes, "not to those who exalt themselves above His flock." Jesus, the letter recalls, did not arrive "clothed in boastful pomp and overweening pride, but in a humble frame of mind."

This much echoes the humility of Jesus, but the author then abruptly shifts tone by defining humility as submission: "You, therefore, the prime movers of the schism, submit to the presbyters, and, bending the knees of your hearts, accept correction and change your minds. Learn submissiveness, and rid yourselves of your boastful and proud incorrigibility of tongue." The Roman author insists on obedience and then proffers a thinly veiled threat: "But should any disobey what has been said by Him through us, let them understand that they will entangle themselves in transgression and no small danger." The parties are joined in a battle for power. The phrase "through us" reveals that the patriarchs in Rome were claiming authority over the teachings of Jesus.

The letter also reveals a disagreement about the presumed return or presence of Jesus, warning doubters: "Wretched are they who are of a double mind, and of a doubting heart; who say, 'These things we have heard even in the times of our fathers; but, behold, we have grown old, and none of them has happened to us.' You foolish ones!" Here we witness the community of Jesus followers several generations after his death, waiting for the return, which *Mark* had promised "in this generation." Apparently, certain followers had grown impatient and doubted the promise. The letter attempts to convince them otherwise. "Let us consider, beloved, how the Lord continually proves to us that there shall be a future resurrection." The author then alludes to a bird that allegedly lived in Arabia:

There is a certain bird, which is called a phoenix. This is the only one of its kind, and it lives five hundred years....it builds itself a nest of frankincense, myrrh, and other spices,

into which, when the time is fulfilled, it enters and dies.
But as the flesh decays a certain kind of worm is produced,
which, being nourished by the juices of the dead bird, brings
forth feathers. Then, when it has acquired strength, it takes
up that nest in which are the bones of its parent, and bearing these it passes from the land of Arabia into Egypt.... The
priests inspect the register of dates and find that it has
returned exactly as the five hundredth year was completed....
Do we then deem it any great and wonderful thing for the
Maker of all things to raise up again those who have piously
served Him in the assurance of a good faith, when even by
a bird He shows us the mightiness of His power to fulfill
His promise?

With this charming tale, the author of the Clement letter, on
behalf of the Church in Rome, claims to prove the physical resurrection. For those who still doubt, he demands faith.

We are not justified by ourselves, nor by our own wisdom,
or understanding, or godliness, or works which we have
wrought in holiness of heart; but by that faith through which,
from the beginning, Almighty God has justified all men.

Here we meet Paul's doctrine of faith, raised to God's ultimate
criterion of judgement and opposed to the idea of expressing spiritual understanding through good deeds, as Jesus had taught.
Clearly, the Roman elders stood in opposition to Jesus followers
who valued compassionate acts over doctrinal faith, and experienced Jesus' presence through those actions. This letter includes
no references to the Gospels, but a subsequent letter attributed to
Clement, likely written between 140 and 160 C.E., paraphrases the
Gospel of Thomas as it takes up the debate about a resurrection:

...we know not the day of the appearing of God. For the Lord Himself, being asked by one when His kingdom would come, replied, "When two shall be one, that which is without as that which is within, and the male with the female, neither male nor female."

This passage paraphrases *Thomas* 22, but with a slight twist. In *Thomas*, Jesus tells his disciples they enter the kingdom "when *you* make the two into one." The Roman Church letter, however, rejects the idea that a disciple is the active agent, presuming that the faithful's only responsibility is to wait and keep the faith. God makes the two into one. Jesus, however, clearly urged his followers to dispel duality through personal experience and to exercise compassion as the means to enter the kingdom.

The second century represents a netherworld between the lifetime of Jesus and the earliest extant gospel manuscripts. The beliefs of Jesus followers at this time remain diverse and the historical figures obscure. By the mid-second century, at least in some circles, Jesus' personal humility had been transformed into institutional obedience, and his consignment of personal responsibility had become faithfully waiting for God to return with the promised kingdom. These changes represent a monumental shift in emphasis.

CHAINED TO LEOPARDS

Roman Church legend records that there lived, during the second century, a patriarch in Syria named Ignatius. According to Eusebius in the fourth century, Ignatius became Bishop of Antioch, following Evodius. A tenth-century manuscript, the *Martyrium Ignatii*, claims that Roman Emperor Trajan visited Ignatius in Antioch, had him arrested for his teachings, and sent him to Rome for execution by wild beasts. Allegedly, along the way, Ignatius wrote seven letters to seven Christian churches in Asia Minor and Rome.

These letters, even if they do not reflect authentic history, tell us a great deal about the development of Christian theology and what became of Jesus' teachings.

According to the *Martyrium*, Emperor Trajan wanted to make an example of Ignatius, to discourage Christians from spreading their ideas. The persecution, however, backfires, as Christians along the route flock to Ignatius, inspired by his courage and faith. The Ignatius letter to the Romans describes the conditions of his journey:

> From Syria even to Rome I fight with wild beasts, by land and sea, by night and by day, being bound amidst ten leopards, with a company of soldiers, who only grow worse when they are kindly treated.

One may find it difficult to imagine how Ignatius, chained to leopards, managed to draft seven letters filled with scores of scriptural references, how he obtained ink and papyrus, or why Roman soldiers would allow a condemned traitor to deliver subversive doctrinal letters to his supporters. It appears unlikely that Emperor Trajan would trouble himself to visit an obscure sect leader in a distant province, or, if he considered him a threat, why he would not execute him on the spot. The convoy's public assemblies along the way appear to undermine Trajan's reported intentions to suppress Christian teachings. No Roman sources confirm Trajan's visit with Ignatius, the journey, or the execution in Rome. The letters, variously dated by scholars between 135 and 165 C.E., well after the reign of Trajan, suggest several authors, redactions, and inconsistencies concerning Ignatius.

The letters cannot be taken as history. According to William Schoedel, professor emeritus of classics at the University of Illinois, "the letters of Ignatius themselves represent a confusing tangle of textual and literary problems." The historical usefulness of these letters arises from their revelations regarding second-century Church doctrine.

The Ignatius letters occasionally reflect Jesus sayings. To the Ephesians, the author writes, "The tree is known by its fruit." A later Ignatius letter advises, "In all circumstances be wise as a serpent, and perpetually harmless as a dove." We recognize these passages as authentic Jesus principles from *Thomas* and Q. The author possibly had access to early versions of these sayings collections, or he may have drawn these ideas from the oral tradition. Nevertheless, the Ignatius letters were written to establish doctrine, and they make a specific point of attacking two competing groups of Jesus followers: Jews and the so-called Docetists.

Regarding the Jews, the letters advise, "Be not seduced by strange doctrines nor by antiquated fables.... It is monstrous to talk of Jesus Christ and to practise Judaism." The author criticizes Docetists, who believed Jesus was a god, not human, and that his resurrected apparition only appeared human. To counter this idea, the Ignatius letters maintain that Jesus was indeed human, as well as a god, that he ate, drank, suffered, and died, and furthermore that his resurrection was physical, not a "vision" or spiritual "presence."

A letter addressed to the congregation at Smyrna, on the Aegean coast of Asia Minor, provides the first known use of the Greek word *katholikos*, the modern "catholic," meaning "universal," to describe the network of churches centred in Rome. As with the Clement letters, the Ignatius letters demand obedience to this church:

> Wherever the bishop appears, there let the people be; as wherever Jesus Christ is, there is the universal Church. It is not lawful to baptize or give communion without the consent of the bishop. On the other hand, whatever has his approval is pleasing to God.

Thus, in no uncertain terms, the author of this letter claims for the Christian hierarchy in Rome absolute authority over the legacy of Jesus. Furthermore, the author equates the bishop's ruling on any matter with the wishes of God. Just as the priests of Akhenaten or Cyrus enjoyed a monopoly over religion, a handful of patriarchs in Rome had presumed to speak on behalf of a one-and-only God and in the name of Jesus.

Ignatius's alleged home of Antioch had served as the original hub of Paul's Gentile mission, and the Ignatius letters quote and paraphrase passages from Paul: "Out of love, be patient," a letter advises the Ephesians; "by their injustices I am becoming a better disciple," he explains to the Romans; and "In the face of their error, be steadfast in the faith," he instructs the Colossians. These passages rely directly on Paul, although the letters do not cite sources. According to the Ignatius letters, while his Roman convoy lingered in Smyrna, Ignatius met a local church elder, Polycarp, another mysterious letter writer and admirer of Paul.

KNOWING JOHN

We possess no independent secular references to confirm the existence of Polycarp, but later Church commentators, including Eusebius, recount his extraordinary deeds, and attribute to him a single letter to the church in Philippi, north of Smyrna. The Polycarp letter paraphrases gospel stories about Jesus, but primarily draws inspiration from the epistles of Paul, who, the author claims, "accurately and steadfastly taught the word of truth." The author borrows passages both from authentic Paul letters and from later imitations attributed to Paul, including the two letters to Timothy and the Hebrews from the New Testament, suggesting a formidable Paulist tradition around the Aegean during the second century.

The Polycarp letter adjudicates a conflict in Philippi concerning certain elders, Valens and his wife, accused of "covetousness."

The letter implores the congregation to be "moderate in regard to this matter," invoking Paul's teaching that "the saints shall judge the world." Valens and his wife should be welcomed back as "suffering and straying members." However, Polycarp reserves this compassion for material, not philosophical, crimes. "For whosoever," the author insists, "says that there is neither a resurrection nor a judgement, he is the first-born of Satan." Several second-century doctrines merge here: the physical return of a universal messiah, a final judgement by a universal God, absolute Church authority, and opposition to that authority equated to incarnate evil, the creature "Satan." None of these ideas can be traced to Jesus.

The ultimate purpose of the Polycarp letter is to establish Roman Church authority, specifically by claiming that Polycarp knew John Zebedee, an apostle of Jesus. The lone witness for this claim is our familiar fourth-century imperial historian Eusebius, quoting an alleged lost letter from one Irenaeus, Bishop of Lyon. Eusebius records that Irenaeus met Polycarp as "a boy" and was "able to describe the very place in which the blessed Polycarp sat...and the accounts which he gave of his intercourse with John and with others who had seen the Lord." This tenuous claim — made 200 years after the alleged events — links the Roman patriarchs to Jesus. No other evidence corroborates that a real Polycarp ever met a real John Zebedee, and problems persist with this hypothesis.

Eusebius's general credibility and the unsubstantiated reference to a vanished letter present the first problem. Secondly, Ignatius, bound to leopards, allegedly met Polycarp but does not mention that Polycarp knew John. Finally, Polycarp himself, in his alleged letter to the Philippians, fails to mention meeting John Zebedee. Since the Polycarp letter goes to some length to establish his authority, failing to mention his audience with a real apostle is inexplicable. Rather, Polycarp's letter glorifies Paul, who never met

Jesus. Polycarp, then, by his own record, gained his inspiration from Paul, not from the Galileans John and Jesus.

The fourth-century Apostolic Constitutions provide a list of bishops supposedly ordained during the lifetime of the apostles, but make no mention of either John or Polycarp in Smyrna. The fragmentary *Life of Polycarp*, also from the fourth century, mentions Polycarp but does not mention John, a significant exclusion if John Zebedee had actually ordained Polycarp as Bishop of Smyrna.

Perhaps to cement this fragile link to Jesus through the apostle John, Eusebius also cites Irenaeus concerning another obscure second-century church elder, Papias, who allegedly was a "hearer of John, and a companion of Polycarp." Eusebius credits Irenaeus with citing five books by Papias, of which we possess only scarce fragments that appeared after 325 C.E. Eusebius quotes from Papias's *Interpretation of the Oracles of the Lord*, for which we have no other record, claiming that Papias wrote:

> If, then, any one came, who had been a follower of the elders, I questioned him in regard to the words of the elders, what Andrew or what Peter said, or what was said by Philip, or by Thomas, or by James, or by John, or by Matthew, or by any other of the disciples of the Lord.

Papias, if a real person, does not claim to have known an apostle John, but only "followers of the elders," who told him about John. You may recall that this same Papias, according to Eusebius, first identified the gospel authors Matthew and Mark. Our only source for these claims remains Eusebius in the fourth century. Even if Papias and his "oracles" could be proven authentic, the information remains second-hand, since he takes the word of "any one" who came by claiming to have known the elders. The chain of evidence then runs from "elders" to their "followers," to "Papias," who was identified by Eusebius only two centuries later.

Irenaeus, cited by Eusebius and likely a real second-century elder in Lyon, tried hard to establish the legitimacy and primacy of the "universal church" in Rome. In *Against Heresies*, Irenaeus insists, "We must obey the priests of the Church who have succession from the Apostles," while denouncing those with "perverse opinion" who "assemble in unauthorized meetings."

Irenaeus also makes the claim that this Roman church was founded by both Peter and Paul in Rome. On the contrary, we know that Paul did not originate the church in Rome, because he wrote a letter to the Roman congregation confirming that he had not yet been there. Acts of the Apostles places Paul in Rome near the end of his life, but the account remains uncorroborated and embroidered with fanciful legends. It does not suggest Paul founded a church there, and does not mention Peter being with him. The legend that Peter visited Rome appears in Acts of Peter, composed in about 185 C.E., concurrent with Irenaeus. Eusebius embellishes this report two centuries later by adding that both Peter and Paul were executed in Rome during Nero's persecutions, but he cites no source and gives an erroneous date, casting doubt on his research. No viable evidence suggests that either Paul or Peter founded a church in Rome, and it remains unlikely that the Galilean fisherman Peter ever went there.

To understand how the message of Jesus became interpreted or misinterpreted, we rely almost entirely upon internal Church documents, which often appear obscure and inconsistent. To know what Jesus actually said, we refer to collections of sayings, letters, gospels, and decrees written between the mid-first and late second centuries. To determine the credibility of events and authors in the second century, we rely on accounts composed in the third and fourth centuries, generally by writers defending the Roman *katholikos* branch of the Jesus tradition. The three centuries between the death of Jesus and the claims of Eusebius represent some fifteen or twenty generations of Jesus followers.

The link from these later legends to a living Jesus and his authentic teachings remains ambiguous. Paul, who tells us the least about the historical Jesus, achieves the greatest influence. The *Thomas* Gospel, on the other hand, which provides the most extensive range of Jesus teachings, appears lost in many accounts, and is denounced in some. Mary, one of Jesus' closest allies and devotees, who perhaps understood some teachings better than anyone, disappears both in Paul and in the letters of the Church fathers.

Perhaps, in effect, we have little actual history of second-century Jesus followers to rely on. If Polycarp and Papias were real people, they, and their link to Jesus, remain obscure. Clearly, however, by the mid-second century, some who spoke on behalf of Jesus jealously guarded their authority to do so. These claims of authority reach their climax in the dramatic tale of Polycarp's demise.

THE WITNESS OF PIONIUS

A century after Polycarp supposedly lived, one Pionius, perhaps in Smyrna, reported a vision during which Polycarp's spirit led him to a written account of Polycarp's execution by an irate mob. Pionius claims that he found the hidden manuscript "almost worn out from age" and made a copy. The document, *The Martyrdom of Polycarp*, survives in five medieval Greek manuscripts dated between 900 and 1300. Eusebius quotes the document, placing its composition in or before the fourth century. As we might expect, the document is not considered historical.

The Martyrdom of Polycarp, however, plays a vital role in the dispute over the legacy of Jesus and the search for his authentic teachings. Purportedly written in the second century, when a variety of Jesus sects flourished, the document attempts to establish the "apostolic succession" promoted by Irenaeus and Eusebius. The

alleged author, Pionius, claims that the document had been produced by a scribe in Corinth, one Socrates, who had copied it from
another scribe, Gauis, who had copied it "from the papers of Irenaeus." Pionius does not claim that Irenaeus wrote the original
account, and a variant version places Irenaeus in Rome at the time of
Polycarp's death. The original witness and author remain unnamed.

. In the narrative, Roman authorities arrest the 100-year-old
Polycarp in Smyrna and haul him into the theatre for execution. At
this time, the Romans used the term "atheist" to describe Christians, Jews, or anyone who refused to honour Roman deities. A
local proconsul implores Polycarp to renounce his beliefs:

> "Swear by the genius of Caesar; repent and say, 'Away with
> the atheists.'" Then Polycarp with solemn countenance
> looked upon the whole multitude of lawless heathen in the
> stadium, and waved his hand to them; groaning and look-
> ing up to heaven he said, "Away with the atheists."

Here, Polycarp outwits the proconsul. Without flinching, he
turns the slur "atheist" back onto the bloodthirsty mob. The crowd,
enraged by Polycarp's insult, builds a wooden pyre to burn him,
assisted by "extremely zealous Jews." The authorities then bind
Polycarp, place him on the pyre, and ignite the wood. The flames,
however, form a great sail on either side of the victim, and he glis-
tens within, "as gold and silver glowing in a furnace." The image
recalls Daniel glowing in the furnace before Babylonian King
Nebuchadnezzar. The startled executioners lose patience and stab
the flame-resistant Polycarp with a dagger. The elder perishes, but
a dove flies from his wound and his blood extinguishes the flames.

We know from Pliny's letter to Emperor Trajan that Christian
groups suffered persecution under the Romans in the second century, so this story may reflect actual events, even if embellished

with miracles and lost manuscripts. The Pionius account matches
Ignatius in naming "Jews" as enemies of the Christian faithful, a
theme that will grow familiar and more violent over time. In the
second century, this indictment confirms a clear break with the
Jewish branches of the Jesus movement, from Syria to Egypt.
Indicting Jews as enemies and refuting opposing views form the
thrust of this document. Pionius affirms authority to speak on
behalf of Jesus, an authority allegedly "received from the saint,"
that is, from Polycarp's John.

The document survives in two variations. The first and earlier
version appears in four Greek manuscripts from the tenth and elev-
enth centuries. A thirteenth-century manuscript, held in the Library
of the Holy Synod in Moscow, includes additions by a later Church
authority. In the first version, the author implores Jesus to "gather
me also with His elect into His heavenly kingdom; to Whom be the
glory with the Father and the Holy Spirit for ever and ever. Amen."

The second version adds "the Son," reading: "...to Whom be
the glory with the Father and the Son and the Holy Spirit for ever
and ever. Amen." These original stories emerged precisely as communities of followers debated doctrines about the divinity of Jesus
and his relation to God. Here, we see the Son added to the Father
and the Spirit, perhaps to place the trinity doctrine into the earlier
story. More importantly, whereas the first version reads, "Gaius
copied this account from the papers of Irenaeus, a disciple of Polycarp," the second version reads:

> Gaius copied this account from the papers of Irenaeus. The
> same lived with Irenaeus who had been a disciple of the
> holy Polycarp. For this Irenaeus...instructed many; and
> many most excellent and orthodox treatises by him are in
> circulation. In these he makes mention of Polycarp, saying
> that he was taught by him. And he ably refuted every heresy,

and handed down the catholic rule of the Church just as he had received it from the saint.

The all-important line — "And he ably refuted every heresy, and handed down the catholic rule of the Church just as he had received it from the saint" — documents three critical points that justify the single, apostolic, universal, and allegedly infallible Church:

1. Polycarp received an endorsement from an apostle of Jesus, namely John.
2. Irenaeus studied with Polycarp and successfully refuted every opposing point of view.
3. Thus, Polycarp and Irenaeus confer sacred authority over Jesus to the Roman bishops.

Signed, sealed, and delivered, this document provided the fourth-century Roman Church with a paper trail to back up their claim that they represented Jesus. As such, this witness of Pionius signals an earth-shaking moment in human history. We might feel somewhat cheated that we cannot identify the original author, who allegedly witnessed Polycarp's execution, or that we have no information about the person of Pionius, when or where he lived, his profession, his associates, or where he "discovered" the lost document supposedly revealed to him by the spirit voice of Polycarp. We may wonder because a tremendous amount of later history rests on these claims.

The alleged Polycarp letter does not reveal what teachings of Jesus the travelling elders conveyed to him, so we cannot know how accurate they were, or how they differed from the teachings revealed by *Thomas, Mary, Philip, Mark, Matthew,* or *Luke.* We don't know because he doesn't tell us. Even if Polycarp's letter proved authentic, one might wonder: What distinguishes this alleged lineage, beginning with John Zebedee, taught second-hand to Polycarp, passed on to Irenaeus, and witnessed by Pionius?

And finally, we might wonder: What happened to the lineages of Thomas, Philip, and Mary Magdalene? What other traditions existed in the second century that might cast light upon the teachings of Jesus?

THE POOR ONES

Even in the fourth century, various Jesus sects survived and threatened the Church of Rome's supremacy. To help eradicate these sects, Roman bishops entrusted the prominent Cyprian scholar Epiphanius to once again refute all opposing views. In his report, *Panarion*, Epiphanius denounces eighty "heresies," a term derived from the Greek *haireomai*, "to choose," meaning a choice, or faction. Over time, the term "heresy" became an epithet for wrong choices or unauthorized beliefs. Among these eighty factions, Epiphanius provides the best available evidence regarding the Jewish Ebionites, who claimed to represent the "original apostles."

As we have seen, after the death of John the Baptist, some of John's followers adopted Jesus as their leader. After Jesus' death, his brother James led the group, and when James was executed, another brother of Jesus, Simon, appears to have taken a leadership role. This Jewish group survived the Roman bloodbath in the year 70 and expanded north from Jerusalem into Galilee, Syria, and beyond, to the headwaters of the Euphrates River, ancestral home of the Aramaic Jewish sects who called God "El." They claimed an unbroken lineage from the apostles of Jesus, especially Peter and James, and called themselves *ebionim*, the poor ones.

The Ebionites may have been associated with Galilean Nazoreans, and may indeed have evolved from the original Jewish apostles. They used an early version of the *Matthew* Gospel, without the birth and infancy stories. They had once believed that John the

Baptist was the rightful high priest and messiah of the Israelites but had shifted their hopes to Jesus after John's death. To the Ebionites, Jesus remained entirely human, the first son of Mary and Joseph. The Ebionite Gospel, like *Mark*, opens with John's baptism of Jesus and depicts a voice from the sky saying: "You are my favoured son. I fully approve of you.... Today I have become your father."

A favoured or chosen son is a specific role in Jewish tradition for a righteous person given special responsibility by God. We know from attacks by Epiphanius that the Ebionites rejected the idea of Jesus as a god. They did not believe in the virgin birth, the trinity, or the physical resurrection. They believed that Jesus modelled the ethical life of the new kingdom, and therefore assumed a special mission on behalf of God. In the Ebionite Gospel, Jesus says of this mission: "I came to do away with sacrifices."

This claim fits with Jesus' rejection of conventional rites and dietary laws. The Ebionites depict Jesus as a Jewish reformer who abolished the requirement for animal sacrifices through his own personal mission. Although they believed in a future age of social justice, they also believed that the social ethics of Jesus gave "the kingdom" a living existence in the here and now. After his death, the Ebionites preserved the "presence," or *parousia*, of Jesus through their own acts of sharing and compassion.

Recall that Paul's letters appear to have been written in the context of conflicts with opponents, and the Ebionites comprised at least one group that disavowed Paul's version of the Jesus message. In Paul's second letter to the congregation in Corinth, he defends himself against accusers and insists, "I am not in the least inferior to these special apostles." These opponents may be the Ebionites or similar Jewish disciples loyal to Jesus and his authentic teachings.

Paul, on the other hand, did not know Jesus, and clashed with almost everyone who did know Jesus. The mysterious Church fathers Clement and Polycarp, according to later documents, adopted Paul's theology: faith in Iēsous Christos, with the additional provision of absolute authority for the bishops in Rome. The Ebionites stood in direct opposition to this presumed authority.

In his *Ecclesiastical History*, court historian Eusebius criticizes the Ebionites for considering Jesus "a plain and common man... the fruit of the intercourse of a man with Mary," who was exalted "because of his superior virtue." He denounces the Ebionite belief that followers "could not be saved by faith in Christ alone," but rather by a "corresponding life," a life of good works such as Jesus modelled. Eusebius also faults the Ebionites for rejecting Paul, and blames an "evil demon" for tricking them with false doctrine. He polishes off his attack by mocking the Ebionite name, "the poor ones." Eusebius writes: "The ancients quite properly called these men Ebionites, because they held poor and mean opinions concerning Christ....Wherefore, in consequence of such a course they received the name of Ebionites, which signified the poverty of their understanding."

A generation later, the Roman Jerome took up the attack, calling the Ebionites "a most pestilent heresy." Jerome declares that Jews should not be allowed in the Church, and denounces their gatherings in "synagogues of Satan." Eusebius invents a spurious story about their name to discredit them, and both Eusebius and Jerome equate the Ebionites' worship to the work of a demon or to Satan. We might note that nowhere in these attacks do we hear anything remotely like a reasonable argument to show why the Ebionites' beliefs should be rejected.

In spite of Roman Church persecution, the Ebionites may have survived into the Middle Ages. Some evidence suggests Muslim historians knew of them in the tenth and twelfth centuries. Even today, certain Jewish followers of Jesus identify with the Ebionites, and claim to represent "the living continuation of the Jewish religious movement of Yeshua." The Yahad Ebyoni, founded in 1985, portray Paul as a "false teacher...outside of the Way taught by Yeshua...son of Maria and Yosef." They believe that following Jesus demands a life that they describe as "exhibiting good works."

The original Ebionites, however, are long gone, purged and forgotten for sixteen centuries. Scarce archaeological evidence only hints at their existence in Judea and Galilee. We know them through their critics. We know that Cynics and Platonic philosophers likely influenced Jesus, and that Gnostics, Docetists, Ebionites, and other factions flourished among the earliest followers of Jesus. Some accurately portrayed his teachings, and all groups probably embellished those teachings with their own beliefs. Among the eighty or more factions of followers accounted for by Epiphanius, some of the earliest, those claiming to be "original," described themselves as poor peasants who believed that salvation came not through Paul's faith, but rather by emulating the compassionate deeds of Jesus.

BY MY WORKS

The discovery of the complete *Gospel of Thomas* near the Egyptian village of Nag Hammadi included thirteen leather-bound, codex-style books written in Coptic, containing stories of Jesus, visions, cosmologies, and prayers. The manuscripts — available in English in *The Nag Hammadi Library* edition edited by James M. Robinson — include gospels attributed to Philip, Peter, and James, plus the poem "Thunder: Perfect Mind" and the *Pistis Sophia* ("Faith Wisdom"). The collection provides insight into the teachings of Jesus as understood by second- and third-century disciples of his message, among those who opposed Roman authority.

These texts, known as the Gnostic Gospels of Jesus, represent a variety of schools, and none refer to themselves as "Gnostic." Roman Church critic Irenaeus first used "Gnostic" to attack congregations that promoted direct knowledge of the divine. The term comes from the Greek *gnosis*, meaning "knowledge," both esoteric knowledge and direct self-knowledge gained from personal experience. Some sects that produced these manuscripts claimed to possess secrets revealed only to accomplished initiates. Others linked direct knowledge to the sort of self-awareness taught by Jesus, Socrates, and the Buddha: "Know yourself."

We learn from these writings that various factions of Jesus followers — from the Ebionites to the Roman bishops — busied themselves expounding complex cosmologies that they had inherited from more ancient philosophers, notably from Plato. The central idea borrowed from Plato portrays the physical world, known through the senses, as a corruption of divine perfection, which is known through deeper insight. Aristotle and others saw spirit in matter, knowable through observation and self-knowledge, but in Plato's world, the spirit remains forever locked in conflict with the degraded body. This "dualism" of Plato haunts humanity to this day.

Most Gnostic sects believed in Plato's separation between a deficient material world and a perfect heaven. However, they presumed a supreme essence beyond this dualism of light and dark or male and female. This essence was known variously as the *monad* ("the one"), *teleos* ("perfection"), or *bythos* ("the depth"). Emanations from this godhead supposedly descend to earth to either corrupt or help humanity. The three most revered of these divine intermediaries, called *aeons*, were Sophia, the feminine manifestation of divine wisdom; Seth, alleged to be the third son of Adam and Eve, chosen by God to receive secret teachings; and later, Jesus, or Yeshua, "the Saviour," also called the Logos, or "divine word."

Some sects considered the feminine emanation, Sophia, to be the cause of humanity's problems, because she descended from the perfect essence without a proper consort and fell victim to her desires: the primal uppity woman. Some sects considered Jesus the antidote to this problem, as he could serve as her consort and male balance. Again we find the patriarchy excluding and scorning feminine divinity, reflecting the status of women in a male-dominant society. Some Gnostic sects honoured women as equals, as did Jesus, and some honoured "Sophia and Yeshua," Wisdom and the Saviour, as a divine couple.

At least three Gnostic texts are attributed to Jesus' brother James, alleged leader of the Ebionites. Two distinct Apocalypse of James documents recount his life, suffering, death, and role in heaven. "Apocalypse" means a revelation of secret teachings, not the end of the world, as often assumed. In the first Apocalypse, James alludes to seven women disciples of Jesus, and names Mariam, Salome, Martha, and Arsinoe. James rebukes "the twelve" for their lack of complete knowledge, suggesting some conflict with competing apostolic stories.

The Apocryphon of James, or "secret writing of James," likely composed in the early second century, quotes Jesus. Like the Ebionites, the author and his congregation reject both Roman Christian authority and the physical resurrection. The author denies that Jesus' death represents atonement for sins, and believes rather that the kingdom of heaven exists within the person who gains knowledge. Jesus speaks to James and the disciples:

No one will ever enter the kingdom of heaven at my bidding, but only because you yourselves are full.... Unless you receive this through knowledge, you will not be able to find it.... know yourselves. For the kingdom of heaven is like an ear of grain after it had sprouted in a field. And when it had ripened, it scattered its fruit and again filled the field with ears of another year.

A letter attributed to James also appears in the New Testament, recounting conflicts between the rich and poor and defending a life of good work against the Paulist doctrine of faith:

> The religion that is pure and undefiled before God, the Father, is this: to care for orphans and widows in their distress, and to keep oneself unstained by the world.... Can faith save you? ... faith by itself, if it has no works, is dead.... I by my works will show you my faith.

The *James* letter was composed by an educated Greek writer after James's death and the destruction of Jerusalem. It is addressed to a Jewish audience, the "twelve tribes dispersed." The letter parallels Ebionite ethics and merges ideas from three traditions — Jewish, Gnostic, and Christian. Sects from all three traditions embraced James as an authority, often in opposition to Paul.

The conflict between Paul and "Jerusalem" — James, Peter, and others — comes to life in these documents, regardless of the historical genuineness of their claims. The adversaries in the battle for the legacy of Jesus routinely linked their ideas and authority to presumed apostles, as we witnessed with Polycarp. Those claiming authority commonly associated themselves with James or Peter, who emerge from the record as authentic people.

The messages in the *James* accounts about a kingdom of self-knowledge and good works agrees with *Thomas*, *Mary*, *Mark*, *Matthew*, and *Luke*. Although the cosmologies and theologies vary, the message remains consistent: Remove the timber from your own eye, see what is before your face, make the inside like the outside, and practise common decency. Many Jesus followers and communities around the Mediterranean believed that humility, self-knowledge, and compassion represented Jesus' message to those who seek the divine kingdom.

THE NAME OF A DEAD MAN

Two letters attributed to Peter appear in the New Testament, both written by a Greek scholar, not by a Galilean fisherman. The first, addressed to a persecuted audience in Asia Minor, affirms a mixed Gentile-Jewish, Gnostic-Christian community of Jesus followers. The letter promotes faith in Christianity against pagan doubters, but not against Jews. It quotes Jewish scripture, promises salvation, and warns that the flesh withers while "this word" endures. The second New Testament letter from "Peter," written by a Greek-speaking Christian probably in the second century, attacks "false teachers" and "destructive heresies," particularly those who deny the future return of Jesus. As we have seen, some Jesus followers, generations after the promised return, had grown discouraged and doubtful.

The Gnostic collection presents a different portrait of Peter. The Acts of Peter and the Twelve Apostles tells of a long journey by the disciples, during which they meet a mysterious "merchant" who turns out to be Jesus in disguise, and together they serve the poor, who flock to the disciples for comfort. The Apocalypse of Peter, probably from the third century, portrays Simon Peter as rightful heir to Jesus, defending this Gnostic faction's interpretation of Jesus against Church authorities "who name themselves bishop and also deacons, as if they have received their authority from God."

Here, we witness the full fury of the conflict among sects of Jesus followers. The Gnostics strike back against Roman Church patriarchs who claim primacy over the teachings of Jesus. The author, in defiance, quotes Jesus telling Peter that those who claim such authority are

Blind ones who have no guide.... They will cleave to the name of a dead man, thinking that they will become pure. But they will become greatly defiled and will fall into a kind of error, and into the hand of an evil, cunning man and a

manifold dogma...They do business in my word and they
will propagate a harsh fate. Those people are dry canals.

These tough words reflect ferocious competition for authority
over the legacy of Jesus. After the fall of Jerusalem, Jewish followers
faced a severe disadvantage, as their communities were scattered
and impoverished. Meanwhile, Gentile sects of Jesus followers
became progressively more powerful. Still, until the fourth century,
eighty or more factions could compete for the right to tell his story.

Throughout the second century around the Mediterranean,
these congregations flourished and clashed with each other. Certain
factions shared overlapping social allegiances: The poor Galilean
peasant Jews formed the original core, characterized by the Ebionites, Nazoreans, Peter, Thomas, Mary, and Jesus' brother James.
Greek-speaking Jewish followers, including Paul, promoted the
messianic tradition. A later Paulist movement of Greek-speaking
Gentiles became an anti-Jewish Christian movement. The Gentile
congregation in Rome eventually assumed authority over all other
Jesus followers.

During the second century, no "Christian canon" yet existed, so
the factions could freely express their views about the story, teachings, and implications of Jesus, provided they did not offend the
Roman emperor. In virtually every case, we hear authors expressing
personal views through the story of Jesus. Already by the second
century, any notion of an authentic Jesus had become almost hopelessly entangled in private predilections, philosophical theory, and
political machinations. However, pressure from Jewish Ebionites,
Gnostics, and other factions aroused the Church patriarchs in Rome
to commission an orthodox canon. The process of defining a sanctioned history and list of beliefs led to hybrid doctrines, a vanishing
Jesus, and more than a few exceptionally strange bedfellows.

· I O ·

THE EMPEROR'S SAVIOUR

> There are many true things that are not useful for the vulgar
> crowd to know; and certain things, which although they
> are false it is expedient for the people to believe otherwise.
>
> AUGUSTINE OF HIPPO, *CITY OF GOD,* 426 C.E.

The gospel wars among factions of Jesus followers led inexorably
to official canons of accepted books. The Alexandrian Jesus followers were prolific writers, and their treatises circulated throughout
the Mediterranean. Basilides from Alexandria wrote twenty-four
books about the legacy of Jesus, including *Exegetica,* a study of text
analysis regarding the gospel stories. His books were later burned,
so we know about him only through his Christian critics.

Basilides mixed his devotion to Jesus with Zoroastrian theology
and Greek philosophy. He describes an original state of nothing-
ness and defines God as "righteousness." He equates life's torments
to the effects of sin and fashions an early version of Original Sin to
explain why innocent people suffer. Babies suffer, he claims,
because they possess sinfulness, and have not sinned only because
they haven't had the chance. His conjectures notwithstanding,
Basilides makes a fair, economical summation of Jesus' teaching:
"Love all, desire nothing."

Meanwhile, Marcion, the shipowner from the Black Sea who researched the Galilean Jesus, travelled to Rome in 144 to defend his historical Jesus theories. He relied on an early version of the *Luke* Gospel that did not include the infancy stories, and dismissed the Acts of the Apostles as inaccurate. Before the assembled Roman elders, Marcion claimed that Jesus had rejected certain Old Testament laws and had accepted women as equal to men. He claimed that some apostles had misunderstood Jesus and mistakenly regarded him as a messiah.

The scandalized Roman elders rebuffed these ideas and expelled Marcion from the professed "universal" church. Thereafter, he established his own network of congregations throughout the Mediterranean, called himself a bishop, appointed women as priests and bishops, and posed a serious threat to the Church of Rome. The Roman bishops, however, responded with denunciations. In the *Martyrdom of Polycarp*, the author makes a point of denouncing Marcion, saying "...when Marcion...met the holy Polycarp on one occasion, and said 'Do you recognize me, Polycarp?' He said in reply to Marcion, 'Yes indeed, I recognize the firstborn of Satan.'"

The Devil, sex as sin, and the rights of women had become signposts that separated peasant congregations from those of elite patriarchies. Followers of Carpocrates in Alexandria — who, like the Ebionites, believed Jesus was a human, not a deity — also welcomed women into their ranks and claimed to possess secret teachings from Mary Magdalene, Salome, and Martha. The Montanists, a grassroots peasant faction in Asia Minor, followed their founder Montanus and two women, Priscilla and Maximilla, who professed to embody the Holy Spirit and reported visions of Jesus in a feminine form. They promoted a "back to Jesus" movement of direct personal experience with the divine and they spoke in ecstatic tongues, as do modern Pentecostals.

The second-century Egyptian Christian Valentinus adopted the popular belief that God possessed both male and female essence. The masculine aspect of God, which he called the "depth," gives the universe form. The feminine — called the "grace"— gives substance to the universe, and thus creates the lower deities and humans. Valentinus believed that humans could rise above their lower form and realize the divine through self-knowledge, or *gnosis*. A Valentinian blessing reflects the common Jesus axiom that the divine within grows like a mustard seed, albeit in the language of the Egyptian Gnostics: "May the Grace beyond time and space that was before the beginnings of the Universe fill our inner man and increase within us the semblance of itself as the grain of mustard seed."

This "Grace beyond time" represents the feminine qualities of spirit. Valentinus almost became Bishop of Rome, losing a narrow election, apparently to Anicetus, who condemned Gnostics and other "heresies." Anicetus, and popes thereafter, forbade women priests or bishops and insisted that male priests wear short hair, to distinguish them from certain long-haired Gnostics. According to Stephan Hoeller, at the College of Oriental Studies in California, Valentinus pioneered text analysis, understood the roles of both history and mythology, and respected personal spiritual insight. Hoeller believes his election as Pope "would have probably resulted in a general flowering of the Gnosis within the very fabric of the Church of Rome."

However, Valentinus lost, and the Gnostics, like the Ebionites and other rural peasant groups that valued personal insight, accepted women, or doubted the divinity of Jesus, became heretics in the eyes of the Roman patriarchs.

HIDDEN NAMES

Among the Gnostic texts found in Egypt, the *Gospel of Philip* reflects popular Valentinian ideas from the late second century, likely composed in the upper Euphrates hill country of northern Syria, the land of the Ebionites. This gospel contains the famous scene of Jesus kissing Mary Magdalene, associates Mary with divine wisdom, or Sophia, and portrays disciples wondering out loud, "Why do you love her more than all of us?"

Jesus' answer to this question corroborates his instruction that one enters the kingdom when "you make male and female into one." In *Philip*, Jesus encourages disciples to become "as you were before you came into being," before male or female existed, before "life and death." These are not trivial philosophies, but rather vital perceptions of how the universe operates, and therefore how people should act in ethical and spiritual circumstances. In the battle for the legacy of Jesus, a great deal of power hinged on the rights of women, the value of private insight, and personal access to the divine. In Rome, male priests and bishops rejected these ideas and claimed to regulate the doors of heaven. Among the *ebionim*, Gnostics, and Marcion's congregations, women and lowly peasants could appeal directly to God and experience both God's grace (feminine) and God's unspeakable depth (masculine).

Evil, the *Gospel of Philip* suggests, occurs when we separate male from female, yet "great is the mystery of marriage," which unifies the opposites. Humanity, the gospel says, "came into being from two virgins, the spirit, and the virgin earth." However, the gospel rejects the idea of a miraculous conception of Jesus. In addition to a "father in heaven," the gospel tells us, Jesus had "another father," on earth. Recall that *Thomas*, the Q sayings, *Mark*, *Paul*, the Ebionites' *Matthew*, and Marcion's version of *Luke* do not offer any nativity stories. Later gospel writers may have added the virgin conception, birth, and infancy of Jesus in the second century. We possess no clear evidence from the early first century describing Mary's pregnancy or Jesus' birth. On the other hand, popular accounts of virgin births, from the Persian god Mithras to the Greek Dionysus, were common.

We now see that from Sinope on the Black Sea, south along the headwaters of the Euphrates, into the Arabian wilderness, and across the Sinai into Egypt, remnants of peasant Semitic tribes retained a human view of Jesus. These northern Israelites and southern nomadic, tribes merged with Egyptian, Assyrian, and other peasants who believed in divine couples and Asherah's earthly bounty. The rural, oral communities tended to conceive of the universe in cyclical time. They rejected an end, but not a future. They saw life renewing itself in cycles, daily and annually. They considered Jesus a human, albeit an extraordinary human, whose compassion and wisdom brought him into alliance with the divine. The *Mary* Gospel describes Jesus' appearance to her as a "vision." The *Gospel of Philip* says:

> Those who say that the Lord died first and then rose up are in error, for he rose up first and then died. If one does not first attain the resurrection, he will not die.... the soul... is a precious thing and it came to be in a contemptible body.

In this version, Jesus resurrected himself from ignorance, not from literal death. The passage implies that the spirit must become manifest in a body before it can realize "resurrection." The idea is clever, Cynic-like, unifying two sides of a public argument over the source of evil, whether spiritual or material. Here, the spirit and the body work together to overcome evil. The spirit in *Philip* accepts its opposite, the material world, as its source, as Jesus suggested in *Thomas*: "if the spirit comes from the body." The spirit accepts the body, where it may attain this unity, the divine kingdom, through self-knowledge. This "gnosis" marks the end of death, because life and death become as one. The *Philip* Gospel states emphatically, "Knowledge is freedom."

You may recall that the *Philip* author knew Jesus as the Nazorean (or Nazarene), which did not imply someone from Nazareth, but rather "he who reveals what is hidden," a person "set apart" in knowledge. Since stories of Jesus' birth and infancy appear in the record about this same time, it is possible that this title became confused with a birthplace. We do not possess any certain evidence establishing the hometown of Jesus. He may have grown up in a village of Nazareth, but to the community of the *Philip* Gospel, "Nazorean" implied respect for one who had achieved spiritual knowledge.

In spite of persecutions and denunciations, congregations of Jesus followers from the upper Euphrates to the Nile River basin believed that Jesus was a human teacher who encouraged inner self-awareness. These communities did not believe that Jesus' death represented atonement for their own misdeeds. Quite the opposite. They believed their compassionate actions in the world evoked the presence of their teacher. However, self-knowledge and personal responsibility undercut political control. These freethinking congregations faced increased pressure from the Church in Rome as it forged an official set of beliefs that would put an end to philosophical inquiry regarding divine truths.

DEVILS AND VIRGINS

The presence of evil particularly troubled Gnostic and Roman Christians, and they took great pains to justify wickedness in a world created by God. Some blamed evil on the feminine deity Sophia. Others, in the tradition of Plato, blamed evil on physical bodies, on desire, and specifically on sexual desire. Some Christian writers associated evil with a devil, an idea introduced into late, post-exile Jewish tradition by Persian Zoroastrians. In the other, ancient Jewish tradition, Israelite peasants, and Jesus in particular, did not equate evil with a devil. In stories about the Good Samaritan, debtors, corrupt judges, and opportunistic priests, we understand that Jesus attributed evil to human ignorance and poor personal choices.

Greek Cynics and students of Socrates also identified evil with ignorance and poor life choices. Socrates had urged self-awareness and warned against seeking wealth. Diogenes the Cynic insisted, "There is only one evil, namely, ignorance." Likewise, in India, the Buddha had equated evil with the suffering caused by "desire, fear, and ignorance." Such ideas placed responsibility for good or evil on each person, as Jesus did when pointing to the fruits of one's actions.

The Roman Church, however, adopted the Persian idea of a devil, which appears regularly in the New Testament, including Jesus' meeting with Satan in the desert. The fourth-century Christian work the Gospel of Nicodemus describes an alleged descent by Jesus into hell after his crucifixion, during which he meets Satan. These ideas arrive in Christianity from Zoroastrian cosmology and Platonic duality, not from Jesus.

Second-century Church writers used the Devil not only to account for evil and sickness, but also to explain away embarrassing facts of history. For example, they blamed the Devil for slipping Paul's "Last Supper" story into earlier Persian mythologies. This rite with wine and bread, which appears long before Jesus in the historical record, proved an embarrassment for the Catholic Church. According to Justin Martyr in his First Apology,

> Jesus took bread, and when He had given thanks, said, "Do this in remembrance of Me, this is My body;" and...having taken the cup and given thanks, He said, "This is My blood;" and gave it to them alone. Which the wicked devils have imitated in the mysteries of Mithras, commanding the same thing to be done.

Throughout the second century, writers attach ideas such as the Devil or rites such as consuming an incarnate deity to the legend of

Jesus. Justin Martyr, in his *Apology*, often appeals to common folklore as proof of certain Church doctrines. Since the Church patriarchs believed that sexuality was evil, they also adopted the popular Persian and Greek doctrine of a virgin birth for their messiah. Justin justifies this by saying, "When we say also that the Logos, who is the first-born of God, was produced without sexual union...we propound nothing different from what you believe regarding those whom you esteem sons of Jupiter," referring to Mercury, Bacchus, Hercules, Pythagoras, and other famous "sons of god." In chapter 22 of his *Apology*, Justin tells his readers:

> Moreover, the Son of God called Jesus, even if only a man by ordinary generation, yet, on account of His wisdom, is worthy to be called the Son of God...if we affirm that He was born of a virgin, accept this in common with what you accept of Perseus. And when we say that He made whole the lame...we say what seems very similar to the deeds attributed to Aesculapius.

At this stage in the second century, claiming Jesus as a son of God born of a virgin appears no more extraordinary to Justin than the claims of Persian Zoroastrians or Roman worshippers of Jupiter. He is saying, "You have your sons of god, we have ours." The idea of Jesus as a son of God brought up the nagging question of whether God had selected him during his baptism at the Jordan River, or if he was an immortal deity. The Church resolution of this debate led inexorably to the popular doctrine of a divine trinity, three distinct forces that simultaneously comprise one single godhead, another notion that originated in Egypt centuries earlier.

According to Plutarch, the Egyptian trinity consisted of Isis, Horus, and Seth, representing the divine mother, father, and son. The second-century Coptic Gospel of the Egyptians describes a trinity emanating from an invisible, unspeakable godhead, namely, the father, the divine mother, and a son, Seth, in the form of Jesus. The Persians, exhibiting patriarchal prejudice, dropped the mother and added a holy spirit, the version that survived in later Christian doctrine.

Two legendary second-century Church authors, Clement and Athenagoras, place Jesus in association with the Father and the Holy Spirit. The penultimate line of the *Gospel of Matthew* refers to "the Father, Son, and Holy Spirit." The *Gospel of John* depicts Jesus proclaiming, "The Father and I are one." None of these passages explicitly describes a unified trinity. However, in the third century, Latin theologian Tertullian speculated, "There are two, the Father and the Son, and three with the Holy Spirit, and this number is made by the pattern of salvation." Tertullian states, "The unity is distributed in a Trinity." This passage marks the earliest known Christian usage of a unified Trinity.

Tertullian claimed that "simple people" who had rejected multiple deities to accept "one true God" were now confused to hear that the deity is three. Tertullian explains: "He must be believed to be one. It is consistent with his economy, because they judge that economy, implying a number and arrangement of trinity is really a division of unity, whereas unity, deriving trinity from itself, is not destroyed by it but made serviceable." We might imagine that some in his audience remained confused.

The trinity doctrine does not appear in pre-Latin Greek editions of the Bible. However, sixteenth-century Christian theologians introduced the Trinity into the New Testament by revising an ancient Greek manuscript. Vatican scholars found a scribe's note about the Trinity on a Greek manuscript of the First Letter of John. The Greek letter mentions "three that bear witness: the spirit, the water, and the blood." The Latin marginal note equates this to the Trinity. Using this, the sixteenth-century Vatican scholars changed the First Letter of John to read: "There are three that bear witness in heaven: the Father, the Logos [Word], and the Spirit, and these three are one."

The Dutch scholar Desiderius Erasmus correctly suspected trickery, but reluctantly included the passage in the third edition of his Greek Bible, later used as a source for the King James version of the English Bible. This revised Latin passage represents the historic pedigree for the Christian Trinity. Thus we find that the modern Roman and Protestant notion of a Father, Son, and Holy Ghost as one divine essence comes to us as a sixteenth-century forgery of a fifth-century Latin handwritten note, reflecting a Gnostic version of an Egyptian mythology about masculine and feminine deities giving rise to humanity. Here we witness the process by which ancient philosophical doctrines — a devil, a virgin birth, a son of god, and a trinity — were attached to the legacy of Jesus. The historical record reveals no connection between these doctrines and the teachings of Jesus in Galilee.

We have noticed that the *Gospel of John* diverges significantly from the three synoptic Gospels, and from the *Thomas*, *Mary*, *Philip*, and other accounts. We can now see how these Persian and Platonic ideas influenced the *John* authors, who depict Jesus' life as a battle between cosmic forces of good and evil, and blame the Devil for turning Judas, and Jews in general, against Jesus.

CHANNELLED GOSPEL

The earliest complete manuscript of the *Gospel According to John* appears in the fourth century. We possess no historic evidence to confirm the original author or place of origin. Scholars presume a Greek original appeared around the Aegean sometime between 90 and 100 C.E. The Ignatius letters, generally dated to about 150 C.E., make no reference to *John*. The numbered miracles or "signs" in the gospel imply an earlier collection of miracle stories, possibly from Syria, known among scholars as the Signs Gospel.

The *John* text does not name a writer. At the end of the second century, Irenaeus alludes to a tradition that named apostle John Zebedee as the author. Other accounts suggest an elder in Ephesus, or the unknown "beloved disciple" mentioned in the gospel. Some traditions believed that the risen Lazarus wrote the text. Most scholars today presume that a Greek-speaking Jewish "school" composed the gospel and revised it over several decades. This community of educated, urban Jesus followers, possibly in Syria, composed the gospel after being expelled from other communities. Hints of this expulsion appear throughout the work, as when the author recalls, "Anyone who confessed him [Jesus] to be the Messiah would be put out of the synagogue." Although the gospel speaks to a Jewish audience, it portrays the "Jews" in an unflattering light. Later European Gentile Christians used these passages to justify persecutions against Jews.

The literary creation took shape over time and borrowed ideas from Gnostic treatises and Greek discourse, implying authors of refined literary skill. The opening eighteen verses follow a style of high Semitic poetry; the long laments and soliloquies of Jesus suggest Greek theatrical oration; and the closing chapter 21 is a spirited ecclesiastical homily added decades, or perhaps a century, later. *John* is certainly not the work of a first-century Aramaic-speaking fisherman. It reads as an urbane, complex Greek literary composition.

John is a dazzling gospel, brimming with inspired religious exhortation and favourite Christian passages: "God so loved the world, he gave his only son"; Jesus proclaiming, "I am the light of the world"; and the story of Jesus meeting a Samaritan woman at a well. The central theme proclaims Jesus to be a god. For believing this, the reader is offered eternal salvation in heaven. The authors of *John* unambiguously state its purpose: "so that you will believe that Jesus is the Messiah." In that sense, it could be considered one of the most successful documents ever written.

John echoes Paul's gospel of faith, and some scholars believe it was composed in Antioch, where Paul began his mission. Like Paul's letters, this gospel reveals little about the life, ethics, actions, or teachings of Jesus. The Sermon on the Mount — a core collection of authentic Jesus sayings — disappears in *John*. The gospel does not urge followers to seek spiritual resources within themselves. Gone is the admonition to avoid laws and lawmakers, and neither the author nor the audience appears concerned with social justice. Jesus' instructions to give to the poor, heal the sick, and share common food are replaced by proclamations about faith and obedience.

Historians do not imagine that the thousand-word monologues by Jesus are direct quotes. The "I am" proclamations in *John* — "I am the bread of life...the good shepherd...the way...the truth... life...I existed before there was an Abraham" — borrow a Greek theatrical device to acclaim Jesus a god. This self-aggrandizing Jesus in *John* contrasts with the humble teacher we met in *Mark, Thomas,* and the Q verses. Recall that "I am" statements do not appear in Jewish literature or in the early Jesus traditions. These passages in *John* represent the philosophy of the messianic community that composed them.

Some *John* passages sound similar to *Thomas* and the Gnostic Gospels that equate Jesus to a primordial light, suggesting these authors shared sources and folk traditions. Nevertheless, *John* explicitly breaks with these traditions and maligns the apostle Thomas, depicting him as "Doubting Thomas," who does not believe in the resurrected Jesus until he can actually see him. This scene encourages potential believers to accept Jesus as a messiah, while also attacking the rival *Thomas* community concerning Jesus' teachings and the authority to preside over his legacy.

Thomas mentions the kingdom some eighteen times, comparing it to a child, a small seed, a crack in a jar, as invisible leaven, and spread out over the earth for all to see. In the earliest sources, Jesus directs disciples to the kingdom by bringing forth their inner light and serving others. Conversely, *John* mentions the kingdom of God only once (3:3–5), does not describe it, and directs disciples to the kingdom by being reborn "from above," through ritual baptism. In John 18:36, Jesus speaks of "my kingdom" as specifically *not* of this earth. The *John* Gospel represents a monumental shift from a kingdom of immediate self-awareness and good deeds, for anyone, to a future kingdom in heaven available only through the patriarchs and priesthood.

Several stories, including that of the woman at the well, are unique to *John*, while others revise familiar narratives. The three earlier gospels, for example, place the scene of Jesus driving moneychangers from the Temple at the end of his public mission, leading to his arrest. *John* places this scene at the beginning and adds details such as a whip in the hands of Jesus. *John* portrays Jesus' last public act as the healing of Lazarus in Bethany, set in the home of Mary and Martha. In *John*, this healing and a subsequent defection of Jews to Jesus lead to his arrest. These may appear as minor adjustments to the plot, but they reveal extraordinary differences among the communities of followers. In the *John* community, Jesus' execution is linked to miracles, not to his public disruption of elite society.

The eighth-century Latin Muratorian Fragment, presumably copied from an earlier Greek original, provides the earliest known list of the New Testament documents. The fragment names John Zebedee as the author of the *John* Gospel, and describes the alleged composition:

> The fourth Gospel, that of John of the disciples: When his fellow-disciples and bishops urged him, he said: "Fast with me from today for three days, and what will be revealed to

each one let us relate to one another." In the same night it
was revealed to Andrew, one of the apostles, that while all
were to review [the gospel], John in his own name should
write everything down.

This scene represents the official Church history of the *John*
Gospel, described as a group revelation enhanced by fasting. Today,
we might call this "channelling," but even so, historians doubt that
the Muratorian account of this session reflects a historical event.

By the end of the second century, the patriarch Irenaeus
included *John* in his canon, excluded *Thomas*, and declared there
could be only four gospels, "Since there are four directions of the
world in which we live, and four principal winds." Recall that only
one line from *John* parallels *Thomas*, *Mark*, and the Q verses, *John*
4:43: "A prophet gets no respect in his own home country." The
Westar Institute scholars conclude that this represented the only
authentic Jesus quote in *John*. By contrast, that same group of
scholars selected thirty-six sayings and parables from the *Gospel of
Thomas* as likely authentic quotes. The Westar Institute is not infallible, but they do publish their rules of evidence. We might fairly
wonder what criteria Irenaeus and others used to exclude *Thomas*
and embrace *John* in the second-century Catholic Church canon.

COUNCIL OF FROGS

By the end of the second century, the battle for the Jesus legacy
raged from Palestine to Rome, in cities around the Mediterranean,
in Alexandria, Carthage, and Corinth. Impoverished Jewish Ebionites at the Euphrates headwaters, the *anawim* outcasts in Galilee,
and ethnically mixed nomads carrying Gnostic tales between Syria
and Sinai had little chance of winning this battle. The era of a Jesus
legacy stewarded by peasants in rural, oral communities inevitably
waned. Merchant-class Gentile Christians, who enjoyed access to

travel, literary skills, and political patronage, gained influence with each succeeding generation. Authority among these congregations inexorably migrated west and concentrated in Rome.

In this climate, in about 178 C.E., philosopher and social critic Celsus wrote a critique of Christian beliefs, *Alethès Lógos* (*True Reason*), describing the doctrinal battles among competing factions of Jesus followers. Later emperors destroyed his works, so Celsus, like Basilides and others, survives only in Christian attacks on him, principally by Origen in the third century, who preserves almost all of *True Reason*.

Celsus may have lived in Alexandria. He appears as a sophisticated, eclectic intellectual, schooled in the histories of Judea, Persia, Egypt, Greece, and Rome. He directs his sharp social wit at the beliefs of Christians, pagans, and Jews. He pokes fun at idle opinions, and lampoons popular philosophies. His mocking of the uneducated sounds elitist, but Celsus's attacks are not levelled at *ebionim* peasant followers of Jesus. Rather, he targets intellectuals among second-century Christian writers for plagiarizing well-known traditions and failing to employ common reason:

> There is nothing new or impressive about their ethical teaching....One ought first to follow reason as a guide before accepting any belief, since anyone who believes without testing a doctrine is certain to be deceived....Just as the charlatans of the cults...the Christian teachers do not want to give reasons for what they believe.

Celsus repeats common complaints against Christian writers, that they manufacture false history and alter texts. He claims that Jesus learned his magic and wisdom in Egypt, and that the Christian factions bicker among themselves. He repeats a Jewish claim that Christianity has no standing in Old Testament prophecies, and he wonders why Christians would suppose those prophecies refer to their messiah rather than any number of others. Celsus also repeats a rumour that Jesus was born from adultery, and he even names the father as a Roman soldier, Panthera. No real evidence confirms such rumours, but Celsus reveals that many people mistrusted the Christian story.

Accusing Christians of plagiarizing popular myth, Celsus claims, "The writings of the Christians are a lie... [and their] fables are not well-enough constructed to conceal this monstrous fiction." Christian writers, he claims, "alter the original writings... in order to deny the contradictions." He concludes that they revise gospels and forge documents to justify their authority over the people they control. He insists that the Christian teachers take advantage of innocent children and desperate fools, but avoid educated debate. He points out that Plato acknowledged his sources and that even Socrates himself could be persuaded by reasonable argument.

> For why is it an evil to have been educated, and to have studied the best opinions, and to have both the reality and appearance of wisdom? What hindrance does this offer to the knowledge of God? Why should it not rather be an assistance, and a means by which one might be better able to arrive at the truth?

Celsus criticizes the doctrine of faith as an easy dodge for the wicked, for the "thief, housebreaker, poisoner, committer of sacrilege, and a robber of the dead." He believes the Church writers ignore the decent person "who has held steady from the cradle," while promising salvation to the "unjust man" in exchange for blind faith. He laments, "Faith, having taken possession of [their] minds, makes them yield the assent which they give to the doctrine of Jesus."

He questions why a god who made the universe would need to come to earth to reform his creation. Did he not create it properly in the first place? He compares the Christian god to Jupiter as portrayed in a popular comedy, "awaking from a lengthened slumber, [with a] desire to rescue the human race from evil." Celsus raises the agnostic idea that human knowledge cannot necessarily discover the truth about the creation of the universe, and that the best hope of knowing the truth is through rational discourse.

However, Celsus also appears as a naturalist in the tradition of Thales, Pythagoras, and Aristotle. He finds fault with those who "bow down to heaven, but not also to the sun, moon, and stars," and maintains that the natural cosmos reflects God. He wonders why humans think themselves superior to bees or ants or why certain groups believe they enjoy a special relationship with the creator. Celsus compares Christian Church writers to "a council of frogs in a marsh...croaking that the whole world was created just for them to be saved."

Celsus's critique echoes common views held by cosmopolitan Greek, Roman, Egyptian, and Jewish citizens. Recall that an information explosion — driven by camel caravans and papyrus documents — had influenced the Mediterranean world. Since Celsus focuses on second-century literary doctrines rather than the sayings of Jesus, it appears that philosophical writers had become the popular face of Christianity. Interestingly, we do not find Celsus denouncing any of the core teachings that we equate with the authentic Jesus, but rather the doctrines borrowed from other traditions and attached to Jesus by Church patriarchs such as Paul, Ignatius, and Justin Martyr.

THE DISAPPEARING TEACHER

Celsus was not the only contemporary critic. Greek philosopher Porphyry of Tyre, the Roman agnostic Caecilius, and others critiqued the new generation of Christian writers, as they strayed from the original teachings of Jesus. Surprisingly, few Christian apologists in the second century tell us anything substantial about Jesus at all.

We find a growing diversity of Christian opinion concerning deities, evil, and prognoses for the future. We hear about sons of God, holy spirits, and eternal life, but virtually nothing about Jesus, his life, his teachings, or in many cases even his existence. Justin Martyr describes his version of "what Christ himself taught," mixed with his own philosophy regarding women and licentious behaviour. Beyond that, it feels almost as if second-century Christian philosophy did not need a real Jesus, and certainly didn't need an itinerant peasant advocating common decency.

Athenagoras of Athens wrote *A Plea for the Christians* to Emperor Marcus Aurelius in 177. In thirty-seven chapters and over 16,000 words, he finds no occasion to mention Jesus or the example of his life. He mentions a "son of God," but only as the "first product" of the deity, who "had the Logos in himself." His Christianity is a messianic, monotheistic version of Plato that does not need a historical Jesus from Galilee.

Syrian philosopher Tatian wrote an *Apology to the Greeks*, promoting Christian doctrine against other sects. He names the Logos as the creative power of the universe, first-begotten of the Father, but mentions no earthly incarnation. He explains that eternal life is gained directly from God's grace, not by following the example of Jesus. In fact, like Athenagoras, he never mentions Jesus in this treatise, and claims that his own knowledge derives directly from God.

One Theophilus, "friend of god," allegedly served as bishop in Antioch from 168 until 180 and wrote *To Autolycus,* claiming that knowledge of Christian doctrines came through the Holy Spirit. He discusses unspecified gospels and paraphrases some ethical ideas that correspond to Jesus' teachings, but does not attribute these ideas to Jesus. Like others, he claims that the son of God is the male word (Logos) of God, created simultaneously with the female wisdom (Sophia).

Theophilus explains the meaning of Christianity: "We are called Christians, because we are anointed with the oil of God." Theophilus is no idle observer. He is, reportedly, the bishop of Antioch, representing one of the most prominent congregations of Christians in the second century. He never once mentions Jesus in this discourse and states flatly that a Christian is one who is anointed with the oil of God.

One cannot help but wonder what was going on. It appears as if the authentic, living Jesus, his message and teachings, his life and example, became irrelevant to many second-century Christians. Now perhaps we see the effect of Paul's ministry, which also tells us almost nothing about Jesus. The practice of attaching pagan mythologies to the name of Jesus begins with Paul. The historical Jesus is already dim, if not invisible, in Paul, twenty years after his life. By the second century, Jesus had become an interchangeable generic messiah who did not require an actual history. In many Christian accounts, Jesus completely disappears.

Here, we witness mythmaking in full swing. Eventually, however, Roman Christianity would recognize a need to place a history of Jesus back into the legend. For this, we finally arrive at the era of Emperor Constantine, his historian Eusebius, and his mother, Helena.

THE EMPEROR'S NEW RELIGION

By the third century, Roman hegemony over the Mediterranean world had begun to show signs of decay. Gothic warriors slipped along the Black Sea, penetrated Roman borders, invaded the Balkans, and reached the Aegean Sea. In the north, Germanic tribes crossed the Rhine into Gaul. Rome fought back, but relied on foreign mercenaries to defend the vast borders. Inexorably, Rome stumbled toward chaos and dissolution.

Meanwhile, a young Roman patrician, Constantine, began his long rise to power. Constantine's father succeeded Emperor Maximian to the western throne; divorced his first wife, Helena, mother of Constantine; and married Maximian's daughter Theodora. Constantine married his stepmother's sister, Fausta, and took command of Gaul and Britain. The youthful general drove some Germanic tribes back across the Rhine, retook Britain, and then invaded Marseilles and executed his father-in-law, Maximian. At this point, his troops proclaimed him emperor.

In the year 312, Constantine marched to the Tiber River, defeated the domestic Roman army, and entered Rome. Eusebius later claimed that Constantine arrived in Rome under the "sign of the cross" after he and his troops had witnessed "the sun surmounted with the trophy of the cross," as Jesus allegedly appeared to Constantine in a dream. This story, often reported as history, relies on the account written by Eusebius twenty-five years after the fact to explain why the emperor had adopted Christianity. However, as historian Edward Gibbon and many others have pointed out, Constantine's conversion to Christianity occurred over the course of his political career and served to appease his troops, the civilian masses, and powerful bishops.

The Church in Rome had consolidated power within the mouldering empire. Bishops, or overseers, had assumed authority over local elders, and by the year 250, Cyprian, from North Africa, was complaining that some bishops were asserting control over multiple churches. Cyprian insisted that all bishops were equal, but he lost the battle as "archbishops" sponsored by Rome claimed to be "more equal," as George Orwell might have put it. Rome's ecclesiastical overlords, or "metropolitans," ruled from powerful urban centres. By the end of the third century, the three metro-politans in Rome, Alexandria, and Antioch had claimed "first priority" over all other metropolitans. The Bishop of Rome was now just one step away from absolute control of the Jesus legacy.

Constantine would provide this final step as he consolidated his empire by merging political power with the popular new reli-gion. However, at this time, Jesus competed with Mithras and Jupiter as a popular saviour. The Roman Senate considered Con-stantine the head priest of Sol Invictus, the "Invisible Sun" cult, and *pontifex maximus*, commander of Rome's official priests loyal to Mithraism. Roman legionnaires had returned from the East with a Romanized version of Persian Mithraism popular among soldiers, Roman bureaucrats, and imperial officials. Roman Mithraic ritual caves serving the legionnaires have been found from the lower Danube in modern Romania to Hadrian's Wall in northern Britain.

The Mithras congregations kept a secret liturgy and performed secret initiations. They possessed no central text that we know of. Their typical temple was a natural cave or a stone structure made to resemble a cave. Stone altars depict their avatar Mithras killing a bull reminiscent of the equinox sun passing from Taurus to Aries. The Persian rites included a eucharist ceremony during which the congregation consumed the body and blood of Mithras, symbol-ized by bread and wine.

Since Paul's hometown of Tarsus provided an early site for European Mithraism, many historians believe Paul borrowed the Last Supper story from a Greek-speaking congregation in Tarsus. The Church of Rome adopted the bread-and-wine ritual along with other Mithraic doctrines: the trinity, virgin birth, a single god, and so forth, the very doctrines opposed by peasant congregations of Jesus followers such as the Ebionites. Since both Roman troops and Christian bishops had adopted popular Mithraic rites and doctrines, Constantine appears to have merged the two theologies into his brand of Latin Christianity, which then earned special status as the official state religion.

Meanwhile, Constantine's family soap opera seethed. His wife Fausta appears to have accused his eldest son — Crispus, by his previous marriage — of rape, likely to eliminate Crispus as a rival for her own sons. Constantine executed Crispus for the embarrassment, executed his nephew as a bad influence, and had Fausta boiled alive for unknown reasons, perhaps just to get rid of her. Nevertheless, the Eastern Church would name him a saint, and in the Western Church he became known as "the first Christian Roman Emperor."

Constantine and his eastern rival Licinius had issued an edict from Milan in 313 C.E., granting their subjects "the liberty of following whatever religion they please." Constantine later executed Licinius and, according to Eusebius, "exhorted all his subjects to imitate, without delay, the example of their sovereign by embracing the divine truth of Christianity." The later Church and many historians have since credited Constantine with "ending persecutions against Christians," but this hasty assessment misrepresents history. Constantine only ended persecution against *his* Christians. Persecutions actually increased against Christians and other Jesus followers who held dissenting views.

However, one irritating problem remained: No one had yet defined the "divine truth" of Christianity, much less Latin Mithraic Christianity, so Constantine required an official canon, a Church constitution, and documentation of spiritual authority. For this, he appointed Eusebius, a scribe of Greek, Hebrew, and Latin probably from the region of Antioch. Eusebius would become official recording secretary, lawyer, historian, editor, document creator, and librarian of the Roman religion, overseeing the paperwork of an ecclesiastical state. Constantine adopted the role of God's vicegerent on earth, God's administrative deputy, with the power of life, death, and salvation.

ONE IOTA

Eusebius was born within a few years of Constantine. They first met in their twenties, when the young general accompanied Emperor Diocletian to Palestine. Two decades later, in 322, Emperor Constantine instructed Eusebius, now Bishop of Caesarea, to produce a collection of orthodox gospels. The emperor ordered fifty uniform Greek copies as the official state-sponsored sacred scriptures. Under the watchful eye of Eusebius, the best scribes of the realm prepared these on fine hide parchment. In his *Life of Constantine*, Eusebius describes sending "magnificent and elaborately bound volumes," in two public carriages, to the emperor for his "personal inspection."

Historians of the Christian canon lament that Eusebius reveals nothing in his prolific writings about his methodology or rules of evidence for selecting this canon. He cites Papias, whom we only hear about through him, for the names of the four Gospels. No Eusebius/Constantine bibles survived, but they may have been similar to the earliest known *Codex Sinaiticus*, from about 350 C.E. We do not know Eusebius's methods, his precise selection, or the Greek editions he used. We do know that the canon remained unsettled. Churches of the East and West would never agree on a precise New or Old Testament. From Syria and Alexandria to Rome, Jesus congregations raised protests and gospel wars raged.

Bishop Irenaeus in Lyon had proclaimed "only four gospels," but named no definitive canon. Additional "Pauline" letters, forged by Church writers, promoting the authority of the Church and denouncing women and Jews, had augmented the seven authentic letters of Paul. Meanwhile, certain bishops adopted other letters attributed to apostles and included these in orthodox collections. Scribes busied themselves creating these letters and making copies as the Church of Rome created a paper trail to support its alleged apostolic pedigree. Later, Church patriarch Cyril of Jerusalem flatly dismissed the *Gospel of Thomas* in his defence of the Constantine canon:

> The Manicheans wrote a Gospel according to Thomas, which being smeared with the fragrance of the name "Gospel" destroys the souls of those who are rather simple-minded.... whatever books are not read in the churches, do not read these even by yourself.

Besides his historical error about the Manicheans, we hear no evidence from Cyril, but rather a decree to toss out a gospel that modern scholarship reveals as one of the most accurate reports regarding the fundamental teachings of Jesus. Constantine, it appears, did not care about the teachings of Jesus. He commissioned his canon to serve the state-sponsored religion.

Recall that Constantine's mother, Helena, toured Palestine in the fourth century and supposedly discovered certain Christian historical sites, such as the hometown of Mary Magdalene, the birthplace of Jesus, and the "true cross" of Jesus, three centuries after his death. Eusebius reported these alleged discoveries and linked them to gospel stories to create a Church history commissioned by his emperor and patron, Constantine. Nevertheless, Eusebius could not resolve the doctrinal disputes concerning the nature of Jesus' divinity. The debate, as historians have observed since, teetered over one single letter, a Greek *iota*. Was Jesus, *homoiousion*, similar to god, or *homoousion*, the same substance as god? The single iota appears to separate history from mythology; indeed, the iota separates a beloved icon of a Jewish peasant uprising from a Roman emperor's court monopoly.

Congregations of followers had cast Jesus variously as an honourable human teacher, a human adopted by God because of his righteousness, a healer, a righteous king of the poor, a human who became a god, a god in human form, a god who only appeared human, and a deity within a unified trinity. Even inside orthodox Christian churches of the fourth century, debates raged regarding the Resurrection, a virgin birth, women's place in God's plan, and apostolic authority. All this came to a head over the single iota, in a showdown between Presbyter Arius and Bishop Alexander in Alexandria.

In the year 318, Constantine sent a letter to both parties asking them to resolve the schism and decide in what manner Jesus was a god. A synod of bishops in Alexandria in 323 condemned Arius as a heretic, but another in Bithynia reversed the decision and reinstated him. The Cyrenian or "Libyan" bishops backed Arius, so Constantine, fed up with the squabble, summoned the lot of them to a council at his lakefront palace in Nicaea, modern Iznik in northwest Turkey.

At the Council of Nicaea in 325, Constantine presided and Eusebius recorded the proceedings of some 300 assembled bishops. Eusebius also composed the first draft of the "Nicene Creed," thereafter recited by Christians for centuries. The council resolved that Jesus was the "only Son of God" and that he was "begotten, not made," meaning that God did not adopt Jesus during the Jordan River baptism because of his righteousness, but rather God shared "the same substance" with Jesus.

Constantine possessed little patience for debate, and the council confirmed the doctrines quickly and overwhelmingly. No voting record survives, but a tradition holds that only two attending bishops did not sign the creed. Dissenting bishops eventually drafted competing creeds, but without imperial sanction, these had little hope of surviving. According to Eusebius, after Nicaea,

Constantine declared: "...if any book composed by Arius shall be found, it shall be delivered to the fire...if anyone shall be found to have concealed any writing composed by Arius...death shall be his punishment."

Membership in Constantine's Christian faith, and book club, swelled after his edict of Nicaea. The forbidden factions surrendered or disappeared. Constantine died in 337. Eusebius baptized him on his deathbed, presumably enabling him to enter heaven. According to Roman Christian doctrine, Constantine's unbaptized victims — his wife, son, nephew, father-in-law, and other enemies — would not be joining him in the presence of God. Eusebius died two years later, after declaring all "Moravians, Valentinians, Marcionites," and other factions of Jesus followers "enemies of truth," whose books were to be burned and temples "confiscated to the Catholic Church."

THE PURGE

Swiftly, the gospels of *Thomas, Mary*, the Ebionites, Egyptians, and others virtually disappeared from the historical record, along with most of the classical literature of Sophocles, Euripides, Sappho, and others. Wherever rational argument failed, fire triumphed. Acts 19:19 records an early Christian-sponsored book burning in Ephesus:

> A number of those who practiced magic collected their books and burned them publicly. When the value of these books was calculated, it was found to come to fifty thousand silver coins. So the word of the Lord grew mightily and prevailed.

Roman Christianity, merged with Mithraic and pagan rites, overwhelmed all others schools of thought. In 347, Emperor Flavius Theodosius and Ambrose, the powerful Bishop of Milan, drafted a series of decrees to suppress all competing religions, close temples, confiscate property, and execute rival bishops. Theodosius declared that all subjects of the Empire must profess the state-sponsored faith.

In Spain (Roman Gallaecia) Bishop Priscillian had devoted his life to classical study and ascetic simplicity. He accepted women as equal to men and regarded a proper Christian life as a humble, relentless communication with God. Under ecclesiastical law that recognized two accusers as sufficient evidence, Priscillian's enemies charged him with practising magic. Roman authorities tortured him until he confessed, then executed him in 385.

Although the dispute about a human or divine Jesus persisted in the East, the Roman Church excommunicated prominent dissenters and installed bishops loyal to Rome. One such loyalist, Athanasius of Alexandria, became one of the most powerful bishops in the Empire. Athanasius composed three "Discourses Against Arians," explaining that God uttered the Logos (Word) and thereby begot the Son as an "eternal relationship," not an event that took place within time. He later wrote "Letters to Serapion" to explain the divinity of the Holy Spirit and the Trinity. Finally, his Easter letter of 367 C.E. established the orthodox Christian canon, the twenty-seven books that we know as the New Testament.

Meanwhile, Emperor Theodosius surrendered the title of *divi filius*, allowing the Church to claim Jesus as the "only son of God." The emperor also relinquished his Pontifex Maximus title and bestowed it upon the Bishop of Rome, henceforth the head of the state religion. The Bishop thereby assumed "first prerogative" above the other metropolitan bishops, finally assuming absolute authority over the teachings of Jesus.

Egyptian monks, mystics, and so-called heretics had become a particular annoyance to Rome, and in 389 Emperor Theodosius issued instructions to demolish all non-Christian temples in

Alexandria. A mob of Roman soldiers, foreign mercenaries, and local vigilantes looted and demolished the shrine of Serapis, a solar deity associated with healing and fertility. The mob then stormed the famous Library of Alexandria, the greatest store of knowledge in the ancient world. They built pyres of scrolls and books in the street, burned them, and reduced the magnificent depository of Mediterranean science and mysteries to rubble and ash. In the eastern delta town of Tanis, mobs reportedly burned accused heretics along with their books. Half a legion of Roman soldiers pushed south toward Memphis and ravaged the temples of Isis and Osiris along the way.

Human civilization lost priceless collections of stories, legends, discoveries, remedies, ideas, and history that will never be recovered or replaced. The Western world fell, along with Rome, into what historian Charles Freeman has called "the gradual subjection of reason to faith and authority." The dynamism of Egyptian and Greek civilization and the Mediterranean spirit of intellectual investigation were crushed under Roman "law and order."

In 399, the Roman Bishop Siricius became the first pope, or "father," of the Church and issued the original *Epistolae decretales*, papal letters proclaiming absolute authority, including the self-referential claim that the decretals themselves represented irrefutable law. A thousand years would pass, and countless spirited thinkers and innocent healers would perish at the stake, before European society even began to emerge from this assault on intellectual freedom. Global society remains, even to this day, shaped by Roman-ecclesiastical intolerance.

BELLUM DEO

So, where is Jesus in all of this? What happened to his teachings, and his example of humility and compassion? This authentic message of Jesus became an illicit secret, surviving only in a few isolated monasteries in the Levant and Egypt. The decisive stamp of Roman authority over the teachings of Jesus arrives in history with a bright, wild-blooded teenage Algerian Berber entering Carthage in 371, looking for amusement. Augustine, later Bishop of Hippo, recounts in *Confessions* his youthful "unholy loves," thefts, jealousies, and pursuit of hedonistic and intellectual stimulation. He recalls, "My soul floundered in the void." Here Augustine appears raw and searching, almost as a twentieth-century existentialist, and his *Confessions* are considered the first modern autobiography.

Augustine absorbed the classics: Virgil's literature, Plato's philosophy, and Cicero's clever rhetorical tricks. At the age of thirty, he earned the job of imperial professor of rhetoric, or speechwriter, for the governor of Milan, where he met Ambrose, the powerful bishop who instructed him in Latin Christianity. Augustine believed in Platonic dualism — the flesh at war with the spirit — but he began to doubt Plato regarding the value of pursuing truth. Ambrose had introduced Augustine to the letters of Paul, which convinced Augustine that the Christian god had predetermined everything. Truth, he came to believe, came only from this god, not from intellectual inquiry. A case could be made, now as then, that Augustine blundered in both conclusions. We might imagine a different European history if he had accepted honest inquiry regarding truth and simultaneously acknowledged divinity in the world around him, as Jesus did. These may be philosophical points, but not trivial ones.

Augustine's inner conflicts peaked at this time. He describes in *Confessions* a full psychological breakdown, during which he hears children chanting a popular refrain: "Take, read, take, read." He deems this a sign from his god, grabs a book from his table, and opens randomly to a passage from Paul's Roman letter: "Put yourself on the Lord Jesus Christ, and make no provision for the flesh to gratify its desires."

This little episode transformed Augustine from a free-spirited savant into a defender of Latin Christianity, using his prodigious rhetorical skills to promote Rome's authority. Augustine endorsed the Trinity and developed the doctrine of Original Sin to explain why God would cast unbaptized innocents into eternal flames. He proposed the antidote to Original Sin as "grace," a gift from God, but does not explain why his god, who has predetermined everyone's fate, chooses some for grace and others for damnation.

As Bishop of Hippo in North Africa, Augustine took one final leap, rationalizing the use of violence, torture, and war in the pursuit of the Church's goals. He deftly twists "blessed are the peacemakers" from the Sermon on the Mount to justify violence for a "greater peace." He claims that "error has no rights," so dissenters, such as Priscillian in Spain, could be tortured and executed. "Why," he reasons, "should not the Church use force in compelling her lost sons to return?" To shield bishops from direct responsibility for torture and murder, he argues that defying the Church amounts to treason, so those condemned by the bishops should be punished by the state. Finally, he describes a "just war" — *bellum Deo auctore* — as a war waged on behalf of the universal Church's god.

Thus, Augustine, the hot-blooded Berber intellectual, employed his rhetorical wit to pave the way for the medieval Inquisition that would condemn millions to horrific deaths. As we hear from Augustine in the epigraph at the beginning of this chapter, he fully understood that he was playing loosely and freely with the truth. In doing so, he borrowed the tricks of Cicero and foreshadowed the cunning of Machiavelli. Finally, in summary, Augustine declared in his first book of sermons, paraphrased by later editors, "*Roma locuta est; causa finita est*" (Rome has spoken; the case is closed).

Fortunately for us, however, the case was not closed. Sixteen centuries later, we possess the gospels of *Thomas, Mary, Philip,* and

296 THE JESUS SAYINGS

Egyptians; the *Sophia of Jesus Christ*; letters and revelations of James; and other precious historical documents that allow us to glimpse the authentic teachings of Jesus. We possess these documents because a few desert monks and mystics preserved them at their peril, and buried them before the Roman legions and Christian soldiers reached southern Egypt.

The peasant Yeshua of Galilee had vanished from Constantine's Paulist, Mithraic Christianity, but the humble teacher did not entirely disappear from history's record. An authentic Jesus lay buried under the sands of the Nile Valley, in documents scattered about the Mediterranean, and in the core passages of later canonical Gospels. Once Western scholarship had liberated itself from Constantine's legacy of official doctrine and intimidation, archaeologists began uncovering these treasures, and manuscript scholars peeled back the layers of text to reveal the earliest, most reliable accounts. Now, in the twenty-first century, we have the opportunity to give Jesus — the humble sage and healer — the cultural and historical respect he deserves. We can place his teachings on our bookshelves along with those of Lao Tzu, the Buddha, and Aristotle. We may now approach his teachings as we would any other great exponent of compassion and wisdom.

· 11 ·

VOICE OF THE GALILEAN

What was your word, Jesus?
Love? Forgiveness? Affection?
All your words were one word:
Wakeup.

ANTONIO MACHADO,
"PROVERBIOS Y CANTARES," 1912

Wisdom is the currency of peasants as well as scholars, perhaps more so. Jesus, poor and disenfranchised, absorbed the culture around him, distilled it, and revitalized it. He likely acquired insights from parents, relatives, and community elders. He probably heard wandering mystics and met sages from Gadara. As a Jewish peasant boy in Galilee, Jesus almost certainly heard plenty about Hillel, or perhaps studied with him directly. The fact that he put a twist on Hillel's version of the golden rule distinguishes Jesus. The way he applied Cynic shrewdness to life under Roman and Judean authorities suggests a virtuosity of language and social instinct.

We need not worry that the precise details of his life and legacy remain obscure. So do the records of the Buddha and Socrates. Even if we suspected that Jesus or the Buddha never existed as historical figures, the body of wisdom associated with them does exist. Some-one created that body of wisdom. Jesus' contributions to humanity stand out from the ideas he borrowed and from the mythologies attached to his name. We sense a discrete personality radiating an exceptionally luminous humility and intelligence. Like other great social commentators, his signature remains on his work. The words and deeds are sublime, as Thomas Jefferson observed, and original. After his encounter with John the Baptist, Jesus reframed his mentor's idea of a righteous kingdom: We create a divine king-dom here and now by finding our own inner light, speaking out, and helping others.

Jesus mediated the kingdom of God, or "Abba," as he put it, through action. Rather than wait for justice to come from God, he attended to the dispossessed peasants in the real world. We have seen that Roman authorities, Temple priests, and the Herod over-lords felt threatened by his actions. In this sense, Jesus truly did die for others. He knew the fate of John and still offered hope to the poor, knowing full well that the rulers in Jerusalem would resist him violently.

Like great visionaries before him and since, Jesus woke up from the cultural trance of his age and broke with the conven-tions and inertia of society. He experienced a spiritual epiphany that provided him with the motivation for his life's work. There-after, he saw before him suffering humanity, envisioned a better world, and set out to manifest that vision. The authentic Jesus, or Yeshua the Nazorean, brought heaven to earth in the here and now.

Although his message rings clear, authentic words from his lips remain elusive. One must be prepared to dig, compare texts, verify witnesses, and discriminate honest accounting from innocent mis-takes, predisposed mythmaking, and prejudicial manipulation. We also must remain cautious regarding the tendency to reshape historical heroes to serve our own ideas. We must, in simple terms, witness the truth.

After his life, a new, Romanized status quo absorbed and revised his legacy, a common fate of social movements throughout history. Claims of authority, promises of salvation, and threats of damnation dominated later accounts and did not require a historical Jesus. Conversely, understanding his acts of compassion and singular wisdom does require an appreciation of this authentic person. His record of deeds, stories, and aphorisms remains a world treasure. Those who truly get the message will reveal their understanding through action, as he asked. Francis of Assisi, Albert Schweitzer, and my grandmother come to mind. Those who don't get it will appear, in comparison, as presumptuous hypocrites, quoting scripture, inventing doctrines, taking bows, and claiming the best seats at dinner. Pedophiles in the Vatican and warmongering radio evangelists come to mind.

The Jesus who actually walked the earth — the Galilean peasant, healer, sage, rebel, and teacher — gave himself to the world. His teachings belong to humankind, as do the teachings of Lao Tzu, Susan B. Anthony, and Martin Luther King. No one owns these teachings or possesses any particular authority to interpret his message. The sayings, parables, and lessons of this Jewish mystic enrich world heritage, and any scholar or curious reader may enjoy access to the insights, warnings, and pleadings of this brilliant and compassionate observer of humanity who lived 2,000 years ago.

Historians do not necessarily agree on the details regarding Jesus' deeds, but they follow rules of evidence and understand the limitations of the record. All serious scholars understand that Jesus wrote nothing, his ideas circulated by word of mouth, and the nuances of his history have been lost and often obscured by later accounts. Nevertheless, historians can reconstruct a reasonable sequence of events by comparing Jesus stories to each other and to the record of the age. The following description summarizes the most likely events in the historic life of the Jewish peasant Jesus.

THE ACTS OF YESHUA

In about 4 B.C.E., before the death of Herod the Great, Jesus first opened his eyes on Galilee, possibly in Nazareth, born to a mother Miriam by a father Yosef, or perhaps by an unknown father. Jesus had four brothers, James (Yacov), Yoses, Yudas, and Simon, and at least two sisters, possibly Miriam and Salome. His childhood remains obscure. Birth and infancy accounts appear late in the record, contradict each other, clash with known history, and reflect popular motifs about divine births. Jesus, almost certainly, was not born in Judea, and his later sayings appear to reflect a Galilean cultural heritage.

He grew up in a Jewish cultural tradition, although his heritage may have been mixed and his influences appear to have been diverse. In thinking of Jesus as a Jew, we must differentiate between Galilean peasants and Judean urbanites, and notice that he consistently rejects Jewish social convention. He lived and taught near trade routes between the Mediterranean and the East, and his teachings reflect worldly ideas of his era.

Jesus first appears in history as a disciple of John the Baptist, a renegade prophet with a following in the wilderness east of the Jordan River. The relative assurance of this derives from later attempts to recast Jesus' relationship with the famous and much-loved John. In the tradition of the Jewish prophet Ezekiel, the Baptist foretold a divine intervention that would liberate Israel. He forgave sins for free, in defiance of the Jerusalem priests' monopoly, drew crowds, and paid with his life on the orders of Herod Antipas. After John's execution, some of his disciples became followers of Jesus, who attracted other devotees, both men and women.

Jesus' epiphany, perhaps during his time with John, appears to have stimulated profound insight, and thereafter Jesus radiated extraordinary charisma. He adopted Capernaum as a second home, but remained an itinerant teacher. He travelled the regions around the Sea of Chinnereth (Sea of Galilee), possibly reaching Sidon on the northwest Phoenician coast, Caesarea Philippi in the northern hills, and Gadara to the southeast. He may have travelled east across Persia, or perhaps met Eastern sages trekking west.

Archaeologists have not found first-century synagogues in Galilee, and historians interpret the use of "synagogue" in Jesus stories as meaning a gathering, not a solid structure. Jesus spoke in private homes, public squares, and the countryside. He primarily addressed a Jewish peasant audience, but he accepted all races and persuasions of followers. He consorted with social outcasts, the poor, the sick, and even despised tax collectors. He directed his audience to enter the kingdom through self-awareness and righteous action. He healed people and held communal meals as part of a central ritual. People believed in his healing powers, which likely contributed to his success. He cured a lame man in Capernaum, where scholars accused him of wielding the power of demons.

High-ranking Pharisees were not common in Galilee or in the adjoining countryside. Nevertheless, Jesus probably did confront religious authorities serving the Jerusalem Temple hierarchy. He openly confronted those who presumed to speak on behalf of God, and chastised them for hypocrisy and failure to help the people. Such authorities would have expected miraculous signs from any real prophet, which Jesus refused to display on demand. The crowds who flocked to him also expected miracles, and may have been rewarded with healings and the benefits of communal sharing. His fame spread throughout the region.

Sometime during the reign of Roman Emperor Tiberius, around the year 30, and during the spring festivals, Jesus entered Jerusalem, perhaps on a donkey, symbolizing Jewish peasant rebellion against foreign oppression. In Jerusalem, he attracted crowds of devoted followers and embarrassed the Temple elite. He likely shared a final communal meal with his closest followers. Irritated authorities arrested him and executed him. The details of his trial and execution remain obscure. The evidence suggests that Jewish authorities collaborated in the arrest, and that someone close to the movement betrayed him, although the name "Judas" may be a fiction used to blame Jews.

Only the Roman prefect, Pontius Pilate, possessed the authority to order his death. Pilate, a notorious thug, not the ambivalent moralist later portrayed for a Roman audience, would have executed Jesus without so much as a shrug, as he did other rebel leaders. An actual appearance before Pilate would not have been necessary. An order from Pilate to neutralize troublemakers in Jerusalem during Passover would have been carried out with ruthless precision, and likely without troubling the prefect. Roman soldiers tormented Jesus, marched him to Golgotha, or Skull Place, somewhere near Jerusalem, perhaps along the western road to Emmaus, and crucified him. Being efficient, the Romans almost certainly executed others with him. Meanwhile, his male supporters avoided attention during and after the execution, while his mother Mary, Mary Magdalene, Salome, and other women witnessed his suffering and attended to the body.

Some of these details may not have happened as they appear here, and other recorded details may bear some historical truth, but this account outlines what we can reasonably say about an authentic Jesus of history. All the rest remains either highly speculative or transparently invented. Some stories about Jesus are borrowed from other sources: the divine birth, blood atonement, conversations with demons, the spring sacrifice and rebirth of Tammuz, and the suffering righteous one.

After Jesus' death, his brother James, Mary Magdalene, and Capernaum fisherman Simon Peter emerged as leaders among his disciples. James held an important position in Jerusalem and possibly among the Ebionites. The Gospel of Hebrews depicts James as a leader, and the *Thomas* Gospel has Jesus naming him as his successor. James was executed in 62 C.E. by high priest Ananus, an event Josephus blames for the Jewish defeat by the Romans.

Considerable evidence suggests that Mary Magdalene enjoyed a special relationship with Jesus, that she deeply understood the teachings and adopted them in practice. No evidence confirms a marriage or intimate relationship, although accounts such as the *Gospel of Philip*, have Jesus kissing the Magdalene. Some historians suggest the wedding at Cana could recall their marriage, but extrapolations from this to an alleged modern bloodline remain entirely speculative. Mary likely anointed Jesus in a ceremony of peasant kingship, became an accomplished disciple, and sustained the teachings after his death. She likely resurfaced in Egypt and, based on later legends, possibly reached Ethiopia, and may have crossed the Mediterranean to southern France.

Later accounts portray Jesus variously as a rebel, a prophet, a Greek-style hero, a wise sage, a Cynic philosopher, a healer, an anointed king, and a saviour. He appears more modest in his own descriptions of himself as a son of Adam, a human. Among his poor neighbours, he made the promised kingdom accessible. His work would have demanded unworldly courage in the face of imperial oppression. Local Roman collaborators and Herodian sycophants did not want their privileged lives spoiled by a zealous preacher from Galilee who exposed their hypocrisy and stirred up revolution. Jesus daringly and humbly exposed truth before power on behalf of the oppressed.

MULTITUDES

All histories are reconstructions. Every piece of surviving evidence about Jesus reflects a later individual or group *impression* of what he said and did. We possess not a single first-person claim by an eyewitness to the life of Jesus. The *Gospel of Thomas* comes close by claiming, "These are the secret sayings that the living Jesus spoke and Didymos Judas Thomas recorded," but at least some of these passages are second-hand, some echo common lore, and others appear as later additions.

Crossan, one of the most highly respected scholars of Jesus history, points out that our search is encumbered by three "giant filters," since ancient history was recorded by (1) the elite, (2) the literate, and (3) males. We mitigate these biases by understanding oral peasant culture and women's voices. Any quest for an accurate view of Jesus is also encumbered by the dearth of physical evidence or unbiased testimony. We must bridge the gaps of translation from lost Aramaic to Greek, to Latin, and to English, accounting for honest mistakes and duplicitous misrepresentations compiled over two millennia. We face nuances of cultural meaning and diverse views of cosmology and society interwoven with the words of Jesus.

Finally, we must overcome our own biases and the hope that history will conform with our private viewpoint. Jesus Seminar scholars warn: "Beware of an idea of Jesus that is too congenial to you." Jesus disturbed the status quo of his time, so we should not be surprised that he occasionally disturbs us, perhaps with his warnings about family conflict, presumptuous authority, or spiritual pride. We occasionally find ourselves simply mystified: How is the kingdom like a cracked jar?

Our historical mission, to the extent possible, is to arrive inside history, to witness events from the era's own perspective, and to understand Jesus and his followers not from the twenty-first century — or from the fourth or fifteenth centuries — but from the first century, through the dust of ancient streets and through the eyes of peasants yearning for a better world. The characters we wish to know — Jesus, Mary Magdalene, and the others — were humans, struggling with very real needs, fears, and hopes. To know them, we must look behind the metaphors and mythologies to discover the authentic human experience.

· Jesus grew up only a short walk from a trade route between the shipping ports on the eastern Mediterranean and the entire Eastern world, stretching from Damascus to Persia, India, and China. We have seen that Jesus borrowed ideas from this rich cultural landscape. He lived at the zenith of the so-called "Axial Age" of humanity, roughly 700 B.C.E. to 200 C.E., when the world's classic philosophies and spiritual cosmologies appear in written records. Advances in travel and literature had triggered an information explosion. This outbreak of refined thinking and storytelling eventually succumbed to empires, kings, and their franchised priests, who attempted to control humanity's story as a means of clinging to power.

First-century Palestine stood at the epicentre, in both time and space, where ancient tribal, peasant mythology collided with imperial, written, urban history; where ancient *mythos* met an emerging *logos*. We can learn a great deal from this era of history, not only through the messages of Lao Tzu, Aristotle, Jesus, and Mary Magdalene, but also by observing the way they saw the world, with myth and reason more equally balanced than they are today. Around the Mediterranean during the four centuries after Jesus, the Roman hierarchy indeed controlled the human story, culminating in Emperor Constantine's establishment of state religion and the purge of competing ideas. The heirs of the Roman Empire have attempted to manage knowledge and religion ever since, advancing the notion that there exists only one, orthodox way to experience or articulate spirituality.

By pushing back through these later filters into the first century, we have discovered that many common notions about Jesus and his colleagues must be abandoned. We have seen that the "first Christians" were not Christians at all. They were rural Jewish and nomadic peasants who did not think of Jesus as a messiah, but as a model of courage and decency. We have seen that Jesus was indeed Jewish, but that his influences, if not his actual heritage, were diverse and worldly.

We have seen that much of what became Roman Christianity, and later Protestant Christianity, can be traced to pagan, Egyptian, and Persian sources adopted by Paul, Justin Martyr, Constantine, Eusebius, and Augustine, but not at all by Jesus. Paul, who had persecuted Jesus' followers, introduced the messiah tradition into the written record, likely arising from a congregation in Antioch, Syria. We have seen that Jesus, both his person and his ideas, virtually disappeared from second- and third-century "Christianity." Many modern Christian rituals, such as Easter, reflect medieval rituals borrowed from ancient pagans, recalling Ishtar, Asherah, and Tammuz.

We have seen that Jesus never said, "Believe in me and you'll go to heaven." He never claimed to be a god or that his mother was a virgin. He never instructed disciples to create an institution and hierarchy of priests, to accumulate wealth or curry power. He did not advance the Augustinian idea that his followers should go to war on behalf of God. In fact he counselled the exact opposite: nonviolence, simplicity, modesty, and generosity.

We have seen that Jesus' aphorisms and parables circulated orally among independent congregations — Ebionites, Egyptians, a Q community, the *Mark* and *Matthew* communities — and that some congregations compiled anthologies of sayings and stories. After the fall of Jerusalem in 70 C.E., gospel stories written for both Jewish and Gentile audiences embellished his story with folklore and legend. These gospels endured three centuries of editing until some were rejected and others assembled as a canon in the fourth century. Scholars identify traces of an authentic Jesus in dozens of other documents, including the *Didache, Dialogue of the Saviour,* the gospels of *Philip* and *Peter,* the Egerton and Egyptian gospels, and the mystic poem "Thunder: Perfect Mind."

We have made special use of the *Gospel of Mary,* which likely appeared in a Greek version by the early second century. The *Mary* Gospel serves this discussion because it represents the earliest known account of Jesus from a woman's point of view, which otherwise has been purged from the historical record. From *Mary* we hear familiar Jesus ideas in a unique voice: "The seed of true humanity exists within you. Follow it!" The "mind is the treasure" that "sees the vision," and "anyone with a mind should use it to think!" We hear that all forms in nature co-exist with each other, and that there is no sin except by acting contrary to one's nature. The mature soul is one that has "slain" the desire and ignorance that binds it to despair. These passages may reflect worldly ideas of the era, but they also record an authentic feminine perspective on Jesus' teachings.

We found the most genuine core of Jesus' message in the earliest editions of three collections, namely *Mark, Thomas,* and the Q sayings. We have seen that a fair summary of this core message survives in the Sermon on the Mount in *Luke* and *Matthew,* drawn from the earliest Q layers. Although scholars do not agree on every line, a ranking of the most authentic sayings has emerged from the textual analysis of the past two centuries. Although Jesus' message has been redacted and obscured, any curious and rigorous seeker may discover the key threads that make his teachings unique and relevant.

By comparing and contrasting these sources and weighing chronology, corroboration, and historical convergence, we can identify the essence of what a radical, Aramaic-speaking, Jewish Jesus might have said to an assembled crowd in Galilee. Imagine the multitudes gathering on a mountainside or on a plain, by the seaside, in a village square, or crammed around the courtyard of a private home. Mary, Thomas, Peter, and other disciples would sit nearby. Infirm peasants would press around him. Jesus would be tired, dusty, and wearing a ragged tunic, yet his eyes would shine with uncommon brilliance, and his voice would reverberate with earth-shaking courage and charisma. He possessed no script but would react to the events around him. He might say something like this:

A Voice in Galilee

You wish to be healed and forgiven for your sins, and so it shall be, but my dear friends, you don't know how lucky you are. You are fortunate to be poor and hungry. Your suffering brings you closer to the true kingdom of God. The rich are distracted by pleasures and power. Look, they stand away at a distance. They will gather up more riches and you will be deprived, but you are the lucky ones.

The kingdom cannot be bought. Nor is it something grand that will come tomorrow and be handed to you. Here, this is the kingdom. These children. Be like these innocents. See? Their kindness is natural. The kingdom is for ones such as these. It is like a tiny mustard seed, almost invisible, but look how it grows wild in the fields and provides a home for the birds and little animals.

Seek this kingdom in yourself. Look within. There is a light inside, and if you look, you will find it. Everything hidden will be revealed to those who seek. When you find this light, don't keep it to yourself. Who would light a lamp and then put it under a basket? Shine your light from the hilltops. Speak out. Tell others. Do as we do.

Look. We have nothing. No staff, no food, no extra clothes. Don't worry about what you will eat or wear. Look at the birds. See these lilies. They don't slave away or worry, yet they are fed and adorned more gloriously than the kings. Your father in heaven loves you as much as those birds and flowers. Accept what is given to you from this bounty and take care of others. That is the Father's kingdom on earth.

The lawmakers there say we have sinned because we healed our neighbours on the holy day. We have no day of rest. Even the birds have nests and the foxes have their holes. Yet a human has nowhere to lay one's head. The holy day was made for us; we weren't made to serve the holy day.

Those of you with two good ears had better listen.

Do you want to live in this kingdom? Then don't call me master, but act on what I am telling you. Don't just hear these words, but do as we do. Go among your neighbours, share whatever you have, give to anyone who asks. You can heal the sick yourselves. Tell them the kingdom is here.

But don't act like those who pretend to speak for God, parade around in fine robes, and demand the best seats in the synagogue. These priests take the keys to the kingdom, but they won't enter and they won't let you enter. Don't be fooled. Be sly as a snake, but gentle as a dove.

I swear to you, I ask no one for authority. I speak from what I know myself. Love your enemies. Pray for them. Share even with those who rebuke you. If someone strikes you on the cheek, offer them the other. If someone wants your coat, give your shirt also. If you are ordered to walk a mile, go another mile also. What do you care? You have nothing. What can they take from you?

Have you not heard? Treat others as you wish to be treated. Be merciful and forgive others, just as you wish to be forgiven. Don't take your neighbour to the court of law.

Settle your disputes among yourselves. Decide yourself what is right and wrong.

And don't judge your neighbours. Before you point out the splinter in your friend's eye, maybe you should think about the timber in your own eye. Do you see? Can the blind lead the blind?

Wake up. Look around you. The kingdom is here, spread out over the whole world, and some people still don't see it. Imagine a merchant who gets a huge shipment of goods, but inside he finds a perfect tiny pearl. Wouldn't he want to keep the pearl for himself and sell everything else? The kingdom is like that. It is like a treasure buried in a field. The landlord has no idea, but you can have that treasure.

Be generous, not just to your family and neighbours, but to anyone in need. A man was robbed and beaten on the road and left in the ditch. A priest and a Pharisee walked by and ignored him. But a Samaritan passed by, cleaned his wounds, and put him up in an inn. So who is your true neighbour?

Look. You know who is righteous. What someone puts into their mouth neither defiles or purifies them. What comes out of one's mouth defiles or purifies. Don't just wash the outer layer like the priests and forget the inside. Make the inside like the outside. This is the kingdom. You create good and evil by what you do. Goodness comes from the good that a person builds up in the heart from a life of common decency. Evil comes from evil work stored up in the heart. Those who try to save their life will lose it. Don't gather treasures that will only be lost. Store up treasures that remain.

Don't worry about sins. The lawyers can't tell you what sin is. Sin comes when you act contrary to your nature. But when you know yourself, when you follow your nature, that is righteousness. Male or female doesn't matter. In the kingdom there is no male or female.

Start now. Do you think you cannot take up a holy life until you have raised your children or buried your parents? Don't wait. Let the dead bury the dead. Commit now. A slave can't serve two masters.

Beware. Your own family may cast you out, but look at us. We have each other; this is our family.

In the kingdom, the first is last, the last is first. This little child, pure in spirit, is greater than the prophets. Who has something to eat? Bring it out. Share it with your neighbour. The kingdom is here.

SIN AND PURITY

Nothing in this message requires a miracle or supernatural beliefs. Jesus never defines "God" for his audience, other than referring to Abba, or the father in heaven, who will provide sustenance. The only term he uses for God in the Sermon on the Mount is "the highest." Listeners in the crowd may have harboured any number of different ideas about deities, but still could have understood and adopted his message to love their enemies or give to anyone who asks.

Recall that both John the Baptist and Jesus addressed four concerns important to first-century peasants: purity, atonement, authority, and acts of righteousness. The public obsession with purity reflects very real first-century peasant existence. Several millennia of agriculture had triggered population growth and urban development, while also financing a social elite protected by imperial armies, fed with the taxed toil of the peasantry. By the first century, however, humanity had experienced its first population decline, made worse by warfare, but more significantly caused by poor urban sanitation and the spread of disease. The fixation on clean and unclean food, purity rituals, and itinerant healers reveals the public response to the health crisis in society. Jesus shifted the focus to action by equating purity with inner awareness and outer generosity rather than ritual.

Jesus, as we've seen, consorted with outcasts, not only the poor, but also tax collectors and sinners. One common first-century tradition equated sin with the body, with sex, and specifically with women. Jesus rejected this and accepted women among his disciples, a policy every bit as radical in his culture as healing on the Sabbath. In *Thomas*, he equates sin to hypocrisy when he says that by simply fasting or performing rituals, without good deeds, "you bring sin upon yourself." The *Mary* Gospel equates sin to "violating your nature."

The *Mary* Gospel provides an invaluable balance against the overwhelming elite, male voices that drafted the orthodox canon, and especially the malicious patriarchal voices that later excluded and demonized women. The *Gospel of Thomas* names only Thomas, Peter, Matthew, James (likely Jesus' brother), and two women: Salome and Mary. *The Sophia of Jesus Christ* counts seven women and twelve men among the disciples. The second-century Apocalypse of James reports seven women, and adds that Mary possessed advanced understanding of the teachings. The canonical Gospels and the *Didache* list of community rules introduce the tradition of exclusively male disciples.

The evidence of Pliny in the second century records women as deaconesses among Christian groups. Second-century Christian leaders Marcion and Valentinus honoured Mary and Salome as disciples, and appointed women priests. These practices so thoroughly clashed with both Jewish and Roman social convention that they suggest a special origin, going back to Jesus, who treated women as equals. His most devoted followers maintained this egalitarian practice.

According to the gospel record, a woman, likely Mary Magdalene, anointed Jesus with oil from an alabaster jar, earning praise from the teacher. Peasant followers would have naturally associated her with "the people's queen," the daughter of Asherah. Recall Jesus' answer to a question by disciples about entering the kingdom, from the *Gospel of Thomas*: "When you make the two into one... the inner like the outer... male and female into a single one... then you will enter [the kingdom]."

Jesus interpreted purity as a consequence of self-knowledge and public action, not observance of religious ritual. Jesus behaved as one who saw divine unity behind common dualities. His spiritual epiphany appears to have revealed to him the magic, more-than-human realm in which the unexpected happens, where people can be healed, and where both men and women move beyond the precincts of gender.

ATONEMENT

The second plank (after purity) in the social program advanced by John and Jesus examines atonement, or forgiveness. For Jesus, if sin does not follow from breaking religious laws, then those laws do not confer atonement. Jesus made forgiveness immediate and unconditional. Without relying on religious status, Jesus would merely say, "Your sins are forgiven." His simple prayer to Abba in heaven asks only that one be forgiven "as we forgive others."

In modern Pennsylvania, on October 2, 2006, a disturbed young man, Charles Roberts, entered a schoolhouse in Nickel Mines and shot eleven Amish schoolgirls, four of whom died. The horrified community met on the evening of the shooting with mental health counsellors to process their grief and support their traumatized children. Then, without hesitation, they organized a horse-and-buggy caravan to visit the Roberts family, the parents of the shooter, with food and condolences. The Amish may appear strange to some people, since they reject technology and live simply, but in doing so, they preserve the lifestyle instructions of Jesus. They also preserve his fundamental message: Love your neighbour, even your enemy. Like Jesus, the Amish in Pennsylvania broke the cycle of revenge with forgiveness.

Jesus taught that unadorned, unconditional compassion is the kingdom made manifest. By forgiving, one is forgiven. We have seen that the two most common images Jesus used to describe the kingdom are the tiny mustard seed and the leaven in bread. The kingdom is something small and natural that grows to produce profound effects. Politically, first-century listeners might have interpreted such images as surreptitious rebellion. Ethically, among the people of the land, the images might suggest humility and perseverance. Leaven speaks directly to the community around the hearth, and wild mustard growing in a landlord's neatly sown fields evokes both daily labour and steadfast resistance to oppression.

In the Jewish scriptures, leaven is only mentioned in its absence, as a sacrifice to mark Nissan, the spring equinox, when the Passover lamb is eaten with bitter herbs and unleavened bread. So this image from Jesus would sound radical to devout Jews. The mustard seed would sound radical in contrast to the Jewish image of the giant cedar, with its massive roots and expansive canopy. Jesus links these images to the patient determination of genuine spirituality in the here and now. Those who sipped from the spring of knowledge that Jesus tended throughout his life learned to safeguard that infinitesimal kernel of understanding until it grows naturally into something that will have impact in the world.

Matthew and *Luke* record Jesus saying, "The kingdom has come" and "the kingdom is among you." We have seen that in *Thomas*, God's kingdom is both "within you" and "spread out on earth." The hidden will be revealed when we know what is in front of our faces.

A common first-century view espoused by John the Baptist and by later Christian writers held that God's own divine action would, someday, bring about the kingdom. Statements by Jesus, therefore, that the kingdom was available here and now sound original to him. Whatever Jesus believed regarding El, Yahweh, or Abba, he rejected waiting around for deities to do the work.

It will not come by watching for it. It will not be said, "Look, here!" or "Look, there!" Rather, the kingdom is spread out upon the earth, and yet people don't see it.

Jesus asks those who will listen to help transform the world now, by helping the disadvantaged. Those who equate spirituality with transcending the physical world in space or time miss this important lesson. Authentic spirituality appears everywhere in nature —"Turn over a stone; I am there"— and in the quality of attention that each individual applies in the most mundane of acts. This message remains relevant today.

Those of us who can afford the time to write or read books are the lucky ones. Two-thirds of humanity lives in poverty, and nearly a billion destitute people barely cling to life. Nine million starve to death every year, 25,000 per day, most of them children. Meanwhile, 2 percent of humanity owns half the wealth. Indeed, as Jesus foretold, the rich got richer and the poor continued to suffer. In this regard, we might view 2,000 years of social progress as rather undistinguished. Masses of homeless poor still suffer from disease in virtually every city in the world. The modern skid-row corner mission, offering a soup kitchen, free clinic, and encouragement to the homeless, might be the most Jesus-like, Christian institution to survive two millennia of cultural evolution.

Jesus understood these social conditions, perhaps intuitively. Francis of Assisi, Albert Schweitzer, and Mother Teresa understood the message of Jesus and applied it to their world. However, giving hope to the disenfranchised remains as politically unpopular today as it was in the first or twelfth centuries. We still hear the comfortable and powerful dismiss advocates for the poor as bleeding hearts, or worse, implying something sinister or criminal in compassion. We have made human greed our economic doctrine, as if the dispossessed of the world are poor because they aren't trying hard enough to compete.

In the first Jesus healing story in *Mark*, set in Capernaum on the Sea of Galilee, Jesus tells the paralytic, "Your sins are forgiven," just like that, without ritual or pretense. This bold assertion of forgiveness removed the power of atonement and healing from the priests and handed it to the poor themselves. Jesus confronted the system of privilege and patronage, inciting the prying scholars at the scene to wonder: Who gave Jesus the right to forgive sins?

PERSONAL POWER

After purity and atonement, the third element of the Jesus social program, echoing John the Baptist, concerns personal authority. Jesus, like John, healed on his own word, based on his own knowledge. He did not hold a licence from the Temple priests or claim to speak for God. He may have felt inspired by his god, but he did not presume to hold a franchise from that god. Jesus broke the priests' monopoly by healing on his own personal conviction. He instructed disciples to move among the villages as he did, helping those in need. These emissaries had glimpsed the light inside and offered it to others without reservation.

Jesus put his own stamp on healing in three important ways. First, he gave it away without obligation, without asking his beneficiaries to honour him as their patron. "Don't call me master; do as I do." Secondly, he encouraged disciples to heal others, creating a network of healed healers. Rather than claim special powers, he handed his gift to others, sharing the power before it froze in his hand and corrupted his purpose. Finally, he healed on his own authority, without appealing to religious convention or divine sanction. Jesus offered free, universal, unbrokered compassion.

Had Jesus remained in one place, say Capernaum, and established a school, as Hillel and Honi did, his enterprise might have brought beneficial economic spin-offs to the community. He would have become a patron for his disciples, who would, in turn, have become patrons for others. However, Jesus rejected the entire web of imperial patronage and the commercialization of peasant life in Galilee. He didn't apply for a foundation grant, design a logo, and register his method as a trademark. He gave his kingdom away to all.

His itinerancy was neither forced nor idle, but rather a living example to follow. The disciples were not simply wandering around scamming free meals. Jesus taught them to decline all trappings of privilege: family, social, or imperial. Recall that an unanswered question remains regarding why Jesus spoke of rejecting, even hating, one's family. In his rejection of privilege, we glimpse an important piece of that puzzle. Jesus rejected family hierarchy and privilege that helped promulgate injustice. He rejected family and social practices, for example, that conferred on a father the right to sell his daughters into slavery, or murder his children for believing in a foreign deity.

Jesus' itinerancy reflected an absolute refusal to allow his message to become a public franchise or an economic hedge fund for his friends. Instructions to his most ardent followers remain clear: No money, no extra possessions, no staff or sceptre. Give it up. Heal each other. Share your food. Share whatever you have. Inspire others to do the same. Then, move on and provide healing and sustenance to the next person who needs help. This mission implied a radical response to oppression, violence, and social privilege, and it remains a radical response today. His unique courage, not posthumous doctrines and mythologies, provides the signature of a living, breathing Jesus that can still inspire humanity in the twenty-first century.

Rare is the person who achieves fame and does not attempt to leverage it into some other personal benefit. Jesus was such a person. He did not exalt himself or send his audience to holy scripture for insight; he sent them back to their own experiences, thoughts, and desires. The authority that Jesus assumed derived from personal knowledge, and he directed his listeners to seek their own personal knowledge.

Self-reflection appears as a motif of the Jesus message in *Mark*, *Thomas*, the Q sayings, the *Gospel of Mary*, *Dialogue of the Saviour*, and other accounts. See the timber in your own eye. Look within. In *Mark*, Jesus explains his parable about seeds that fall on poor or fertile ground: "The final group...are the ones who listen to the message and take it in and produce fruit." The *Mary* Gospel says, "The seed of true humanity exists within you." In *Thomas*, Jesus says: "When you know yourselves, then you will be known, and you will understand that you are children of the living Father. But if you do not know yourselves, then you live in poverty."

Still today, one might observe real human tragedies driven by the insatiable ego, old habits, resentments, and vengeance. Self-awareness provides the remedy to these obstacles of the ego and represents timeless wisdom. Jesus talks about seeing the reflection of oneself that existed "before you were born," a common image in Vedic and Buddhist traditions. Jesus may have heard about the importance of self-knowledge as taught by Socrates or Gautama Buddha, but he put his own spin on it. Jesus told disciples that when they look inside, they will find a light, and encouraged them to impart this light to their neighbours. These ideas became a focal point of his teachings.

Finding this light is not an intellectual process, but rather intuitive; it is a quality of attention, not a doctrine to be memorized.

For Jesus, self-knowledge is not a private concern, but the beginning of a public concern. Self-awareness is the first step in being an effective agent of social justice in the world. With this, we reach the heart of the matter: For Jesus, authentic spiritual insight appears in the quality of one's action in the world. Spirituality is measured by the consequences it produces in the living world.

ACTION HERE AND NOW

The itinerant, modest, culture-crashing style of Jesus emulated the Cynic sages, but Jesus and his disciples were not out to simply mock wealthy hypocrites or score philosophical points. The Jesus mission intended to actually make life better for others by healing them and teaching them to share whatever they had.

The instruction to give freely is particularly interesting since Jesus spoke primarily to the poor. He encouraged them not to dwell on their own poverty and troubles, but rather to give to others. Giving to others appears in Jewish scriptures — Ezekiel, Deuteronomy, and Job — but again, Jesus adds his own emphasis. He provides the example of the Good Samaritan, who gave unconditionally. Even sinners love their families and friends, he says; that's nothing special. Be better than that. Love foreigners, those with other beliefs, even those who rebuke and attack you.

When Jesus speaks of love, the Greek manuscripts predominantly use the word *agape*, from the root *agan*, meaning "much," signifying abundance and sharing, quite distinct from *eros*, "romantic love"; *phileos*, "friendship"; or *storge*, instinctual "family love." Jesus spoke Aramaic, so we may not know his precise term, but Greek translators used *agape*. Some English translations render this as "love," but we should note that it means "sharing." For Jesus' first-century audience, his instruction would imply sharing God's natural gifts, the abundance of the world, distributed equitably to all.

Jesus showed the poor that giving rather than hoarding provided enough for everyone. In large crowds, he instructed his disciples to share whatever food they had, and indeed, no one went hungry. Later writers recorded these events as miracles, and perhaps in some sense they were. Even today, it might appear miraculous if people in a large modern city fed the hungry on a daily basis.

Although Jesus experienced a spiritual awakening, he remained a man of earthly purpose. As much as he borrowed from philosophers and ethical teachers, he was not satisfied with philosophy or ritual. His central point remains unambiguous: Spiritual insight is revealed by deeds. Talk is cheap. Action counts. In *Matthew* we hear: "Wisdom is vindicated by her deeds," echoing a common axiom that Jesus could have heard from an uncle or a wandering sage. Nevertheless, he made the principle his own by becoming a living example.

The golden rule — treat others as you wish to be treated — may represent the most common piece of ancient wisdom in the world, and Jesus likely had heard it in the Hillel version since childhood: "What is hateful to you, do not do to your neighbour." Jesus flips this around, making it positive and active: "Whatsoever you wish others should do to you, do so to them." Jesus consistently asks for action, for physical evidence of understanding. The Buddhists refer to such enlightened action as "achieving the meaning."

Of course, this is no small task. Love those who rebuke us? Who among us can face insult or physical abuse without dreams of revenge? How often have organized Christian churches failed this simple mandate? Witness the Inquisition, witch-burnings, the violence of modern empires, or the cycle of revenge in the Middle East. Jesus taught action, but not violence. "Turn the other cheek," he insisted. No violence or warfare anywhere, any time, honours the authentic Jesus. The papal armies of Innocent III and the U.S.

Corpus Christi nuclear submarine represent insults to his memory. Unconditional generosity is the challenge Jesus set before the world. Jesus did not have to invent this idea, since it appears as common wisdom, but actually living it became his great gift to the future of humanity. A simple act of unconditional kindness is the tabernacle of Jesus' message.

WITNESS YOURSELF

On the morning of December 21 — the first day of Hanukkah, eve of the solstice, and five days before Christmas in 2003 — I muted the television and watched the blinking images of cluster-bomb victims in the al-Dora neighbourhood of Baghdad. The scene reminded me of my only visit to Baghdad many years earlier: the yellow-grey stone, homes with dirt floors, and dusty, timeless sandalled citizens at the mercy of history by the rivers of Babylon, the great city of Nebuchadnezzar, Cyrus, and Alexander. Now, as then, generals whispered state secrets inside the gates that retainers would deny in public. I watched the modern empire stagger in pursuit of desert riches and global supremacy and I imagined all the armies that had forded the Euphrates River in a similar quest. I remembered standing before the massive stone tomb of King Cyrus, 600 kilometres to the east in Persia, bearing witness to the cold fate of colonial pride. Empires fade, great kings die and turn to dust, but the human story and struggle for survival endure.

History matters because it tells us how we arrived in our present circumstances and how we might respond. History is the evidence that verifies or refutes social philosophy. Doctrines come and go, harboured by the status quo, drafted to protect power, and parroted to justify self-interest. Truth remains elusive, as any serious student of history knows. Certainty remains the realm of ideologues. "The whole problem with the world," wrote Bertrand Russell, "is that fools and fanatics are always so certain of themselves, and wiser people so full of doubts." The lessons of history cannot be found in lists of rules, but might be glimpsed as a distant ship passing in a fog.

Official history gets dressed up to serve the culture that writes it. The counter-history of every age springs from those who are not intimidated by the consequences of acting on their conscience rather than convention: Jesus, Gandhi, Rosa Parks. Like other innovators, Jesus cracked open the cultural inertia of his age with pure authenticity and unadorned compassion for humanity. Rare is the spiritual experience that cuts through cultural norms and social convention to reveal raw, unprogrammed awakening. Jesus the Galilean appears to have experienced just such an epiphany. He found his neighbours drunk on illusion, but few thirsty for knowledge. He exposed the hypocrisy of privilege and offered hope to those left out, the dispossessed, the losers.

To understand our past, we cannot set the historical issues aside and simply cling to mythologies of former ages. Nor can we set aside the mythologies to understand the historical facts. Truth emerges from both stories and factual evidence. We don't do Jesus or ourselves any service by accepting shoddy fourth-century scholarship, mistaken translations, or politically biased rewrites as the real message of Jesus. Ideas have their time in history, and the time has certainly arrived in the twenty-first century to honour Jesus as any other historical figure. Regardless of what I or you or anyone believes about Jesus or Mary Magdalene, they deserve honest inquiry. We don't dishonour Jesus by asking: Did he really exist? What did he actually say and do? What did he believe or intend? On the contrary, such questions are precisely what Jesus would expect. Like the victim of a dysfunctional family, society has failed to know its own history, unable to escape the double bind of the lie itself and the taboo against talking about it.

I recently attended a literary conference in Victoria, B.C., and delivered a seminar called "Writing History." After the seminar, in the hallway, an attendee asked if I would talk to her about the history of Jesus, and we went to a coffee shop. She appeared curious, but cautious and even distressed. We talked for about an hour and I gave her a list of books to read — Crossan, Karen King, Rosemary Ruether, the Nag Hammadi Library — and some websites to visit. Finally she gazed at me with a look of panic and asked, "If I read these will I lose my faith?" I did not know what her faith was, so I could not answer her question. I felt helpless. If I could see her now, I would like to say, "If you believe that your god created you, including your intelligence, then why would you ever fear using that intelligence to learn about the world or about someone else's religious ideas? What is there to fear in knowledge?"

Spiritual insight may be a private affair, but we all share the same pool of spiritual wisdom recorded throughout history. We have nothing to fear from knowing about Rama, Gaia, Jupiter, Jesus, or Muhammad riding Buraq the white horse into heaven. Even if we learn that certain legends are mythology, not history, we will find that they still reveal secrets about human experience and emotion. The stories mean things, important things, about how people cope with each other and the world. We do not have to confuse myth with history to absorb its treasures. We are not stuck in an intellectual limbo where we can't "prove or disprove" alleged miraculous events that appear in cultural myth. We make such judgements every day to distinguish fact from fiction and genuine insight from delusion and manipulation.

We do not serve the memory of Jesus by denying the dark side of religion, the horror of children abused in religious institutions, the victims of the Inquisition, or the casualties of sectarian violence in Belfast or Jerusalem. We often don't talk about religion's shadow because we do not want to offend, but our silence buys suffering. Perhaps if we achieved a better relationship with our own religious traditions, we would find the insight and courage to make peace with other traditions. Ethics is not about beliefs, but rather about the actual experience of joy or anguish. Our actions, not our doctrines, count in the world.

History is not on autopilot, but emerges as the summation of choices and actions performed by the living. "What will be, will be" is a proverb for laziness. "What will be" is the result of the choices we make and the actions we take. Jesus lived and taught this lesson. How we act to our neighbour, our enemy, to the unfortunate, to the earth itself, measures our humanity. Jesus encouraged his audience to wake up. Witness yourself. Witness what is before your eyes. Be as a child, alive with wonder and natural generosity. We honour Jesus when we distinguish his teachings from the proclamations of Paul, the machinations of Constantine, the travelogues of his mother Helena, or the historical revisions of Eusebius. We cannot have it both ways. There is no historical or cultural value in pretending that the mythic constructions of Roman sycophants or clever rationalizations of Augustine are a substitute for Jesus.

The historical problem with the later-sixteenth-century Reformation is that it did not reform any of these previous errors, or the brutality and pretence of the Romanized revision of Jesus, but only divided the power structure and carried on with atrocities and counterfeit doctrines. The time has come for a real Reformation, a simple return to the authentic message of Jesus. Dominican and Episcopal scholar Matthew Fox has written that a "New Reformation will be Interfaith...female with male.... It will worship a God that loves creation." A real Reformation would worship creation itself. We will learn that spirit and matter are not at war with each other, as Plato and the Gnostics surmised and as patriarchal rulers proclaimed. If spirit comes from matter, that is the wonder of wonders!

We live inside the miracle every day, but we miss it because of our preoccupation with control over nature for our advantage. Jesus warned that those who seek to save their lives will lose life. Our modern ecological crisis is a crisis of spirit. Humanity sought salvation in all the wrong places and forgot to worship the one great gift set out before us, the abundance of the natural world. While we cobbled together promises of paradise, we bought and sold the earth's bounty. We have decimated half the forests that once existed, burned the petroleum, depleted the fish, scattered our toxins, turned farmland into desert, and now we melt the icecaps, dragnet the ocean bottom, and wage war to squeeze the last drop of oil from stone. We appear as little more than the great Babylonian or Roman empires, with fancier technology, and a longer reach.

Jesus had faith in humanity, and this knowledge bolsters my faith in humanity. It may take a miracle, or a complete disaster, but perhaps humankind can rediscover simple living, common decency, everyday compassion, and reverence for the earth. We don't need mythic superheroes; we need ordinary heroes who will witness the truth and speak up for those deprived of a voice. Perhaps the living presence of Jesus — the peaceful dream of the Ebionites, Cathars, and Quakers — will endure. Perhaps this presence appears in the actions of Iqbal Masih, the twelve-year-old murdered for opposing child slavery in Pakistan; or in Mairead Corrigan, who marched for peace in Ireland; or in the courage of Aung San Suu Kyi in Burma.

I now know that as a child, when my sister and I opened the little doors on the Advent calendar, we unwittingly honoured the advent of that presence, the *parousia* of the Ebionites. I felt that presence in the grace of my grandmother Elizabeth Goodwin. I sensed it in the life of Francis of Assisi. I witnessed it in the courage of Dorothy Day and Martin Luther King. If that presence survives, if Jesus lives, I suspect he lives in the deeds of ones such as these.

APPENDICES
THE CORE JESUS SAYINGS

1. THE *THOMAS*, MARK, AND Q (LUKE/MATTHEW) CONVERGENCE
Twelve common sayings and parables in the three earliest sources

The language varies among the sources. The most likely—usually the earliest and simplest—near-original version is quoted.

1. **The kingdom is like a mustard seed.**
   Thomas 20; *Mark* 4:30–32; Q: *Matthew* 13:31–32, *Luke* 13:18–19.
   "The kingdom...is like a mustard seed. It is the smallest of all seeds, but when it falls on prepared soil, it produces a large plant and shelter for birds of the sky." (*Thomas*)

2. **Don't hide your light.**
   Thomas 33; *Mark* 4:21; Q: *Matthew* 5:15, *Luke* 8:16, 11:33.
   "No one lights a lamp and puts it under a basket or in a hidden place. Rather, one puts it on a lampstand so that all who pass will see its light." (*Thomas*)

3. **The hidden will be revealed.**
   Thomas 5, 6; *Mark* 4:22; Q: *Matthew* 10:26, *Luke* 12:2.
   "There is nothing hidden that will not be revealed." (*Thomas*)

4. **The rich get richer: Who has receives, who has nothing is deprived.**
   This statement is probably a common maxim used by Jesus.

Thomas 41; *Mark* 4:25; Q: *Matthew* 25:29, Luke 19:26.
"To those who have, more will be given, and from those who don't have, even what they do have will be taken away." (*Mark*)

5. **Action, not ritual.**
Thomas 14; *Mark* 7:15; Q: *Matthew* 15:11 use "It's not what goes in the mouth."
"What goes into your mouth will not defile you; rather what comes out of your mouth will defile you." (*Thomas*)
Thomas 45; Q: *Matthew* 7:16, 12:33, *Luke* 6:44 (and *James* 3:12) use "good fruits."
"You'll know who they are by what they produce. Since when do people pick grapes from thorns or figs from thistles?" (*Matthew* 7:16)

6. **Unity from duality, two into one, move mountains.**
This widely attested maxim was likely common lore. The "Faith moves mountains" version is a *Paul* adaption (1 *Corinthians* 13:2), not Jesus language.
Thomas 48, 106; *Mark* 11:22–23; similar idea in *Luke* 17:6.
"When you make the two into one, you will become children of Adam (human), and when you say, 'Mountain, move,' it will move." (*Thomas* 106)

7. **Entering a strong man's house.**
Thomas 35; *Mark* 3:27; Q: *Matthew* 12:29, *Luke* 11:21.
Matthew and *Luke* may have copied *Mark*, so there are only two sources.
"One can't enter a strong person's house and take it by force without tying his hands." (*Thomas*)

8. **First and last.**
Thomas 4; *Mark* 10:31, Q: *Matthew* 20:16, *Luke* 13:30.
"The last will be first and the first last." (*Matthew*)

9. **Kingdom not in the sky, not by watching, but is here before you.**
Thomas 113, 3, 51; *Mark* 13:21; Q: *Luke* 10:16; *Mary* 4:3–4.
"The kingdom...will not come by watching for it. It will not be said, 'Look, here!' or 'Look, there!' Rather the Father's kingdom is spread out upon the earth, and people don't see it." (*Thomas* 113)

10. **Ask, seek, and knock, and you will find.**
Thomas 2, 92, 94; *Mark* 11:24; Q: *Luke* 11:9–10; *Mary* 4:7. Also found in P. Oxy. 654:2; *Gospel of the Hebrews* 4; *Dialogue of the Saviour*. The *Mark* passage is a

similar idea ("trust you will receive everything you pray and ask for"), not a direct parallel.

"Seek and you will find." (*Thomas* 92)

11. **Mission: travel to towns, without money, and heal**.
     Thomas 14; *Mark* 6:7–13; Q: *Matthew* 10:5–15, *Luke* 10:4–11.
     Parallels can be found in *Dialogue of the Saviour* and *Didache*. Precise instructions vary but *Mark*, *Luke*, and *Matthew* agree: Go among the towns without a bag, money, or second tunic; stay with whoever takes you in and heal the sick.

12. **Blaspheming the Holy Spirit won't be forgiven**.
     Thomas 44; *Mark* 3:28–30 = *Matthew* 12:31, 32b; Q: *Matthew* 12:32, *Luke* 12:10; *Didache* 11:7.
     Many scholars doubt this saying comes from Jesus. John Dominic Crossan believes it does. *Matthew* copies both Q and *Mark*.
     "Whoever utters a word against the son of Adam (humanity) will be forgiven, but whoever blasphemes against the Holy Spirit won't be forgiven." (*Luke*)

II. THE EARLIEST WIDELY ATTESTED SAYINGS FROM
THE JOHN DOMINIC CROSSAN INVENTORY
Thirty ideas from Jesus, recorded before 60 C.E.
with three or more independent sources

Crossan examines "complexes," shared ideas, not necessarily equivalent language, ranking the units based on early evidence and number of attestations. He includes authentic events (such as the Crucifixion), events merged with legend (Last Supper), and sayings from common lore (golden rule) or later writers (descent into hell). This list of Jesus sayings excludes those ideas with another origin. Notice the overlap among lists and the frequency of the *Thomas* and Q sources. For the full Crossan inventory and explanation of independent sources, see Crossan's *The Historical Jesus* (HarperCollins, 1992) or online at www.wiki.faithfutures.org. The second number is the Crossan rank. These ideas were likely spoken by Jesus.

1/1. **Mission and Message** (No money, go to towns, heal the sick)
      Thomas 14; *Mark* 6; Q1: *Matthew* 10:7–14, *Luke* 9:1, 10:4; 1 *Corinthians*, D.Sav.
2/4. **Ask Seek Knock** (And you will receive)
      Thomas 2, 92, 94; *Mark* 11:24; Q1: *Matthew* 7:7–8, *Luke* 11:9; G. Hebrews; *John* 14–16.

3/8. **Kingdom When and Where** (Not in the sky, but here)
Thomas 3, 51, 113; Q2: *Matthew* 24:26, *Luke* 17:23.

4/9. **Who Has Ears Should Listen**
Frequent in *Thomas, Mark, Matthew, Luke,* and *Mary*; likely a common expression.

5/10. **Receiving (Rejecting) the "One who sent me"**
Mark 9:36; Q1: *Matthew* 10:40, *Luke* 10:16; *Didache*; *John* 5, 12, 13.

6/15. **Against Divorce**
Mark 10:10–12; Q: *Matthew* 5:31–32, *Luke* 16:18; *Paul 1 Corinthians*; Shepherd of Hermas.

7/19. **In the Mouth, Out** (What causes defilement)
Thomas 14; *Mark* 7:14–15; Q: *Matthew* 15:10–11, *Acts* 10:14, 11:8b.

8/20. **Kingdom and Children**
Thomas 22; *Mark* 10:13–16; *Matthew* 18, 19; *Luke* 18:15–17; *John* 3–5.

9/21. **The World's Light** (A light within)
Thomas 24; *P.Oxy.* 655; *Matthew* 5:14; *Dial. Sav.* 14, 34; *John* 8, 11, 12.

10/22. **Prophet's Own Country** (Get no respect)
Thomas 31; *Mark* 6:1–6; *Matthew* 13:53–58; *Luke* 4:16–24; *John* 4:44.

11/23. **All Sins Forgiven** (Blaspheme and atonement)
Thomas 44; *Mark* 3:28–30; Q: *Matthew* 12:31–32, *Luke* 12:10; *Didache* 11:7. Some scholars believe this is later Christian, not from Jesus.

12/24. **Blessed the Womb** (That has not conceived)
Thomas 79; Q: *Luke* 11:27–28; *John* 13:17; *James* 1:25.

13/27. **Forgive Us as We Forgive Others** (Prayer)
Mark 11:25; Q: *Matthew* 6:12–15, *Luke* 11:4; plus Clement and Polycarp letters.

14/31. **First and Last**
Thomas 4; *Mark* 10:31; Q: *Matthew* 19, 20, *Luke* 13:30; P. Oxy. 654.

15./32. **Hidden Made Manifest**
Thomas 5, 6; *Mark* 4:22; Q: *Matthew* 10:26, *Luke* 12:2; P. Oxy. 654.

16./34. **The Sower** (Seeds on good and bad ground)
Thomas 9; *Mark* 4:3–8; Q: *Matthew* 13:3–8, *Luke* 8:5–8; 1 Clement 24:5.

17/35. **Kingdom Is Like a Mustard Seed**
Thomas 20; *Mark* 4:30–32; Q: *Matthew* 13:31–33, *Luke* 13:18–19.

18/36. **Lamp and Bushel** (Don't hide your light)
Thomas 33; *Mark* 4:21; Q: *Matthew* 5:15, *Luke* 8:16, 11:33.

19./38. **Serpents and Doves** (Be clever and gentle)
Thomas 39; P. Oxy. 655; *Matthew* 10; Gospel of Nazareth 7; Ignatius's letter to Polycarp.

20/40. **Who Have Receive, Those Without Deprived** (The rich get richer)
Thomas 41; *Mark* 4:25; Q: *Matthew* 25:29, *Luke* 19:26.

21/43. **Blessed Are the Poor** (Fortunate, close to the kingdom)
Thomas 54; Q: *Matthew* 5:3, *Luke* 6:20; James 2:5; Polycarp letter.

22/46. **The Tenants** (Who beat the landlord's servants)
Thomas 65; *Mark* 12:1–12; Q: *Matthew* 21, *Luke* 20; Shepherd of Hermas.

23/48. **Blessed Are the Persecuted**
Thomas 68, 69; Q: *Matthew* 5, *Luke* 6:22; Polycarp; *Gospel of Peter*.

24/49. **Temple and Jesus** (I will destroy this temple)
Thomas 71; *Mark* 14, 15; Q: *Matthew* 26, *Luke* 23; *Acts* 6:11–14; *John* 2:18–20.
Some scholars consider this to be post-70 C.E. Christian origin, not Jesus.

25/50. **Harvest Is Great** (But workers are few)
Thomas 73; Q: *Matthew* 9:37, *Luke* 10:2; *John* 4:35.
Possibly post-70 C.E. Christian origin, not Jesus.

26/53. **Knowing the Times** (Know the one before you)
Thomas 91; Q: *Matthew* 16:2–3, *Luke* 12:54; Gospel of Nazoreans 13; possible link to *John* 6:30.

27/55. **Coin, Caesar, and God** (Give to God what belongs to God)
Thomas 100; *Mark* 12:13–17.

28/57. **For or Against** (With me or against me)
Mark 9:40; Q: *Matthew* 12:30, *Luke* 11:23; P. Oxy. 1224.

29/59. **Blessed Are the Sad**
Q: *Matthew* 5:4, *Luke* 6:21; Dial. Sav. 13–14; *John* 16:20, 22.

30/63. **Who Tries to Save One's Life Will Lose It**
Mark 8:35; Q: *Matthew* 10:39, *Luke* 17:33; *John* 12:25.

III. THE HIGHEST-RANKED SAYINGS FROM THE JESUS SEMINAR
Thirty sayings that likely came from Jesus

The Jesus Seminar scholars vote on each saying attested to Jesus: (1) Yes, this is an original Jesus saying; (2) Jesus likely said something like this; (3) not from Jesus, but may reflect an idea he employed; or (4) Jesus did not say this. They vote on each individual line from each source, and assign a percentage that reflects the likelihood that the saying can be attributed to Jesus. The thirty sayings below received a ranking of 69 percent or higher. For a complete listing and explanation, see *The Five Gospels*, by Robert W. Funk and Roy W. Hoover (Scribner, 1993). For an explanation of the methodology, see this book or visit www.westarinstitute.org.

1. **Turn the other cheek**: Q: *Matthew* 5:39, *Luke* 6:29.
2. **If someone asks for your coat, give your shirt also**: Q: *Matthew* 5:40, *Luke* 6:29.
3. **Blessed (fortunate) are the poor**: *Thomas* 54; Q: *Matthew* 5:3, *Luke* 6:20.
4. **Go the second mile**: Q: *Matthew* 5:41.
5. **Love your enemies**: Q: *Matthew* 5:44, *Luke* 6:27-35; this common saying appears as "Pray for your enemies" in P. Oxy. 1224 and Didache, and appears widely outside the Jesus tradition.
6. **The kingdom is like leaven**: *Thomas* 96; Q: *Matthew* 13:33, *Luke* 13:20-21; Paul, *Galatians* 5:9, uses the metaphor to explain the impact of his own teachings, but does not attribute it to Jesus.
7. **Coin, Caesar, and God** (Give to God what belongs to God): *Thomas* 100; *Mark* 12:17, Q: *Matthew* 22:21, *Luke* 20:25; Egerton Gospel 3:1-6.
8. **Give to one who begs from you**: *Thomas* 95; Q: *Matthew* 5:42, *Luke* 6:30; Didache 1:5.
9. **Good Samaritan**: *Luke* 10:30-35
10. **Blessed are the hungry**: *Thomas* 69; Q: *Matthew* 5:6, *Luke* 6:21.
11. **Blessed are those who weep**: Q: *Matthew* 5:4, *Luke* 6:21; Dial. Sav. 13; *John* 16:20-22.
12. **The shrewd manager** (Settling his master's debts): *Luke* 16:1-8
13. **Vineyard laborers** (The first will be last): *Matthew* 20:1-15
14. **Abba, Father** (Prayer): Q: *Matthew* 6, *Luke* 11; "Abba" is used widely in *Thomas*, Q, and *Mark*; (*Thomas* 15, 16, 27, 40, 44, 50, 57, 76, 96, 98, 113; Father's kingdom, 61, 64, 69, 79, 83, 99).
15. **The kingdom is like a mustard seed**: *Thomas* 20; *Mark* 4:30-32, Q: *Matthew* 13, *Luke* 13.
16. **Don't worry** (Trust in God, look at the birds and lilies): *Thomas* 36; Q: *Matthew* 6, *Luke* 12.
17. **Lost coin** (Woman will search for her lost coin): *Luke* 15:8-9.
18. **Foxes have dens** (A son of Adam has nowhere to rest his head): *Thomas* 86; Q: *Matthew* 8:20, *Luke* 9:58; this saying is similar to both Buddhist and Taoist sayings; see chapter 8.
19. **A prophet gets no respect at home**: *Thomas* 31; *Mark* 6:4; Q: *Matthew* 13:57, *Luke* 4:24; *John* 4:44; the one saying that the *John* Gospel shares with *Thomas*, *Luke*, *Matthew*, and *Mark*.
20. **A friend visits at midnight** (Parable to illustrate "seek and you'll receive"): *Luke* 11:5-8.
21. **You cannot serve two masters** (Money and God): *Thomas* 47; Q: *Matthew* 6:24, *Luke* 16:13.

22. **The kingdom is like a hidden treasure in a field**: *Thomas* 109; *Matthew* 13:44; this parable illustrates that who seeks finds.

23. **Lost sheep** (Disciples helping one lost person): *Thomas* 107; Q: *Matthew* 18, *Luke* 15.

24. **What goes in the mouth and out** (What causes defilement): *Thomas* 14:5; *Mark* 7:14–15; *Matthew* 15.

25. **Corrupt judge** (Even a corrupt judge can administer justice, so God will): *Luke* 18:2–5

26. **Prodigal son** (Rejoicing at the return of the lost person): *Luke* 15:11–32

27. **Leave the dead** (To bury the dead; commit now): Q: *Matthew* 8:22, *Luke* 9:59–60.

28. **Eunuchs; castrating oneself for the kingdom**: *Matthew* 19:12; a cryptic saying. Jesus might have said something like this, but his purpose remains unknown. Church father Origen may have castrated himself over this passage; see Origen, *Antithesis of Law and Adultery*.

29. **By their fruit** (Know the true disciples by their action): *Thomas* 45; Q: *Matthew* 7:16, *Luke* 6:44b.

30. **The wedding feast** (Bring anyone, the lowly, the last shall be first): *Thomas* 64; Q: *Matthew* 22, *Luke* 14.

IV. MISCONCEPTIONS

Sayings and ideas that Jesus did not originate or say

Three catagories describe sayings erroneously attributed to Jesus: (1) common wisdom and lore that Jesus or gospel authors borrowed; (2) ancient cosmologies, theologies, and philosophies adopted by Judaism and Christianity; and (3) later doctrines formulated by Greek and Latin Christians and attributed to Jesus.

1. Common Sayings and Lore That Jesus Likely Borrowed

Jesus probably repeated these ideas gleaned from his cultural environment. His application of popular wisdom to his circumstances often sounds inventive and radical.

The golden rule is probably the most common ancient aphorism. It is mentioned by Confucius in *The Analects*, by Herodotus in *The Histories*, and in the Hindu *Mahabharata* and Zoroastrian *Dadistan-I-Dinik*. Jesus likely heard the Jewish Hillel version: "What is hateful to you, do not unto your neighbour." Jesus makes it positive, as recorded by *Matthew* in the Sermon on the Mount: "Treat people the way you want them to treat you."

"Love your enemy" is a universal concept, recorded in Akkadian, Buddhist, and pagan traditions. The Taoist version states simply, "Return love for hatred."

"Know yourself" was inscribed over the entrance to the Apollo temple at Delphi. The aphorism is attributed to Soctrates, Thales, Pythagoras, Heraclitus, and many others. The Buddha said, "Know your own mind." Kabir wrote, "I'll tell you the truth. The God whom I love is inside."

"Don't judge others" belongs to common wisdom. Hillel says (*Avot* 2, 4): "Judge not your neighbour until you are in his place."

"Commit now" is common in Buddhism and other traditions. Jesus might have heard the Hillel statement (*Avot* 2, 4): "Say not, 'When I have time I shall study,' for you may never have any leisure." Jesus made the point creatively as "Let the dead bury the dead."

"Whoever has ears, should listen" recalls an everyday refrain.

"A good tree is known by its fruits" reflects common proverbial wisdom.

"Healthy people don't need a doctor, the sick do," originates with the Cynic sages.

2. Ancient Concepts Adopted by Judaism or Christianity

Writers often attributed theological and cosmological concepts from Egypt, Babylon, and Persia to Jesus or erroneously presumed he believed and advocated these ideas. The following doctrines entered Judaism from Egyptian or Zoroastrian tradition after Persian King Cyrus began to influence Jewish scriptures. Jesus did not originate any of these ideas:

Angels
A trinity of deities
The end of the world
Resurrection of the dead
Judgement Day

Eternal life

Paradise in heaven

A fiery hell

Devils and demons

Ritual requirements through priests to attain heaven

Purification by water, baptism

Redemption of sins only through priests and sacrifice

A transcendent messianic saviour

Son of God, human children of the deities: Osiris, Horus, Mithras, Hercules, Bacchus, Pythagoras, Attis, Tammuz, Thor in the Baltic, Beddru in Japan, and many others

Virgin mother: attributed to Horus, Attis, Mithras, Adonis, Dionysus, Krishna, and others

Divine birth on the solstice, or three days after (December 25)

One single male deity: This concept comes from Egypt and Persia, associated with single male, all-powerful kings. The Jewish scriptures (Old Testament) mention El, Elohim, El Elyon (the Most High), Aveer, Shaddai, and the god of Moses, YHVH. The Old Testament also mentions Asherah, the Queen of Heaven, and Tammuz, the resurrected son, often to denounce them, which tells us that the authors opposed the popularity of these deities in Jewish society. Jesus mentions El, Elohim, Abba, and the Most High. El is a Canaanite god associated with a council of deities, including his consort Asherah. Elohim is sometimes plural in the Old Testament, and Most High is a relative term for a primary deity among others. Peasant Jews in northern Israel were not necessarily monotheistic, and Jesus never mentions YHVH or declares that there is only one deity. We cannot know what Jesus believed regarding deities because he does not specifically tell us, but the evidence does not establish that he believed in a single, unique deity.

Evil matter opposing perfect heaven: Jesus does not advocate this idea from Plato, Zoroastrianism, and the Gnostics.

Eucharist meal, wine and bread as the blood and body of a saviour: Jesus does not claim this idea, borrowed from Persian Mithraism, introduced by Paul, and incorporated into later gospels. Jesus' ritual meal honoured communal sharing, not the consumption of an embodied deity.

Many Bible stories — the Last Supper, Lazarus, the twelve disciples — are borrowed from Egyptian and Persian sources. For more details about ancient mythology in the Old and New Testament, see *The Hero with a Thousand Faces* by Joseph Campbell (Paladin, 1949); *The Pagan Christ* by Tom Harpur (Thomas Allen, 2004); *Ancient Christian Gospels: Their History and Development* by Helmut Koester (Trinity Press, 1990); and *The Root of All Religion* by Alvin Boyd Kuhn (Kessinger Publishing, 1993).

3. Later Christian Ideas

Jesus as a messiah ("Christos"): Jesus does not make this claim. Paul introduces the idea, which later Greek-speaking and Latin Gentile groups developed.

Blood atonement; Jesus dying for sins: Jesus associated forgiveness with forgiving others. He told the infirm, "Your sins are forgiven," without condition, except that they must forgive others.

Original Sin: Jewish theology does not include this doctrine, and Jesus never mentions it. The idea originated in the fourth century with Augustine, later adopted by Roman Catholic theologians and Protestant reformers such as Martin Luther and John Calvin.

To gain heaven, believe that Jesus is a divine messiah: Jesus does not say this. The concept begins with Paul, is augmented by the *John* Gospel author, and is later developed by the Roman and Protestant churches.

Male disciples and male priests: Later Greek and Latin Christian writers adopted this patriarchal idea, expunged goddesses and priestesses, denounced women in churches, and slandered Mary Magdalene. Jesus included Mary and other women among his closest disciples.

"Those who want to come after me should deny themselves, pick up their cross, and follow me." (*Mark* 8:34). "The sun will be darkened, and the moon will not give off her glow, and the stars will fall from the sky, and the heavenly forces will be shaken! And then they will see the son of Adam coming on the clouds with great power and splendor." (Mark 13:24–26)

These passages and many others are the creation of the author or later Christian editors, relying on Jewish scriptures (Daniel, Ezekiel, Joel, Psalms, etc.). The statements do not come from Jesus. Evidence shows that gospel authors searched Jewish scriptures to make the new religion appear foretold, but they relied on Greek translations. They give away their methodology by putting Greek idioms on the lips of Jesus, including the un-Jewish "I am" statements (*ego eimi*) in the *John* Gospel. Jesus spoke Aramaic and taught by his own authority and knowledge, not by appealing to scriptures, especially in Greek translation.

For a survey of gospel sources, later editing, and doubtful attributions to Jesus, see *Misquoting Jesus* by Bart D. Ehrman (Harper, 2005); *The Canon of the New Testament: Its Origin, Development and Significance* by Bruce M. Metzger (Clarendon Press, 1987); and *The Five Gospels* by Robert W. Funk and Roy W. Hoover (Polebridge/Scribner, 1993).

NOTES AND SOURCES

THE COMPLETE GOSPELS

We possess no Aramaic, Hebrew, or first-century New Testament manuscripts. The earliest Greek manuscripts employ different words, verses, and even entire chapters. English editions of the Bible suffer from erroneous sources, later redaction, and poor translation. Beyond the popular gospels, some 200 sources — gospels, sayings collections, dialogues, commentaries, and other accounts — contribute to an understanding of what Jesus might have said. Historians make no substantial distinction between canonical and non-canonical literature.

The following primary sources used in this book provide a comprehensive foundation of the complete gospels:

i.   *The New Oxford Annotated Bible* (Oxford University, 1973, 1994): A reliable modern translation with notes explaining the problems, uncertainties, and history of revisions. *The New Revised Standard Version* is edited by Bruce M. Metzger and Roland E. Murphy. The translation panel includes thirty-four renowned contributors, including John Knox, Herbert G. May, John Breck, Leslie J. Hoppe, and Mary C. Callaway.

ii.   *The Complete Gospels*, ed. R. J. Miller (Polebridge Press, 1992): This volume includes the New Testament and seventeen additional gospels and fragments, including *Thomas*, *Mary*, Ebioinites, Nazoreans, Hebrews, Egerton, Dialogue of the Saviour, the *Gospel of Peter*, and others. The *Scholars Version* translations are edited by Robert W. Funk, Vanderbilt University; Daryl D. Schmidt, Texas Christian University; Julian V. Hills, Marquette University; Ron Cameron, Wesleyan University; and Karen L. King, Harvard University and Occidental College.

iii. *The Five Gospels*, Robert W. Funk, Roy W. Hoover (Scribner, 1993): Includes the four canonical gospels, and the *Thomas* Gospel, with a commentary on statements attributed to Jesus. The authors compile the opinions of hundreds of scholars to examine sayings and parables that Jesus borrowed from common tradition, those attributed to Jesus by later writers, and those he may have originated and spoken. The translation panel includes Ron Cameron, Karen L. King, Julian V. Hills, John Dominic Crossan, John S. Kloppenborg, Helmut Koester, Mahlon H. Smith, Marvin W. Meyer, and others. Each of the contributors are experts in their fields of Greek, Hebrew, Aramaic, and Coptic languages, Middle Eastern history, and text analysis.

iv. *The Nag Hammadi Library*, ed. James M. Robinson (Harper & Row, 1988): The complete contents of the thirteen books found near Nag Hammadi, Egypt in 1945, plus four manuscripts from Oxyrhynchus, Egypt. A team of thirty-eight translators, contributors, and distinguished scholars includes Elaine H. Pagels, Helmut Koester, Marvin W. Meyer. The forty-seven texts include the gospels of *Thomas, Mary, Philip*, Egyptians, the Gospel of Truth, *Pistis Sophia, Dialogue of the Saviour*, "Thunder: Perfect Mind," and the Apocalypses of James and Peter.

v. *The Gospel of Mary of Magdala*, Karen L. King (Polebridge Press, 2003). The *Mary* Gospel merits particular focus due to the purging of the feminine voice in the historical record.

vi. Early Christian Writings compiled by Peter Kirby at www.earlychristianwritings.com: Alternative translations and commentaries for each of 155 significant texts from the first three centuries after the life of Jesus, including *Didache*, Epistle of Barnabas, Shepherd of Hermas, *Gospel of Judas*, commentaries by Church patriarchs such as Ignatius and Origen, and evidence from historians such as Titus and Pliny.

vii. *The New Strong's Exhaustive Concordance of the Bible*, James Strong (Thomas Nelson, 1991): The classic source for definitions of Hebrew and Greek words used in the Bible. *Strong's Dictionary and Concordance* is available online at www.htmlbible.com.

Translations: All quotations attributed to Jesus, including the earliest Greek versions, reflect reconstructed, paraphrased renderings. English renderings in this book rely primarily on the sources above. Unless otherwise mentioned, quotations from the Old and New Testaments rely on *The New Oxford Annotated Bible, New Revised Standard Version* and *Scholars Version* translations. I attempt to balance academic precision with common language where these versions diverge or offer alternatives. The renderings in *The Jesus Sayings* sometimes merge sources.

For example, I substitute the traditional "kingdom" for the *Scholars Version* translation of "imperial rule" or "domain" because "kingdom" sounds more like the metaphoric language of a peasant teacher.

Abbreviations: I have dropped subtitles on books, unless they provide significant information.

Bibliography: Sources appear throughout the notes, and additional reading suggestions appear by subject at the end of each chapter section in the Notes. Since, in this day and age of search engines, one may find sources relatively easily, I give short-form references for books and websites. See additional sources and information at the author's website, www.rexweyler.com.

CHAPTER NOTES

INTRODUCTION: A REAL JESUS

Elizabeth and Francesco

1. **Poor Clares:** A Franciscan order of nuns named after Clare (Chiara) Offreduccio, who heard Francis speak in 1209 and became his confidant. She founded the Poor Ladies, guided the group for forty years, and died in 1253 at the age of fifty-nine. Modern Poor Clare nuns follow a life of prayer, poverty, and silence.
2. **Francesco di Bernardone:** Francis of Assisi's full name is Giovanni Francesco di Pietro di Bernardone, taking Pietro from his father and Giovanni from his mother.

Innocent of What?

3. **Innocent III's war on the Cathars:** See *A Most Holy War* by Mark Gregory, who argues that the Cathars did not exist as a unified movement and that the war targeted anyone who denied Roman Church authority. Cistercian Abbot Arnaud-Amaury, "Slay them all!" is quoted from Caesarius of Heisterbach (c. 1180–1250) in *Caesarius Heiserbacencis monachi ordinis Cisterciensis, Dialogus miraculorum*, ed. J. Strange (J. M. Heberle, 1851).
4. *La Civiltà Cattolica*: "Catholic Civilization," an Italian magazine founded by Jesuits in 1850 and brought under direct Vatican control in 1885. In 1880, *La Civiltà Cattolica* depicted the Jews as "insolent children, obstinate, dirty, thieves, liars, ignoramuses, pests." See David Kertzer, *The Popes Against the*

Jews (Knopf, 2001), on the role of *La Civiltà Cattolica* in nineteenth- and twentieth-century anti-Semitism.

5. **Buddha, Mahatma Gandhi, Dorothy Day, Martin Luther King, Susan B. Anthony:** These social reformers link civil rights to spiritual awareness. Dorothy Day led the Catholic Worker Movement for thirty years; see her memoir, *Loaves and Fishes* (Harper & Row, 1963). Quaker pacifist Susan B. Anthony led the U.S. women's suffrage movement from 1861 until her death in 1906.

A Real Jesus?

6. **Ernest Evans on Marcion:** *Tertullian: Adversus Marcionem* (Oxford University Press, 1972).
7. *Excavating Jesus*, John Dominic Crossan and Jonathan Reed (HarperCollins, 2001).

Ways of Knowing

8. **Mythos and Logos:** *The Battle for God*, Karen Armstrong (Ballentine, 2000).
9. **Gospel is not history:** John Dominic Crossan, "Dateline NBC," February 26, 2004.
10. Buddhist Aung San Suu Kyi leads the democracy movement in Burma; Catholic Mairead Corrigan co-founded the Community of Peace People in Ireland; both women received the Nobel Peace Prize.
11. Dalai Lama quoted by Matthew Fox in *A New Reformation*, Wisdom University Press, 2005.

FURTHER READING

Francis and Clare: St. *Francis of Assisi: A Biography*, Omer Englebert (Servant Ministries, 1979). *Francis and Clare: The Complete Works*, Regis Armstrong and I. C. Brady; (Paulist Press, 1986).

Pope Innocent III: *Innocent III: Vicar of Christ or Lord of the World?* Edited by James Powell (Heath & Co. 1963). *Inquisition*, Edward Peters (The Free Press, 1988).

Abuse of religious authority: *Vows of Silence*, Jason Berry and Gerald Renner (The Free Press, 2004); *Confronting Power and Sex in the Catholic Church*, Bishop Geoffrey Robinson (John Garratt Publishing, 2007); *Church, Charism and Power*, Leonardo Boff on church collusion with South American dictatorships (The Crossroad Publishing Company, 1985); *Christianity, Patriarchy and Abuse*, Joanne Carlson Brown and Carole Bohn (Pilgrim, 1989); *Vicars of Christ: The Dark Side of the Papacy*, Peter De Rosa (Poolbeg Publications, 2000); *Papal*

Sin, Garry Wills (Doubleday, 2000); *Sex, Priests, and Secret Codes*, Thomas P. Doyle, A. W. Richard Sipe, and Patrick Wall (Volt Press, 2006); and see Doyle's research and bibliography of Papal abuse of power at www.reform-network.net.

Modern analysis of religious conflict: Sam Harris, *The End of Faith: Religion, Terror and the Future of Reason* (W. W. Norton. 2004) and *Letter to a Christian Nation* (Knopf, 2006); John Shelby Spong: *Liberating the Gospels* (HarperCollins, 1997), *Why Christianity Must Change or Die* (HarperCollins, 1998), and *The Sins of Scripture* (HarperCollins, 2005); *Chaos, Creativity, and Cosmic Consciousness*, Rupert Sheldrake, Terrence McKenna, Ralph Abraham, and Jean Houston, Ph.D. (Inner Tradition, 2001); *The God Delusion*, Richard Dawkins (Houghton Mifflin, 2006); *God Is Not Great*, Christopher Hitchens (McClelland & Stewart, 2007).

Historical precedents: *The Varieties of Religious Experience*, William James (Collins, 1971); *Letters and Papers from Prison*, Updated Edition, Dietrich Bonhoeffer, a priest and prisoner in Nazi Germany writes about the authentic message of Jesus (Touchstone, 1997); *Why I Am Not a Christian*, Bertrand Russell, (Touchstone, 1957); *Natural Grace*, Matthew Fox and Rupert Sheldrake (Doubleday, 1977); *Lost Christianity*, Jacob Needleman (Doubleday, 1980).

CHAPTER 1: WITNESS

1. **"King of the Jews":** *John* 16:31; see Translations on page 338.

The Earliest Bible

2. **P52 Fragment:** John Rylands Library, Manchester, U.K. For translation, see "P52: A Fragment of the Gospel of John" at www.kchanson.com; Bruce Metzger: *Manuscripts of the Greek Bible*, (Oxford University Press, 1981) and *The Early Versions of the New Testament* (Oxford University Press, 1977); and "The Use and Abuse of P52: Papyrological Pitfalls in the Dating of the Fourth Gospel," Brent Nongbri, *Harvard Theological Review* 98, 2005.
3. Constantin von Tischendorf, *When Were Our Gospels Written?* (American Tract Society, 1866); the excerpt of "The Discovery of the Sinaitic Manuscript" can be accessed online at www.rosetta.reltech.org.
4. **Apollos from Alexandria:** Acts of the Apostles 18:24
5. **Travel times, first-century Mediterranean:** *Hammond Atlas of World History*, ed. G. Garraclough, R. Overy (HarperCollins, 1978, 1997), p. 89.

For This I Was Born

6. **Yehuda, Yehudi, Yacov, Yeshua:** There is no "J" sound or letter in Hebrew and Aramaic languages. The modern "J" (Judea, Jesus) appeared in the sixteenth century. See chapter 2.

7. *John 18:37,* "This is why I was born," is based on Robert T. Fortna's translation, *The Complete Gospels* (1994).

Tender Youth and Servant Maids

8. **Pliny letter to Trajan:** Pliny, Epistle x:96.

9. **"Yeshu":** *The Soncino Babylonian Talmud, Tractate Sanhedrin, Folio* 43, ed. Rabbi Dr. Isidore Epstein, trans. Rabbi Jacob Shachte (The Soncino Press, 1948).

10. **"Christus":** Tacitus, *Annals,* book 15, chapter 44.

A Wise Man

11. **Flavius Josephus quotes:** *The Works of Josephus,* trans. William Whiston (Hendrickson Publishers, 1980). See *Josephus and the New Testament,* Steve Mason (Hendrickson Publishers, 1980).

12. **"Domitian":** *The Life of Flavius Josephus,* chapter 76, the closing lines of his personal memoir.

13. **"Iēsous, a wise man":** *Jewish Antiquities,* 18:3:3, trans. Louis H. Feldman (Loeb Classical Library, 1965)

An Elusive Jesus

14. **Messiah, MSYH:** Derived from the Hebrew verb *mashach,* "to rub with oil," as Samuel rubbed the head of Saul, anointing him king. The Aramaic *m'shikha* means "anointed." The Greek *Christos* converts the verb and adjective to a noun, "the anointed one."

A Historical Jesus

15. Mythicist scholars doubt Jesus existed as a single, historical figure. See *The Jesus Myth,* G. A. Wells (Open Court, 1998), which suggests Jesus is a composite figure; *Deconstructing Jesus,* Robert M. Price (Prometheus Books, 2000) examines early Jesus sects; and *The Jesus Mysteries,* Timothy Freke and Peter Gandy (HarperCollins, 2000) discusses the influence of pagan avatar deities. See also *The Jesus Puzzle,* Earl Doherty (Canadian Humanist Publications, 1999) and a summary of Doherty's arguments at www.jesus-puzzle.humanists.net. Other writers (Robinson, Loisy, Drews) agree with the mythic view. Burton Mack writes in *A Myth Of Innocence* (Augsburg

Fortress, 1998), "Much of the evidence [for Jesus] is secondhand, all of it is later."

16. **William R. Inge, "No materials for a life of Christ.":** Howard Marshall, *I Believe in the Historical Jesus* (Eerdmans Publishing Company, 1977).

17. **Thomas Jefferson:** *The Life and Morals of Jesus of Nazareth* (compiled in the 1820s, published in 1904); a modern edition, *Jefferson's Bible*, ed. Judd Patton (American Book Distributors, 1997). The letters to Dr. Benjamin Rush and William Short are from the *Memorial Edition of Jefferson's Writings*, vol. 10 and 11.

FURTHER READING

Jesus as a Jew: Géza Vermes: *Jesus the Jew* (Augsburg Fortress, 1981) and *Jesus In His Jewish Context* (Augsburg Fortress, 2003); *Jesus and Judaism*, E. P. Sanders (Augsburg Fortress, 1987); *Rabbi Jesus*, Bruce Chilton (Image, 2002); *Jesus of Nazareth, King of the Jews*, Paula Fredriksen, (Vintage, 2000); and *A Marginal Jew: Rethinking the Historical Jesus*, John P. Meier: vol. 1. *The Roots of the Problem and the Person* (Anchor Bible, 1991), vol. 2. *Mentor, Message, and Miracles* (Anchor Bible, 1994), and vol. 3. *Companions and Competitors* (Anchor Bible, 2001).

The early quest: *An Apology for the Rational Worshipper of God*, Hermann Reimarus (1774); *The Life of Jesus Critically Examined*, David F. Strauss (1835); *The Quest of the Historical Jesus*, Albert Schweitzer (Adam & Charles Black, 1948); and *The History of the Synoptic Tradition*, Rudolf Bultmann (Hendrickson Publishers, 1990).

The modern quest: John Dominic Crossan: *The Historical Jesus*, (HarperCollins, 1992); *Jesus: A Revolutionary Biography* (HarperCollins, 1994); *The Essential Jesus* (HarperSanFrancisco, 1994), which examines the earliest sayings and images of Jesus; and *Excavating Jesus*, with Jonathan L. Reed (HarperCollins, 2001). For a rebuttal of Crossan's conclusions about a historical Jesus, see Earl Doherty's review of *The Birth of Christianity* (HarperCollins, 1999) at www.jesus-puzzle.humanists.net.

Burton Mack: *Christian Myth* (Continuum Books, 2001) and *Who Wrote the New Testament?* (HarperCollins, 1996); *The Historical Figure of Jesus*, E. P. Sanders, (Penguin, 1996); *The Historical Jesus: A Comprehensive Guide*, Gerd Theissen (Augsburg Fortress, 1998); *Honest to Jesus*, Robert Funk (HarperCollins, 1997); *Rediscovering the Teaching of Jesus*, Norman Perrin (HarperCollins, 1976); *From Jesus to Christ*, Paula Fredriksen, (Yale University Press, 2000); and *Jesus After 2000 Years: What He Really Said and Did*, Gerd Lüdemann (Prometheus Books, 2001).

Writers reconciling Christian faith with a historical Jesus: Marcus J. Borg, *Jesus* (HarperCollins, 2006); and N. T. Wright: *The Resurrection of the Son of God* (Augsburg Fortress, 2004) and *The Original Jesus: The Life and Vision of a Revolutionary* (Eerdmans, 1997).

A historical Jesus in modern literature: Mikhail Bulgakov's *The Master and Margarita* (Russian original first published in English, Harper & Row, 1967) includes a subplot about Jesus ("Yeshua ha-Notsri"). Bulgakov's sources include Strauss's *Life of Jesus Critically Examined*, *The Life of Christ* by Frederic Farrar (1874), Josephus's Jewish history, and Jacques Thibault's *Le procurateur de Judée* (1892). *The Gospel According to Jesus* by José Saramago (Harcourt Brace, 1994) offers a mythic/historical portrayal of Jesus. See also *The Man Who Died*, D. H. Lawrence (Harper, 1995); *The Last Temptation of Christ*, Nikos Kazantzakis (Touchstone, 1998); and *The Gospel According to the Son*, Norman Mailer (Random House, 1999).

Historical Jesus web sites: "The Real Jesus" at www.mystae.com offers scholarly opinion on Jesus and is compiled by Richard Shand. "The Historical Jesus" course syllabus compiled by Dr. James F. McGrath, Department of Religion, Butler University can be viewed at www.blue.butler.edu, and includes a survey of Jesus historians and links to their work. "Historical Jesus Theories" can be seen at www.earlychristianwritings.com. Westar Institute and Jesus Seminar scholars — Robert Funk, Karen Armstrong, Marcus Borg, John Shelby Spong, and others — can be researched at www.westarinstitute.org and "The Jesus Seminar Forum" at www.virtualreligion.net. "The Jesus Project" website is www.jesus-project.com.

CHAPTER 2: SAUL OF TARSUS

1. **Opening epigraph, Matthew Fox:** *A New Reformation* (Wisdom University, 2005).
2. **"Wait on tables" (Acts 6:2):** Some translators render this statement as, "in order to keep accounts."

The Mysterious Saul

3. **Acts of the Apostles as history:** Acts has been attributed to Luke, but the author remains unknown. Paul's letters and Acts do not mention each other, and their accounts diverge with regards to the Jerusalem meeting and other points. The earliest manuscripts — *Codex Sinaiticus* and *Codex Bezae* —

contain different content. Ferdinand Christian Baur in *Paulus, der Apostel Jesu Christi* (1845) and Werner G. Kummel in *Introduction to the New Testament* (Abingdon Press, 1975) conclude that Acts is historically unreliable. Gerd Lüdemann's *Early Christianity According to the Traditions in Acts* (Augsburg Fortress, 1989) suggests Acts combines history and mythology. See also Hans Conzelmann, *Acts of the Apostles* (Augsburg Fortress, 1987) and *History of Primitive Christianity* (Abingdon Press, 1973). *The Book of Acts in the Setting of Hellenistic History* by Colin J. Hemer (Eisenbrauns, 1990) offers some evidence for historicity in Acts. For a discussion of history in ancient texts, see *The Historian and the Believer* by Van Harvey (Macmillan, 1966).

4. **Josephus mentions Saul in *The Jewish Wars* 2:20 and in *Antiquities* 20:9:** "Costobarus and Saulus themselves put together a multitude of wicked wretches, because they were of the royal family... They used violence with the people, and were very ready to plunder those that were weaker than themselves." In *Jesus the Brother of James*, Robert Eisenman makes the case that Josephus's devious aristocrat is Paul the letter-writer.

The Jerusalem Deal

5. Paul mentions Aretas IV (2 Corinthians 11:32) and famine (Galatians 2:10).
6. **Five inconsistent versions of Paul's visitation:** Acts 9:1–19, 22:6–11, and 26:12–18; Paul's Epistle to the Galatians 1:11–17; and Paul's Second Epistle to the Corinthians 12:2–4.
7. **The importance of James:** See Robert Eisenman, *James the Brother of Jesus* (Viking Penguin, 1997); and *Excavating Jesus*, John Dominic Crossan and Jonathan L. Reed (HarperCollins, 2001), pp. 33–48.
8. Barnabas and Paul hear the voice of the Holy Spirit: Acts 13:1.

The Loner

9. **Assigning "Nazareth" to a first-century town raises three problems:**
   i. **The difficulty of reconciling Mark 1:9:** "Nazareth" with "Nazorean" (or Nazarene), which is used elsewhere as a title, not a reference to a town, suggesting to some scholars that Mark 1:9 is a later addition.
   ii. **The lack of historic corroboration of a first-century Nazareth:** Josephus names forty-five towns in Galilee, and none of them is Nazareth. Nazareth is not mentioned in the Old Testament, Paul's letters, the Talmud, or by ancient historians before the fourth-century report by Constantine's mother Helena and court historian Eusebius (Historical Ecclessiastes 1:7–14); see *The History of the Church from Christ to Constantine*, Eusebius, ed. Andrew Louth, trans. G.A. Williamson (Penguin, 1965).

iii. **Scarce archaeological evidence:** Excavations by Benedict Vlaminck (1892), Prosper Viaud (1889–1909), and Bellarimo Bagatti (1950s) uncovered pre-Israelite, Canaanite tombs (2000–1000 B.C.E.) and eighteen tombs from about 200 B.C.E. The citizens of Yafa, about one kilometre away, used caves in the Nazareth region for burial. Pottery dates from about 900 B.C.E., but no evidence confirms a first-century settlement. Structural evidence suggests human habitation "near the time of the gospels" (Richard Carrier) and "in the Roman period" (Jack Finegan), i.e. 70 C.E. to the fourth century. After the Jewish revolt in 135 C.E., refugees settled the Nazareth site, leaving pottery, lamps, and glass vessels. See *The Archaeology of the New Testament*, Jack Finegan (Princeton University Press, 1969, 1992); Finegan's summary, "Nazareth in History and Archaeology," at www.spiritus-temporis.com; *Archaeology and the Galilean Jesus*, Jonathan L. Reed (Trinity Press International, 2000); *Excavations in Nazareth*, Bellarmino Bagatti (Franciscan Press, 1969); *Beyond the Basilica: Christians and Muslims in Nazareth*, Chad Emmett, (University of Chicago Press, 1995); and "Biblical Archaeology" at www.bibarch.com.

10. **Nazoreans:** In addition to "set apart," a second possible meaning comes from the Hebrew root *natsar*, "to guard or protect." Perhaps the Nazoreans considered themselves "guardians" of people or righteousness.

11. **Hebrew names for the poor in the Bible:** *ebionim*, "the poor ones"; *anah*, *anawim* (Aramaic), "the poor"; *dal*, "the weak, lean"; *rash*, "those left out"; *yarash*, "utterly left out, expelled"; *muwk*, "wax poor, poorer"; *machcowr*, "poverty"; *micken*, "a poor man"; *anav*, "meek, humble"; *aniy*, "afflicted, lowly." Psalms and Job use *ebyon* and *aniy* together as "the poor and lowly," the oppressed outcasts, deprived of all dignity, food, clothing, and shelter.

12. **On Paul versus Peter:** *Paulus, der Apostel Jesu Christi*, F. C. Baur (1845), and *Paul and the Competing Mission in Corinth*, Michael Goulder (Library of Pauline Studies, 2001).

13. **Acts 15:7 quotes Peter:** "God selected me from your number to be the one from whose lips the Gentiles would hear the message."

14. **Irenaeus on the Ebionites:** Against Heresies, i.26.2.

15. **Kingdom like a child:** *Thomas* 22, 26, 4; *Mark* 10:14, 10:31; *Matthew* 11:11, 19:14, 20:16; and *Luke* 18:16, 13:30.

16. **F. C. Baur on Jesus:** *Church History of the First Three Centuries* (1853), trans. Allan Menzies, (London, 1878).

17. **Paul's disease:** Malaria was common. Epilepsy is suggested by the statement, "You did not reject me" (Galatians 4:13–14). The Greek word *ekptuo*, literally

"to spit out," is possibly linked to the ancient practice of spitting at epileptics to purge the contagion. Paul's description in Galatians 4:15, "You would have torn out your own eyes and given them to me," suggests ophthalmia, with eye infections and periodic blindness, which might explain his temporary blindness in Acts 9:9.

18. **Physical description of Paul:** Various translations use "crooked nose," "bandy-legged," and "large eyes." See "Acts of Thekla," Dennis R. MacDonald, *Anchor Bible Dictionary* (Anchor Bible, 1998); *Apollonius's Apology and Acts, and Other Monuments of Early Christianity,* W. J. Conybeare (London, 1894); *Lost Christianities,* Bart Ehrman, (Oxford University Press, 2005); and *Saint Paul,* Michael Grant, (Scribner, 1976).

Iēsous Christos

19. The name of Jesus, *Yeshua,* could be a title, meaning "saviour," Greek *soter.* Nevertheless, the name Yeshua was common in ancient Jewish culture.

20. **Earliest Paul letters:** Papyrus collection of Chester Beatty held in Dublin. F. C. Baur (1845) first identified Titus, Timothy, Colossians, Ephesians, Philemon, and Philippians as "inauthentic." See *Saint Saul,* Donald H. Akenson, (McGill-Queen's University Press, 2000), p. 125; and *The First Edition of the New Testament,* David Trobisch, (Oxford University Press, 2000).

21. **Paul on money and wages:** "Who tends a flock," 1 Corinthians 9:2–7; "collection" Corinthians 16:1; "pleased to share their resources," Romans 15:25–29; and Paul in his Italian home, Acts 28:30.

22. Paul, "deserting" and "different gospel" (Galatians 1:6–9); Paul "persecuting the church" (Galatians 1:13).

Paul's Jesus

23. **"Love your enemy":** Robert Funk and Roy Hoover in *The Five Gospels* on *Matthew* 5:43 and *Luke* 6:27–36: "The two evangelists created independent complexes out of the love saying."

24. **Mithraic Eucharist:** Virtually nothing survives from Mithraic accounts of rituals, so we rely on later references. Justin Martyr (1 Apology, ch. 66) confirms that the Mithraic Eucharist literature existed. Plutarch's reference to Mithras worship in Tarsus appears in *The Life of Pompey* (24:1–8, c. 100 C.E.). See *The Origins of the Mithraic Mysteries,* David Ulansey, (Oxford University Press, 1991); *The Ancient Mysteries,* ed. by Marvin W. Meyer (University of Pennsylvania Press, 1999); *Bible Myths and Their Parallels in Other Religions,* Thomas W. Doane, (Kessinger Publishing, 1997); and *Mithras: The Secret*

God, M. J. Vermaseren, (Chatto & Windus, 1963). In *The Pagan Christ*, Tom Harpur traces Christian rituals to pre-Persian sources in Egypt.

Paul's Kingdom

25. Pamela Eisenbaum, *The Jewish Heroes of Christian History* (Scholars Press, 1997).

FURTHER READING

The life and times of Paul: *From Jesus to Paul*, Joseph Klausner, trans. William Stinespring (MacMillan, 1943); *Saint Saul*, Donald Harman Akenson (McGill-Queen's University Press, 2000); *Paul: A Critical Life*, Jerome Murphy-O'Connor (Clarendon Press, 1996); *The Life and Epistles of St. Paul*, W. J. Conybeare and J. S. Howson (University of Michigan Press, 2005, an excerpt can be viewed at www.austinbiblechurch.com); Peter Richardson's University of Toronto course outline, "The Historical Paul," www.chass.utoronto.ca; and "Paul as Herodian," Robert Eisenman, www.depts.drew.edu/jhc/eisenman.

Paul's mission and theology: *Psychological Aspects of Pauline Theology*, Gerd Theissen, (T & T Clark, 1999); *Paul and the Competing Mission in Corinth*, Michael Goulder (Hendrickson Publishers, 2001); *What Saint Paul Really Said*, N. T. Wright (Eerdmans, 1997); E. P. Sanders: *Paul: A Very Short Introduction* (Oxford University Press, 2001) and *Paul and Palestinian Judaism* (Augsburg Fortress, 1983); *The Mythmaker: Paul and the Invention of Christianity*, Hyam Maccoby (HarperCollins, 1987); and *Social Science Commentary on the Letters of Paul*, Bruce J. Malina (Augsburg Fortress, 2006).

CHAPTER 3: DOWN BY THE RIVER

1. **Epigraph:** *The Secret Gospel*, Morton Smith (Harper & Row, 1973)

The Biblical Baptism

2. *Jesus of Nazareth*, Joseph Ratzinger/Benedict xvi (Doubleday 2007).
3. *Jesus the Jew*, Géza Vermes, (Augsburg Fortress, 1973); his comments on the Ratzinger book appeared in *The Times*, London, May 19, 2007.
4. **Gospel of John, chapter 1, literary styles and redaction history:** Commentary in *The Complete Gospels* (1992), *The New Oxford Annotated Bible* (1994), and *The Five Gospels* (1993); "The Gospel According to John," Raymond E.

Brown in *An Introduction to the New Testament* (Doubleday, 1997); and "An Exegetical Study of the Prologue of *John* (John 1:1–18)," Richard Van Egmond, McMaster University, at www.mcmaster.ca

Greater than John

5. **John the Baptist as Elijah:** *Matthew* 17:12–13.
6. **The Baptist in the womb:** *Luke* 1:41.
7. **Mark's Baptist story:** *Mark* 1:9–11.
8. **Gospels of Hebrews and Ebionites:** See *The Complete Gospels*, ed. R. J. Miller (Polebridge Press, 1992).
9. Ignatius letter to Smyrna, 1:1; Roberts–Donaldson translation, www.early-christianwritings.com.

At the Jordan River

10. **Josephus on John:** Antiquities of the Jews, Book 18, 5:2. *The New Complete Works of Josephus*, trans. W. Whiston, commentary by Paul L. Maier (Kregel, 1999). The Whiston translations appear online at earlychristianwritings.com.
11. Josephus on Banus, *Vita*, ch. 2.

Preventing Mischief

12. **Herod and Baptist:** Mark 6:17–20; Josephus, *Antiquities*, Book 18, 5:2.
13. Deng Xiaoping quoted in *The Deng Xiaoping Era*, Maurice Meisner, (Hill and Wang, 1996, p. 482). The J. Edgar Hoover FBI memo, March 4, 1968, from the 1976 Senate Select Committee on Intelligence; see *Orders to Kill*, Dr. William Pepper (Warner Books, 1998), and *Murder in Memphis*, Mark Lane (Thunder's Mouth Press, 1993).
14. **Dates for John the Baptist:** John's death in 36 C.E. is based on Josephus references to historic events such as the reigns of Tiberius and Aretas. See "Dating of John According to Josephus," in *John the Baptist and Josephus*, online at J. G. Goldberg's Flavius Josephus website, members.aol.com/fljosephus/JohnTBaptist. An earlier date that conforms with the orthodox gospels is possible according to Christiane Saulnier, "Herode Antipas et Jean le Baptiste," *Revue Biblique* 91:362–376 (1984).

Impending Cataclysm

15. For a dialogue among scholars about whether or not Jesus believed in an imminent end of the world, see *The Apocalyptic Jesus: A Debate*, with Dale Allison, Marcus Borg, John Dominic Crossan, and Stephen Patterson

(Polebridge Press, 2001); and *Jesus: Apocalyptic Prophet of the New Millennium*, Bart Ehrman (Oxford University Press, 1999).

16. **Literary dependence:** See *The Gospel of Mary of Magdala*, Karen L. King (Polebridge Press, 2003) and "Written Gospels or Oral Tradition," Helmut Koester, *Journal of Biblical Literature*, 113.2, 1994.

17. **"John appeared in the countryside":** Presumed "original" details appear nearly verbatim in *Matthew* and *Luke*. See *The Formation of Q*, John Kloppenborg (Trinity Press, 2000); *The Lost Gospel*, Burton Mack, (HarperCollins, 1993). These early source verses are examined in chapter 4. The rendering here relies on: (1) Burton Mack, *The Lost Gospel* (HarperCollins, 1993); (2) Arland D. Jacobson in *The Complete Gospels*, ed. R. J. Miller (Polebridge Press, 1992); (3) *The New Oxford Annotated Bible* (Oxford University Press, 1973, 1994); and (4) a technical translation by John S. Kloppenborg, James M. Robinson, and others, which is available at www.chass.utoronto.ca.

18. **"The head of prophecy":** *Secret Book of James* (*Apocryphon*), trans. Francis E. Williams, *The Nag Hammadi Library*, Robinson (1988). This and Ron Cameron's translation appear online at www.gnosis.org.

Like a Child

19. **A child, greater than John:** From Thomas 46, *Scholars' Translation* by Stephen Patterson and Marvin Meyer in *The Complete Gospels*; available online at www.misericordia.edu. The "Q" source verses (Luke 7:28 and Matthew 11:11) set this saying after Jesus sends John's messengers away, and is an example of how written gospels attached narrative to raw sayings recorded in Thomas.

FURTHER READING

Flavius Josephus, *Antiquities of the Jews* 18:5, *The New Complete Works of Josephus* (Kregel, 1999). For the social context of John the Baptist and Jesus, see Richard Horsley: *Bandits, Prophets, and Messiahs: Popular Movements in the Time of Jesus* (Trinity, 1999) and *Archaeology, History, and Society in Galilee* (Trinity Press, 1996); Helmut Koester: *Introduction to the New Testament, Volume II: History & Literature of Early Christianity* (Walter de Gruyter, 2000) and *Ancient Christian Gosepls* (Trinity Press, 1990); *The Historical Jesus*, John Dominic Crossan (HarperCollins, 1992), "John and Jesus," Chapter 11; and *John the Baptist and Jesus*, W. Barnes Tatum (Polebridge Press, 1994). For a Christian perspective on John's example of righteousness, see *John the Baptist*, Alexander J. Burke (Saint Anthony Messenger, 2006).

CHAPTER 4: CHILD IN THE KINGDOM

The Source

1. **Q verses in *Matthew* and *Luke*:** See *The Lost Gospel: The Book of Q*, Burton Mack (HarperCollins, 1993) for a reconstruction of the presumed Q source. In *The Historical Jesus,* John Dominic Crossan suggests that the Q verses likely appeared within thirty years of Jesus' death, in Galilee, possibly in the town of Tiberias.

2. **Strata in the Q verses:** John Kloppenborg, from the University of Toronto, first recognized independent layers of Jesus tradition within the Q material: *The Formation of Q*; (Augsburg Fortress, 1987); *Q Parallels* (Polebridge Press, 1988); *Excavating Q: The History and Setting of the Sayings Gospel* (T & T Clark, 2000); Kloppenborg and Marvin W. Meyer, Stephen J. Patterson, Michael G. Steinhauser, eds., *Q Thomas Reader* (Polebridge Press, 1990); Kloppenborg and Leif E. Vaage, eds., *Early Christianity, Q and Jesus* (Scholars Press, 1991); and Kloppenborg, James M. Robinson, and Paul Hoffmann, eds., *The Critical Edition of Q* (Augsburg Fortress, 2000). For a critique of Kloppenborg's stratification of Q, see "Q-Community and Implications for Historical Yeshua" by Dennis Ingolfsland, *Journal of the Evangelical Theological Society*, June 2003, online at BNET Research, www.findarticles.com.

   Further resources include *The Four Gospels: A Study of Origins*, Burnett H. Streeter (Macmillan, 1930); *The First Gospel: An Introduction to Q*, Arland D. Jacobson (Polebridge Press, 1992); *The Jesus Tradition in Q*, Dale C. Allison (Trinity Press, 1997); *The Quest for Q*, David R. Catchpole (T. & T. Clark, 1993); and *Q: The Sayings of Jesus*, Ivan Havener (Michael Glazier Books, 1987).

Treasure among the Tax Receipts

3. **Grenfell and Hunt discoveries:** *City of the Sharp-Nosed Fish*, Peter Parsons (Weidenfeld & Nicolson, 2007); *Excavating Q*, John Kloppenborg (T & T Clark, 2000), Chapter 7, "Putting Q on the Map."

4. **"These are the...sayings":** Translation of the Greek *Thomas* by Marvin W. Meyer, Stephen J. Patterson, in *The Complete Gospels* (Polebridge Press, 1992).

A Light Within

5. *Logia Iesou: Sayings of Our Lord from an Early Greek Papyrus*, Bernard Grenfell and Arthur Hunt, modern edition (Kessinger, 1996).

Cops and Outlaws

6. *Nag Hammadi Library*, ed. James M. Robinson (Harper & Row, 1978), with commentary on the discovery, the manuscripts, and the texts. An account of the discovery, with images and maps appears, in "The Nag Hammadi Library," www.naghammadi.com.

Basileia

7. Kingdom: For an explanation of *basileia* translated as "imperial rule," see *The Complete Gospels,* ed. R. J. Miller (Polebridge Press, 1992), page 12, and *The Five Gospels,* Robert W. Funk and Roy W. Hoover (Scribner, 1993), pp. 40 and 136.
8. **Kingdom inside and outside:** *Thomas* 3, with parallels in *Thomas* 89, *Mark* 13, *Matthew* 24, *Luke* 17, and Job 28.
9. **Woman with a jar of meal:** *Thomas* 97.

Moving Mountains

10. *Thomas-Q-Mark* sayings: Translation from Meyer and Patterson (see note 4 on page 351.) Helmut Koester writes in *Ancient Christian Gospels* (p.95, 150): "The materials which the *Gospel of Thomas* and Q share must belong to a very early stage of the transmission of Jesus' sayings."
11. **Nine Thomas-Q-Mark sayings; variations on the core Jesus message:**
    What is hidden, revealed: *Thomas* 5, 6; *Mark* 4: 22; Q (*Luke* 12:2, *Matthew* 10:26).
    Fruits of action: *Thomas* 14, 45; *Mark* 7:14–23; Q (*Luke* 6:44, *Matthew* 7:16); *James* 3:12.
    Mustard seed: *Thomas* 20; *Mark* 4:30–32; Q (*Luke* 13:18–19, *Matthew* 13:31–2).
    Light and lamp: *Thomas* 33; *Mark* 4:21; Q (*Luke* 8:16, 11:33, *Matthew* 5:15).
    Rich get richer, the poor are deprived: *Thomas* 41; *Mark* 4:25; Q (*Luke* 19:26, *Matthew* 25:29).
    Kingdom in knowledge, not in a place: *Thomas* 3; *Mark* 13:21–23; Q (*Luke* 17:20–25, *Matthew* 24:23–28).
    Last shall be first: *Thomas* 4; *Mark* 10:41; Q: (*Luke* 13:30, *Matthew* 20:16).
    Unity from duality, move mountains: *Thomas* 106, 48; *Mark* 11:22; Q (*Luke* 17:6, *Matthew* 17:20)
    Entering a strong person's house: *Thomas* 35; *Mark* 3:27; Q (*Luke* 11:21–22, *Matthew* 12:29).

A Little Something for Everyone

12. The mustard seed saying parodies the Old Testament image of a giant cedar in Ezekiel 17:22–3 and Daniel 4:10–12.

13. **Kingdom like leaven:** *Thomas* 96 and Q (*Luke* 13:20–21, *Matthew* 13:33); see *The Five Gospels*, Robert W. Funk and Roy W. Hoover, (Scribner, 1993) p. 195.
14. **Child, greater than John:** *Thomas* 46 and Q (*Luke* 7:28, *Matthew* 11:11).
15. **Children in the Kingdom:** The *Thomas* version is paralleled in *Mark* and likely copied from there into *Luke* and *Matthew* (*Thomas* 22, *Mark* 10:14, *Matthew* 19:14, *Luke* 18:16).
16. "History is philosophy acquired from evidence," or "philosophy learned by example," attributed to Thucydides (c. 460–395 B.C.E.), who wrote *The History of the Peloponnesian War*, and to Dionysius Halicarnassus (c. 60–7 B.C.E.), who wrote commentary on Thucydides.
17. Black Elk, an Oglala Lakota spiritual leader, and Rosa Parks, who helped launch the U.S. civil rights movement, typify the tradition of nonviolent social justice advocacy based on personal spiritual awareness.
18. Mohandas K. Gandhi, *The Collected Works of Mahatma Gandhi*, vol. 37 (Government of India, 1970), quoted in *The Gospel According to Jesus*, Stephen Mitchell (HarperCollins, 1991).

FURTHER READING

Gospel sources: See notes 1 and 2 in this section. See also Burton Mack's, *A Myth of Innocence: Mark and Christian Origins* (Augsburg Fortress, 1988); *The History and Theology of the New Testament Writers*, Udo Schnelle, (Augsburg Fortress, U.S./SCM, London, 1998); *The New Testament: A Historical Introduction to the Early Christian Writings*, Bart Ehrman (Oxford University Press, 1999); and *Studying the Synoptic Gospels*, E. P. Sanders and Margaret Davies (Trinity Press, 1990).

The Thomas Gospel: Meyer and Patterson translation in *The Complete Gospels* (1994) and online at www.users.misericordia.edu. *The Gospel of Thomas*, Marvin Meyer (HarperCollins, 1992); *The Gospel of Thomas: Discovering the Lost Words of Jesus*, John Dart, Ray Riegert, and John Dominic Crossan (Ulysses, Seastone, 2000); and *The Gospel of Thomas: A Guidebook For Spiritual Practice*, Ron Miller and Stevan L. Davies (Skylight Paths, 2004).

For an examination of *Thomas* in relation to oral tradition, the *John* Gospel, women disciples, Gnosticism, ritual, and asceticism, see: *Thomas at the Crossroads*, ed. Uro Risto (T & T Clark, 1998) and *Beyond Belief: The Secret Gospel of Thomas*, Elaine Pagels (Random House, 2003). Pagels describes how the "Doubting Thomas" story in *John* denounces the rival *Thomas* community, and how this clash continued into the fourth century.

CHAPTER 5: INTO THE TOWNS

1. **Epigraph:** John Kloppenborg, "Alms, Debt and Divorce: Jesus' Ethics in Their Mediterranean Context," *Toronto Journal of Theology* 6:182–200, 1990.

2. **Jewish polytheism in Galilee:** Mark S. Smith: *The Early History of God: Yahweh and the Other Deities in Ancient Israel*, (Eerdmans, 2002) and *The Origins of Biblical Monotheism: Israel's Polytheistic Background and the Ugaritic Texts* (Oxford University Press, 2003); *Canaanite Myth and Hebrew Epic*, Frank Moore Cross (Harvard University Press, 1997); *The Bible Unearthed: Archaeology's New Vision of Ancient Israel and the Origin of Its Sacred Texts*, Israel Finkelstein and Neil A. Silberman, (Touchstone Books, 2001).

    Israelite ancestors as agrarian, polytheistic Canaanites, pastoral nomads, and Semitic slaves from Egypt, and Judaism emerging within Canaanite society: *Who Were the Early Israelites and Where Did They Come From?*, William G. Dever (Eerdmans, 2006); G. E. Mendenhall: *Ancient Israel's Faith and History* (John Knox Press, 2001) and *The Tenth Generation: The Origins of the Biblical Tradition* (Johns Hopkins University Press, 1974). In *A Marginal Jew*, vol. I, II, and III, John Meier refines the idea of Jesus as a Jew, distinguishing his Galilean traditions from mainstream temple Judaism, and showing how Jesus further marginalised himself by rejecting ritual, law, and religious authority.

    Evidence that Old Testament scriptures were revised during the Persian empire (c. 539–330 B.C.E.): *The History of Israel*, Martin Noth, (Harper & Row, 1960); *Essays on Old Testament History and Religion*, Albrecht Alt (Doubleday, 1968).

Am Ha-aretz

3. **Humans in Galilee, Ubeidiya, near the Sea of Galilee, about 1.5 million years ago:** *On the Palaeo-Ecological History of the Site of Ubediya*, E. Tchernov and O. Bar-Yosef (Israel Academy of Sciences and Humanities, 1972). Eight millennia before Jesus, stone-age cave dwellers cultivated native emmer wheat in the region. The farmers eventually moved from hillside caves into stone buildings near their fields. Some kept dead rulers in stone rooms that became shrines for ancestor-heroes, comprising the earliest known temples. Julian Jaynes discusses these sites in *The Origin of Consciousness in the Breakdown of the Bicameral Mind* (University of Toronto Press, 1976) pp. 149–75.

4. **YHVH (or YHWH):** The Hebrew letters "YHVH" refer to the God of Moses, although in Jewish tradition, the name of god is not spoken. See chapter 8 for other names of Jewish deities, and chapter 8, note 24, regarding YHVH.

5. *"Separate from people of the land":* Book of Ezra 10:11.

6. E. P. Sanders, *Jesus and Judaism* (Augsburg Fortress, 1985) p. 222.

Testimony of Eusebius

7. **"Oral tradition":** Helmut Koester, "From Jesus to Christ," PBS, *The Importance of the Oral Tradition*, at pbs.org.
8. **Gospel names:** *The Five Gospels*, p. 20. According to Tertullian (*Against Marcion*, 4:2), the second-century Marcion did not ascribe an author to the *Luke* Gospel. Eusebius in the fourth century is the principal source for the modern gospel names. See *The Nicene and Post-Nicene Fathers, Volume 1*, Philip Schaff and Henry Wace (Hendrickson, 1995); "Early Christian Texts Quoted by Eusebius on the Authorship of the Gospels," Felix Just, at www.catholic-resources.org.

Let the Dead Bury their Dead

9. **Jesus' relationship with his family:** *The Gospel According to Jesus*, Stephen Mitchell (HarperCollins, 1993) pp. 48–54; and *The Gospel According to Jesus Christ*, Jose Saramago, English trans. by Giovanni Pontiero (Harcourt Brace, 1994).
10. **Jewish family law:** Deuteronomy 13:7–11.
11. **"Let the dead bury their dead":** *Luke* 9:59–62.

Behaviour in the Kingdom

12. **Paul, "a follower of the Way":** Acts 24:14.
13. **"When you go into any region" instructions:** *Thomas* 14.

A Labourer's Wages

14. **The coin:** *Thomas* 100.

The Dogs of Philosophy

15. **Diogenes and Alexander:** Dio Chrysostom, *Fourth Discourse*; Cicero, *Tusculanae Quaestiones*, 5.32; Plutarch in *Alexander*, chapter 14.
16. **Diogenes to Hicatea:** *The Cynic Epistles*, ed. Abraham Malherbe (Society of Biblical Literature, 1986), by an unknown author, attributed to Diogenes.
17. **Gadarene swine:** *Matthew* 8:28; three deaf mutes healed: *Mark* 7:31–37.
18. **"Cynic dog, Menippus"** from *A Descent into Hades*, Lucian Menippus (120–200 C.E.).
19. **"Tread softly":** Meleager quoted in *Select Epigrams from the Greek*, J. W. Mackail (Longmans, Green, and Co., 1890), available online at www.jollyroger.com. See also "Ancient Gadara City of Philosophers," at www.research.haifa.ac.il.

20. **Jesus parallels with cynics Dio Chrysostom, Crates, Epictetus, and Seneca:** Francis Gerald Downing, *Cynics and Christian Origins* (T & T Clark, 1992) and *Christ and the Cynics: Jesus and Other Radical Preachers in First-Century Tradition* (Continuum Books, 1988), online at www.users.cyberone.com.au.

Tossing the Knapsack and Staff

21. **"Unclean places":** From "The Life of Diogenes" 6:63, *The Lives and Opinions of Eminent Philosophers*, Diogenes Laertius, trans. C. D. Yonge, (Henry G. Bohn, 1853), online at "Peithô's Web," www.classicpersuasion.org. "Physicians" quote from D. Laertius on Antisthenes, 6:6.

22. Epictetus, "The Way of a Cynic," *Discourses*, 3.22, from *The Creed of Epictetus*, Ulysses G. B. Pierce, (Beacon Press, 1916), quoted in *The Historical Jesus*, John Dominic Crossan (HarperCollins, 1992), p. 79.

Common Decency

23. **Crates, "women not inferior":** Downing, *Christ and the Cynics*, see note 21 above.

24. **Musonius Rufus:** *Essays III*, "That Women Too Should Study Philosophy."

FURTHER READING

Jesus' mission: *Jesus: A Revolutionary Biography*, John Dominic Crossan (HarperCollins, 1989); *Sheep among the Wolves: A Study on the Mission Instructions of Q*, Risto Uro (Suomalainen Tiedeakatemia, Helsinki, 1987); and *Asceticism and the New Testament*, Leif E. Vaage (Routledge, 1999).

Jesus and Cynic philosophers: *The Greek Cynics*, Farrand Sayre (Furst, 1948); *A History of Cynicism: From Diogenes to the 6th Century A.D.*, Donald R. Dudley (First published in 1937; Duckworth, 1996); and Francis Gerald Downing: *Christ and the Cynics* (Continuum Books, 1988); *Cynics and Christian Origins* (T & T Clark, 1992); and *Jesus and the Threat of Freedom* (Trinity Press, 1988).

CHAPTER 6: THE MAGDALENE

Seed of Humanity

1. *Gospel of Philip* **on Mary Magdalene:** Translation by Wesley W. Isenberg, *The Nag Hammadi Library*, ed. James Robinson (Harper & Row, 1988); Isenberg and Paterson Brown translations are online at www.earlychristianwritings.com.

2. **The "Holy Blood" hoax:** *The Da Vinci Code* borrowed its bloodline premise from *Holy Blood, Holy Grail* by Michael Baigent, Richard Leigh, and Henry Lincoln (a.k.a. Henry Soskin). The story began as a French restaurant promotion in 1953, when Noel Corbu opened the Villa Béthanie restaurant and planted a rumour that mysterious parchments had been discovered in his church. In 1955, Corbu met Nazi con artist Pierre Plantard, who promoted himself as a descendent of Merovingian French kings. With the help of academic Philippe de Chérisey, Plantard forged parchments to create the "Priory of Sion" legend and link himself to Jesus, and then slipped these forgeries into the French Bibliothèque Nationale. An actual Priory of Sion — a Catholic monastic order in ancient Jerusalem (Zion or Sion) — existed until 1617. Plantard simply resurrected the obsolete name for his bogus 1956 forgeries. Surrealist author Gérard de Sède embellished the hoax in his book *L'Or de Rennes*. Plantard bickered with Sède over royalties and testified in court that he had forged the parchments.

American astrologer Liz Greene (Leigh) read Sède's story and wove the royal bloodline into a novel about French psychic Nostradamus. Her brother Richard Leigh and boyfriend Michael Baigent then teamed up with Henry Lincoln to write *Holy Blood, Holy Grail*. French scholars claim they warned Baigent, but the *Holy Blood* authors insisted on depicting the hoax as real. Dan Brown weaved the premise into his novel, which led to the popular movie. For more information about the Jesus bloodline ruse, see *The Da Vinci Hoax*, Carl E. Olson and Sandra Miesel (Ignatius Press, 2004); and "The Da Vinci Con," by Laura Miller, *The New York Times*, February 22, 2004, online at cesnur.org.

3. **Mary in France:** Irenaeus, c.180 C.E., in *Against Heresies* (1:25:1–3), claims Carpocratian missionaries in southern France reported revelations directly from Mary Magdalene. Legends of Mary living out her life in Southern France, Egypt, Ethiopia, or Ephesus are all possible, though none of these stories can be confirmed.

4. **"Thunder: Perfect Mind":** Translation by George W. MacRae in *The Nag Hammadi Library in English*, ed. James M. Robinson (HarperCollins, 1978).

5. *Gospel of Mary* **translations:** Karen King, *The Gospel of Mary of Magdala*, (Polebridge Press, 2003), compares the Coptic and Greek versions; King's translation with variations reconciled appears in *The Complete Gospels*, ed. R. J. Miller (Polebridge Press, 1992). A translation from the Coptic by George MacRae and R. M. Wilson appears in *The Nag Hammadi Library*, ed. James M. Robinson (HarperCollins, 1978).

Body and Soul

6. *Tao Te Ching*, **Chapter 34:** See translations by Gia-Fu Feng and Jane English (Vintage, 1972), Ursula K. Le Guin (Shambala, 1998), and Stephen Mitchell (HarperCollins, 1992).

7. *Thomas* **translations:** Meyer and Patterson, *The Complete Gospels*, ed. R. J. Miller (Polebridge Press, 1992).

A Vision

8. **Vision, visitation:** The earliest mention of a future coming of Jesus appears in *Matthew*, from about 80 C.E. Mahlon H. Smith, from Rutgers University, believes the *Matthew* author transformed the coming kingdom into a coming person. "Early writers had a tendency to confuse the two," writes Smith.

9. **Buddha:** *The Dhammapada: The Sayings of the Buddha*, Thomas Byrom (Vintage, 1976).

10. *Ramayana* is rendered in prose by William Buck (University of California Press, 2000).

11. **Buddhist and Hindu influence:** In *The Life of Jesus*, Earnest Renan suggests that "wandering Buddhist monks" and Indian sages had influenced the Chaldeans, Babylonians, and Essenes.

What Are You Thinking?

12. **Male/female conflict:** In the Greek version Peter asks whether Jesus considered Mary "more worthy." The Coptic version adds, "Did he choose her over us?" Karen King suggests in *The Complete Gospels* that this shift reflects theology from "a later time."

Miriam

13. **Mary Magdalene and other women who followed Jesus:** *Mark* 15:40; *Matthew* 27:55; *Luke* 8:2. *Mark* names Mary Magdalene; Salome, possibly Jesus' sister or aunt; and Mary "the mother of James the younger and Joses," likely Jesus' mother since *Mark* names James and Joses as his brothers. *Matthew* drops Salome and adds, "the mother of the sons of Zebedee," possibly the same person.

Sorting Out the Marys

14. Elaine Pagels on women disciples: *The Gnostic Gospels* (Vintage, 1979), pp. 68–73; and Tertullian on women: *De Virginibus Velandis* 9, quoted in *Gnostic Gospels*, p. 72.

15. Jane Schaberg, *The Resurrection of Mary Magdalene* (Continuum Books, 2004)

16. **John William Draper on Pope Gregory:** "A History of the Intellectual Development of Europe" at www.h-net.org.
17. **Adam and Lilith:** *Hebrew Myths: The Book of Genesis*, Robert Graves and Raphael Patai (Doubleday, 1964), pp. 65–69.
18. **Variations in the anointing of Jesus by a woman with ointment:**
    Mark 14:3–9: Bethany, alabaster jar, anointing on the head.
    Matthew 26 6–13: Copies *Mark*.
    Luke 7:36–45: Capernaum, alabaster jar, woman "sinner," Pharisee complains about the oil.
    Luke 10:38–42: Certain village, road from Galilee, Martha and Mary.
    John 11:2: Bethany, Lazarus, Martha, and Mary anointed Jesus' feet, wiped with hair.
    John 12:1–3: Bethany, Martha, and Mary; Judas complains about the oil.
19. *Mark* **introduces Mary:** *Mark* 15:40–41.

Venus in the Spring

20. **Matriarchial society or gender balance:** *The Myth of Matriarchal Prehistory*, Cynthia Eller (Beacon Press, 2001).
21. **Ancient feminine spirituality:** *Goddesses and the Divine Feminine*, Rosemary Radford Ruether (University of California Press, 2005).
22. **Procession of the equinox:** A natural phenomenon of the earth's wobbling movement on its axis. See "The Platonic Year" by Andrew Raymond at www.revealer.com and *The Origins of the Mithraic Mysteries*, David Ulansey (Oxford University Press, 1991). Ulansey makes the case that images of Mithras slaying a bull depict the equinox sun moving from Taurus into Aries in about 2280 B.C.E. His summary, "The Cosmic Mysteries of Mithras," with procession diagrams, is posted at www.well.com/user/davidu/mithras.

Anath and Tammuz

23. **Asherah in the Bible:** With prophets (I Kings 18:19), vessels (II Kings 23:4), denounced (I Kings 15:13), "altars of incense" and stone pillars linked to Baal (Judges 6:28). See *Asherah and the Cult of Yahweh in Israel*, Saul Olyan (Scholars Press, 1988) and *Asherah: Goddesses in Ugarit, Israel, and the Old Testament*, Tilde Binger (Sheffield Academic Press, 1997).
24. **Day of Atonement, Tammuz, Suffering Servant:** *Goddesses and the Divine Feminine*, Rosemary Radford Ruether (University of California Press, 2006); *The Suffering Servant*, ed. Bernd Janowski and Peter Stuhlmacher (Eerdmans, 2004); *The Messiah before Jesus*, Israel Knohl (University of California Press, 2002); *The Legend of Ishtar and Tammuz*, Elizabeth Goldsmith

(Kessinger Publishing, 2006); *Myths of Babylonia and Assyria*, Donald A. Mackenzie (Kessinger Publishing, 2004), Chapter v, "Myths of Tammuz and Ishtar," is available online at ww.sacred-texts.com.

25. **The grain of Tammuz:** *John* 12:23.
26. **Jesus' death modelled after Tammuz and Attis:** Proposed by David F. Strauss and Bruno Bauer in the nineteenth century and later by Arnold Toynbee and John M. Roberston. See *Mythology: The Voyage of the Hero*, David Adams Leeming (Oxford University Press, 1998) and *The Hero with a Thousand Faces*, Joseph Campbell (Princeton University Press, 1968).

The Magdalene

27. **"Dalmanutha":** *Mark* 8:10 and "Magadan": *Matthew* 15:39 in parallel passages. Josephus calls the region "Taricheae" in *Jewish Wars*, III, 10:6. There are no biblical references to "Magdala."
28. **"Magdalene" as a title:** See *Mary Magdalene: Bride in Exile*, Margaret Starbird (Bear & Co., 2005) pp. 52–63. See also *The Woman with the Alabaster Jar*, Margaret Starbird (Inner Tradition, 2001).
29. **Tower of the flock, plowshares, and little clans:** Micah, Chapter 4.
30. **Weeping for Tammuz:** Ezekiel 8:14.
31. **Mary weeps for Jesus:** *John* 20:13.
32. **Mary "favoured with visions":** *The Gnostic Gospels*, Elaine Pagels (Vintage, 1979) p. 26.

FURTHER READING

Mary Magdalene: *The Gospel of Mary of Magdala*, Karen L. King (Polebridge Press, 2003); *Which Mary?: Marys in the Early Christian Tradition*, ed. F. Stanley Jones (Society of Biblical Literature, 2002); *Mary Magdalene: Myth and Metaphor*, Susan Haskins (Harcourt Brace, 1994); *Mary Magdalene: The First Apostle*, Ann Brock (Harvard University Press, 2002); *The Resurrection of Mary Magdalene*, Jane Schaberg (Continuum Books, 2004); Margaret Starbird: *Mary Magdalene: Bride in Exile* (Bear & Co. 2005), *The Woman with the Alabaster Jar* (Inner Tradition, 2001), and *The Goddess in the Gospels* (Inner Tradition, 2001).

Feminine Spirituality: Rosemary Radford Reuther: *Goddesses and the Divine Feminine* (University of California Press, 2006) and *Religion and Sexism*, ed. (Simon and Schuster, 1974). Elaine Pagels: *The Gnostic Gospels* (Vintage, 1979) and *Adam, Eve and the Serpent* (Vintage, 1988). Karen L. King: *Images of the Feminine in Gnosticism*, (Trinity Press, 2000), and *Women and Goddess Traditions in Antiquity and Today* (Augsburg Fortress, 1997). *The Chalice and the Blade*,

Riane Eisler (Harper & Row, 1988); *The Spiral Dance*, Starhawk (HarperCollins, 1999); *The Language of the Goddess*, Marija Gimbutas (HarperCollins, 1995); and *The Gospel According to Woman*, Karen Armstrong (Hamish Hamilton, 1986).

CHAPTER 7: KINGDOM OF DECENCY

Their Hearts Are Distant

1. **Eagerton Gospel:** "Eagerton Gospel," Jon B. Daniels's translation and commentary can be found in *The Complete Gospels*, ed. R. J. Miller (Polebridge Press, 1992) and *The Other Gospels*, ed. Ron Cameron (Westminster, 1982), pp. 72–75. Cameron dates Egerton "in the middle of the first century." The line about lip service comes from Isaiah 29:13.

The Passion

2. **"I'm Thirsty":** Psalms 69:21.
3. **Crucifixion study:** *The Death of the Messiah*, vol. 2, Raymond E. Brown (Doubleday, 1994; Anchor, 1999), including Marion L. Soards's essay, "The Question of a Premarcan Passion Narrative." For a critique of Soards's analysis, see *The Passion in Mark*, ed. Werner H. Kelber (Augsburg Fortress, 1976).
4. Passion scenes from Psalms 22:1, "My god, why have you forsaken me," and 22:18, "They cast lots for my clothing."
5. **Suffering Servant:** Isaiah 52:13 to 53:12: "He grew up...like a root out of dry ground...he was despised and rejected...he was wounded for our transgressions...upon him was the punishment that made us whole."
6. **Crucifixion "a Roman job":** Allen D. Callahan, associate professor of New Testament, Harvard Divinity School, on PBS, "From Jesus to Christ," www.pbs.org.

Common Wisdom

7. **Cynic proverb, "no need of a physician":** *Mark* 2:17, *Matthew* 9:12, and *Luke* 5:39.
8. **Pagan prayer, "all men's happiness"** is quoted in *Five Stages of Greek Religion*, Gilbert Murray (Kessinger Publishing, 2003).
9. For common secular proverbs in the New Testament, see *The Five Gospels*, Robert W. Funk and Roy W. Hoover (Scriber, 1993) p. 286.
   Barren fig tree: *Luke* 13:6–9.
   Sower, good and bad soil: *Thomas* 9; *Mark* 4:3–8, *Matthew* 13:3–8, *Luke* 8:5–8.
   Wine and wineskins, old and new: *Thomas* 47; *Mark* 2:22, 5:37, *Matthew* 9:17, *Luke* 5:39.

10. **"Christos":** 1 Corinthians 15:3–5; *Mark* 8:31.

11. **Greek Septuagint scriptures attributed to Jesus:** For example, *John* 4:48, *Matthew* 4:1–11.

12. **Jesus "growing up":** *The Five Gospels*, Robert W. Funk and Roy W. Hoover (Scribner, 1993) p. 287.

The Essence

13. The Jesus Seminar has been criticized for its voting method to evaluate the authenticity of Jesus sayings, although academic polls are a tradition of Bible scholarship. In 1611, James Stuart of Scotland convened a committee to resolve discrepancies in Greek translations, resulting in the King James English Bible, which nevertheless suffered from poor originals and translation errors. In 1979, a United Bible Society panel updated the Greek New Testament. In 1989, a U.S. National Council of Churches panel assembled the New Revised Standard Edition of the Bible.

14. **Generosity in the Sermon on the Mount:**
    Give your coat and shirt: *Matthew* 5:40, *Luke* 6:29.
    Go the second mile: *Matthew* 5:41.
    Give to those who ask: *Luke* 6:30, *Matthew* 5:42, *Thomas* 95, Didache1:5a.
    By their fruits, compassionate action: *Thomas* 45, *Matthew* 7:16, *Luke* 6:44.
    Giving to others in the Jewish scriptures:
    "Does not…require a pledge for a loan": Ezekiel 18:16.
    "Give some of your food": Tobit 4:16.
    "Giving them food and clothing": Deuteronomy 10:18.
    "I rescued the poor who cried for help": Job 11–13.

15. **The Good Samaritan:** *Luke* 10:30–35.

What Did You See?

16. **Loaves and fishes story:**
    First version: *Mark* 6:31–44; *Matthew* 14:13–21 and *Luke* 9:10–17 copy *Mark*.
    Second version: *John* 6:5–15 adds a boy with food and disciple Andrew.
    Third version: *Mark* 8:1–9 and *Matthew* 15:32–39.

17. **Elisha feeding multitudes:** II Kings 4:42–44.

18. **David receives priest bread from Ahimelech:** I Samuel 21:3.

Miracle of Generosity

19. *Agape*, **"sharing":** John Dominic Crossan and Jonathan L. Reed, *Excavating Jesus* (HarperCollins, 2001), p.175.

Heal the Sick

20. **Stevan Davies, Jesus as healer, carpenter:** Quoted from Jeffrey L. Sheler, "Who was Jesus?" *U.S. News & World Report*, December 1993. Davies concludes that *Mark* used *Thomas* as a source; see "further reading," chapter 4 notes.

21. **John the Baptist reborn:** *Mark* 6:13–14.

22. **Healing a youth in Nain:** *Luke* 7:11–16, borrows from the Greek Book of Kings 17:8–23, with Jesus in the place of Elijah. See *The Acts of Jesus*, Robert Funk (Polebridge Press, 1998), p. 91, and *Gospel Fictions*, Randal Helms (Prometheus Books, 1988) p. 64.

23. **Healing stories:** John Dominic Crossan believes the rare corroboration among healing accounts suggests "Jesus, as a magician and miracle worker, was a very problematic and controversial phenomenon not only for his enemies but even for his friends." (*Historical Jesus*, HarperCollins 1993, p. 311).

24. **The Devil as a Greek and Christian concept:** Henry A. Kelly: *Satan: A Biography* (Cambridge University Press, 2006) and *The Devil, Demonology, and Witchcraft*, (University of California Press, 1968; Wipf and Stock Publishers, 2004). See also *The Origin of Satan*, Elaine Pagals, (Random House, 1995).

25. **Jesus to Peter, "Get out of my sight, you Satan":** *Mark* 8:33 and *Matthew* 16:23.

26. **Beelzebul controversy, "He's out of his mind":** *Mark* 3:20–30.

27. **Teacher of Righteousness:** Jesus shares many traits — historic and mythic — with the Essene Teacher of Righteousness and the humble teacher in Amos 7:14: "I am no prophet…I am a herdsman and a dresser of sycamore trees…"

28. *The Spell of the Sensuous*, David Abram (Pantheon, 1996).

29. **Placebo effect:** Daniel Bruns and John Mark Disorbio, "Chronic Pain and Biopsychosocial Disorders," *Practical Pain Management*, November/December 2005; Jerome Schofferman, et. al., "Childhood psychological trauma correlates with unsuccessful lumbar spine surgery," *Spine* 17, (1992), pp. 138–44; Arthur Kleinman: *Patients and Healers in the Context of Culture* (Universtiy of California, 1981) and *The Illness Narratives* (Basic Books, 1989).

    Placebo results, salicylic acid and warts: Sam Gibbs, Ian Harvey, Department of Dermatology, Ipswich Hospital, University of East Anglia, Norwich, U.K., posted at www.pubmedcentral.nih.gov.

    Penicillin V and pain: "Randomised, Double-Blind, Placebo-Controlled Trial of Penicillin V in the Treatment of Acute Maxillary Sinusitis in Adults in General Practice," J. G. Hansen, et. al, *Scandinavian Journal of Primary Health Care*, August 8, 2000.

Anti-depressants: Helen. S. Mayberg et al., "The Functional Neuroanatomy of the Placebo Effect," *American Journal of Psychiatry*, 159, May 2002.

A Radical Cure

30. **"Magic...keeping the world alive":** *The Spell of the Sensuous*, David Abram (Pantheon, 1996).
31. Gerd Theissen, "Itinerant Radicalism: The Tradition of Jesus Sayings from the Perspective of the Sociology of Literature," *Radical Religion*, 2, 1975, pp. 84–93; *The Shadow of the Galilean* (Augsburg Fortress, 1987).

FURTHER READING

Jesus as healer: *Jesus the Magician*, Morton Smith (Barnes & Noble, 1993); *Jesus the Healer*, Stevan L. Davies (SCM, 1995); *From Jesus to Christ*, Paula Fredriksen (Yale University Press, 1988, 2000); *The Greek Magical Papyri in Translation*, Hans Dieter Betz (University of Chicago Press, 1992); *The Faith Healers*, James Randi (Prometheus Books, 1989); and *Religion, Science, and Magic*, Jacob Neusner, E. Frerichs, P. Flesher, eds., (Oxford University Press, 1992). The third-century *Books of Jeu* (*Ieou*) identify Jesus as the "holy comforter;" available online at www.earlychristianwritings.com. See also *The Books of Jeu*, Carl Schmidt and V. Macdermot (Brill Academic, 1997).

CHAPTER 8: ON WHOSE AUTHORITY?

1. **Epigraph:** Bhagavad-Gita 4:6–10, Krishna to Arjuna.
2. **Blue snake:** John Izzo, personal communication. Izzo is the author of *Second Innocence* (Barret-Koehler, 2004) and *The Five Secrets You Must Discover Before You Die* (Barret-Koehler, 2008).

Humility and Integrity

3. **The unforgiving slave:** *Matthew* 18:23–34. The *Matthew* author adds the punishment from God interpretation (*Matthew* 18:35).
4. **Jesus on humility:**
   Timber in your own eye: *Thomas* 26, Q (*Luke* 6: 41–42, *Matthew* 7:3–5).
   Do not pass judgement: *Mary* 9:12, Q (*Luke* 6:37, *Matthew* 7:1).
   First shall be Last, ask a child: *Thomas* 4, Q (*Matthew* 20:16, 19:30; *Luke* 13:30), *Mark* 10:31.
   Left and right hands: *Thomas* 62, *Matthew* 6:3.

5. **Pharisees, scribes, and hypocrisy:**
    Taking the keys to knowledge: *Thomas* 39, 102; *Luke* 11:52, *Matthew* 23:13.
    Pharisees' privileges: *Mark* 12:38, *Matthew* 23:6, *Luke* 20:45–47.

6. **Ordinary mind:** *Zen Mind, Beginner's Mind*, Shunryu Suzuki, (Weatherhill, 1970, 1983); *Cutting through Spiritual Materialism*, Chogyam Trungpa (Shambala, 1987). "Eventually," Trungpa writes, "we must give up trying to be something special."

7. **Jesus instructs action not praise:**
    Why do you call me good?: *Mark* 10:18.
    Why do you call me Master?: Q (*Luke* 6:46, *Matthew* 7:21).
    Lip service: Egerton 3:5.

I Am that One

8. I am not your judge: Q (*Luke* 12:13)

9. Jesus asks, "Who am I?": *Thomas* 13, *Mark* 8:27–30, *Matthew* 16:13–20, *Luke* 9:18–22, *John* 1:35–42.

10. *Gospel of John*, **"I am" statements:** See an analysis in *The Five Gospels*, p. 419.
    "I have come down from heaven," *John* 6:38.
    "I am the light of the world," *John* 8:12.
    "I am the way, the truth, and the life," *John* 14:6.
    "I am the authentic vine," *John* 15:1, 5.

Foxes and Humanity

11. **"Adam" means human:** Maryanne Cline Horowitz, "The Image of God in Man — is woman included?" *Harvard Theological Review*, v.72, n.3-4, July-Oct, 1979.

12. **Daniel's vision, the Son of Adam:** Daniel 7:9–14.

13. *Mark* 13:26–37, the coming "son of Adam," borrows from Daniel 7:13, 9:27, 11:31, 12:11; Isaiah 13:10, Deuteronomy 13:2–4, Ezekiel 32:7, 1 Maccabees 1:54, and 4 Ezra 13:1–3. The passage was likely written with the Jewish scriptures at hand, not recalled by Jesus on the spot.

14. Son of man forgives sin: *Mark* 2:10.
    Son of man rules the Sabbath: Mark 2:28, Luke 6:1–5, Matthew 12:1–8.

15. **Foxes have dens:** *Thomas* 86, Q (*Luke* 9:57–62, *Matthew* 8:20).

16. **The humble human:**
    Buddha, *Dhammapada* 7.2, translated by Marcus Borg in *Jesus and Buddha* (Ulysses Press, 1997), p. 81.
    Lao Tzu, *Tao Te Ching*, 20, trans. Gia-Fu Feng and Jane English (Vintage, 1972)

"Thunder, Perfect Mind" 15, trans. G. W. MacRae, *Nag Hammadi Library*, ed. James M. Robinson (Harper & Row, 1988).

One God

17. **Name of God in *Luke* 1:68:** The author refers to "YHVH Elohay Yisrael," evoking the ineffable, supreme God of Israel. Jesus does not use the Moses designation, "YHVH."

18. **One God:** According to Greek historian Herodotus, Persians adopted the Egyptian god, renamed Ahura Mazda. They imagined angels to mediate with human priests, who performed baptisms, foretold a virgin birth to a divine human saviour, and assured believers that they would be resurrected after death and escorted to heaven. The Persian Zoroaster (Zarathustra) allegedly met the one god on a mountain, and later worshippers celebrated the birth of Mithras three days after winter solstice. Following the Jewish exile to Babylon, c. 540 B.C., these ideas appear in Jewish doctrines and then later in the Christian New Testament. See *The Religious Experience of Mankind*, Ninian Smart (Fontana, 1969): "After the exile of the Jewish people . . . Zoroastrian concepts influenced Jewish thought"; and *Testament*, John Romer (Konecky, 2004): "After the period of exile, other major themes of both Judaism and Christianity also begin to appear in the Bible."

19. **El:** The Canaanite El represented a supreme deity, *El ôlam* "the eternal"; Amorite *El abīka* was "god of our father"; the Ugarit *El abū banī 'ili*, "father of the gods"; and *Tôru El* or "bull god" appeared as the equinox sun rose in the constellation Taurus, c. 3000 B.C.E. See *Canaanite Religion*, Gregorio Del Olmo Lete (Eisenbrauns, 2004) and *The Faces of God: Canaanite Mythology as Hebrew Theology*, Jacob Rabinowitz (Spring Publications, 1998).

Converging Gods

20. **Abraham:** In Genesis 17:1, God tells Abraham, "I am El-Shaddai." Abraham had allegedly travelled through Amorite communities near the Euphrates headwaters, and El Shaddai may indicate an Amorite deity.

21. **Jacob's deities:** Genesis 49:22–26.

22. **El Shaddai:** *Septuagint* translation, "ample," c. 300 B.C.E. Seventy-two Jewish scribes in Alexandria translate the Torah into Greek. For the Shaddai relation to "breasts," see *Yahweh and the Gods of Canaan*, William F. Albright (Doubleday, 1968) and *The God with Breasts: El Shaddai in the Bible,* David Biale (Universtiy of Chicago Press, 1982).

23. "I will make you exceedingly fruitful": Genesis 28:3; "Be fruitful and increase in number": Genesis 35:11.

24. "I am," introduced to Moses in Exodus 3:15, is not an active verb, but rather simple being. The phrase is sometimes rendered "I am that I am," or "who I am," but is just "I am." An earlier reference in Genesis 4:26—"At that time, people began to invoke the name of YHVH"—is generally deemed a later retrofit. The new name is introduced to Judaism through Moses in Exodus. Jewish tradition forbade speaking the name YHVH except by the High Priest in the Temple, and so referred to this god as "Lord," or "Adoshem" in secular use. Orthodox Hebrew grammar eliminates "I am" from the lexicon, to avoid inadvertently profaning their God, thus "I hungry," rather than "I am hungry." See chapter 5, note 4.

25. **Shomron and Asherah:** The unknown *Shomron* may mean "Samaria" or "our guardian." Throughout ancient Israel and Judah, male and female idols of clay are found. As late as 100 B.C.E., farmers around Jerusalem practiced fertility rituals honouring multiple deities. The Jews who made these idols followed a polytheistic fertility religion, and the Jewish prohibition against idols appears far later than commonly believed.

26. **Deities "El Shaddai" and "YHVH" equated:** Exodus 6:3.

27. **Names of Jewish deities:** El, Elohim, El Shaddai, El Elyon, El Olam, Qanna, Adonai, YHVH, YHVH-Nissi, -Mekoddishkem, -Jireh, -Raah, -Rapha, -Shammah, -Shalom, -Tsidkenu, and YHVH-Sabaoth. See *Dictionary of Deities and Demons in the Bible*, ed. Karel van der Toorn, et. al. (Eerdmans, 1999); *The Early History of God*, Mark Smith (Eerdmans, 2002); and see also chapter 5, note 2.

Abba

28. In *Thomas* 61, Jesus tells Salome that he comes from "what is whole" or "undivided." The next line in this passage, "I was granted from the things of my Father," may be a later addition, similar to lines in *John* 3:35 and 13:3 that have Jesus claiming the father "turned everything over to me." See *The Five Gospels*, p. 507.

29. **Abba, the father:** Primitive, Chaldean, Aramaic; used in *Thomas*, Q, *Mark* and Paul. *Mark* (14:36) and Paul (Romans 8:15, Galatians 4:6) use the Aramaic Abba with a Greek translation, *Pater*, a rare practice suggesting some in their audiences associated Abba with Jesus, and some Greek speakers did not. Literally, "father" in Aramaic is *ab*, whereas Abba is vocative, speaking directly to the father, highlighting the personal relationship with divine spirit that Jesus offered his listeners. Prayer to Abba, Q (*Luke* 11:2–4, *Matthew* 6:9–13).

Murderers and Thieves

30. Entering a strongman's house: *Thomas* 35, *Mark* 3:27, Q (*Luke* 11:21, *Matthew* 12:29).

31. What binds me has been slain: *Gospel of Mary*, 9:27.
32. Leased vineyard, son killed: *Thomas* 65, *Mark* 12:1–9, *Matthew* 21:33–41, *Luke* 20:9–16.

Salt

33. **Salt:** *A Catholic Dictionary*, ed. Donald Attwater (MacMillan, 1961) p. 447.
34. **Sophia (wisdom) and salt:** *Gospel of Philip*, trans. Wesley W. Isenberg, *The Nag Hammadi Library*, ed. James M. Robinson (Harper & Row, 1978).
35. *Holy Vedas, Yajur Veda*, Book 5, 2:1, trans. Ralph T. H. Griffith, from www. sacred-texts.com.

Wisdom East and West

36. David Steindl-Rast, from the Introduction to Martin Aronson's *Jesus and Lao Tzu: The Parallel Sayings* (Ulysses Press, 2000). See also by David Steindl-Rast: *Words of Common Sense for Mind, Body, and Soul* (Templeton Foundation Press, 2002) and *Gratefulness: The Heart of Prayer* (Paulist Press, 1984).
37. **Buddha and Jesus:** *Buddhist and Christian Gospels*, Albert J. Edmunds and M. Anesaki (Kessinger Publishing, 2006); *Jesus and Buddha: The Parallel Sayings*, ed. Marcus J. Borg, (Ulysses Press, 1997); *Living Buddha, Living Christ,* Thich Nhat Hanh (Riverhead Books, 1997); and *The Good Heart: A Buddhist Perspective on the Teaching of Jesus,* Dalai Lama (Wisdom University Press, 1998).
38. **Lao Tzu and Jesus:** *Jesus and Lao Tzu*, Martin Aronson (Ulysses Press, 2000); *The Jesus Sutras: Rediscovering the Lost Scrolls of Taoist Christianity*, Martin Palmer, (Ballantine, 2001).
38. **"Don't store up treasures":** Q (*Luke* 12:33, *Matthew* 6:19).

FURTHER READING

Burnett Hillman Streeter: *The Buddha and the Christ* (Kessinger Publishing, 2004); *The Primitive Church* (Macmillan, 1930; Kessinger Publishing, 2003); and *The God Who Speaks*, Warburton lectures; (Macmillan, 1937). Alvin Boyd Kuhn: *The Root of all Religion* (Kessinger Publishing, 2005), and *Lost Light: An Interpretation of Ancient Scriptures* (Filiquarian, 2007).

Ancient influences on Judaism, Jesus, and Christianity: *Moses the Egyptian: The Memory of Egypt in Western Monotheism*, Jan Assman (Harvard University Presss, 1998); *Zoroastrianism*, Peter Clark (Sussex Academic, 1999); *The Ancient*

Jewish Mysticism, Joseph Dan (Mod Books, 1990); *The Pagan Christ*, Tom Harpur (Thomas Allen, 2004); *The Messiah Texts*, Raphael Patai (Wayne State University Press, 1989); *Mythology's Last Gods: Yahweh and Jesus*, William Harwood (Prometheus Books, 1992).

Wisdom East and West: *Sacred Texts of the World*, ed. Ninian Smart and Richard D. Hecht (Crossroad Publishing Company, 1982; Herder Book Company, 1984); *The Dhammapada: The Sayings of the Buddha*, trans. Thomas Byrom (Vintage, 1976); *The Dhammapada*, Gil Fronsdal (Shambhala, 2006); *Tao Te Ching*, Lao Tsu, trans. Gia-Fu Feng and Jane English (Vintage, 1972, 1997); trans. Stephen Addiss and Stanley Lombardo (Hackett, 1993); and trans. Stephen Mitchell (HarperCollins, 2006).

CHAPTER 9: BATTLE FOR THE LEGACY

1. **Epigraph:** Dionysius, Bishop of Corinth, quoted by Eusebuis, *Ecclesiastical History*, Book IV, ch. 23, v. 12.
2. Josephus calls Menahem the "son" of Judas the Galilean (*Jewish War*, II:17:8), but the chronology suggests he was the grandson.

The Scattered Israelites
3. Going "over to the Romans": Josephus (*Jewish War*, VI:2:4).

The Phoenix
4. **Clement Letter:** Translations by Charles Hoole, J. B. Lightfoot, and A. Roberts/J. Donaldson at earlychristianwritings.com. Clemens (or Clement) addresses his story to "James the Just" in Jerusalem, Jesus' brother, executed in 62 C.E., but this is not considered historical. In *The Anchor Bible Dictionary*, Lawrence Welborn dates the Clement letter between 80 to 140 C.E. The two early versions of Clemens's legend contradict each other. The Clement legend is Romantic fiction.
5. **The Phoenix:** 1 Clement, 25, Roberts/Donaldson trans.
6. **Not justified by ourselves:** 1 Clement, 32.
7. **Neither male nor female:** 2 Clement, 12.

Chained to Leopards
8. **Eusebius on Ignatius:** *Historia Ecclesiastica*, 3:22, online at www.newadvent. org. *The History of the Church*, Eusebius, (325 C.E.; Penguin, 1989). Eusebius

370 THE JESUS SAYINGS

claims Ignatius succeeded the unknown Evodius in Antioch. Another source, Theodoret (*Dialogue Immutable*, I, 4:33), claims Ignatius directly followed Peter the apostle in Antioch. None of this appears historical.

9. **Martyrium Ignatii:** See *Martyrdom of Ignatius*, online at www.newadvent.org.

10. **Ignatius letters:** See "Early Christian Fathers" at Christian Classics Ethereal Library, www.ccel.org; *The Apostolic Fathers*, v.1, Kirsopp Lake (Loeb, 1912). Among thirteen letters attributed to Ignatius, six were exposed as forgeries early, seven claimed authentic by Eusebius. The letters are dated 135–165 C.E. Some nineteenth-century scholars considered seven letters authentic [Zahn (1873), Harnack (1878), Lightfoot (1885, 1889)]. However, many scholars since conclude they are all imitations. See *The Gospel and Ignatius of Antioch*, Ramsay Srawley and Charles Brown (Peter Lang, 2000); *A Study of Ignatius of Antioch in Syria and Asia*, Christine Trevett (Edwin Mellen, 1992); *Ignatius of Antioch: A Commentary on the Letters*, William Schoedel (Augsburg Fortress, 1985); and "The Epistles of Ignatius: Are They All Forgeries?" by Bernard Muller online at www.geocities.com/b_d_muller.

11. **Ignatius letters, gospel parallels**:
   By its fruit: *Thomas* 45, Q (*Luke* 6:43, *Matthew* 12:33).
   Serpent and dove: *Thomas* 39, *Matthew* 10:16.

12. This is the Letter of Ignatius to the Magnesians, chapters 8–10, J. B. Lightfoot translation from *Apostolic Fathers* (1891).

13. "Wherever the bishop appears," to the Smyrnaeans 8, J. R. Willis translation.

Knowing John

14. **Polycarp to the Philippians:** See earlychristianwritings.com, translations by J. B. Lightfoot, Kirsopp Lake, Roberts-Donaldson.

15. **"Firstborn of Satan":** *Polycarp to the Philippians*, ch. VII, "Avoid the Docetae."

16. **Eusebius mentions Polycarp, quoting an alleged letter from Irenaeus to Florinus:** Historia Ecclesiastica 5:20:5–6.

17. **"Companion of Polycarp":** Irenaeus, *Against Heresies* 5:33:4.

18. **Eusebius on Papias:** *Historia Ecclesiastica* 3:39:4–15. Irenaeus on Papias: *Against Heresies*, v:33:4. See Stephen C. Carlson, "External Evidence: Papias" at earlychristianwritings.com; *The Origins of Christianity*, R. Joseph Hoffman (Prometheus Books, 1985); *Early Christian Writings: The Apostolic Fathers*, ed. Staniforth, Maxwell, and Louth, (Penguin, 1987); and Paul Tobin, "The Rejection of Pascal's Wager" at www.geocities.com/paulntobin.

19. **John apostle and presbyter John:** See *John: The Son of Zebedee, The Life of a Legend*, R. Alan Culpepper (Augsburg Fortress, 2006).

20. **Irenaeus on Peter and Paul:** *Against Heresies,* IV:26 and III:3. Fiction in Acts: Paul's miraculous survival from a shipwreck and a poison "viper" on Malta, for example; there have never been any poisonous snakes on Malta.

The Witness of Pionius

21. *Martyrdom of Polycarp,* trans. Kirsopp Lake and Roberts-Donaldson, early-christianwritings.com.

22. **"Pionius" and "Socrates":** *Martyrdom* 22:2: "Gaius copied from the papers of Irenaeus...And I Socrates wrote it down...And I Pionius again wrote it down from the aforementioned copy." In a second version of the story, Pionius places Irenaeus in Rome during Polycarp's execution.

23. **"Refuted every heresy":** *Martyrdom of Polycarp,* Moscow manuscript, version 22:2, trans. Richard Shrout/J. B. Lightfoot, "The Martyrdom of Polycarp," www.ministries.tliquest.net.

The Poor Ones

24. **Gospel of the Ebionites in Epiphanius, Panarion 30.13.6:** *The Panarion of Epiphanius of Salamis,* trans. Frank Williams (Brill Academic, 1987); Ebionite excerpts from Panarion at earlychristianwritings.com; and the *Gospel of the Ebionites* reconstructed in *The Complete Gospels,* ed. R. J. Miller (Polebridge Press, 1992).

25. **Eusebius attacks the Ebionites:** "Poverty of their understanding," *Historia Ecclesiastica,* 27.

26. **Jerome attacks the Ebionites:** "Synagogues of Satan," (Epistles 123, 130)

27. **Ebionite sects:** *The Book of Religious and Philosphical Sects,* Muhammad Shahrastani, trans. William Cureton (Gorgias Press, 2002); *Lost Christianities,* Bart D. Ehrman (Oxford University Press, 2005); *The Ebionites And Gnosticm,* G. R. S. Mead (Kessinger Publishing, 2006); modern Ebionites, Yahad Ebyoni, at www.ebionite.org.

By My Works

28. *The Nag Hammadi Library,* ed. James M. Robinson (Harper & Row, 1978). See Robinson's introduction regarding the discovery, the manuscripts, texts, Gnostic schools, and the philosophies incorporated in the collection.

29. **Entering the kingdom:** Apocryphon of James, 1:30, 7:25, 12:24–25, trans. Francis E. Williams, *Nag Hammadi Library,* ed. James M. Robinson (Harper & Row, 1978).

30. The letter attributed to *James,* 1:27, 2:17–18, *The New Oxford Annotated Bible* (Oxford University Press, 1994).

The Name of a Dead Man

31. **Gnostic Peter:** The Acts of Peter tells a harrowing tale of how a divine force strikes Peter's daughter with paralysis to preserve her virginity.

32. Apocalypse of Peter, 74:14, 79:30, trans. J. Brashler and R. Bullard, *Nag Hammadi Library*, ed. James M. Robinson (Harper & Row, 1978).

FURTHER READING

Heretics: The Other Side of Early Christianity, Gerd Lüdemann (Westminster John Knox Press, 1996); *The Mysterious Origins of Christianity*, Paul Angle (Wheatmark, 2007); *Jews and Christians: The Parting of Ways A.D. 70 to 135*, ed. James Dunn (Eerdmans, 1992). *The Gospel and the Church*, Alfred Loisy, trans. Christopher Home (Charles Scribner's Sons, 1909); *The Writings of the Apostolic Fathers*, Alexander Roberts and James Donaldson (1867; Apocryphile, 2007; Part I, Kessinger Publishing, 2004); *A Myth Of Innocence*, Burton Mack (Augsburg Fortress, 1998); *The Religion of the Earliest Churches*, Gerd Theissen (Augsburg Fortress, 1999). *The Text of the New Testament: Its Transmission, Corruption and Restoration*, Bruce M. Metzger (Oxford University Press, 1968); *Antioch and Rome: New Testament Cradles of Catholic Christianity*, Raymond E. Brown and John P. Meier (Paulist Press, 1983).

CHAPTER 10: THE EMPEROR'S SAVIOUR

1. **Basilides:** "Fragments from the Writings of Basilides," Gnostic Society Library, at www.gnosis.org; and Irenaeus, *Against Heresies*, 1:24:3–7, at early-christianwritings.com.

2. **Valentinus:** Stephan A. Hoeller, "Valentinus: A Gnostic for all seasons," in *Gnosis: A Journal of Western Inner Traditions*, v. 1. Hoeller quotes "grace beyond time" as a "Valentinian blessing." For Valentinian gnosticism, see *A History of Gnosticism*, Giovanni Filoramo, trans. Anthony Alcock (Blackwell Publishing, 1992); *The Gnostic Gospels*, Elaine Pagels (Vintage, 1979); *The Gnostic Scriptures*, Bentley Layton, (Doubleday, 1987); *The Rediscovery of Gnosticism*, v.1: *The School of Valentinus*, ed. Bentley Layton (Brill, 1980).

Hidden Names

3. *Gospel of Philip*, Wesley W. Isenberg trans., *Nag Hammadi Library*, ed. James M. Robinson (Harper & Row, 1978), online at Gnostic Society Library. Jesus depicts the kingdom beyond duality, "before male or female...life and death," similar to the earlier *Thomas, Mark*, and Q versions: *Thomas* 89, 22; *Mark*

7:18; Q (*Luke* 11:39–41, *Matthew* 23:25, 15:1–20). "Knowledge is freedom," is the *Philip* Gospel statement of gnosis, personal knowledge beyond dualism of spirit and body. See *The Gospel of Philip: Annotated & Explained*, Andrew P. Smith (Skylight Paths, 2005) and *The Gospel of Philip: Jesus, Mary Magdalene, and the Gnosis of Sacred Union*, Jean-Yves Leloup (Inner Traditions, 2004).

Devils and Virgins

4. **The Devil:** See chapter 7, note 24 for Kelly and Pagels on the history of the devil.
5. ***Gospel of Nicodemus,* chapters 15, 16, Jesus descends into hell:** "Satan, the prince and captain of death, said to the prince of hell, 'Prepare to receive Jesus of Nazareth.'" Fourth-century manuscripts of the Apostle's Creed do not claim that Jesus "descended into hell." That claim was added in the seventh century. See *The Gospels of Nicodemus from the New Testament Apocrypha*, Charles F. Horne (Kessinger Publishing, 2005) and *The Middle English Harrowing of Hell and Gospel Of Nicodemus*, William Henry Hulme (Kessinger Publishing, 2004).
6. **Justin Martyr, *First Apology*, Chapter 66, "The Eucharist":** See *The Apologies of Justin Martyr*, ed. A. W. F. Blunt (Wipf & Stock Publishers, 2006); and the Roberts-Donaldson translation at earlychristianwritings.com.
    Mithraic Eucharist: *Mithras, The Secret God*, M. J. Vermaseren (Barnes & Noble, 1963).
    Egyptian rite: *The Demotic Magical Papyrus of London and Leiden*, F. Ll Griffith (Cisalpino-La goliardica, 1976), and Richard A. Gabriel: *Gods of Our Fathers: The Memory of Egypt in Judaism and Christianity* (Greenwood Publishing Group, 2001) and *Jesus the Egyptian* (iUniverse, 2005).
7. **Martyr, "What you accept of Perseus":** Translations vary; the Classic Christian Ethereal Library, www.ccel.org, uses "Perseus;" Roberts-Donaldson at earlychristianwritings.com uses "Ferseus." See *New Testament Apocrypha*, ed. Wilhelm Schneemelcher (Westminster John Knox Press, 1989).
8. **Sons of God:** Egypt: Osiris, Horus, and others; Babylon: Mithra; Greek: Hercules, Dionysus, Orpheus, Hermes, Adonis, Pythagoras, Attis, and others; Roman: Bacchus and others; Hindu: Krishna, Rama; Sumerian and Akkadian Tammuz; the Essene Righteous One; Baltic Thor; Japanese Beddru; Siamese Deva Tat; and so forth. A virgin birth is common in these stories. The Christian *Didache* 9:1 records two Christian sons of God, David and Jesus. See *The Canon of the New Testament: Its Origin, Development, and Significance*, Bruce M. Metzger, (Clarendon Press, 1987); *The Egyptian Book of the Dead: The Papyrus of Ani*, E. A. Wallis Budge (Dover Publications, 1967).

9. **Trinity:** Tertullian, c. 200 C.E., "…Father, Son and Holy Spirit": *Adversus Praxeam*, 23:2:156.

    Egyptian trinity: *The Egyptian Origin of Christianity* by Lisa Ann Bargeman (Trafford Publishing, 2006); *The Pagan Christ*, Tom Harpur (Thomas Allen, 2004); and *Egyptian Mythology and Egyptian Christianity*, Samuel Sharpe (Kessinger Publishing, 1997).

    Hindu trinity: *Symbolism of Hindu Gods & Rituals*, A. Parthasarathy (Vedanta Life, 2001) and "Hare Jesus: Christianity's Hindu Heritage," Stephen Van Eck, www.theskepticalreview.com.

10. Desiderus Erasmus, c. 1516, knew the Trinity doctrine did not exist in early Greek Bible manuscripts. The insert into the *First Letter of John* is known as the "Johannine comma," 1 *John* 5:7–8. See *Misquoting Jesus*, Bart D. Ehrman (HarperCollins, 2005), pp. 78–83; and *Text of the New Testament*, Bruce M. Metzger (1992).

Channelled Gospel

11. ***Gospel of John:*** See commentary in *The New Oxford Annotated Bible, The Five Gospels*, and *The Complete Gospels*. Ferdinand Christian Baur: *Critical Investigations concerning the Canonical Gospels* (1847); *An Introduction to the New Testament*, Raymond E. Brown (Anchor Bible; Doubleday, 1997); *The Gospel of John*, F. F. Bruce (Eerdmans, 1983); *The Gospel of John*, Rudolf Bultmann (Westminster, 1971); *The Interpretation of the Fourth Gospel*, C. H. Dodd (Cambridge University Press, 1953); and Elaine Pagels, *Beyond Belief: The Secret Gospel of Thomas* (Random House, 2003).

12. **"Signs source" for *John:*** *The Fourth Gospel and Its Predecessor,* Robert Fortna (Polebridge Press, 1988; T & T Clark, 2004); *Johannine Christianity: Essays on its Setting, Sources, and Theology*, D. Moody Smith (University of South Carolina Press, 1984; T & T Clark, 2005); "Fortna's Signs-Source in John," Edwin D. Freed, R. B. Hunt, *Journal of Biblical Literature*, v. 94, no. 4 (December, 1975); and "The Signs Gospel," earlychristianwritings.com.

13. **"Doubting Thomas,"** *John* **20:27–29:** Elaine Pagels, *Beyond Belief: The Secret Gospel of Thomas* (Random House, 2003), pp. 58, 70–1; and *Resurrection Reconsidered*, Gregory Riley (Augsburg Fortress, 1995).

14. **Muratori canon:** Eighth-century fragment discovered in the eighteenth century by Italian historian Ludovico Muratori. Scholars postulate a second-century Greek original. *New Testament Apocrypha*, Wilhelm Schneemelcher and R. M. Wilson (James Clarke, 1990); *The Canon of the New Testament*, Bruce M. Metzger (Clarendon Press, 1987). The quote is from the Schneemelcher translation.

Council of Frogs

15. **Celsus:** From Origen's *Contra Celsus*, trans. Roberts-Donaldson online at earlychristianwritings.com. The versions by R. Joseph Hoffmann in *Celsus: On the True Doctrine* (Oxford University Press, 1987) are useful, but not direct quotes; Hoffmann combines quotes to reconstruct Celsus's original meaning. See *The Christians as the Romans Saw Them*, Robert L. Wilken (Yale University Press, 1986).

16. "Evil to have been educated" Origen, *Contra Celsus*, Book 3, ch. 59.

17. "Faith, having taken possession," 3:39.

18. God like Jupiter, 6:78; Origen quotes Celsus quoting agnostic ideas from Plato's *Timaeus*.

19. "Council of frogs," 4:23.

The Disappearing Teacher

20. *A Plea for the Christians*, Athenagoras (Kessinger Publishing, 2004); online at "Fathers of the Church," newadvent.org and at earlychristianwritings.com.

21. Tatian, *Apology to the Greeks*; "eternal life" 13:1; see Earl Doherty, "The Jesus Puzzle."

22. *To Autolycus*, Theophilus: "gospels" (III:12); ethical sayings (II:14); Christian means "anointed with oil" (I:12); see Doherty "The Jesus Puzzle."

The Emperor's New Religion

23. **The cross:** The Greek word used in the gospels for the instrument of Jesus' execution is "stauros," stake, as in *Mark*, 15:21–32. Fifth-century Latin translators rendered *stauros* as *crux*, as "cross," and *stauroo* ("impaled") as "crucified." *The Concordant Literal New Testament*, ed. A.E. Knoch (Concordant Publishing, 1983) explains the meaning of *stauroo*: "Fasten on a stake, impale, now by popular usage, crucify, though there was no crosspiece." In *The Companion Bible* (Kregel, 1995), Ethelbert Bullinger concludes that Jesus "was put to death upon an upright stake." The earliest Christian cross image — three intersecting lines (asterisk) forming the Greek letters *iota* and *chi* — was a popular pagan symbol and the monogram of Constantine. See *Illustrated Dictionary of Symbols in Eastern and Western Art*, James Hall (Westview Books, 1996); "Cross Crucifix" at crosscrucifix.com displays historic images of Christian crosses.

24. The Roman Mithraic cave temple is a "mithraeum." In Rome, the twelfth-century San Clemente basilica sits on the foundations of a fifth-century church that replaced a second-century mithraeum, a shrine to the saviour Mithras, an archaeological testament to mythic evolution.

25. **Constantine:** *The Life and Times of Constantine the Great*, D. G. Kousoulas (Rutledge, 2003); *Constantine and the Bishops*, H. A. Drake (Johns Hopkins University Press, 1999).

One Iota

26. **Eusebius's Bible:** *Constantine and Eusebius*, Timothy D. Barnes (Harvard University Press, 2006); *The Canon of the New Testament*, Bruce M. Metzger (Clarendon Press, 1987); *The Biblical Canon*, Lee M. McDonald (Hendrickson Publishers, 2007); "The Development of the Canon of the New Testament," Glenn Davis, www.ntcannon.org; and "The Formation of the New Testament Canon," Richard Carrier, www.infidels.org. *Constantine's Bible*, David L. Dungan (Augsburg Fortress, 2006) offers a sympathetic view of Eusebius's selection.

27. **Eusebius's history:** *The History of the Church from Christ to Constantine*, Eusebius, ed. Andrew Louth, trans. G.A. Williamson (Penguin, 1965); *Life of Constantine*, Eusebius, ed. A. Cameron, S. Hall (Oxford University Press, 1999).

28. **Cyril of Jerusalem attacks the *Thomas* Gospel:** *Catechetical Lectures* 4.36. See *The Catechetical Lectures of St. Cyril, Archbishop of Jerusalem*, trans. John Henry Newman (Kessinger Publishing, 2007); available online at www. newadvent.org.

29. **Arius:** *Arius: Heresy and Tradition*, Rowan Williams (Eerdmans, 2002).

30. **Declaration of Constantine:** From Eusebius, *Life of Constantine*, 3:65; *History of the First Council of Nice*, Dean Dudley (A & B, 1992); *An Anthology of Atheism and Rationalism*, ed. Gordon Stein (Prometheus Books, 1980).

The Purge

31. **Execution of Priscillian:** *Introduction to the History of Christianity*, ed. Tim Dowley, et. al. (Augsburg Fortress, 2002), p. 150; and *A History of the Devil*, Gerald Messadie (Fitzhenry & Whiteside, 1997) p. 272.

32. **Athanasius canon letter:** See "Athanasius: Easter Letter of A. D. 367" at www.scrollpublishing.com.

33. **"Subjection of reason to faith":** *The Closing of the Western Mind: The Rise of Faith and the Fall of Reason*, Charles Freeman (Vintage, 2005) describes how Roman emperors and bishops after Constantine suppressed the Greek intellectual tradition. For modern parallels, see *Dark Ages America*, Morris Berman (W. W. Norton, 2007).

Bellum Deo

34. **Augustine:** *Confessions*, trans. Henry Chadwick (Oxford University Press, 1998); *City of God*, trans. Henry Bettenson (Penguin, 2003).

35. **Church use of force:** Augustine in *The Correction of the Donatists*, see Letter 185, 6:23, at newadvent.org.

36. ***Bellum Deo*:** Augustine in *City of God*; see *The Political and Social Ideas of St Augustine*, Herbert Deane (Columbia University Press, 1966) and *The Just War in the Middle Ages*, Frederick Russell (Cambridge University Press, 1975).

37. **"Rome has spoken":** A truncated paraphrase of Augustine's statement in Sermons 131:10, used by both promoters and opponents of Catholic authority. See *Upon This Rock*, Stephen K. Ray (Ignatius Press, 1999), p. 233, note 187. Ray compares the short version to the original statement.

FURTHER READING

The Social Record of Christianity, Joseph McCabe, (Book Tree, 2000); *When History and Faith Collide: Studying Jesus*, Charles W. Hendrick (Hendrickson Publishers, 1995); *The Just War and Jihad: Violence in Judaism, Christianity, and Islam*, ed. R. Joseph Hoffmann (Prometheus Books, 2006); *A History of Christianity*, Paul Johnson (Penguin, 1976); *Books and Readers in the Early Church*, Harry Y. Gamble (Yale University Press, 1995); *Shadow of the Third Century: A Revaluation of Christianity*, Alvin Boyd Kuhn (Kessinger Publishing, 1992). *Forgery In Christianity*, Joseph Wheless (FQ Classics, 2007); *Gospel Fictions*, Randel Helms (Prometheus Books, 1988); and *Social Reality and the Early Christians*, Gerd Theissen, trans. Margaret Kohl (Augsburg Fortress, 1992).

CHAPTER 11: VOICE OF THE GALILEAN

1. **Antonio Machado:** Quoted from *Times Alone*, trans. Robert Bly (Wesleyan University Press, 1983).

The Acts of Yeshua

2. **Life of Jesus:** See *The Acts of Jesus*, ed. Robert W. Funk (HarperCollins, 1999); *Jesus As a Figure in History*, Mark Allan Powell (Westminster John Knox Press, 1998); *The Historical Figure of Jesus*, E. P. Sanders (Penguin, 1996); *The Historical Jesus*, John Dominic Crossan (HarperCollins, 1992); and chapter 1 notes regarding Vermes, Meier, Theissen, and others; see "The

Real Jesus," Richard Shand, online at www.mystae.com for a review of scholarly opinion.

3. **James, Jesus' brother:** Gospel of Hebrews 9:1–4, *Thomas* 12.

Multitudes

4. **"Giant filters":** *The Historical Jesus,* John Dominic Crossan (HarperCollins, 1991), p. 3.

A Voice in Galilee

5. **Jesus paraphrased:** Based on the likely authentic sayings of Jesus, as examined in this book.

Sin and Purity

6. **"Sin upon yourself":** *Thomas* 14.

7. **"Violating your nature":** Jesus paraphrased from the *Gospel of Mary* 3:3–5, "There is no sin... what belongs to every nature."

8. **"Two into one":** *Thomas* 22.

Atonement

9. **Mustard Seed:** *Thomas* 20; *Mark* 4:30–2; Q (*Luke* 13:18, *Matthew* 13:31). **Leaven:** *Thomas* 96; Q (*Luke* 13:20, *Matthew* 13:33).

10. **Kingdom among you; spread out on earth:** *Luke* 17:20–21, 11:20; *Thomas* 113, 3; *Mary* 4:4–5. See Norman Perrin, *The Kingdom of God in the Teaching of Jesus* (Westminster Press, 1963; SCM, 1984). John the Baptist believed in an imminent intervention by God to restore justice. The *Mark* Gospel has Jesus saying, "Some of those standing here won't taste death before they see God's kingdom arrive with power," i.e. within the lifetime of *Mark*'s audience. Jesus, however, appears to have transformed this idea: The kingdom is here now in awareness and action. For a discussion of future or present kingdom in Jesus, see Marcus Borg, *Jesus* (HarperCollins, 2006) pp. 252–60; *The Five Gospels,* ed. Robert W. Funk and Roy W. Hoover (Scribner, 1993) pp. 136–7; and *The Historical Jesus* by John Dominic Crossan (HarperCollins, 1992), pp. 227–302.

Personal Power

11. **Itinerant Jesus:** Burton Mack, John Dominic Crossan, Marcus Borg, Elaine Pagals, and others point out the importance of itinerancy in understanding Jesus. Crossan suggests Jesus worked around the Sea of Galilee because that was the centre of peasant resistance to Rome. Jesus encouraged itinerancy

to his closest followers, but also offered the kingdom to anyone. Gautama Buddha taught a similar concept regarding the "householder," that is, the practitioner, who does not leave the responsibilities of family, but who nevertheless rigorously pursues spiritual insight. The Buddhist Bodhisattva is one who relinquishes the rewards of knowledge to help others.

12. **Produce fruit:** *Mark* 4:20.
13. **Know yourselves:** *Thomas* 3.
14. **Light within:** *Thomas* 24, 83, 84; Q (*Luke* 12:3, *Matthew* 10:27).

Action Here and Now

15. **Unconditional giving:**
Coat and shirt: Q (*Luke* 6:29, *Matthew* 5:40).
Second mile: *Matthew* 5:41.
Give anyone who begs: Q (*Luke* 6:30, *Matthew* 5:42) and Didache 1:5a.
Good Samaritan: *Luke* 10:30–35.
Lend without return: *Thomas* 95, Q (*Luke* 6:34).
Unconditional Love:
Love your enemies: Q (*Luke* 6:27-35, *Matthew* 5:44).
Pray for your enemies: P.Oxy 1224 6:1a; Didache 1:3.
Love those who rebuke you: Q (*Luke* 6:32, *Matthew* 5:46).
The sun rises on bad and good: Q (*Matthew* 5:45).
Be compassionate, merciful: (*Luke* 6:36) [as God is, as you judge, you will be judged].
Akkadian, Buddhist, Taoist, and Pagan traditions. See chapter 7.
16. *Agape,* **"sharing":** See *Excavating Jesus,* John Dominic Crossan and Jonathan L. Reed (HarperCollins, 2001), p.175. See chapter 7.
17. **Wisdom and deeds:** Q (*Luke* 6:43–45, *Matthew* 7:16–20); *Thomas* 45.
18. **Golden rule, Jesus style:** *Mark* 12:31; *Matthew* 7:12, 22:39; *Luke* 10:25–28.
19. *A New Reformation,* Matthew Fox (Wisdom, 2005; Inner Traditions, 2006).

FURTHER READING

Matthew Fox: *One River, Many Wells* (Tarcher, 2004); *Original Blessing,* (Tarcher, 2000); *The Coming of the Cosmic Christ* (HarperCollins, 1983); *A Spirituality Named Compassion,* (Inner Traditions, 1999); *Illuminations of Hildegard of Bingen* (Bear & Co., 2002); *Meditations with Meister Eckhart* (Bear & Co., 1983); and *Natural Grace,* dialogues with Rupert Sheldrake (Doubleday, 1977). Fox has pioneered honest, respectful spirituality since ordination as a Dominican Catholic priest in 1967. John Shelby Spong says, "History will name Fox one of the great Christian spirits of our age."

Global society and spiritual experience: *Divinity and Diversity*, Marjorie Hewitt Suchocki (Abingdon Press, 2003); *In the Footsteps of Gandhi: Conversations with Spiritual Activists*, Catherine Ingram speaks with the Dalai Lama, Joan Baez, Thich Nhat Hanh, and others (Parallax Press, 1990); *A New Christianity for a New World*, John Shelby Spong (HarperCollins, 2002); *Encountering God: A Spiritual Journey from Bozeman to Banaras*, Diana L. Eck (Beacon Press, 2003); *A Sociable God*, Ken Wilber (McGraw Hill, 1983; Shambhala, 2005); *God & Empire*, John Dominic Crossan (HarperCollins, 2007); *Introducing Liberation Theology*, Leonardo Boff (Orbis Books, 1987); *The Violence of Love*, Oscar A. Romero (Plough Publishing, 1998); Marcus J. Borg: *Reading the Bible Again For the First Time: Taking the Bible Seriously But Not Literally* (HarperCollins, 2002); *From Science to God*, Peter Russell, (New World Library, 2003); *The Rebirth of Nature: The Greening of Science and God*, Rupert Sheldrake (Bantam Books, 1991); and *The Reenchantment of the World*, Morris Berman (Cornell University Press, 1981).

ACKNOWLEDGEMENTS

The author extends gratitude to those who contributed exper-
tise, ideas, encouragement, and critical feedback to the writing
of this book. The project relied on the exceptional publishing team
at House of Anansi Press: publisher Lynn Henry, editors Kevin
Linder and Janie Yoon, copyeditor Jonathan Webb, cover designer
Paul Hodgson, text and map designer Ingrid Paulson, Sarah
MacLachlan, Laura Repas, Martin Litkowski, Alison Charles, and
the entire staff at the House of Anansi Press Inc.

Norm Gibbons and Dr. Roger N. Moss provided crucial feedback and ideas throughout the process of envisioning, researching,
and writing this book, and the project could not have been completed without their help. Marvin Storrow, Stephan Schwartz,
Dr. Yossef Av-Gay, Lisa Gibbons, Bill Gannon, and Linda Gannon
also read the manuscript and provided critical advice and refine-
ments. Matthew Fox, Brother David Steindl-Rast, Rupert
Sheldrake, Alan Clements, Catherine Ingram, and Sindy Taylor
provided inspiration and information to the project. Journalists
Monte Paulsen, Douglas Todd, John Izzo, and Jonathan Roth discussed the concept of this book with me and provided ideas. Some
of the sections of the book first appeared as segments from *The
Standard*, OMNI-10 television, in Canada. Thanks to the historians,

archaeologists, translators, and text scholars who have made these subjects their life's work, contributing the rigorous research and analysis that brings this history to light. It might also be appropriate to thank the brave seekers of the past who defied convention and faced severe persecution to keep the search for truth alive.

Finally, I wish to thank my family — Lisa, Jack, Jonah, and Liam — for their patience and support during the writing of this book.

INDEX

131, 149, 210, 317; as Logos of God, 261, 273, 275, 283–84, 292; as messiah, 19, 28–30, 31–32, 34, 35–38, 40, 53–55, 60, 70, 91, 176, 193, 276–77, 283–84, 306, 335; on money, 56–57, 128–29; as Nazorean, 49, 54, 169, 270–71; peasant audience/followers of, 49–52, 62, 70, 101, 115–18, 121–25, 137, 195–96, 301; return of, as promised by other writers, 53–54, 55, 60, 63, 170, 227, 244–46, 250, 264; social action of, 177, 185–91, 203–206, 298, 319–21; as son of Adam, 215–19, 238, 303; as son of God, 51, 66, 70, 73, 213–15, 255, 273, 283–84, 289–90, 292; trial of, 22, 24, 26–28, 37, 94, 177, 283–84; and vernal equinox deities/rites, 163–68, 171, 180, 193, 303, 306; and women, 140–41, 161, 171–72, 312–13, 335

Jesus, core messages of, 307–11; action here and now, 319–21; atonement and compassion, 313–16; personal power/authority, 316–19; purity, 311–13; self-knowledge (looking within), 101, 261, 318–19

Jesus sayings: authenticity of, 184–91; as common wisdom, 97, 100–101, 133–34, 183–84, 185, 187, 234–38, 297, 320, 326–27, 332–33; Crossan inventory of, 187–88, 328–30; Josephus on, 34–38; and letters of Paul, 57–61, 114; and non-Jesus sayings, 332–36; timeline of, viii–xiv; variations in, 125–30, 208. *See also* Logia Iēsou; Q sayings;

see also individual gospels

Jesus sayings (core texts), 106–10, 138–39, 185–91, 307–11, 326–32; hiding one's light, 96, 107, 186, 308, 326, 329; kingdom of God, 80–81, 83–85, 90–91, 104–106, 108, 110–14, 121–25, 262, 314; leaven parable, 105, 106, 111, 139, 187, 277, 314, 331; mustard seed parable, 105, 106, 107, 110–11, 186, 187, 308, 314, 326, 329, 331; need to be childlike, 51, 85, 112–13, 139, 187, 194, 227, 236, 277, 308, 311, 324, 329; poverty/good works, 84–85, 124, 136, 137, 139, 189–91, 194–95, 319; revealing the hidden, 101, 106–107, 109, 186, 308, 314, 326, 329; serpents and doves, 96, 97, 102, 109, 128, 186, 248, 309, 329; strong person's house, 108, 109, 186, 227–29, 327

Jesus Seminar, 104, 111, 122, 188–89, 304, 330–32

Jewish Antiquities (Flavius Josephus), 32, 74. See also Josephus, Flavius

Jews, 10, 19, 26–27, 35, 45, 215, 216–17, 248; and Church fathers, 248, 255, 259, 265, 288, 302; and Jesus' death, 26–27, 53, 57, 63, 182, 275, 276, 302; as Jesus' followers, 248, 259–60, 265; Josephus on, 32–34, 35, 117, 118; and Roman persecution, 33–34, 47, 239–41, 254

John, Gospel of, 12, 41, 88, 95, 103, 275–79; authorship/origins of, 67–68, 82, 90, 119–20, 275–76, 278–79; Jesus sayings in, 184–85; and John the Baptist, 67, 70; on

ABOUT THE AUTHOR

REX WEYLER is the critically acclaimed author of *Blood of the Land*, which was nominated for a Pulitzer Prize, and *Greenpeace: The Inside Story,* which was a finalist for the Shaughnessy Cohen Award for Political Non-Fiction, the Hubert Evans Award for Non-Fiction, and was named one of the best books of 2004 by the *Ottawa Citizen,* Halifax Public Libraries, *Publishers Weekly,* and the *Seattle Post-Intelligencer.* He is also co-author of the self-help classic, *Chop Wood, Carry Water: A Guide to Finding Spiritual Fulfillment in Everyday Life.* His photography and essays have appeared in such publications as the *New York Times, Smithsonian, Rolling Stone, New Age Journal,* and *National Geographic.* He also appears regularly on Canadian television as a religion commentator and writes for magazines on social issues. He lives in Vancouver, British Columbia.